PENGUIN CLASSICS

THE PROPHECIES

NOSTRADAMUS (1503–1566) was a French doctor, astrologer, and seer believed to have predicted major world events.

RICHARD SIEBURTH is an award-winning translator of works by Maurice Sceve, Henri Michaux, Michel Leiris, Georg Büchner, Walter Benjamin, and Friedrich Hölderlin. His translation for Penguin Classics of Gerard de Nerval's *Selected Writings* won the PEN/Book-of-the-Month Club Translation Prize. Sieburth teaches French and comparative literature at New York University.

STÉPHANE GERSON is an award-winning historian of modern France and the author of *Nostradamus: How an Obscure Renaissance Astrologer Became the Modern Prophet of Doom*. He teaches French history at New York University.

Acclaim for *The Prophecies*

"Never mind the Weather Channel. If the Penguin Classics people are telling me to be afraid, then I am prepared to be very afraid indeed."
—Dwight Garner, *The New York Times*

"A richer, more wrangling read than any other English translator has managed or even attempted . . . [It] offers English readers the experience of reading the [prophecies] steadily and sequentially, rather than piecemeal, and with the original French on facing pages, making it possible to read the prophecies as acts of writing rather than riddles. . . . In keeping faith with the strangeness of these verses Sieburth has succeeded brilliantly in making them at last readable, in all their weird, cruel beauty, their jagged brilliance and spasmodic dash."
—*London Review of Books*

"I devoured this book in one ecstatic sitting and am already eager to do so again. Nostradamus's *Prophecies* is an indispensable classic—enigmatic, captivating, and uncannily prescient. In Richard Sieburth's elegant translation, it is also hauntingly beautiful."
—Caroline Weber, author of *Queen of Fashion: What Marie Antoinette Wore to the Revolution* and *Terror and Its Discontents: Suspect Words in Revolutionary France*

"Is Nostradamus a poet? The form in which he wrote—dark astrological visions of world events—is not one of poetry's frequent modes, though he anticipates the resounding malarkey of Yeats. But it takes a poet to create such haunting, resonant, and mysterious quatrains."
—Richard Wilbur, former U.S. poet laureate and winner of the Pulitzer Prize and the National Book Award

"Astrologically speaking, no prophecies are closer to what the Dada and Surrealist spirit holds sacred than the *Prophecies* of Nostradamus, whose mysterious enigmas are here rendered sparkling, all these centuries later." —Mary Ann Caws, Distinguished Professor of Comparative Literature, English, and French, the Graduate Center, City University of New York

"Richard Sieburth's translation of the *Prophecies* of Nostradamus proves once again that Sieburth ranks first and foremost among the translators of today. Sieburth's artful work demonstrates a keen understanding of Nostradamus that few possess. Accompanied by a masterly introduction by Stéphane Gerson, this translation is one for the ages."
—Lawrence D. Kritzman, John D. Willard Professor of French and Comparative Literature, Dartmouth College

"The avant-garde occult classic *The Prophecies* has found its ideal translator in Richard Sieburth, and Sieburth and Stéphane Gerson have provided superb introductions and notes. . . . *The Prophecies* is riddled with riot, predicting a panoply of possible futures while all the time registering the trauma of its historical moment and, against all odds, our own." —Charles Bernstein, author of *All the Whiskey in Heaven: Selected Poems*

NOSTRADAMUS

The Prophecies

A DUAL-LANGUAGE EDITION WITH PARALLEL TEXT

Translated with an Introduction and Notes by
RICHARD SIEBURTH

Historical Introduction and Supplementary Material by
STÉPHANE GERSON

PENGUIN BOOKS

PENGUIN BOOKS
Published by the Penguin Group
Penguin Group (USA) LLC
375 Hudson Street
New York, New York 10014

USA | Canada | UK | Ireland | Australia | New Zealand | India | South Africa | China
penguin.com
A Penguin Random House Company

This translation first published in the United States of America by Penguin Books,
a member of Penguin Group (USA) Inc., 2012
Published in Penguin Books 2013

This work, published as part of the program of aid for publication, received support from the
French Ministry of Foreign Affairs and the Cultural Service of the French Embassy in the United States.
Cet ouvrage publié dans le cadre du programme d'aide à la publication bénéficie du soutien du Ministère
des Affaires Etrangères et du Service Culturel de l'Ambassade de France représenté aux Etats-Unis.

THE LIBRARY OF CONGRESS HAS CATALOGED THE HARDCOVER EDITION AS FOLLOWS:
Nostradamus, 1503–1566.
[Prophéties. English & French]
The prophecies : a dual-language edition with parallel text / Nostradamus ; translated
with an introduction and notes by Richard Sieburth ; historical introduction and
supplementary material by Stéphane Gerson.
p. cm.—(Penguin classics)
ISBN 978-0-14-310675-3 (hc.)
ISBN 978-0-14-310723-1 (pbk.)
1. Prophecies (Occultism)   I. Sieburth, Richard.   II. Gerson, Stéphane.   III. Title.
BF1815.N8A213 2012
133.3—dc23
2012018576

Set in Sabon

Contents

Historical Introduction

Nostradamus's Worlds

The *Prophecies* of Nostradamus published as a classic? The last time someone tried it in the United States was in 1942, when the Modern Library, Random House's esteemed collection, released the *Oracles of Nostradamus*. Nostradamus had entered the country a century earlier, but he became a household name only during World War II. He was everywhere—in newspapers, on movie screens, even in Nazi propaganda—and Random House's president, Bennett Cerf, paid attention. Priced at ninety-five cents, and with a cover teaser telling readers that the book made "for fascinating reading when related to the catastrophes announced daily while the world is in crisis," the *Oracles* was a hit. Only five Modern Library titles sold more copies that year, among them W. Somerset Maugham's *Of Human Bondage* and Dostoyevsky's *Crime and Punishment*. "We have our ears to the ground as editors," Cerf told a journalist, "and I point to such titles as Nostradamus to prove to you what I mean." Cerf had dug up these *Oracles*—an 1891 publication whose author, an Englishman named Charles A. Ward, had selected and commented on random verses by Nostradamus—and simply patched on an afterword and a new cover. Nostradamus had entered the Modern Library, but strangely enough the *Prophecies* themselves were nowhere to be found.

This tells us a few things about Nostradamus in modern times. His *Prophecies* are ubiquitous, especially during times of crisis, and yet they remain elusive. They often play upon the mercenary instincts of cultural promoters high and low. And the people and institutions that bestow symbolic recognition seldom acknowledge the book's literary qualities. The ever-candid Cerf confessed that he had included the book in his collection with his tongue in his cheek. Could he do otherwise when respected journalists were denouncing Nostradamus's disjointed words and uncouth French? Ever since the Frenchman Michel de Nostredame (pen name Nostradamus) published *Les premières centuries, ou Prophéties* in Lyon in 1555, no secular or religious canon has deemed his predictions fit for inclusion. The book has not made it into school curricula or college syllabi or onto the lists of prestigious publishing imprints. No institution, no political or religious group, has taken on the task of consecrating or preserving the *Prophecies*. If a classic, following one definition, refers to an old work canonized by widespread admiration, then the controversial Nostradamus was doomed. The Nobel Prize–winning novelist J. M. Coetzee once suggested that a classic is a book that has drawn the attention of professional critics and overcome them. This has not been the case with the *Prophecies*.

Until recently, that is. Over the past decade or so, scholars have begun reconsidering this book and its mix of astrology, prophecy, melancholy poetry, magic, and history. The first reputable dissertation on Nostradamus's poetics was defended in Stockholm in 2005, by a scholar named Anna Carlstedt. Other books and articles have followed. Did this happen because of turn-of-the-millennium enthusiasm? Because scholars came to see the modern age as one not only of scientists and engineers but also of magicians and Spiritualists? Or because they had to recognize that Nostradamus's predictions continue to capture the West's collective imagination (if not the world's at this point)? A bit of all three, no doubt. But there is a paradox at work. The *Prophecies* of Nostradamus have outlasted most of the writings published during the late Renaissance. People have read and parsed the work for close to five centuries. And yet, it seems to float in some distant realm, out of our reach, broken up into fragments or hidden behind interpretations.

The time is ripe for a new translation and a new look at a work whose formal organization, stylistics, evocative powers, and enduring resonance defy comparison. Beyond the predictions that may or may not have come true, beyond the intimations of world's end, beyond the strange tales about a wizard who buried himself alive in his grave, the *Prophecies* contain the universe—as the avant-garde writer Max Jacob, a fervent reader of Nostradamus, once proclaimed. The singular book that sought to encompass its worlds—past, present, and future—tells us as much about its era as it does about our own and about yearnings that remain as conflicted today as they were during the Renaissance.

When the first edition of the *Prophecies* came out, Nostradamus (1503–66) was fifty-two and living in the southern French town of Salon-de-Provence, halfway between Avignon and Aix. He was something of a celebrity by then. In the 1530s he had made a regional name for himself as a plague doctor. Epidemics afflicted Provence every other year, and many physicians fled. Nostradamus, however, braved physical danger and potential threats to his reputation (remedies and prophylactics could fail, after all) and stayed. Salon summoned him when the plague reached the town, and he liked its climate enough to settle there, start a family, and set up a medical practice. His diagnostics, like those of other Renaissance physicians, rested on bodily humors as well as the stars, which were believed to govern parts of the body and mirror character traits. Nostradamus soon branched out and began calculating detailed horoscopes that provided insights into people's character and destiny. He knew what his customers expected: not a stream of favorable predictions, but truth and sufficient warning to chart the best course of action. They wanted an astrologer who would unveil the workings of fate and reinforce their faith that humans, if warned, could parry the worst blows. Illness and misfortune were unavoidable, but people also expected a satisfying existence and reason to hope. Nostradamus provided it all. Valleys follow peaks, he said. Pleasure and joy are intermingled with sorrow. But moderation and perseverance outline a sound path forward.

Nostradamus's thriving practice enhanced his reputation. His customers addressed him as their friend, and this was what he provided: friendship as a virtuous bond of equality, reciprocity, and moral commitment between reasonable, virtuous men who shared interests and professional goals and sometimes emotional attachments as well. This was a humanistic notion, and Nostradamus was a Renaissance humanist through and through. He had learned the traditional curriculum in Avignon: grammar, rhetoric, and logic coupled with arithmetic, geometry, music, and astronomy. He had then studied medicine at the University of Montpellier, built a sizable library, and mastered Latin, Greek, Italian, Hebrew, Spanish, and perhaps Arabic in addition to his native French and Provençal. He read widely—poetry, the classics, history—and worked on a French translation of the Greek physician Galen. (Renaissance doctors frequently engaged in such pursuits, partly to garner prestige.) One of his earliest projects was a verse riff on the hieroglyphics of Horapollo, which had been discovered in 1419 and translated into Greek in 1505. He exchanged letters with educated men throughout Europe and interspersed references to Lucillius and other classical authors in his missives.

But Nostradamus ventured beyond such circles. In 1550 he published his first almanac, a short and flimsy publication that contained a calendar, tables of the phases of the Moon (known as ephemerides), and weather forecasts. He wrote at least one almanac per year, along with prose narratives called prognostications, which described weather patterns, epidemics, wars, and even the behavior of men with soft or bellicose temperaments for the year to come. Like his horoscopes, these publications rested on his astrological calculations of planetary conjunctions and revolutions and cosmic cycles. Almanacs had become the popular medium of the day. The world of print was booming: printers and publishers created new genres and altered the ways in which people organized knowledge. Nostradamus flourished in this market, partly because he managed his editorial ventures with skill, and partly because he was in sync with his world. He read other astrologers and classical authors and almanacs and synthesized all this material into publications that were sold across France and abroad as well. His massive output of cheap vernacular publications exemplified the media culture that was now taking form and would grow in the West.

The prose writer was also a poet. He adorned his almanacs with four-line predictive poems—called *présages*, or portents—that he claimed to have composed out of natural instinct and poetic frenzy. Each almanac contained one portent for the whole year, one for each month, and sometimes a fourteenth one at the end. This was Nostradamus's signature. The blend of prose and poetry was characteristic of a man who moved constantly from one realm to the next, who was present in all of them and yet confined to none. He was Catholic and French but a resident of Provence (recently incorporated into France), with two grandparents who had converted from Judaism. His family of middling merchants was close to the local elite, yet not quite part of it. He attended a prestigious medical school but contested his teachers' formal course of study and spent decades on the road, a peripatetic adventurer who followed his curiosity wherever it led him. The French queen Catherine de Médicis invited him to the court of France, but he never became a courtier. Nostradamus was both an insider and outsider, an establishment figure who followed the rules and a maverick who skirted around them. His liminal position enabled him to encounter people from various walks of life, to tap different forms of knowledge, and to grasp the aspirations and fears, the violence and contradictions of his world.

Nostradamus's *Prophecies* built upon his almanacs and went further. The fundamental similarity: the quatrains, which were now arranged in series of one hundred called Centuries. The 1555 edition contained 353 quatrains and a preface to Nostradamus's eldest son, César. Over the next few years, publishers in Lyon and Paris released other editions—sometimes with additional quatrains. In 1568, two years after Nostradamus's death, there came a final edition with 942 quatrains spread over ten Centuries. It also contained a second preface, addressed to the late king Henri II. The odd number of quatrains remains mysterious. We do not know whether Nostradamus intended it as such or simply lacked the time to complete his work. It is also possible that some quatrains went astray in publishers' workshops or, less likely, that he fit as many as he could in the sixteen-page leaves that publishers routinely used. Nor do we know why the last three Centuries were published posthumously. Some commentators believe that someone else composed them after Nostradamus's death, but this is conjectural. Regardless, most readers believed at that time and afterward that Nostradamus had penned the 942 quatrains and two prefaces. This is the core of the book that has traversed the centuries.

There were other book-length predictions and other collections of Centuries during the Renaissance, but none that built on the author's preexisting fame and that mixed poetry, astrology, and prophecy in this fashion. Astrologers provided interpretations of celestial signs according to a method. Prophets, in contrast, were elected by God to convey augurs to humanity; they typically proffered warnings or requested renewed devotion.

Nostradamus did not resemble familiar prophetic types. He was neither a lowly, unorthodox man nor a pure figure who disregarded his body nor a divine envoy who interpreted Scripture to help a leader overcome adversity. After all, he claimed that no human being could comprehend the secrets of God the Creator and assured his readers that he would never arrogate such a sublime title for himself. Still, the book's title is revealing. While he stayed within the boundaries prescribed by the Catholic Church, Nostradamus combined facets of the Jewish prophet who brought together past, present, and future; the Christian prophet who could accomplish nothing without divine power; and the melancholy, Aristotelian prophet who could connect with the soul of the world. Alone in his study, scrutinizing the sky, guided by "natural instinct & accompanied by poetic furor," overcome by prophetic inspiration, and dabbling in white magic (he wore laurel crowns and a sky blue stone ring during these sessions), Nostradamus composed what he called "nocturnal & prophetic calculations."

The Neoplatonists believed that poets could contemplate and render meaningful mysteries that startled ordinary mortals, and in this spirit it is important to emphasize the primacy of words in Nostradamus's enterprise. Like formulas and incantations, words had obtained therapeutic or magical powers during the Middle Ages. They embodied hidden verities and divine ideas and the essence of things and people. By the Renaissance, they brimmed with meaning and could modify the natural world and sometimes transcend the symbolic realm to become analogies of the cosmos.

The following quatrain provides a taste of Nostradamus's words. It is the sixty-fourth of the first Century (1.64):

> At night they shall believe the sun does shine
> When at the half-human pig they get a peek :
> Noise, song, battalions battling in the sky
> Shall be perceived & brute beasts heard to speak.

These verses capture the book's distant authorial voice (Nostradamus rarely uses the first person in the quatrains) and the imposing authority it conveys. They also display the opacity that, even in an age of mystifying prophecies, allegorical engravings, and analogical means of reasoning, befuddled many contemporaries. The prophet seems to have relished obscurity. Perhaps he sought to capture the volatility of his era, the instability of the human condition, the hidden workings of the world, or the mysteries of the cosmos. Perhaps he sought to join a brotherhood of prognosticators whose authority rested on arcane language and expert knowledge. And perhaps he understood the value of dissimulation—and the dangers of exposure—while coming of age in tumultuous times. To succeed as a soothsayer in the sixteenth century, one had better learn how to assuage secular rulers as well as religious authorities.

This quatrain also captures Nostradamus's terse bleakness. Even if readers did not fathom all the verses, they could not miss the gloomy tidings, the harrowing violence, the apocalyptic battles that expressed the eschatological mood spreading across the continent during a century of diseases, wars, marauding armies, inflation, and famine. Signs that the Last Days approached seemed to multiply, from the Protestant Reformation to the sack of Rome by troops of Charles V in 1527 to Ottoman advances. Astrological prophecy, which focused on the Last Judgment and the struggle against Satan, made inroads. Even if many Christians contemplated their future with equanimity, a sense of foreboding permeated European society. Nostradamus voiced the two dimensions of Apocalypticism. Readers of the *Prophecies* could find looming cataclysm and suffering as retribution for a society that had succumbed to sin. They could also uncover a more optimistic horizon, with prospects of universal peace, empathy for people who had sinned out of ignorance rather than evil, and a merciful God whom devout and humble Christians could placate.

In this quatrain as in others, Nostradamus left no domain untouched. He wrote about princely marriages, losses of property, and religious councils. This was a world in which all lives, eminent as well as base, were interconnected, and all human activities had an impact on one another. Nostradamus piled it on, but he also created connections between all realms, from the highest political reaches to the ordinary concerns of everyday life. His enumerations and repetitions express the abundance of his world as well as the dread of emptiness—what contemporaries called *horror vacui*. Nostradamus did not invent a literary form—other writers penned prose prognostications or quatrains—but he stretched the boundaries of existing ones and filled them with words that were at once precise and evanescent. His taut, bulging concentrates of the mundane and the arcane are filled with infinite possibilities and a forcefulness that belongs to Nostradamus alone.

In one respect, we may read the *Prophecies* as exactly what their title indicates: perspectives on the future. Certainly many readers were awed by his apparent predictive powers, even if Nostradamus was less precise here than in his almanacs. The book mentions only nine dates, from 1588 until 3797, which some have linked to the end of the world and others to the end of *a* world. And yet, nothing was straightforward. The author explained that he could distinguish neither the present from the past nor the past from the future. The book contains a cyclical notion of time, in which past figures and political states return at set intervals, with cycles of growth, renewal, and decline. There is also a biblical conception of time, with its progressive unveiling of a hidden message and the ineluctability of the Apocalypse. Finally, there is the Roman idea of Fortuna, with unpredictable yet formidable disturbances. Nostradamus spoke in one of his almanacs of "transmutations of time," as if time had a dynamic energy of its own and could alter, perfect, and destroy. While time moves in some quatrains, there is no flow, no steady progression, no sense that the words are confined to any single era. Nostradamus sometimes uses the present tense and sometimes no verb at all, giving his verses the feeling variously of predictions, comments on current affairs, and considerations on human passions and interactions. They tell universal stories about human choices, conflicts, emotions, and consequences—the present, future, and eternal stuff of life.

In terms of geography, too, the book straddles boundaries. Editions of the *Prophecies* often included the following subtitle: *Represents Part of What Is Now Happening in France, in England, in Spain, and in Other Parts of the World.* The innumerable place-names contained within the book are stopovers in a far-flung exploration that begins in France and ranges from Scandinavia to the Mediterranean, via eastern Europe and Italy and the Ottoman Empire. The *Prophecies* are at once a screen on which realms distant in place or time are projected and a mirror on which the European maelstrom of the time is reflected. Many of Nostradamus's contemporaries recognized in the pages of the *Prophecies* depictions of the era's hardships and the major shifts that altered the way they saw the world. The Copernican revolution was removing humanity from the center of the universe while providing a rational purchase on the cosmos. The discovery of the Americas and its pagan inhabitants emboldened new conquests while shifting the borders of the known world and making some people wonder whether Christ had truly spread the good word to all. The printing press broadened the intellectual landscape and spread ideas while undermining dominant institutions. The Protestant Reformation's assault on Catholicism, finally, fed yearnings for true spirituality and social equality while outlining strikingly different ways of being a good Christian.

Everything was in flux, and so was Nostradamus. The man and the words that hovered between realms captured this founding moment of Western modernity in its full tension, with its shifting fault lines and the conflicting forces that propelled the Renaissance in chaotic and often disconcerting ways. Nostradamus seemed to have special knowledge about the emotions of sovereigns and the hidden forces that governed people's lives. There were other such cornucopian texts, but the *Prophecies* had a scope, a sharpness, a plasticity, and an urgency of their own. The cryptic book distilled sinister moods and anxieties into fragmented yet meaningful stories, as if their author, the man who circulated across realms without fully belonging to any one of them, had grasped each one from the inside *and* from the outside. The references to strange figures, plots, and collusions unveiled the workings of this chaotic world. The hundreds of quatrains named the era's confusion, made it visible and tangible, and expressed what readers sensed but could not—or dared not—put into words. Opacity and darkness could prove meaningful for people who contemplated the present and future with bewilderment or trepidation— especially with the verses anchored in regular, codified series of quatrains, in which surprises and reversals take the same form and the same words recur again and again. Everything holds together in the *Prophecies*. And, in Nostradamus's view, things happen for a reason.

Some writers responded to formidable calamities by accepting the limitations of language, its inability to express what was unspeakable. They wrote about what they could *not* express, or told readers that the meaning of such catastrophes was that there was no meaning. The *Prophecies*, in contrast, spoke about catastrophes head-on, endowed them with dramatic form, and placed them in continuums that exuded mysterious power. His words resonated during the French Wars of Religion (1562– 98) and continued doing so afterward—when the French monarchy faced a political rebellion around 1650 (the Fronde), in the midst of the English Civil War and Glorious Revolution, in the wake of the fire of London in 1666, during the French Revolution, and then throughout most modern wars. (The appendix delves into Nostradamus's presence during such collective crises.)

The French poet Guillaume Apollinaire once referred to these wars and other collective crises as "Martian periods"—in which people feel they are living through an era of anxiety, with time growing slower and denser, obsessional concern with future developments, the norms that regulate what is acceptable and what is not changing almost overnight, events seeming to unfold outside one's sway, and outlets for action hovering out of reach. Apollinaire wrote about this in 1915, from the trenches of World War I; earlier that year, he had lauded Nostradamus as a great poet. Why do people consult the *Prophecies* during such periods? To name and make sense of cataclysms and forces that seem distant. To feel the tremors of events that, however violent and irrepressible, acquire a majestic, world-historical grandeur. And to uncover horrendous tidings about other people, countries, or even eras and then return to their own hardships with greater fortitude. Immediate and yet distant, Nostradamus's vast predictions make it possible to reframe distressing circumstances and substitute a specific, imminent fear for floating anxieties. Whereas anxiety tends to draw people apart, fear pulls them together. Nostradamus's evocative words can thus make fear palatable as a controlled, communal feeling that displaces the solitary terror of the unknown. The book's presence in the West has changed over the centuries, and so have the ways in which people from different countries and backgrounds have perceived and made sense of the quatrains. But some things have endured.

By World War I, Nostradamus's original almanacs and prognostications had vanished, but his *Prophecies* continued to circulate across western

Europe. There have been hundreds of editions since his death. Unlike most classics, which rarely change once they are in print, this book was at once fixed and unstable. The quatrains and prefaces remained, but competing publishers added subtitles, biographical sketches, and guides to his anagrams and metaphors. Some publishers even inserted new predictions (including fifty-eight six-line poems, the *sixains*, in 1605). If there is a parallel, however distant, it is the Bible, but there is a major difference, too. No institution or collective group embraced the singular *Prophecies*, and this left it free from norms and controls. Open and open-ended in all senses of the words, the *Prophecies* could thus lure all kinds of people, from different backgrounds and religions. Besides publishers, there have been compilers, translators, forgers, and innumerable interpreters. These individuals have tended to reside or end up on the fringes of society, within a Nostradamian underworld, as it were. They have conversed and competed with one another, reframed the *Prophecies*, and sometimes broken the book down into its component parts. But they have also kept Nostradamus visible and vibrant within the mainstream.

This autonomy has freed the *Prophecies* from gatekeepers. No one has decreed who could parse these predictions and how. This is not the kind of book that one needs to read silently, or in one go. One may start anywhere, stop and resume at any time, and engage with it as one sees fit. Over the centuries, its readers have ranged from monarchs to prelates, lawyers to military officers, social workers to retirees. Some have relished the challenge of decoding arcane predictions, gaining confidence in their interpretive powers and making their own world legible. Others have beheld with awe mesmerizing words and forces that they could not understand but that still proved meaningful. Others have approached the quatrains as a political template, fodder for whatever ideological or religious cause they embraced, or a source of delight and entertainment. And still others have delved with a mix of feelings into a supernatural realm that hovers precariously between prophecy and superstition. Curiosity and ambivalence could overlap with sentiments of shame that people did not always acknowledge to themselves. These men and women have both read the words of Nostradamus and *done* things with them, whether annotating its margins, sharing quatrains and debating their meaning, or even imitating them for themselves or others. Many have also moved from one way of apprehending Nostradamus to another. Words that speak to such distinct yearnings, that lend themselves to so many relationships between words and their readers—without external constraints or policing—are bound to appeal across social, cultural, and religious divides.

The *Prophecies* are too mystifying, however, to provide easy or rapid access. One nineteenth-century commentator—his name was Pierre Chaillot—asked his readers whether they had "the noble courage to venture into the labyrinth of the Centuries." Courage might help, though other readers presumably yearn for something more tangible, such as a road map. There are plenty to be found. A cottage industry of interpreters has long come into being, fully convinced that Nostradamus had seen or said something of importance but expressed it in coded language. By using the right method, it is possible to untangle this thicket of words and provide clarity of meaning. It is all about the key. Chaillot's resided in what he called the "torch of erudition." Drawing from his knowledge of Latin and mythology, he linked quatrains to past events and clarified their grammatical constructions, their classical references, and the true meaning of their anagrams. He and others have suggested, for instance, that the great "Chyren" designates King Henri or Henry (*Henryc* in Provençal), "Rapis" Paris, and "Car." or "Carcas.," the French town of Carcassonne. The "lion" is a warchief; the "Castulon monarque" is Emperor Charles V. "Snakes" stands for heretics, "hell" for the Châtelet prison, and "whites" and "reds" for French magistrates who wore robes of those colors. Other interpreters have insisted that, below the surface of the quatrains, there lies another, deeper layer of meaning. Take quatrain 1.53:

> Alas one shall see a great nation bleed
> And the holy law & all of Christendom
> Reduced to utter ruin by other creeds,
> Each time a new gold, silver mine is found.

According to one François Buget in 1862, the references to gold (*d'or*) and silver (*d'argent*) in the last verse pointed to the d'Orléans family, New Orleans, and the marquis d'Argenson, president of the Council of Finances. Having established this, Buget considered numbers. He added 153, 1555 (the *Prophecies*' date of publication), and 5 and 3 to arrive at a total of 1716. This was the year in which the Scottish economist John Law—recently appointed Controller General of Finances by the French regent Philippe d'Orléans—had set up the Banque Générale in Paris. Shortly thereafter, Law issued handwritten notes for the development of Louisiana—a scheme that led to a bubble that burst in 1720. The marquis d'Argenson resigned after the collapse. Nostradamus, Buget concluded, had seen it all two centuries earlier.

Readers of the present edition will decide for themselves what to make of this and other keys, and whether Nostradamus looked to the past or commented on the present or projected himself into the future. Perhaps he did all three. Regardless, the arcane *Prophecies* remain open to all readings and projections. This has been a central reason for its enduring appeal over the centuries.

Success has not, however, endowed the book with legitimacy and cultural worth. The elusive author and his predictions seemed suspect and came under attack from the start. They were too powerful and popular, too seductive and dangerous. Many people recoiled before the prognosticator who was everywhere and nowhere, before verses that captured the contradictions of the modern West, and before predictions that said so much and yet could not be pinned down.

In the sixteenth and seventeenth centuries, detractors went after the *Prophecies* and the man himself—a poor astrologer, a false prophet, an impostor, a satanic envoy, or a charlatan. By the eighteenth century, they targeted credulous, superstitious followers who trusted their passions rather than reason. A century later, they denounced the interpreters and publishers who used Nostradamus to attack science, spread magical thinking, and become celebrities in their own right within a consumerist society. By the twentieth century, finally, Nostradamus captured the fear and panic that, like a disease, fed conspiracy theories and predictions of world's end while whittling away at modern civilization from the inside. For close to a half millennium, then, the all-encompassing Nostradamus has also proven appealing as a way of denouncing threats linked to change and modernity, distancing oneself from offensive yet seductive forces, and reaffirming norms. In this respect, too, the *Prophecies* reside at the core of the modern West.

Which brings us back to the Modern Library's 1942 edition. It is easy to include *Oracles of Nostradamus* in a story in which the media and propaganda outfits exploit and distort the quatrains, play up the darker overtones, dismiss their wondrous or moral dimensions, and oftentimes leave the verses themselves behind. All that remains, from this vantage point, are unfathomable pronouncements that frighten people into accepting irrational forces instead of contemplating the injustice of the world. The elusive quatrains thus accrue power during an era that is governed by fear, an era that searches in vain for trustworthy authorities, an era that pledges allegiance to recognized facts while lacking the time or desire to ascertain them.

And yet, to immerse oneself in the dense, unsettling *Prophecies* is also to witness the immensity of time and history in the making. The verses continue to dramatize the haphazard and sometimes catastrophic violence of our world and the pain, the afflictions, the sorrow that ensue— all of them marks of the human condition. In so doing, they remind us of our frailty, allow us to express oft-concealed vulnerabilities, and put us in touch with emotions that, from resentment to desolation to empathy, we cannot always pinpoint. As in the Renaissance, they provide deeper knowledge and reprieve from too much information. We can still delve into horror while keeping it at a remove; we can still participate in our own fate while securing protection and a sense of community. At once ephemeral and covered with the dust of ancient origins, Nostradamus's cascade of words draws us into past worlds, the worlds in which we must live and those that we anticipate, and perhaps deeper within our internal world as well.

This is enough to meet some definitions of a classic. Unless of course it is the opposite, and the *Prophecies* deserve our attention as an *anti-classic*, a work that has endured by charting a course of its own. After all, the writers who have found the quatrains most enthralling belong to avant-gardes that, by definition, distrust canons and academies and the very idea of a classic. In 1916, the Romanian artist Marcel Janco came across the *Prophecies* on the shelves of a Zurich bookstore. Janco, a founder of the Dada movement, was so enthused that he purchased the book and promptly read selections during one of the group's soirées at the Cabaret Voltaire. His fellow poets and artists, he later related, were astounded by this suggestive, mystic, abstract verse. "The sound, the associations, the alliteration—it was these that made it a true new poetry."

The Dadaists felt a shock of recognition before opaque mash-ups that upended grammatical and social conventions and unleashed the playful and corrosive powers of language. By fusing high and low cultures and pushing against the outer limits of expression and understanding, the *Prophecies* invited readers to consider their world, and themselves as well, with greater discernment. The poet Tristan Tzara found these verses so powerful that he slipped fragments into his writings. "[T]o the north by its double fruit / like raw flesh / hunger fire blood." Tzara circulated in different circles from Bennett Cerf, but he would have agreed with the American publisher on one point: Nostradamus makes for fascinating reading in a world in crisis.

STÉPHANE GERSON

Suggestions for Further Reading

Over the past two decades, several French editions of the *Prophecies* have been reissued with some form of scholarly apparatus. The first edition of 1555 can be found in *Les premières centuries, ou Prophéties,* ed. Pierre Brind'Amour (Geneva: Droz, 1996). For the second edition, of 1557, see *Prophéties,* ed. Bruno Petey-Girard (Paris: Garnier-Flammarion, 2003). Michel Chomarat provides a facsimile of the 1568 edition in *Les Prophéties: Lyon, 1568* (Lyon: Michel Chomarat, 1993). The standard English-language edition has long been Edgar Leoni, *Nostradamus and His Prophecies* (Mineola, NY: Dover, 2000 [1961]). See also the translation by Peter Lemesurier, *The Illustrated Prophecies* (Alresford, Hampshire, UK: O-Books, 2003). Bernard Chevignard collects and analyzes all of Nostradamus's portents (the quatrains that he included in his almanacs) in *Présages de Nostradamus* (Paris: Le Seuil, 1999). Nostradamus's original letters (in Latin) and French summaries can be found in his *Lettres inédites,* ed. Jean Dupèbe (Geneva: Droz, 1983). English translations by Peter Lemesurier and the Nostradamus Research Group are available at http://bit.ly/mNdCOK.

Patrice Guinard has recently published a detailed study of the *Prophecies*' successive editions: "Historique des éditions des *Prophéties* de Nostradamus (1555–1615)," *Revue française d'histoire du livre* 129 (2009): 7–142. The best guide to French-language publications by and about Nostradamus (up to 1989) is Robert Benazra, *Répertoire chronologique nostradamique: 1545–1989* (Paris: La Grande Conjonction, 1990). There are useful complements in Michel Chomarat with Jean-Paul Laroche, *Bibliographie Nostradamus: XVIe-XVIIe-XVIIIe siècles* (Baden-Baden and Bouxwiller: V. Koerner, 1989); Chomarat, *Supplément à la Bibliographie lyonnaise des Nostradamus* (Lyon: Centre Culturel de Buenc, 1976); and Chomarat, "Nouvelles recherches sur les 'Prophéties' de Michel Nostradamus," *Revue française d'histoire du livre,* new ser., 48, 22 (1979): 123–31. For earlier bibliographies, see De Rg., "De quelques ouvrages contenant des prédictions," *Le bibliophile belge* 5 (1848): 91–113; and Graf Carl v. Klinckowstroem, "Die ältesten Ausgaben der 'Prophéties' des Nostradamus: Ein Beitrag zur Nostradamus-Bibliographie," *Zeitschrift für Bücherfreunde* (March 1913): 361–72.

Scholarship on Nostradamus's *Prophecies* is relatively sparse (especially in English). The standard biography is Edgar Leroy, *Nostradamus: Ses origines, sa vie, son oeuvre,* new ed. (Marseille: Jeanne Laffitte, 1993 [1972]). See also Peter Lemesurier, *The Nostradamus Encyclopedia* (New York: St. Martin's Press, 1997); Ian Wilson, *Nostradamus: The Man behind the Prophecies* (New York: St. Martin's Press, 2003); Elmar Gruber, *Nostradamus: Sein Leben, sein Werk und die wahre Bedeutung seiner Prophezeiungen* (Bern: Scherz, 2003); and Richard Smoley, *The Essential Nostradamus: Literal Translation, Historical Commentary, and Biography,* 2nd ed. (New York: J. P. Tarcher, 2010). Patrice Guinard's online Corpus Nostradamus provides a trove of well-documented articles (http://cura.free.fr). Scholars have recently sought to place Nostradamus and his *Prophecies* in their cultural world. On Nostradamus as a Renaissance humanist with a historical bent, see Michel Chomarat, Jean Dupèbe, and Gilles Polizzi, *Nostradamus ou Le savoir transmis* (Lyon: Michel Chomarat, 1997); and Roger Prévost, *Nostradamus, le mythe et la réalité: Un historien au temps des astrologues* (Paris: Robert Laffont, 1999). Jean Céard situates Nostradamus in the sixteenth-century culture of wonder in his *La nature et les prodiges: L'insolite au XVIe siècle, en France* (Geneva: Droz, 1977). Pierre Brind'Amour provides a fascinating portrait of Nostradamus as an astrologer in his *Nostradamus astrophile: Les astres et l'astrologie dans la vie et l'oeuvre de Nostradamus* (Ottawa: Presses de l'Université d'Ottawa, 1993). On the sources and ramifications of Nostradamus's predictions, see Chantal Liaroutzos, "Les prophéties de Nostradamus: Suivez la Guide," *Réforme, Humanisme, Renaissance* 12, 23 (December 1986): 35–40; Claude-Gilbert Dubois, "L'invention prédictive dans les 'Prophéties' de Nostradamus," in Richard Caron et al., eds., *Ésotérisme, gnoses et imaginaire symbolique: Mélanges offerts à Antoine Faivre* (Leuven, Belgium: Peeters, 2001), 547–57; and Dubois, "Un imaginaire de la catastrophe: Nostradamus, témoin du présent et visionnaire du futur," *Eidôlon* 58 (2001): 69–81.

Other scholars take the *Prophecies'* title seriously and view Nostradamus as first and foremost a prophet. See Olivier Pot, "Prophétie et mélancolie: La querelle entre Ronsard et les Protestants (1562–1565)," *Cahiers V.-L. Saulnier* 15: *Prophètes et prophéties au XVIe siècle* (Paris: Presses de l'ENS, 1998), 189–229; as well as Pierre Béhar, *Les langues occultes de la Renaissance: Essai sur la crise intellectuelle de l'Europe au XVIe siècle* (Paris: Desjonquères, 1996), ch. 5. Denis Crouzet places Nostradamus within a surge of astrological prophecy, increasingly focused on the Last Judgment and the struggle against Satan, in his *Les guerriers de Dieu: La violence au temps des troubles de religion (vers 1525–vers 1610),* 2 vols. (Seyssel, France: Champ Vallon, 1990). More recently, Crouzet has presented Nostradamus's predictions as a hermeneutics that took form in dialogue with evangelical currents. See his

Nostradamus: Une médecine des âmes à la Renaissance (Paris: Payot, 2011).

Still other scholars insist that Nostradamus was fundamentally a poet. François Crouzet first made the argument in his *Nostradamus, poète français* (Paris: Julliard, 1973). Yvonne Bellenger added stones to this edifice in "Nostradamus prophète ou poète?" in M. T. Jones-Davies, ed., *Devins et charlatans au temps de la Renaissance* (Paris: Université de Paris-Sorbonne, 1979), 83–100; and "Sur la poétique de Nostradamus," in François Marotin and Jacques-Philippe Saint-Gérand, eds., *Poétique et narration: Mélanges offerts à Guy Demerson* (Paris: Honoré Champion, 1993), 177–90. More recently, the Swedish scholar Anna Carlstedt has depicted Nostradamus as a melancholy poet in her "La poésie oraculaire de Nostradamus: Langue, style et genre des Centuries" (PhD dissertation, University of Stockholm, 2005); and "Nostradamus mélancolique: Un poète déguisé en prophète?" *Nouvelle revue du seizième siècle* 22, 2 (2004): 41–55. For a close analysis of Nostradamus's poetic language, see David Shepheard, "Pour une poétique du genre oraculaire: À propos de Nostradamus," *Revue de littérature comparée* 60 (January–March 1986): 59–65.

The reception of the *Prophecies* over the centuries is a vast topic, which some of the works above broach intermittently. On Nostradamus's detractors, see Olivier Millet, "Feux croisés sur Nostradamus aux XVIe siècle," *Cahiers V.-L. Saulnier 4: Divination et controverse religieuse en France au XVIe siècle* (Paris: Presses de l'ENS, 1987), 103–21. Studies of Nostradamus's posterity since the Renaissance began with François Buget, "Études sur Nostradamus," a series of nine articles in the *Bulletin du bibliophile et du bibliothécaire* (1857–63). One should also consult Hervé Drévillon, *Lire et écrire l'avenir: L'astrologie dans la France du Grand Siècle, 1610–1715* (Seyssel, France: Champ Vallon, 1996); Drévillon and Pierre Lagrange, *Nostradamus: L'éternel retour* (Paris: Découvertes Gallimard, 2003); Jean-Paul Laroche, *Prophéties pour temps de crise: Interprétations de Nostradamus au fil des siècles* (Lyon: Michel Chomarat, 2003); Yvonne Bellenger, "Nostradamus au fil du temps," in Fiona McIntosh-Varjabédian and Véronique Gély, eds., *La postérité de la Renaissance* (Lille: Université Charles-de-Gaulle-Lille 3, 2007), 115–27; and Stéphane Gerson, *Nostradamus: How an Obscure Renaissance Astrologer Became the Modern Prophet of Doom* (New York: St. Martin's Press, 2012). On the *Prophecies*' translations, consult Martine Bracops, ed., *Nostradamus traducteur traduit: Actes du colloque international tenu à Bruxelles le 14 décembre 1999* (Brussels: Editions du Hazard, 2000).

Finally, regarding Tristan Tzara's discovery of the *Prophecies* during World War I and Bennett Cerf's use of the book during World War II, see Gordon Browning, "Tristan Tzara: La grande complainte de mon obscurité," *Europe* 555–56 (1975): 202–13; transcript of a CBS radio interview with Bennett Cerf, 16 January 1943, in "Of Men and Books," *Northwestern University on the Air* 2, 16 (1943): 4; and Gordon B. Neavill, "Publishing in Wartime: The Modern Library Series During the Second World War," *Library Trends* 55 (Winter 2007): 583–96.

STÉPHANE GERSON

Translator's Introduction

The Poetics of Futurity

When I was initially approached about undertaking a fresh translation of Nostradamus's complete *Prophecies*—or the *Centuries*, as they are also known—I had never read a single line of his work. Even for someone who considered himself relatively well versed in the canon of sixteenth-century French poetry, Nostradamus was simply off the map—a name vaguely associated with the heavy breathers of apocalypse, dotty maiden aunts, late-night viewers of the History Channel, or those consumers of astrology columns whose mass delusions Theodor Adorno had, during a visit to Los Angeles in 1953, so trenchantly exposed in *The Stars Down to Earth and Other Essays on the Irrational in Culture*. But as I made my way into the project (thanks in part to the encouragement of my colleague Stéphane Gerson), I discovered in Nostradamus a compelling *poet*, perhaps not one of the magnitude of his French contemporaries Maurice Scève, Louise Labé, Pierre de Ronsard, or Joachim du Bellay, but a genuine poet nonetheless, certainly deserving of inclusion, in his own homespun and wayward fashion, within that larger visionary company defined by the vatic tradition of Virgil, Dante, D'Aubigné, Du Bartas, Milton, and Blake.

As a versifier, Nostradamus exhibits a formal range that is slight indeed, especially if compared to the exuberant strophic and prosodic experiments of the poets of the Pléiade. With the exception of a few spurious late six-line *sixains*, the entirety of his published poetic corpus is composed of rhymed (*abab*) decasyllabic quatrains—a popular vehicle in the French sixteenth century for matters as various as biblical psalms, Calvinist hymns, humanist adages, courtly epigrams, and moral instruction for the young. Nostradamus's *Prophecies*, the first installment of which was issued in 1555, were designed to add up to one thousand such quatrains in all, subdivided into ten books (or Centuries) of a hundred quatrains each. Fifty-eight quatrains are missing from the work's seventh Century—no doubt because of the editorial vagaries involved in the serial composition and publication of an endeavor of this scope; as a result, when the complete edition of the *Prophecies* appeared posthumously in 1568, its 942 quatrains fell somewhat short of the millenary originally envisaged. The nearest contemporary equivalent to this arithmetic permutation of identical poetic modules is Scève's 1544 *Délie*, composed of 449 decasyllabic *dizains* of ten lines each. In both cases, the reiterative hammering home of a single poetic chord, each time the same, each time warped into a slightly different overtone, produces what John Ashbery (speaking of Scève) has termed "a fruitful monotony, ideal for repetitions with minimal variations"—either a hallmark of modernist composition by field or grid, or a symptom of that black and brooding melancholia from whose anatomy Renaissance humanism never quite manages to escape.

Although they have been more or less continuously in print in French for nearly five hundred years—bibliographers count some two hundred different editions—the *Prophecies* were in fact *not* the work that catapulted Nostradamus into European celebrity: the belated translation of the complete *True Prophecies* into English by Theophilus de Garencières in 1672 is proof that his magnum opus did not really take off until the seventeenth century. Instead, during his lifetime, his meteoric rise to fame was fueled by the almanacs he published on a yearly basis from 1550 until his death in 1566. Also known as his *Présages* or *Prognostications*, these ephemeral chapbooks benefited from the success of that vast body of predictive astrological literature that, with the spread of printing, already had become so bloated that it was ripe for parodic puncture in Rabelais's satirical *Pantagrueline Prognostication for the Year 1533*. Nostradamus's almanacs observed the standard conventions of the genre, featuring as they did calendars, ephemerides, lists of movable feasts, and weather forecasts, as well as increasingly alarmist prose vaticinations that provided monthly auguries of the latest news of the world, as espied from the prophetic vantage point of his provincial hometown of Salon de Craux in southern France. By the end of his life, the steady sales of his almanacs, together with his far-flung network of wealthy (and sometimes royal) clients seeking private horoscopic advice, had made Michel de Nostredame a prosperous man.

Scholars have ventured several explanations for the extraordinary "Nostradamus effect" that generated countless imitations, plagiarisms, and translations of his *Présages* during the late Renaissance. Some point to the deep eschatological anxiety that held Europe in its grip during this period of fierce religious and political strife; others invoke the environmental, epidemiological, and economic disasters that beset the plague- and famine-ridden continent during the severe climate changes of what has been called its Little Ice Age. Cultural historians in turn underscore the swift expansion of a reading public hungry for titles in the vernacular and the concomitant explosion of the book trade, especially in places like Lyon—where Nostradamus's publishers savvily merchandised him as a brand name, issuing additional volumes of his pharmaceutical recipes and paraphrases from Galen to buttress his reputation as a "Doctor of Medicine" (which was how he appeared on the title page of all his almanacs). But the characteristic innovation that set his chapbooks off from those of his competitors was (starting with his *Prognostication nouvelle* of 1555) the introduction of portentous quatrains keyed to the various months of the year. By fusing science with prophecy, astrology with vernacular poetry, Nostradamus had hit upon a winning formula.

Here is what these calendar poems sounded like in English in a cheap eight-page *Almanacke for the Yeare of Oure Lorde God, 1559, Composed by Mayster Mychael Nostradamus, Doctour of Phisike*:

February

> Grayne, corruption, pestilentiall ayre, locustes.
> Sodayn fall, newes, newes shall rise,
> Captives yroned, swift, high, lowe, heavy,
> By his bones, evil which wold not be to the King.

August

> The earthen potte found, the citie tributory,
> Fields divided, newe begylynges,
> The Spaniard hurt, hunger, warly pestilence
> Obstinate mockery, confusedness, evyl, ravying.

As a trained apothecary and herbalist, Nostradamus tended (like his fellow student at the Faculty of Medicine in Montpellier, François Rabelais) to organize his universe into lists—hence, in the above quatrains, the agrammatical declension of nouns and modifiers, elliptically spliced together by commas and featuring virtually no verbs to govern logical sequence. Though they might initially strike one as sixteenth-century Dada, these crude English translations—without rhyme or apparent meter—nonetheless manage to register the basic architectonics of Nostradamus's verse, whose decasyllables are invariably cut in two by a strong rhythmic and semantic break falling after the fourth syllable, creating a caesura that often has the force of a colon. Thus one might repunctuate (and modernize) a few of the above lines as follows:

> Sudden fall : news, news shall rise
> Fields divided : new beginnings
> Obstinate mockery : confusion, evil, raving

To my ear at least, this rings uncannily like the kind of folksy sententiousness one finds in Ezra Pound's translations from the archaic Chinese of *The Confucian Odes*—a model I have kept in view throughout my translation.

But to the English ear of 1559, just in the process of discovering the mellifluous Petrarchan syntax of Wyatt and Surrey, this kind of choppy, paratactic verse not only sounded uncouth: it was deemed positively subversive. As one contemporary commentator remarked of the above almanac, "our craftye Nostradamus coulde wrappe hys prophesyes in such darke wryncles of obscuritye that no man could pyke out of them either sence or understandying certayn." Like "the devyll at Delphos" who inspired the oracles of Apollo, these quatrains were "obscure, double, and suche as myght chance both waies." Given the still-fragile condition of the English polity—the young, untested Elizabeth Tudor had just been made queen that same year after fraught contentions for the crown—Nostradamus's "blinde enigmatical" ambiguities threatened to cause the populace so to "waver" that they would abandon the "heavenly fountayne of hope" for "the bottomlesse pytte of utter desperation." Dismissed as arrant nonsense, yet at the same time feared because they invited their readers into a world teetering on an alarming surplus (or abyss) of meaning, Nostradamus's almanacs spawned a slew of doomsday imitators in Elizabethan England. Shakespeare, writing a generation after the craze, unerringly captures all the rhetorical and astrological commonplaces of Nostradamian dread in Horatio's speech at the outset of *Hamlet*, just before the appearance of the Ghost:

> As stars with trains of fire and dews of blood,
> Disasters in the sun; and the moist star
> Upon whose influence Neptune's empire stands
> Was sick almost to doomsday with eclipse.
> And even the like precurse of feared events,
> As harbingers preceding still the fates
> And prologue to the omen coming on,
> Have heaven and earth together demonstrated
> Unto our climatures and countrymen.

The distant shade of Nostradamus can even be heard haunting the battle-fields of *Richard II*:

> The bay-trees in our country are all wither'd
> And meteors fright the fixèd stars of heaven;
> The pale-faced moon looks bloody on the earth,
> And lean-looked prophets whisper fearful change . . .

From age forty-seven onward, during the last sixteen years of his life, Michel de Nostredame churned out almanac after almanac, saturating the market while whispering fearful change. His *Prophecies*, by contrast, composed over a short span of four years (1554–58), define a notable parenthesis within his more commercial output. Far more ambitious in scope, more carefully designed and composed, they would seem to represent his attempt to legitimize his work in the eyes of educated readers while hoping to attract royal patronage of Henri II—although, curiously enough, precious few direct references to his magnum opus on the part of his contemporaries have survived. The first edition of the *Prophecies* of

"M. Michel Nostradamus"—the more gentlemanly "Monsieur" having replaced the "Doctor of Medicine" of the almanacs—appeared in Lyon in May 1555, under the imprint of Macé Bonhomme. Handsomely printed, with a title-page woodcut of its full-bearded author seated at his table with open book and armillary sphere as he looks out at the starry firmament beyond his window, it consisted of 354 quatrains, preceded by a preface addressed to his son César. A second Lyon edition, published by Antoine du Rosne in 1557, cumulatively expanded the number of Centuries to seven (though mysteriously cutting off halfway through the final section). A third edition, comprising the last three Centuries (eight through ten), was apparently brought out by Lyon publisher Jean de Tournes in 1558, though not a single copy of it has ever turned up. If this edition is indeed not apocryphal, it would provide proof that Nostradamus had with his huge new work-in-progress attracted the attention of the leading humanist circles of Lyon: Jean de Tournes was after all the highly respected publisher of Aesop, Ovid, Dante, Petrarch, Du Bellay, Labé, and Scève. After a rather inexplicable ten-year hiatus, the complete edition of the *Prophecies* (still missing fifty-eight quatrains, but including an epistle to [the late] king Henri II inserted as a preface to the final three Centuries) was issued by Benoist Rigaud in Lyon in 1568, two years after its author's death. Some scholars have doubted the authenticity of the three hundred new quatrains included in this posthumous edition, suggesting possible editorial mischief on the part of Nostradamus's faithful amanuensis, Jean-Aimé de Chavigny. Having closely pored over this final portion of the poem—the zaniest of the lot—all I can say is that its author's idiosyncrasies of diction and syntax are palpable in every line.

The first page of the *Prophecies* invited its readers of 1555 to imagine the Magus alone at night in his study, seated on a metaphorical bronze tripod like the Pythia of yore, intoxicated by the vapors emanating from the pit where Apollo once slew the Python, and moved to prophetic utterance by the flickering flame of the gases produced by its decomposing body—a description derived from the *De mysteriis Aegyptiorum* of Syrian Neoplatonist Iamblichus and the *De occulta philosophia* of German occultist Cornelius Agrippa:

> Estant assis de nuict secret estude
> Seul reposé sus la selle d'aerain :
> Flambe exigue sortant de solitude,
> Fait proferer qui n'est à croire en vain.

This was first rendered into English by Theophilus de Garencières in 1672 as:

> Sitting by night in my secret Study
> Alone, resting upon the Brazen stool.
> A slight flame braking forth out of that solitude,
> Makes me utter what is not in vain to believe.

Garencières justified his literal translation by claiming that "the Crabbedness of the Original in his own Idiome can scarce admit a Polite Eloquency in another." But on closer inspection, his translation proves far less literal than it pretends, for he invents first-person pronouns ("*my* secret Study," "makes *me* utter") where there are none in the original, entirely missing the point that these *Prophecies* enact a proto-Mallarméan "elocutory disappearance of the poet who henceforth leaves the initiative to words"—indeed, in the entire thirty-five-thousand-word corpus of the *Prophecies*, there are only five occurrences of the pronoun "I." Within this poetics of vatic anonymity, the crucial verb that leaps out in the lines above is *proferer*—from the Latin *pro-ferre*, "to carry forward," hence "to utter"—a verb whose subject is not a person, but rather the "narrow flame" emanating from (decomposed) tradition. In my translation of this same quatrain, I have inflected this verb toward its etymological cognate, "prophecy"—from the Greek *pro-phetes*, "one who speaks beforehand," or perhaps more accurately, "the one who speaks *for*, that is, who translates the vaporous images of the oracle into concrete poetry:

> Being seated at night in secret study
> Alone upon a stool of bronze at ease :
> Slim flame issuing forth from solitude
> Fuels prophecies not futile to believe. (1.1)

Still paraphrasing Iamblichus in Latin, the subsequent quatrain moves from Delphi to the ancient oracle of Didymus at Branchidai (or Branchus) in Asia Minor. Nostradamus maintains his impersonation of a female sibyl (in the third person this time), while throwing in an erudite pun (capitalized so the printers would get it) on the branchlike legs of the tripod:

> Wand in hand set in the midst of BRANCHES,
> With water he wets both his hem & feet :
> Vapor & voice aquiver in his sleeves :
> Splendor divine. The god here takes a seat. (1.2)

In the original French the closing hemistich reads, "Le divin près s'assied." Or in Marsilio Ficino's terse neo-Latin, "subito deus adest."

In the volume's preface, addressed to his infant son César, Nostradamus further elaborates upon these moments of divine visitation. Arising, as they do, as he studies at night, scanning the stars for signs, their sacred intensity (or *furor*) guarantees the authenticity—and, more importantly, the veracity—of his prophetic utterance:

But, my son, I'm speaking to you here a bit too abstrusely: as for the occult vaticinations inspired in us by that subtle spirit of fire which sometimes exercises our minds as we sit up nights contemplating the stars on high, finding myself (to my surprise) prophesying, I write it all down, pronouncing myself without fear, free from immodest loquacity. How so? Because all these things were flowing from the almighty power of Eternal God, from whom all bounty proceeds.

He continues (paraphrasing the Latin of the Italian firebrand Savonarola):

Note, however, my son, that if I have made mention of the term prophet, far be it from me to arrogate a title this exalted, this sublime, in these present times: *For he that is now called a Prophet was beforetime called Seer* [I Samuel 9:9]: for a Prophet, my son, is properly speaking someone who sees distant things with the natural knowledge possessed by all creatures.

Nostradamus is proceeding with extreme caution here. Lest he be accused of arrogance, madness, or, worse, heresy—Savonarola's public incineration by a Borgia pope was still within recent memory—he prefers to present himself as a "seer" (*videns*), in the same eidetic sense that Rimbaud will later use the term *voyant*. Although he alludes in this same preface to his "hereditary gift of prophecy"—in which some commentators have seen a veiled allusion to his distant Jewish ancestry—and although he mentions being seized by "trances of epilepsy" during what appear to be veritable episodes of automatic writing, he is careful to insist that he has abjured all the occult arts of magic and that he does not claim for himself "the name or function of a prophet, but that of a mortal man possessed of revealed inspiration, whose senses are no less distant from heaven than his feet from the ground : *I can err, fail, be deceived*, there is no greater sinner on this earth than I, subject to all the afflictions of man." Which was apparently good enough for the Catholic Church, for his *Prophecies* never appeared on its newly established Index of forbidden books.

William Blake observed in 1798 that "Prophets, in the modern sense of the word, have never existed. Jonah was no prophet in the modern sense, for his prophecy of Ninevah failed. Every honest man is a Prophet; he utters his opinion both of private & public matters. Thus: If you go on So, the result is So. He never says, such a thing shall happen let you do what you will. A Prophet is a Seer, not an Arbitrary Dictator." For today's readers, it seems to me, the Nostradamus who will matter as a poet is the Seer and not the authoritative prognosticator of the future. If he has typically been read in the latter fashion, it is because (as he argues in this same preface) he was convinced that his divinely inspired "imaginative impressions" were validated by what the Renaissance unanimously accepted as a legitimate science, namely, "judicial astrology." This art of forecasting future events on the basis of the recurrence of planetary alignments or "conjunctions" was a practice that reached back to seventh-century Baghdad, subsequently popularized in Europe by the medieval translation of Albumasar's *De magnis conjunctionibus*. For a poet inhabiting the vast Renaissance echo chamber of sympathies and similitudes (see Michel Foucault's *Order of Things*), the doctrine of conjunctions was bound to appeal to his sense of *rhyme*; he even coined a lovely adjective for it, "harmotic"—from the Greek *harmotikos*, "fit for joining." The stately, inevitable procession of the planets through the houses of the zodiac in turn provided him with a corresponding master *rhythm*: lesser conjunctions occurred every 20 years, major ones every 240 years, great ones every 960 years—the rarer the conjunction, the more disastrous its impact. Conjunction and procession, rhyme and rhythm: as in the heavens, so on the page.

Richard Roussat's *Livre de l'estat et mutation des temps* (1550) encouraged the Nostradamus of the *Prophecies* to move from the merely annual and short-term calendrical predictions of his almanacs into a sweeping, millennial vision of universal history, divided into three great celestial cycles of 2,380 years, each ruled by a different planet. The current third cycle had begun with the reign of Saturn in 329 B.C.E., followed by Venus (116), Jupiter (470), Mercury (824), Mars (1179), Moon (1533), Sun (1887), and finally, at the End of Days (2242), Saturn again. Here is Nostradamus translating Roussat into verse, with a rare appearance of the first-person singular and an even rarer specification of date (only nine explicit dates occur throughout the entire *Prophecies* and their prefaces):

> Now that the Moon for twenty years has reigned, [i.e., 1553]
> Seven thousand more shall it last as king : [biblical chronology]
> When the Sun resumes its remaining days, [i.e., in 1887]
> My prophecy's fulfillment it shall bring. (1.48)

> Long before the above things come to pass,
> Those from the East by virtue of the moon
> In seventeen hundred shall launch attacks,
> Bringing much of the North under their rule. (1.49)

As a prophet who described himself as driven by "melancholy inspiration," Nostradamus was especially susceptible to the influence of Saturn. According to Roussat, the next great renewal of this distant planet would occur around 1789–91, a fact not lost on the readers of the *Prophecies* after the French Revolution:

> Ten revolutions of dread Saturn's scythe
> Shall effect changes in ages & reigns :
> It assumes its place in the mobile sign
> Where the two are equal, their angles same. (1.54)

Rewriting Virgil's celebrated Fourth Eclogue ("redeunt Saturna regna"), the poet forecasts the transfer of empire (*translatio imperii*) to a mysterious place called Brodde (from the Latin *Ebrodunum*, a region of the Alps?), if and when (?) a vulture (?) plucks out an eye (kills a leader?) in a particular town on France's southern coast near the border of Spain:

> The world's final age drawing ever close,
> Slow Saturn again making a return :
> Empire transferred toward the nation of Brodde,
> Vulture plucking out the eye at Narbonne. (3.92)

At times he is capable of a fierce, almost Blakean irony, as in this quatrain where the conjunction of Saturn ("Scythe") and Jupiter ("Tin") in Sagittarius produces a "renovation" that proves to be merely another screw-turn of horror:

> Toward Sagittarius, Scythe joined to Tin,
> And at the APOGEE of ascension :
> Plague, famine, death at military hands,
> Thus does the age approach renovation. (1.16)

Contemporaries of Nostradamus such as Laurent Videl were quick to pounce on his incompetence as an astrologer; more recently, Pierre Brind'Amour's *Nostradamus astrophile* (1993) has provided a devastatingly detailed critique of his amateurish dabbling in star lore. The current scholarly consensus has it that the astrology-based predictions of the *Prophecies* are well-nigh worthless as futurology. I tend to see them as T. S. Eliot took the theological lumber of Dante's *Divine Comedy*, that is, as a mere scaffolding device—somewhat akin to the wheels and gyres that inform the verse of the later Yeats. The latter described the cosmological gimcrackery of *A Vision* in a 1937 letter as "a last act of defense against the chaos of the world"—and so it was for Nostradamus living through what he called a most "sinister age," with early modern Europe crashing down about his ears. But the spirits also said to Yeats: "we have come to bring you metaphors for poetry."

To dismiss Nostradamus as a reliable futurologist, however, is not to deny the immense force of the *futural* that lies stored within his *Prophecies*. I know of no other long poem in any language that is cast so consistently in the future tense—a tense that (somewhat like the imperfective aspect of biblical Hebrew) cumulatively contains within itself that which once was, that which still is, and that which lies ahead. In my translation I have therefore made use of the slightly archaic auxiliary verb "shall" throughout to indicate not just simple futurity, but also (according to the Usage Note in the *American Heritage Dictionary*) various shades of determination, promise, command, and compulsion, often colored by the more optative uncertainties of doubt, anxiety, and desire. The Nostradamian sublime, linked as it is to this uncanny apprehension of time past as time future, places its reader into a state of acute anticipatory angst, hermeneutically alert to tokens and traces portentous of great changes to come—Shakespeare's "precurse of feared events, /As harbingers preceding still the fates /And prologue to the omen coming on."

Omens—signs taken for wonders—occasion the most dramatic intimations of futurity in the *Prophecies*. In his important study *La nature et les prodiges: L'insolite au XVI siècle*, historian Jean Céard has called the chaotic period between 1552 and 1559 in France "the golden age of marvels." Like his fellow poets (notably Ronsard), Nostradamus found inspiration in the extremely popular *Book of Prodigies* of Julius Obsequens, which had been recently reissued (with illustrative woodcuts) in 1552. A fourth-century epitome (or abridgment) of the Roman historian Livy's annals, Obsequens's book offers a compendium of the wonders and portents recorded in Rome during the second and first centuries B.C.E. The *Prophecies* are infused with the cultural memory of ancient divination:

> Of kings & princes images they'll unfurl,
> Haruspices, augurs, their crooks raised high :
> Victims' horns, gold, lapis lazuli, pearl,
> Entrails to be interpreted for signs. (3.26)

Among his many stray abridgments of Roman historians, Nostradamus evokes the ominous darkening of the skies after the death of Julius Caesar:

> The moon obscured within the shadows' maze,
> Its brother wan, as dull as iron rust (1.84)

Or, via Suetonius, the portents announcing the birth of Augustus—

> Near her royal bed the lady apprehends
> A snake : not a dog shall bark that night (4.93)

—or the assassination of Emperor Domitian:

> When the crow shall caw for seven hours
> Without cease upon its high brick tower :
> A death foretold, statue running with blood,
> Tyrant stabbed, people praying to the gods. (4.55)

Most frequently, however, Nostradamus introduces the kinds of spectacular prodigies and marvels that were the staple of contemporary almanac literature—comets streaking through the sky, lightning strikes, earthquakes, hailstorms, eclipses, plagues, hermaphrodites, amphibious fish, rains of frogs, monstrous births (such as the celebrated "Monster of Ravenna," discovered by invading French troops in 1512 and thought to have augured their subsequent military reverses in Italy). Nostradamus's strategy is to heap omen upon omen until a kind of mantic hysteria is achieved:

> Milk, blood, frogs showering Dalmatia,
> Battle breaking out, plague near Balenna :
> A great cry throughout all Slavonia,
> Then monster born near & in Ravenna. (2.32)

Often the causal relation between the monstrous portent (announced in the first distich) and its aftermath (in the second) remains completely garbled. Colons replace logical connectives:

> Sans foot or hand & sharp & strong of tooth,
> Born of ram & sow, with a glob for a face :
> The traitor sidles toward the gate : the moon
> Shines : led away are the small & the great. (2.58)

We end up with something like a series of screaming tabloid headlines—or prophetic tweets:

> A golden flame from sky to earth is seen :
> Struck from on high : a newborn babe amazes :
> Major massacres : the lord's nephew seized :
> Deaths at the theater : the proud one flees. (2.92)

> The spear of the sky shall streak far & wide :
> Many executed, talking as they die :
> Stone striking tree : proud people on its knees :
> Man-beast monster born : purge & purify. (2.70)

Always monitory, always remindful of the violent and inexplicable designs of God, these traumatic omens bespeak the prophet's deep anxiety about humanity's Job-like sufferings in a world so clearly fallen from grace. But much as these portents point forward in time, they also hearken back to an equally uneasy past. Nostradamus has a whole series of quatrains featuring persons or objects that have been entombed and forgotten and that now enigmatically resurface, enacting a kind of pre-Freudian return of the repressed. In a scene straight out of a horror film, someone who was mistakenly buried alive during an attack of apoplexy returns from the grave, announcing the burning of a heretic (Savonarola again?):

> Not dead when buried, just apoplectic,
> He shall be found to have his hands all gnawed:
> When the city condemns the heretic
> Who, so it seemed to them, had changed their laws. (3.36)

Having grown up near the impressive Roman ruins of Glanum in Saint-Rémy-de-Provence, Nostradamus was fascinated by the ghostly persistence of the past: his *Prophecies* are the direct contemporaries of the sonnets of Du Bellay's *Les antiquitez de Rome* (1558). The quatrains of his great serial poem are filled with archaeological allusions to buried treasure or to the chance and ominous resurgence of antiquities from beneath the ground. For instance, heavy flooding in southern France in 1557 had led to the discovery of various pagan artifacts from the ruined temple of Diana, originally thrown into the Sacred Lake of Nîmes with the coming of Christianity:

> When the ever-burning lamp is unearthed
> Within the Temple of Diana's walls,
> Flame found by a child, working with a sieve :
> Floods destroy Nîmes, Toulouse's market halls. (9.9)

> A potter digging away for fresh clay
> Shall unearth silver likenesses untold
> Of Hermes & Diana in the lake :
> He & his ilk shall have their fill of gold. (9.12)

These thematics of concealment echo another quatrain apparently evoking contemporary Spain's disastrous greed for the fabulous reserves of silver and gold lying buried in the New World—although, as Gerson points out, one nineteenth-century commentator preferred to read the following lines as intimating the Louisiana Bubble of John Law. Whatever the case may be, Nostradamus seems to be presciently registering the emergence of a whole new gold-driven colonial era:

> Alas one shall see a great nation bleed
> And the holy law & all of Christendom
> Reduced to utter ruin by other creeds,
> Each time a new gold, silver mine is found. (1.53)

One of the archaeological discoveries that most fired the prophet's imagination was the unearthing of the bones of Emperor Augustus in his Roman mausoleum in 1521 (which he may have read about in Bandini's *Dell' obelisco di Cesare Augusto* of 1549). The ruins of Glanum near Michel de Nostredame's birthplace also included a celebrated mausoleum— hence his frequent allusions to the local place-name Saint-Paul-de-*Mausole* throughout the *Prophecies*, a site better known today as the location of the

mental hospital where Van Gogh was interned toward the end of his life.
But to open a tomb—or to interpret or translate these *tombeau*-like qua-
trains?—is to risk desecration of the dead:

> The bones of the Triumvir shall be found
> While seeking cryptic treasures of the dead :
> No peace for those who lie in nearby ground
> When they go digging for marble & lead. (5.7)

Read as a malefic portent, the uncovering of Augustus's bones in 1521
was historically conjoined by Nostradamus to the (equally disastrous)
emergence of Protestantism in Europe—Luther had just been threatened
with excommunication by the pope the previous year:

> At the founding of the sect deemed so new,
> They shall dig up the great Roman's remains :
> The marble-clad tomb shall come into view :
> Earthquake in April, burial in May. (6.66)

In another quatrain, Nostradamus similarly connects the ominous reap-
pearance of ancient artifacts (sometimes referred to in his French as *sim-
ulachres*) to the sham and deceitful (*faincte*) philosophy of the new
Protestant sects whose Reformation threatened to bring about a complete
reversal of traditional values:

> The scythe shall expose the topography,
> Earthen pots revealed at the ancient sites :
> Sects pullulate, & sham philosophy :
> New mistaken for old, & black for white. (7.14)

In what is believed to be a quatrain about the city of Toulouse (Sodom?),
a city associated with the ancient Roman sacrifice of bulls and in the
mid-sixteenth century a redoubt of French Protestantism, the forces of
change are denounced as mere atavistic regressions to barbarous heathen
practices—a common trope in anti-Protestant pamphlets of the day
(just as it was in Huguenot polemics against the pagan idolatries of the
Catholic Church):

> In the city of Fertsod most murderous,
> Where plow-ox risks sacrifice on altar,
> They'll return to the worship of Artemis,
> And bury their dead in Vulcan's honor. (9.74)

Characteristically, the eruption of the archaic into the present, or of myth
into the real, is registered as taking place in the future. All tenses are si-
multaneous in the great time warp of the *Prophecies*. History, a nightmare

from which the prophet is trying to awake, offers itself as a single, unremitting trauma.

After the extraordinary flowering of its medieval chansons de geste, the history of French literature is dotted with a series of failed (or utterly arid) verse epics: with the possible exception of Hugo's *Légende des siècles*, it possesses nothing on the order of Ariosto, Tasso, Camões, Spenser, or Milton. In his manifesto for the modernization of national culture, *La deffence et illustration de la langue françoyse* (1549), Du Bellay had called for a "long poem" that might exemplify the new vernacular literature while vying with the epics of the Ancients. Ronsard promptly took up the challenge and in the following year began to sketch out what would eventually become *La Franciade*, an account of the adventures of Francus, the son of Hector who had escaped from the sack of Troy and gone on to establish the Frankish kingdom. In this foundation myth, the French were thus descended from the Trojans and could therefore claim kinship with the Romans, who owed their origins to Aeneas, another survivor of Troy. Modeling himself on Virgil, Ronsard hoped to publish his epic as an homage to the nation-building of the current king, Henri II, but, all attempts at securing royal patronage having failed, he had to wait until 1572 to bring it out, thanks to the generous influence of the queen mother, Catherine de Médicis, on the new young monarch, Charles IX. Though considered among Ronsard's least successful poems, the incomplete *Franciade* had at least provided the house of Valois with its legitimizing epic—and its poet received a handsome priory in exchange.

As the Epistle to Henri II preceding the final three Centuries of his poem demonstrates, Nostradamus likewise sought to put his *Prophecies* at the service of the Valois dynasty. Filled with fawning allusions to his visit to the court in 1555 and dated June 1558, this epistle was rendered nugatory by Henri II's unexpected death in a duel the following year—a singular lapse of prophetic foresight on Nostradamus's part (which may account for the fact that it had to wait ten years for posthumous publication). Henri II's demise notwithstanding, the seer remained in the good graces of the court, as evidenced by the ever-superstitious Catherine de Médicis' visit to his hometown of Salon in October 1564, accompanied by her fourteen-year-old son, Charles IX—during which Nostradamus performed a series of astrological consultations that were rewarded by three hundred crowns and his appointment as Counselor and Physician in Ordinary to the King.

As a long poem written to glorify (and instruct) the Valois dynasty, the *Prophecies* would seem a poor candidate for epic. Its crabbed and willfully archaic idiom—which at times slips into the poet's native Provençal—hardly represents the streamlined vernacular advocated by Du Bellay for the celebration of a modern nation-state under a centralized monarchy.

Furthermore, the poem as a whole lacks that most minimal requirement of an epic—a hero whose noble exploits and tribulations take place within a culturally intelligible grammar of narrative. Instead of epic sweep, Nostradamus provides scattered miniatures.

A dramatic naval battle that another poet would have taken pages to develop is condensed into four telegraphic, imagistic lines:

> Night shall overtake the battle at sea,
> Fire shall devastate the Western ships :
> Newly ruddled red shall the galleon be :
> Merciless defeat : victors in the mist. (9.100)

Instead of the leisurely catalogs and enumerations of epic description, we are assaulted by a fusillade of monosyllables whose only grammar is the shriek:

> Pleurs, crys & plaincts, hurlement, effraieur,
> Coeur inhumain, cruel, noir, & transy :
> Leman, les iles de Gennes les majeurs,
> Sang espancher, frofaim, à nul mercy.

> Tears, shrieks & moans, vociferation, fright,
> Inhuman heart, cruel, & blacker than stone :
> In Leman & Genoa's greater isles,
> Bloodshed, no wheat to eat, no mercy shown. (6.81)

Nostradamus's profound agrammaticality is evident at every level of the work. Just as its individual quatrains are disrupted from within by punctuation and rhetorical figures (syllepsis, hypallage, hyperbaton, asyndeton, etc.) designed to cloud their syntactical clarity—he wrote his son that he intended to shroud his poem "sous figure nubileuse"—so their larger sequencing into Centuries appears utterly aleatory, following no discernible narrative pattern. The poem as a whole observes what in the Renaissance was called *ordo neglectus*—digressive and dispersive in the serial fashion of Montaigne's *Essais*. Like Montaigne's immense cento of citations, it thereby gradually acquires the density of a palimpsest: events or texts quoted from the past or from earlier portions of the poem are constantly cut up (in William Burroughs's sense) and recycled throughout its pages to create a bleakly Nietzschean (or, more precisely, Benjaminian) vision of the Eternal Return of the Same—history petrified into brittle allegory, with mankind bound, Ixion-like, on the relentless wheel of Fortuna.

And yet from this virtually Dantescan Inferno, there occasionally flash forth a few eschatological gleams of hope. Much of Nostradamus's 1568 Epistle to Henri II is taken up by a rambling, apocalyptic prophecy in prose concerning the future of the Barren Lady—presumably the Church—in which, somewhat incoherently, at least three different advents of the millennium are predicted, in conjunction with the arrival of at least three separate antichrists. Much of this material is patchworked together from the *Mirabilis liber,* a popular compilation of prophecies ranging from Pseudo-Methodius and Joachim of Fiore to Savonarola and Fra Bonaventura. Originally published in Paris in 1522, this volume (as Alexandre Haran has shown in his *Le lys et le globe: Messianisme dynastique et rêve impérial en France*) was assembled as part of the propaganda effort to create an aura of messianic inevitability around the Valois reign of François I—especially urgent, given that his Hapsburg archrival, Charles V, had just recently been anointed Holy Roman Emperor in 1519. The core myth of the Messianic King—subsequently used to justify ventures as dubious as the Crusades, the expulsion of the Jews from Spain, and the conquest of America—reached back to a fourth-century prophecy attributed to the Tiburtine sibyl (also included in the *Mirabilis liber*). A leader descended from the Greeks and Romans by the name of Constans would reestablish the unity of the Roman Empire, vanquish the infidels, baptize them by force, and take possession of the Holy Land; there he would rule in peace and prosperity, before handing over his empire to God the Father and Jesus Christ his Son; the end of this millennium would then usher in the final battle with the Antichrist, eventuating in the Last Judgment. This dream of an enlightened temporal monarch who would institute a lasting world peace transcending the corrupt and divisive politics of the papacy was first influentially formulated in the fourteenth century by Dante's *De monarchia* and then subsequently developed in Ariosto's equally Ghibelline idealization of Charles V as a solar Carolingian emperor in his epic *Orlando Furioso* (1516–32)—which in turn inspired Spenser's encomium of Astraea-Elizabeth, astral virgin queen of the golden age, in *The Fairie Queene* (1590–96). Rooted in the same politico-prophetic soil as these other Renaissance epics, the *Prophecies* anagrammatize Henri II into the larger-than-life figure of "Chyren" (from the Provençal spelling of his name, "Henryc"), a mythic, "selenian" moon-king destined to institute universal harmony and justice on earth and, more importantly, to bring about that Saturnian "renovation" in which a Valois monarch would finally displace the Hapsburgs (as well as the papacy and the Ottomans) as the wise and peace-loving *restorator orbis*—Restorer of the World.

An epic, as Ezra Pound once observed, is "a poem including history." By this definition, the *Prophecies,* nonnarrative though the poem may be, certainly deserves inclusion at the margins of the genre. Jean-Aimé de Chavigny, Nostradamus's secretary and general amanuensis—who had gotten his job with the prophet through the good offices of Jean Dorat, erstwhile mentor of the Pléiade poets and later appointed Poète du Roy—was the first to present Nostradamus as a genuine historian-prophet in his 1594 anthology, *La première face du Janus françois*, subtitled, "Summarily Containing the Troubles, Civil Wars & Other Remarkable Things that Occurred in France from 1533 to the End of the House of Valois in 1589." Though one might remain skeptical about Nostradamus's predictions of the establishment of the Bourbon monarchy by Henri IV in 1589—after all, he finished writing his *Prophecies* some thirty years earlier—Chavigny nonetheless seized upon the Janus-like "retrospective future" that was his master's most head-turning trope. Veiled in allegory (the French are often called "Trojans," the Spaniards "Hesperidians," the Milanese "Insubrians," and the Turks "Punics" or "Barbarians") and jumbled almost beyond recognition, the *Prophecies* are nonetheless permeated with allusions to history past and present. Threaded throughout their quatrains lies a hidden tapestry of sixteenth-century Europe, some of whose scope I have tried to indicate in my annotations.

The "matter" of the poem, as one says of the old French epics and romances, revolves around a titanic clash of civilizations (the Christian West vs. the Islamic East), internecine European strife (Protestants vs. Catholics), and the shifting alliances and conflicts among Spain, France, and England for imperial supremacy over land and sea. Here is a sample of some of the military and political matter rehearsed within the great (and troubled) memory theater of the poem—the historical "facts" behind Nostradamus's great phantasmagoria of the Disasters of War: the French triumph over the Holy League at Ravenna (1512); Turkish gains in the Balkans, Austria, Hungary, and the capture of Rhodes (1521–22); the Hapsburg-Valois wars in Italy, resulting in the French loss of Milan and Genoa (1522); Charles V's subsequent invasion of Provence and Italy (1524); the crushing defeat of the French at Pavia (1525), leading to the imprisonment of François I in Spain and his forced signing of the Treaty of Madrid (1526); the sack of Rome by the Imperial forces (1527); Süleyman the Magnificent's invasion of Hungary and besieging of Vienna (1529); the corsair Hayreddin Barbarossa's predations along the North African, French, and Italian coasts (1533–38); Charles V's reconquest of Tunis (1535) and triumphant entry into Rome after having ravaged southern France (1536); Barbarossa's defeat of the Spanish fleet under the command of Andrea Doria (1538); the sack of Buda by the Turks and Calvin's establishment of a theocracy in Geneva (1541); the massacre of the French Protestant Waldensians in the Lubéron and the convening of the Council of Trent to counter the Reformation (1545); the death of François I (1547); the revolt in southwestern France against the new king Henri II's salt tax, leading to fears of English invasion (1548); the decision of Henri II, allied with the Protestant elector of Saxony, to go to war against Charles V, with the battle for Metz pitching the Duke of Guise against the Duke of Alba (1552); the defeat of the French fleet by Andrea Doria in Corsica (1553), etc.

All these events, even if conjugated in the future, took place years before Nostradamus embarked upon his *Prophecies* in 1554. As the poem progresses, however, its historical ground grows asymptotically ever closer to the present, particularly in the last three Centuries. After Charles V abdicated in 1555, leaving his son Philip the Spanish empire and his brother Ferdinand the crown of Holy Roman Emperor, Nostradamus predicted (falsely, it turned out) that tensions between the two would open an avenue for French ambitions (9.35). Toward the end of the poem, however, the Spanish have entered into alliance with the English as a result of Philip's marriage to Queen Mary: their combined forces would inflict a devastating defeat on the French at Saint-Quentin in 1557, which led to the capture of Montmorency (9.18), even though the fortress would be retaken by the dashing Duke of Guise the following year—together with Calais, England's last surviving enclave in France (9.29). In April 1558, just as Nostradamus was bringing his tenth Century to a close, the fourteen-year-old dauphin François married Mary Stuart, Queen of Scots and niece of the Duke of Guise (10.55), inspiring Nostradamus's hope that this union might allow the Valois to diplomatically outflank the Hapsburgs as leaders of a new Catholic Anglo-French empire. Which might explain the rather curious concluding quatrain of the *Prophecies*:

> By England shall great empire see the day,
> More than three hundred years' powerful sway :
> To the discomfort of the Portuguese,
> Its great forces shall sweep over land & sea. (10.100)

But for the house of Valois, ever more mired in France's grim Wars of Religion, this world-historical mission envisaged by the prophet would remain forever unrealized: Henri II was killed in a duel in 1559; his son François II ruled for a mere eighteen months, dying at age sixteen; François's brother Charles IX assumed the throne at age ten and, after being married off to a Hapsburg by his mother, Catherine de Médicis, died at twenty-three; Charles was succeeded by another brother, Henri III, without issue. By 1589, the dynasty was extinct.

During Nostradamus's actual composition of the *Prophecies*, however, the future still looked relatively auspicious for the Valois. Though the prophet warns, Cassandra-like, against France's continued foreign involvement in the Italian Wars (e.g., 3.23) while condemning its savage persecution of the Protestants (4.63), he remains optimistic that it will produce a ruler capable of ushering in a golden age:

> Born in shadows & day as dark as night,
> With sovereign benevolence he shall rule :
> From the ancient urn he'll refresh his line,
> Remake the age of bronze an age of gold. (5.41)

The name he most frequently applies to this messianic sovereign-to-come is "Ogmion," or the "French Hercules"—an appellation that appears in Erasmus's 1502 Latin translation of Lucian's *Death of Peregrinus*. In celebration of Henri II's royal entry into Paris in 1549, the new king was depicted on an arch of triumph as the "Gallic Hercules." Unlike the Spanish Hercules, Charles V, often represented as enfettering the columns of Hercules (i.e., Gibraltar) by his sheer strength, the French Ogmion instead was here shown binding his subjects together by his *word*—with delicate gold and silver chains running from his tongue into their listening ears (see 1.96). Governing not simply by military power, but rather by the force of eloquence, the figure of Ogmion incarnates Nostradamus's humanist ideal of an enlightened and cosmopolitan French monarch in the tradition of that great patron of arts and letters François I, who even created a chair for the study of Arabic at his new Collège des Lecteurs Royaux:

> A Libyan prince with influence in the West
> Shall so inflame François for Arab matters
> That in his knowledge of letters he shall abet
> The translation of its language into French. (3.27)

The traditional emblem of the French monarchy, the fleur-de-lis—which recalls the lily of the valley of the Song of Songs—will in turn transform France into an Arcadia akin to the "green and pleasant land" of Blake's redeemed Albion:

> There peace & abundance shall find its land,
> With the lily growing wild everywhere :
> The dead shall be brought in by sea and land,
> In the vain hope of being buried there. (4.20)

As in Plutarch's *Parallel Lives*, everything in Nostradamus's poem happens (at least) twice: every *event* past or present is parsed as an *advent* of the future. Toward the very end of the *Prophecies*, Nostradamus quotes the dying Augustus's boast that "I found a Rome of bricks and left it to you of marble," while predicting that his fifty-seven-year reign as emperor will provide the paradigm for a great Pax Augusta to come:

> In marble shall the walls of brick now rise,
> Seven & fifty years of lasting peace,
> Aqueducts restored, joy to all mankind,
> Health, abundant fruit, blissful honeyed times. (10.89)

In Virgil's celebrated Fourth Eclogue, the imminent return of the golden age under Saturn's sway was interpreted in the Middle Ages as announcing the coming of Christ—born under the reign of Augustus. This soteriological figure, however, is virtually absent from the *Prophecies*. The poem contains but a single glancing mention of the Messiah ("The great Messiah shall rule through the Sun," 5.53) and but a single quatrain that might possibly allude to his brief and ultimately imperiled parousia as a "shepherd":

> Lost, found, in hiding for so long a while,
> Shepherd as demigod shall be honored :
> Before the moon completes its full cycle,
> By other vows shall he be dishonored. (1.25)

In the meantime, in a world whose God is at best inscrutable and at worst utterly riven by religious schism—the word "God" occurs only three times over the course of the entire poem—the only fitting response is therefore a watchful silence, in the patient expectation that, sooner or later, the awaited one might arrive, always imminent, always deferred:

> The rose at the core of the greater world,
> New allegations civic bloodshed feed :
> One's mouth shall be closed, if the truth be told,
> The awaited one late in time of need. (5.96)

RICHARD SIEBURTH

A Note on the Translation

Translations are always fated to be clearer than their originals. In the case of Nostradamus, I have taken the smudged and almost indecipherable woodcuts of his quatrains and tried to sharpen their quality of (Latin) epigrammatic incision, always seeking to imagine what, in his mind's eye, the seer might have actually "seen." I have cleaved close to his French decasyllabic meter, attempting to re-create in English the measures and caesurae of nonaccentual verse: the syllable has therefore been (as Charles Olson put it) the "kingpin" of my prosody. Nostradamus's prophecies are unthinkable in a universe without rhyme: in addition to his standard alternating scheme (*abab*), I have played with couplets, mono-rhyme, and all the resources of assonance, consonance, cross-, near-, slant-, and eye-rhyme in order to register a cosmos where homophony and homology constantly collide. If many of the quatrains therefore come out sounding like the doggerel of disaster (or like the nonsense stanzas of Edward Lear), this, too, is part of the popular culture from which they emerged.

Nostradamus himself started out as a translator: his first literary work (unpublished) was a casting of Horapollo's treatise on Egyptian hieroglyphics into rhymed "epigrams." His *Prophecies* can in turn be approached as a massive translation machine, in which Latin word order is literally transferred into vernacular French and in which the past is continually ferried into the future in the service of a vast vision of *translatio imperii*. The poem has in turn called up myriads of further translations over the centuries—if one includes under this broad rubric not only rewordings into other languages (including modern French), but also all forms of plagiarism, imitation, exegesis, commentary, and outright hermeneutic delirium (still proliferating on the World Wide Web). My new verse version is thus merely the latest afterlife (*Nachleben*) of Nostradamus's serial work-in-progress.

As was the case for my previous translation of Scève's *Délie*, my worn copy of Cotgrave's 1611 *Dictionarie of the French and English Tongues* has never been far from my side. Also on my desk: Edgar Leoni's 1961 *Nostradamus and His Prophecies* and Peter Lemesurier's 2003 *Nostradamus: The Illustrated Prophecies*. Leoni provides a literal, word-for-word account of the poem, based on a rather corrupt version of the original text. Although his readings are therefore far from dependable, his edition of the complete *Prophecies*—especially its indices and appendices—contains much that will be of interest to the serious student of the prophet. Lemesurier's *Illustrated Prophecies* provides a "New and Authoritative Translation" of the poem to commemorate the five hundredth anniversary of Nostradamus's birth. While certainly an interpretative advance on Leoni's humble literalism and informed by admirable scholarship, Lemesurier's verse translation addresses itself primarily to British ears of a bygone Edwardian era. I have tried to look further back—and forward.

RICHARD SIEBURTH

A Note on the Text

The original from which a translation—or any interpretation—derives is usually assumed to be in some sense authoritative. Nothing could be further from the truth in Nostradamus's case. The original texts of his *Prophecies* are notoriously unstable, laced as they are with printer's errors that arose during the oral dictation of the fair copies to harried compositors plucking type from dwindling sets of font. Given the distance between Nostradamus's hometown of Salon and the publishing epicenter of Lyon, the proofreading of his texts was often desultory, if not downright garbled. There is therefore no truly credible "original" of his *Prophecies*—just a welter of different printings (or different "translations"), which philologists have attempted to collate.

The first modern critical edition of the 1555 Macé Bonhomme printing of the initial 353 quatrains was provided by the late Pierre Brind'Amour in 1996. This Canadian scholar brilliantly reconstructed Nostradamus's (hypothetical) original, reimagining and, above all, *rehearing* its meanings behind all the acoustic distortions of the typographers. In a somewhat controversial move, Brind'Amour also repunctuated the text, occasionally inserting additional (spaced out) colons to clarify the rhythmic and semantic phrasing of the quatrains—a practice I have followed in my English versions. His philology in turn established the basis for Bruno Petey-Girard's 2003 Garnier-Flammarion version of *Les Prophéties*, which brought the poem up to its second 1557 printing by Antoine du Rosne (i.e., to the end of its seventh Century). This is the edition on which I have based my en-face translation, even though the punctuation of the quatrains occasionally varies, preferring as I do Brind'Amour's (and du Rosne's) sense of the Nostradamian colon. In addition, I have restored all the ampersands Petey-Girard silently corrects into the French *et*: the ampersand (where "&" can at once mean "and" and "or"—as in "soon & late") is absolutely crucial to the poem's logic and visual prosody. The final installment of the *Prophecies*—Centuries 8 through 10—still awaits editing. In the absence of such an edition, I have followed (with minimal modernization of its spelling) what is thought to be the most reliable extant printing: the posthumous edition of the "complete" poem (with its intercalated prefatory matter), published by Benoist Rigaud in 1568. Its lackadaisical orthography and punctuation have proved to be at once a nightmare and an inspiration. In my annotations to this edition, I have underscored Nostradamus's references to actual historical events of his times and to real geographical places. Above all, I have tried to be attentive to his onomastics, for the *Prophecies* are founded on the poetics of the Proper Name—the only stable (and magically eucharistic) symbol left in a world torn asunder by religious and political schism.

RICHARD SIEBURTH

Chronology

1503	December 14: Michel de Nostredame is born in Saint-Rémy-de-Provence. He is the eldest child of Jaume de Nostredame, a notary and occasional moneylender, and Reynière de Saint-Rémy. His paternal side includes converted Jews, probably of Spanish origin, who changed the family name to Nostredame.
1515	François I succeeds Louis XII as king of France.
1517	Martin Luther posts his Ninety-Five Theses against papal indulgences on a church door in Wittenberg.
ca. 1518–21	Nostradamus studies the humanities at the University of Avignon.
1519–56	Reign of Charles V, Holy Roman Emperor.
ca. 1521	Nostradamus begins medical studies at the University of Montpellier. Interrupts them to travel and study botany across southern France. Reenrolls in 1529 and probably graduates in 1532.
1521–59	Intermittent wars between France and the Spanish Hapsburgs, who win the Italian war of 1521–26. Spanish troops enter Provence in 1526 and 1536.
1524	February: Great planetary conjunction of Saturn, Jupiter, and Mars under the sign of Pisces generates fears of a universal, apocalyptic deluge.
ca. 1530–46	Nostradamus travels throughout southern France and northern Italy. Practices medicine, collects plants, and helps people afflicted by the plague. Among other cities, lives in Toulouse and Agen, where he befriends and then quarrels with the scholar and physician Julius Caesar Scaliger. Loses his wife and two children, probably to the plague, in 1539.
1533	Caterina de' Medici, daughter of Lorenzo II de' Medici, marries the future Henri II of France.
1536	John Calvin publishes his *Institutes of the Christian Religion* in Geneva. Alliance between François I and Turkish ruler Süleyman the Magnificent against Charles V. Joint military operations in the 1540s and 1550s. Ottoman fleet winters in Toulon in 1543/44.
1545–63	Council of Trent, called to examine Roman Catholic doctrine in response to the Protestant Reformation.

ca. 1545   Nostradamus writes a long and personal poetic rendering (in French) of the hieroglyphics of Horapollo. The eighty-six-page manuscript was rediscovered in 1967.

1546   Aix-en-Provence summons him for medical assistance during a plague epidemic.

1547   Small Provençal town of Salon de Craux (now called Salon-de-Provence) calls upon Nostradamus when the plague hits. In November, he marries the local widow Anne Ponsarde Gemelle, with whom he has six children between ca. 1551 and 1561. Their eldest son, César, will become a respected magistrate, historian, and mayor of Salon.

1547   François I dies, succeeded by Henri II.

1547–50   Nostradamus travels in France and Italy, but grows more sedentary and settles in Salon. Practices medicine and opens a successful horoscope practice, with clients visiting and writing from all corners of western Europe.

1548   Violent tax riots and repression in southwestern France.

1550   Nostradamus presumably publishes his first almanac. Other annual almanacs and prognostications signed "Nostradamus" or "Nostredame" follow until his death, sometimes more than one per year.

1552   Publishes a collection of recipes for jams, preserves, love philters, and cosmetics (*Le vray & parfaict embellissement de la Face, & la manière de faire des confitures*).

1555   Publishes the first edition of the *Prophecies* in Lyon (pub. Macé Bonhomme). It contains 353 quatrains, divided into four Centuries, and a preface addressed to César.

       Summer: Catherine de Médicis invites Nostradamus to the court to provide horoscopes of her children. He reportedly predicts that all of her sons will accede to the throne.

ca. 1556–58   First translations of Nostradamus's almanacs into German, Italian, and English.

1556   Antoine Couillard's *Les Prophéties du seigneur du Pavillon les Lorriz* (published in 1560) lambastes the all-too-popular Nostradamus. Other French and English detractors join the fray during the following years.

1557   Second edition of the *Prophecies*, published in Lyon by Antoine du Rosne. Contains 642 quatrains. Nostradamus also writes a French adaptation of a treatise by the Greek physician Galen.

1559   Publishes a short essay on the plague (*An Excellent Tretise, Shevving Suche Perillous, and Contagious Infirmities*). The English translation alone has survived.

       Treaty of Cateau-Cambrésis marks the end of hostilities between France and Spain and England. That summer, Henri II dies following an accident in a jousting tournament in Paris (he is succeeded by his son François II). At court and elsewhere, people claim that Nostradamus had predicted this calamity.

Tensions between French Protestants (the Huguenots), Catholics, and the crown grow more acute. Secret Protestant synod; arrest and execution of Protestant leaders. Violence intensifies during the following years.

Marguerite de Valois, daughter of Henri II and Catherine de Médicis, consults Nostradamus.

1560 Poet Pierre de Ronsard vindicates Nostradamus as a Catholic poet whose prophecies have been confirmed by recent marvels.

December: François II dies, succeeded by his ten-year-old brother Charles IX. Catherine de Médicis appointed regent. People in France link Nostradamus's quatrains to these events.

1560s–70s Several forgers and imitators publish works attributed to Nostradamus or one of his kin.

1560–61 Catholic peasants from Salon hound local Protestants. Some accuse Nostradamus of being a covert Huguenot. He takes refuge in Avignon for two months.

1562 French Wars of Religion begin. Intermittent strife between Catholics and Protestants until 1598.

1564 October 17: The French court makes an overnight stop in Salon while traveling across the provinces. Catherine de Médicis summons Nostradamus for a private audience and names him Counselor and Physician in Ordinary to the King. Charles IX reportedly consults him during ensuing months.

1566 Afflicted by arthritis, dropsy, and arteriosclerosis, Nostradamus writes his will on June 17. He dies in his Salon home on July 2. His secretary, Jean-Aimé de Chavigny, later claims that Nostradamus had predicted his death a day earlier.

1568 First complete edition of the *Prophecies*, containing 942 quatrains divided into ten Centuries and a second preface (to the late French king Henri II). Published in Lyon by Benoist Rigaud.

1594 Chavigny publishes the first biographical sketch and book-length interpretation of Nostradamian quatrains, taken from his almanacs as well as the *Prophecies* (*La première face du Janus françois*).

1605 Some editions of the *Prophecies* incorporate fifty-eight six-line poems (*sixains*) under the title *Admirable Predictions for the Current Years of This Century*. Reportedly recovered by a doctor and flour merchant named Vincent Seve, these verses were most likely forgeries. Still, they have entered the Nostradamian corpus.

1672 First complete English translation of the *Prophecies*, by the French-born apothecary Theophilus de Garencières, published in London.

The Prophecies

Preface of
M. Michel Nostradamus
To his Prophecies
To César Nostradamus His Son

LONG LIFE & HAPPINESS

Your late arrival, César Nostradame my son, has caused me to devote a great deal of time, spent in continual nightly vigils, to reveal in writing & to leave behind to you as a memory, after my own physical demise, & for the common benefit of mankind, such knowledge as the Divine Being has granted me, thanks to the revolutions of the stars.

And since it has pleased God that you should have appeared on this goodly earth, but that your years are still too small to number, adding only up to two successive months of March, your tender understanding cannot yet fathom what it is I am compelled to bring to completion at my death:

& seeing that it is possible to leave something behind to you in writing which would otherwise have been obliterated by time, for this hereditary gift of prophecy shall not survive me:

& considering that all human ventures come to an uncertain end & that everything is ruled & governed by the incalculable power of God, finding our inspiration not in Dionysian frenzy, nor in the furor of madness, but in astrological considerations, *Only those who are inspired by the divine spirit & the prophetic breath can predict particular things.*

Given that I have for a long time repeatedly predicted well in advance what has since come to pass & in what particular region, attributing this accomplishment to God's power & inspiration, as well as having predicted on a more short-term basis other fortunate & unfortunate events that were to take place throughout the world,

& having wanted, for fear of causing offense, to keep my silence & refrain from putting into writing the majority of these events, not only those of the present but also those of the future, because kingdoms, sects, & religions shall undergo such dramatic changes, changes so diametrically opposed to the present state of things, that if I were to reveal what the future brings, the people of the kingdoms, sects, religions & faiths would find it so discordant to the fancy of their ears that they would condemn that which in centuries to come will be recognized as having been actually seen & witnessed.

Also considering this dictum by our True Savior, *Give not that which is holy unto the dogs, neither cast ye your pearls before swine, lest they trample them under their feet, & turn again & rend you,* which has been the cause of my withholding my tongue from the vulgar & my pen from paper, I have since then decided to extend myself, declaring to the common assembly by means of abstruse & puzzling utterances the things of the future, even the most imminent ones, & those that I have seen, however much these might disrupt & scandalize their fragile ears, & the whole thing written in nebulous figures rather than palpably prophetic.

Because *thou hast hid these things from the wise & prudent,* that is, from the powerful & the kings, & *hast revealed them unto the small amid the poor* & to the Prophets: by the grace of everlasting God & the good angels these have received the spirit of prophecy, by which they see distant causes & come to foresee future events, for nothing can come to pass without Him, whose power & goodness is so great to his creatures that even if He remains withdrawn into Himself, one & indivisible, nonetheless to each according to its proper shape & genius this prophetic heat & power visits us as do the rays of the sun whose influence works upon bodies both elementary & non-elementary.

As for ourselves, mere humans, neither our natural knowledge nor the bent of our ingenuity can lead us to know anything about the dark secrets of God the Creator, *It is not for you to know the times or the seasons &c.*

Although it is possible that even today there may appear & exist people to whom God the Creator has deigned to reveal, through imaginative impressions, some of the secrets of the future by recourse to judicial astrology, just as in the past a certain power & faculty of will were given by the gods, appearing like a flame of fire which, acting to inspire them, allowed others to judge of their human & divine inspiration.

For those divine works which are totally absolute are accomplished by God: medial works, in the middle, by angels: the third kind, by evil spirits.

But, my son, I'm speaking to you here a bit too abstrusely: as for the occult vaticinations inspired in us by that subtle spirit of fire which sometimes exercises our minds as we sit up nights contemplating the stars on high, finding myself (to my surprise) prophesying, I write it all down, pronouncing myself without fear, free from immodest loquacity. How so? Because all these things were flowing from the almighty power of Eternal God, from whom all bounty proceeds.

Note, however, my son, that if I have made mention of the term prophet, far be it from me to arrogate a title this exalted, this sublime, in these present times: *For he that is now called a Prophet was beforetime called Seer:* for a Prophet, my son, is properly speaking someone who sees distant things with the natural knowledge possessed by all creatures.

But it can happen that the Prophet, infused with the perfect light of prophecy, receives a manifest revelation of things both divine & human, which is normally impossible, given the huge span of future prediction.

For the secrets of God are inscrutable, & effective virtue, which is ultimately contingent on the far reach of natural knowledge & whose most immediate source lies in free will, causes things to appear which, in & of themselves, cannot attract the knowledge either of human clairvoyance or any other occult power in this world below, precisely because of the fact that eternity contains within itself all of time.

But precisely because eternity is indivisible, things can be known through the Herculean trances of epilepsy, through the movement of the heavenly stars.

I am not saying, my son (lest you misunderstand me, given that knowledge of such matters cannot yet imprint itself upon your tender mind), that the very distant things of the future lie beyond the knowledge of any reasonable creature: on the contrary, the intellective soul can grasp things both present & distant if they are not too occult or too closed off: but the perfect knowledge of things cannot be acquired without divine inspiration, seeing as how all prophetic inspiration derives its prime moving principle from God the creator, then from good fortune & nature.

It is thus that, any given thing being produced or not produced in a given fashion, the prophecy is in part fulfilled as predicted.

For intellectual understanding cannot predict which way things of the future shall tend, unless it be through the voice heard at the hem by means of the slender flame.

Moreover, my son, I beg you never to devote your mind to such fancies & vanities which desiccate the body, drive the soul to perdition, troubling the feeble faculty of judgment: to wit, the vanity of that more than execrable magic that was long ago condemned by the Holy Scriptures & the canons of the Church, with the exception of the judgment of judicial astrology, by means of which & thanks to the inspiration & divine revelation accorded by continuous nightly vigils & calculations, we have drawn up our prophecies in writing.

And because this occult Philosophy is disallowed, I have never wanted to offer to view its heady persuasions, even if a number of volumes hidden for ages did come into my hands.

But for fear of what might happen, after reading them I offered them up to Vulcan, & while the fire was devouring them, the flames that licked the air gave off an unaccustomed brightness, brighter than any natural flame, like the fulguration of a jet of fire at once illuminating the entire house as if it had suddenly burst into flames.

For this reason, lest you one day be deceived by the pursuit of the perfect transmutation of silver or gold, or of those uncorruptible metals buried in the earth or hidden underwater, I reduced these books to ashes.

But as concerns that prophetic judgment which is rendered perfect by divine inspiration, let me explain it to you: it is this judgment that enables you to have knowledge of future things, projecting into the distance the fabulous imaginings of things to come &, under supernatural inspiration, precisely locating the particularity of places, attuning the places & dates to their celestial figures thanks to a virtue, a power & a faculty divine possessed of occult properties, for which the three dimensions of time are comprehended within eternity & whose revolution includes things past, present & future: *all things are naked & opened &c.*

Thus, my son, despite your tender mind, you can easily grasp that those things which are bound to happen can be foretold by recourse to the stars in the heavens at night (which are natural) & by the spirit of prophecy, not that I arrogate for myself the name or function of a prophet, but that of a mortal man possessed of revealed inspiration, whose senses are no less distant from heaven than his feet from the ground : *I can err, fail, be deceived*, there is no greater sinner on this earth than I, subject to all the afflictions of man.

But sometimes surprised over the course of the week by prophetic inspiration & my lengthy calculations lending a pleasant scent to my nightly studies, I composed prophetic books each of which contained one hundred quatrains of astronomic predictions, which I intentionally cobbled together somewhat obscurely: these being perpetual prophecies which reach from now to the year 3797.

Some might well raise their brows, seeing such a great extension of time, yet these things, my son, shall take place & shall be known within our sublunar realm: which is to say universally & throughout the earth.

And if you live until the age of your natural manhood, you shall see these future events take place even in the specific skies of your own native clime.

For the only eternal God is He who alone knows the eternity of the light that proceeds from Him, & I frankly maintain that to those to whom He has chosen to reveal, in their long & melancholy inspiration, the immensity of His grandeur (which is without measure & incomprehensible), by means of this occult thing which is the manifestation of the divine, He infuses one of the two principal things which shape the understanding of the inspired Prophet, clarifying the supernatural light to the person who makes predictions on the basis of astrology & who prophesies by inspired revelation, which inspiration provides a definite participation in the eternity of God, allowing the prophet to come to judge what his divine guiding spirit has revealed to him through God the Creator & through natural instigation: which is to say, what he predicts is true & of celestial origin: & this light & slender flame is efficacious & most sublime, no less than the natural brightness or natural light that bestows certainty upon philosophers who, reasoning forth from the principles of the first cause, manage to penetrate into the deepest depths of the loftiest truth.

But, my son, lest I digress into matters too deep for the future capacity of your mind, & because I feel that the world of letters shall undergo such a massive & incomparable collapse, I find that so many deluges & major floods shall befall the world before the universal conflagration that there shall remain scarcely any land that is not covered by water, & that this shall go on for such a long time that, were it not for the surviving oenographies & topographies, all would be completely lost: likewise, before & after these inundations, in many lands the rains shall be so slight & so much fire & so many white-hot stones shall fall from the sky that nothing shall remain that has not been consumed: & all this shall come to pass, in short, before the final conflagration.

But now that the planet Mars is completing its cycle & is at the end of its latest period, it shall recommence again: but with some of the planets grouped in Aquarius for several years, others in Cancer for longer & continuous periods.

And now that we are governed by the Moon, under eternal God's omnipotent sway, before it has completed its full circuit, the Sun shall reign & then Saturn.

For according to the celestial signs, the reign of Saturn shall return, the whole thing having been calculated, the world is approaching a revolution that breaks wholly with the past:

& from the present day on which I am writing this until before one hundred seventy-seven years, three months & eleven days, the world shall be so diminished by plagues, by extended famines & wars & even more by floods, between this moment & the time I have just indicated, before & after this repeatedly, the world shall be so diminished that no one shall be found willing to work the fields, which shall remain fallow for as long a time as they were subjected to the plow:

& all this, by interpreting what is seen in the stars on high : even though we be in the seventh millennium which brings everything to a close, we are approaching the eighth, the seat of the firmament of the eighth sphere, at the altitude where great God most eternal shall accomplish the revolution by which the signs of the zodiac shall return to their movements & to that higher movement which renders our earth stable & firm & *which shall not vary from age to age*: except that all this come to pass as His will be done, but not otherwise.

Whereas by ambiguous opinions exceeding all natural reasonings by Mohammedan dreamings, it shall come to pass that on several occasions God the creator, through the ministry of his messengers of fire, should propose to our exterior senses (& even to our eyes), in the form of this expediting flame, the causes of our predictions of the future, causes that are the signs of those future happenings which are bound to occur to persons engaged in prognostication.

For the prediction that is shaped by outer light infallibly ends up contriving with & depending on inner light, even though in truth that part which seems to see through the eye of understanding does so only by inhibiting the imaginative faculty: the reason for this is only too obvious, for everything is predicted through the afflatus of God & through the angelic spirit breathed into the man who prophesies, illumining him, stirring his fantasy with various nocturnal visions, to the same extent that, during the certainty of day, he prophesies on the basis of astronomy, in conjunction with that most holy prediction of the future, which moreover derives from nothing less than the exercise of free will.

Now come listen, my son, as I divine by my calculus of revolutions, in accord with the inspiration that has been revealed to me, how the sword of death now threatens to lay us low by plague, by a war more horrible than seen in three generations, & famine, a sword that shall swoop down on earth & shall often return, for the stars are in harmony with the revolution, & moreover our Lord has said: *Then will I visit their transgression with the rod, & their iniquity with stripes,* for the mercy of our Lord shall not have had the time to work its effect, my son, before most of my prophecies shall be fulfilled & accomplished in due revolution.

Then at several points during these ominous storms, the Lord shall say *I will not pity, nor spare, nor have mercy, but destroy them & therefore will I also diminish thee; neither shall mine eye spare, neither will I have any pity,* & many other things shall occur through the floods & continual rains, as I have set out more clearly in writing in my other prophecies which are composed throughout in prose, in which I stipulated the places, the times, & the preordained ends which those who come after us will be able to see, realizing how these events infallibly occurred just as we have noted them down in other prophecies, speaking more clearly: even though their meaning shall be hidden in a cloud: *but when ignorance is cast aside,* the thing will become clearer.

To bring this to a close, my son, accept this gift from your father M. Nostradamus, in the hope that one day he might explain to you each of the prophecies included here. Begging immortal God that He might grant you a long life in lovely & prosperous happiness. From Salon, this first of March, 1555.

CENTURIE I

I.1
Estant assis de nuict secret estude
Seul reposé sus la selle d'ærain :
Flambe exigue sortant de solitude,
Fait proferer qui n'est à croire vain.

I.2
La verge en main mise au milieu de BRANCHES,
De l'onde il moulle & le limbe & le pied :
Vapeur & voix fremissent par les manches :
Splendeur divine. Le divin près s'assied.

I.3
Quand la lictiere du tourbillon versée,
Et seront faces de leurs manteaux couvers :
La republique par gens nouveaux vexée,
Lors blancs & rouges jugeront à l'envers.

I.4
Par l'univers sera faict un monarque,
Qu'en paix & vie ne sera longuement :
Lors se perdra la piscature barque,
Sera regie en plus grand detriment.

I.5
Chassés seront sans faire long combat,
Par le pays seront plus fort grevés :
Bourg & cité auront plus grand debat,
Carcas. Narbonne auront cœurs esprouvés.

I.6
L'œil de Ravenne sera destitué,
Quand à ses piedz les ælles failliront :
Les deux de Bresse auront constitué,
Turin, Verseil que Gaulois fouleront.

I.7
Tard arrivé l'execution faicte,
Le vent contraire lettres au chemin prinses :
Les conjurez xiiij. d'une secte :
Par le Rousseau senez les entreprinses.

CENTURY I

1.1
Being seated at night in secret study
Alone upon a stool of bronze at ease :
Slim flame issuing forth from solitude
Fuels prophecies not futile to believe.

1.2
Wand in hand set in the midst of BRANCHES,
With water he wets both his hem & feet :
Vapor & voice aquiver in his sleeves :
Splendor divine. The god here takes a seat.

1.3
When whirlwind turns the litter upside down,
And faces are covered over by cloaks :
The republic shall be vexed by new folk,
The whites & reds judging the wrong way round.

1.4
In the world one monarch shall be proclaimed
Who shall have little peace & little reign :
Then shall the fisher's barque now lose its way,
Be steered toward ever greater disarray.

1.5
They'll be dispatched without much resistance
And greatly harried through the countryside :
Town & city shall fight with more persistence :
At Carcas., Narbonne their courage be tried.

1.6
The eye of Ravenna shall be deposed
When his wings finally fall at his feet :
The two of Brescia having thus proposed,
The Gauls shall sack Turin & Vercelli.

1.7
Arrived late, execution taken place,
Wind against them, letters seized en route :
The conspirators, fourteen of a sect :
By the Redhead their schemes shall be approved.

1.8

Combien de foys prinse cité solaire
Seras changeant les loys barbares & vaines :
Ton mal s'approche. Plus seras tributaire,
La grand Hadrie reovrira tes veines.

1.9

De l'Orient viendra le cœur Punique
Facher Hadrie & les hoirs Romulides
Accompagné de la classe Libyque
Trembler Mellites & proches isles vuides.

1.10

Serpens transmis dans la caige de fer,
Où les enfans septains du roy sont pris :
Les vieux & peres sortiront de l'enfer,
Ains mourir voir de son fruict mort & crys.

1.11

Le mouvement de sens, cœur, piedz, & mains,
Seront d'accord. Naples, Leon. Sicille :
Glaifves, feux, eaux ; aux puis nobles Romains,
Plongés, tués, mors par cerveau debile.

1.12

Dans peu dira faulce brute fragile,
De bas en hault eslevé promptement :
Puis en instant desloyale & labile,
Qui de Veronne aura gouvernement.

1.13

Les exilez par ire, haine intestine,
Feront au Roy grand conjuration :
Secret mettront ennemis par la mine,
Et ses vieux siens contre eux seditions.

1.14

De gent esclave chansons, chantz & requestes,
Captifs par Prince, & Seigneur aux prisons :
A l'advenir par idiotz sans testes,
Seront receuz par divins oraisons.

1.8

How often shall you be taken, City
Of the Sun, change laws barbaric & vain :
Your doom draws nigh. Sucked ever more dry,
Adria the great reopens your veins.

1.9

The Punic heart shall emerge from the East
To vex Adria & Romulus's heirs
Accompanied by the Libyan fleet :
Malta shall tremble & nearby isles lie bare.

1.10

Serpent is placed into the iron cage
Where the king's seven children now do pine :
From this hellhole the forebears shall emerge,
Die, having seen the death throes of their line.

1.11

The motion of the senses, hearts, feet, hands,
Naples, Leon, Sicily shall unite :
Sword, fire, flood : into wells noble Romans
Plunged, killed, dead because of a feeble mind.

1.12

It shall soon be said that this false frail brute
Shall be swiftly lifted from low to high :
Then soon turn disloyal & swing in mood,
He who shall have seized Verona's reins.

1.13

In rage & intestine hate the exiles
Shall hatch a most bold plot against the king :
Secretly send enemies through tunnels,
Among allies of old foment sedition.

1.14

The songs & chants & prayers of the enslaved
Kept captive in prisons by princes & lords :
In the future these shall all be rated
Divine supplications by headless dolts.

1.15
Mars nous menasse par sa force bellique,
Septante foys fera le sang espandre :
Auge & ruyne de l'Ecclesiastique,
Et plus ceux qui d'eux rien voudront entendre.

1.16
Faulx à l'estaing joinct vers le Sagitaire,
En son hault AUGE de l'exaltation :
Peste, famine, mort de main militaire,
Le siecle approche de renovation.

1.17
Par quarante ans l'Iris n'aparoistra,
Par quarante ans tous les jours sera veu :
La terre aride en siccité croistra,
Et grans deluges quand sera aperceu.

1.18
Par la discorde negligence Gauloise,
Sera passaige à Mahommet ouvert :
De sang trempé la terre & mer Senoise,
Le port Phocen de voilles & nefz couvert.

1.19
Lors que serpens viendront circuir l'are,
Le sang Troyen vexé par les Espaignes :
Par eulx grand nombre en sera faicte tare :
Chef fuyct, caché aux mares dans les saignes.

1.20
Tours, Orleans, Bloys, Angiers, Reims, & Nantes,
Cités vexées par subit changement :
Par langue estrange seront tendues tentes,
Fleuves d'arenes, terre & mer tremblement.

1.21
Profonde argille blanche nourrir rochier,
Qui d'un abisme istra lacticineuse :
En vain troublez ne l'oseront toucher,
Ignorans estre au fond terre argilleuse.

1.15

Mars threatens us with his power of war,
Seventy times shall he cause blood to flow :
Bringing the Church to new heights & new lows,
Plus those who'd rather not be in the know.

1.16

Toward Sagittarius, Scythe joined to Tin,
And at the APOGEE of ascension :
Plague, famine, death at military hands,
Thus does the age approach renovation.

1.17

For forty years the rainbow shall not shine,
For forty years be seen every day :
The parchèd earth waxing ever more dry,
And great flooding should it show in the sky.

1.18

The quarrelsome negligence of the Gauls
Shall open a passage to Mohammed :
The Sienese land & sea soaked in blood,
The Phocaean port covered with sails & ships.

1.19

When the altar is encircled by snakes,
Trojan blood by the Spaniards shall be vexed :
By them a great number shall meet their fates :
The chief fleeing, hidden among marsh reeds.

1.20

Tours, Orléans, Blois, Angers, Reims, & Nantes,
Cities beset by all too sudden change :
Tents shall be pitched by those of foreign tongues,
Sandy rivers, land & sea all aquake.

1.21

Nourishing the rock the deep white clay
From a cleft below takes its milky birth :
No one dares touch it, needlessly afraid,
Unaware clay soil lies beneath the earth.

1.22

Ce que vivra & n'ayant aucun sens,
Viendra leser à mort son artifice :
Austun, Chalon, Langres & les deux Sens,
La gesle & glace fera grand malefice.

1.23

Au moys troisiesme se levant le Soleil,
Sanglier, Liepard, au champ Mars pour combattre :
Liepard lassé, au ciel extend son œil,
Un Aigle autour du Soleil voit s'esbatre.

1.24

A cité neufve pensif pour condemner,
L'oisel de proye au ciel se vient offrir :
Après victoire à captifz pardonner,
Cremo. & Mant. grans maulx aura à souffrir.

1.25

Perdu trouvé, caché de si long siecle,
Sera pasteur demy Dieu honoré :
Ains que la Lune acheve son grand cycle,
Par autres veux sera deshonoré.

1.26

Le grand du fouldre tumbe d'heure diurne,
Mal est predict par porteur postulaire :
Suivant presaige tumbe d'heure nocturne,
Conflit Reims, Londres, Etrusque pestifere.

1.27

Dessouz le chaine Guien du ciel frappé,
Non loing de là est caché le tresor
Qui par longs siecles avoit esté grappé :
Trouvé mourra, l'œil crevé de ressort.

1.28

La tour de Bouq gaindra fuste Barbare,
Un temps, long temps après barque hesperique :
Bestail, gens, meubles tous deux feront grant tare,
Taurus et Libra quelle mortelle picque !

1.22

That which shall survive lacking any sense
Shall give its progenitor no respite :
At Autun, Chalon, Langres, & the two Sens,
Untold harm shall be caused by hail & ice.

1.23

In the third month with the Sun on the rise,
Boar & leopard meet on the battlefield :
Weary leopard lifts his eye to the sky,
Around the Sun he sees an eagle reel.

1.24

In New City, the brooder is reproved
By bird of prey appearing in the sky :
After victory, the captives pardoned,
At Cremo. & Mant. great hardships in sight.

1.25

Lost, found, in hiding for so long a while,
Shepherd as demigod shall be honored :
Before the Moon completes its full cycle,
By other vows shall he be dishonored.

1.26

During daytime a great clap of lightning,
Ill omen from the bearer of tidings :
The following portent falling at night :
Conflict in Reims, London, Tuscan blight.

1.27

Beneath the Guyenne oak struck by lightning,
Not far from there the hidden treasure lies
Which was seized countless centuries ago :
Who finds it dies, lockspring blinding his eye.

1.28

Off Tower of Bouc Barbary galley's sails,
Long long after the armada of Spain :
The two destroying cattle, people, chattel,
From Taurus to Libra what deadly raids !

1.29
Quand le poisson terrestre & aquatique,
Par forte vague au gravier sera mis,
Sa forme estrange suate & horrifique,
Par mer aux murs bien tost les ennemis.

1.30
La nef estrange par le tourment marin,
Abourdera près de port incongneu :
Nonobstant signes de rameau palmerin,
Après mort, pille : bon avis tard venu.

1.31
Tant d'ans les guerres en Gaule dureront,
Oultre la course du Castulon monarque :
Victoire incerte trois grands couronneront,
Aigle, coq, lune, lyon, soleil en marque.

1.32
Le grand empire sera tost translaté,
En lieu petit, qui bien tost viendra croistre :
Lieu bien infime d'exiguë comté,
Où au milieu viendra poser son sceptre.

1.33
Près d'un grand pont, de plaine spatieuse,
Le grand lyon par forces Cesarées
Fera abbatre hors cité rigoureuse :
Par effroy portes luy seront reserées.

1.34
L'oyseau de proye volant à la senestre,
Avant conflict faict aux Françoys pareure :
L'un bon prendra, l'un ambigue sinistre,
La partie foyble teindra par bon augure.

1.35
Le lyon jeune le vieux surmontera,
En champ bellique par singulier duelle :
Dans caige d'or les yeux luy crevera,
Deux classes une, puis mourir, mort cruelle.

1.29

When the fish terrestrial & aquatic
By a mighty wave is tossed on the beach,
Its form weird, tallowy & horrific,
The enemy shall reach the walls by sea.

1.30

The storms at sea shall force the foreign ship
To make for land near an uncharted bay :
Despite the warning signs by palm fronds waved,
Death, then pillage : good advice, coming late.

1.31

For many years the wars grind on in Gaul,
Well after the reign of the king of Spain :
Uncertain victory shall three lords crown,
Eagle, Cock, Moon, Lion, Sun be marked again.

1.32

The empire shall soon find itself retired
Into a small place which shall fast expand :
A tiny space within a narrow shire
In midst of which his scepter he shall plant.

1.33

Near a great bridge amid the rolling plain,
The great lion with his Caesarean might
Shall start bombarding the defiant town :
Gates flung open to him in utter fright.

1.34

The bird of prey flying toward the left
Appears to the French before the battle :
A good omen to one, ill to the next,
Weaker party hoping it augurs well.

1.35

The young lion shall overcome the old
On the field of battle in single duel :
He'll put out his eyes in his cage of gold,
Winner taking all, then a death most cruel.

1.36

Tard le monarque se viendra repentir,
De n'avoir mis à mort son adversaire :
Mais viendra bien à plus hault consentir,
Que tout son sang par mort fera deffaire.

1.37

Un peu devant que le soleil s'esconse,
Conflict donné grand peuple dubiteux :
Profligés port marin ne faict responce :
Pont & sepulchre en deux estranges lieux.

1.38

Le Sol & l'aigle au victeur paroistront,
Responce vaine au vaincu l'on asseure :
Par cor ne crys harnois n'arresteront
Vindicte, paix par mors s'y achève à l'heure.

1.39

De nuict dans lict le supresme estranglé,
Pour trop avoir subjourné blond esleu :
Par troys l'empire subrogé exanclé,
A mort mettra : carte & paquet ne leu.

1.40

La trombe fausse dissimulant folie,
Fera Bisance un changement de loix :
Hystra d'Egypte qui veut que l'on deslie,
Edict changeant monnoyes & aloys.

1.41

Siege en cité & de nuict assaillie,
Peu eschapés : non loin de mer conflict :
Femme de joye, retours filz defaillie,
Poison & lettres cachées dans le plic.

1.42

Le dix Kalende d'Avril le faict gotique,
Resuscité encor par gens malins :
Le feu estainct, assemblée diabolique,
Cherchant les us Adamant & Pselin.

1.36

The monarch shall later come to repent
Not having put his adversary to death :
But shall have to bow to something higher,
Which shall spill his blood until he expires.

1.37

Just before the sun goes into hiding,
A great nation caught up in dubious war :
Port affords defeated no asylum :
Bridge & sepulcher on two foreign shores.

1.38

Sun & eagle to the victor shall appear,
Vain assurance given to the vanquished :
Hue & cry shall not cause the troops to veer
From vengeance, peace alone assured by death.

1.39

By night the emperor, having outlived his use,
Shall be strangled in bed : the fair elect,
The empire being claimed by three & ruined,
Does the deed : note in packet left unread.

1.40

The deceitful trump that feigneth folly
Shall cause Byzantium to change its creed :
From Egypt comes one eager to be freed,
A change in coins & alloys he'll decree.

1.41

The town besieged by night they shall attack,
Few escape the skirmishes by the shore :
Mother shall faint with joy that son is back :
Poison & sealed note tucked in envelope.

1.42

Tenth Calends of April, the Gnostic rite
By wicked persons shall now be revived :
Lights out, the assembled devils shall writhe
In the filth Origen, Psellus describe.

I.43

Avant qu'advienne le changement d'empire,
Il adviendra un cas bien merveilleux :
Le champ mué, le pillier de porphire
Mis, translaté sus le rocher noilleux.

I.44

En bref seront de retour sacrifices,
Contrevenans seront mys à martire :
Plus ne seront moines, abbés, novices :
Le miel sera beaucoup plus cher que cire.

I.45

Secteur de sectes grand preme au delateur :
Beste en theatre, dressé le jeu scenique :
Du faict antique ennobly l'inventeur :
Par sectes monde confus & schismatique.

I.46

Tout auprés d'Aux, de Lectore & Mirande,
Grand feu du ciel en trois nuictz tumbera :
Cause adviendra bien stupende & mirande,
Bien peu après la terre tremblera.

I.47

Du lac Leman les sermons fascheront,
Des jours seront reduictz par les sepmaines :
Puis moys, puis ans, puis tous deffailliront,
Les magistratz damneront leurs loix vaines.

I.48

Vingt ans du regne de la Lune passés,
Sept mil ans outre tiendra sa monarchie :
Quand le Soleil prendra ses jours lassés,
Lors s'accomplir, miner ma prophetie.

I.49

Beaucoup beaucoup avant telles menées,
Ceux d'Orient par la vertu lunaire
L'an mil sept cens feront grand emmenées,
Subjugant presque le coing Aquilonaire.

1.43

Before the transfer of empire occurs,
A marvel most great shall cause quite a shock :
The field shall shake, the porphyry pillar
Change place, translated to the knobby rock.

1.44

Sacrifices shall soon return in force :
Those who object shall be placed on the rack :
Monks, abbots, novices shall be no more :
Honey shall be more expensive than wax.

1.45

The bane of sects shall reward every spy :
The beast is brought onstage, the scene now set :
Deviser of this ancient rite made knight :
The world a mess, schism'd because of sects.

1.46

Not far from Auch, Mirande, & Lectoure
Lightning shall strike for a full three nights :
A most stupendous marvel shall occur,
And in its wake all the earth shall quake.

1.47

Lake Leman's sermons shall prove tiresome :
Days shall be as long as weeks, weeks as months,
Months as years, before they all come undone :
Magistrates shall damn their mumbo jumbo.

1.48

Now that the Moon for twenty years has reigned,
Seven thousand more shall it last as king :
When the Sun resumes its remaining days,
My prophecy's fulfillment it shall bring.

1.49

Long before the above things come to pass,
Those from the East by virtue of the moon
In seventeen hundred shall launch attacks,
Bringing much of the North under their rule.

I.50

De l'aquatique triplicité naistra,
D'un qui fera le jeudy pour sa feste :
Son bruit, loz, regne, sa puissance croistra,
Par terre & mer aux Oriens tempeste.

I.51

Chef d'Aries, Jupiter, & Saturne,
Dieu eternel quelles mutations !
Puis par long siecle son maling temps retourne :
Gaule, & Itale quelles esmotions !

I.52

Les deux malins de Scorpion conjoincts,
Le grand seigneur meurtry dedans sa salle :
Peste à l'Eglise par le nouveau roy joincts
L'Europe basse & Septentrionale.

I.53

Las qu'on verra grand peuple tourmenté,
Et la Loy saincte en totale ruine
Par autres loix toute Chrestienté,
Quand d'or, d'argent trouvé nouvelle mine.

I.54

Dix revoltz faictz du maling falcigere,
De regne & siecles faict permutation :
De mobil signe à son endroict s'y ingere,
Aux deux egaux & d'inclination.

I.55

Soubz l'opposite climat Babylonique
Grande sera de sang effusion
Que terre & mer, air, ciel sera inique :
Sectes, faim, regnes, pestes, confusion.

I.56

Vous verrés tost & tard faire grand change,
Horreurs extremes, & vindications :
Que si la lune conduicte par son ange,
Le ciel s'approche des inclinations.

1.50

From water's triplicity shall be born
One who shall make Thursday his day of feast :
His fame, praise, reign, & power shall increase,
By land & sea he shall war his way east.

1.51

Saturn & Jove at the head of Aries,
Eternal God, all the mutations !
Then the slow round brings back bad times again :
Gaul & Italy, what perturbations !

1.52

In Scorpio the two wicked ones conjoined,
The grand seigneur is murdered in his room :
A plague on the church : the new king shall join
Lower Europe to the Septentrion.

1.53

Alas one shall see a great nation bleed
And the holy law & all of Christendom
Reduced to utter ruin by other creeds,
Each time a new gold, silver mine is found.

1.54

Ten revolutions of dread Saturn's scythe
Shall effect changes in ages & reigns :
It assumes its place in the mobile sign
Where the two are equal, their angles same.

1.55

Over against where Babel used to stand
Blood shall be spilled in such great effusion
As to defile sky & air, sea & land :
Sects, famine, kingdoms, plagues, confusion.

1.56

Sooner or later you shall see great change,
Extreme horrors & retaliations :
That if the moon be led by its angel,
The sky shall know no more trepidation.

1.57
Par grand discord la trombe tremblera
Accord rompu dressant la teste au ciel :
Bouche sanglante dans le sang nagera,
Au sol sa face ointe de laict & miel.

1.58
Tranché le ventre, naistra avec deux testes,
Et quatre bras : quelque an entier vivra :
Jour qui Aquilloye celebrera ses festes,
Fossen, Turin, chef Ferrare suyvra.

1.59
Les exilés deportés dans les isles,
Au changement d'un plus cruel monarque
Seront meurtrys & mis deux des scintiles,
Qui de parler ne seront estés parques.

1.60
Un Empereur naistra près d'Italie,
Qui à l'Empire sera vendu bien cher :
Diront avec quelz gens il se ralie,
Qu'on trouvera moins prince que boucher.

1.61
La republique miserable infelice,
Sera vastée du nouveau magistrat :
Lors grand amas de l'exil malefice,
Fera Sueves ravir leur grand contract.

1.62
La grande perte las que feront les lettres,
Avant le cicle de Latonia parfaict :
Feu, grand deluge, plus par ignares sceptres,
Que de longs siècles ne se verra refaict.

1.63
Les fleaux passés diminué le monde :
Long temps la paix terres inhabitées :
Seur marchera par ciel, terre, mer, onde :
Puis de nouveau les guerres suscitées.

1.57
Great Discord shall cause the trumpet to sound,
Accord broken, her head raised to the sky :
Her bleeding mouth shall be aswim in blood,
Face to the ground, smeared with milk & honey.

1.58
The belly slit, it'll be born with two heads
And four arms & live a full year at least :
The day Aquileia celebrates its feasts,
Fossan, Turin shall lead Ferrara's chief.

1.59
All the exiles deported to the isles
When a crueler king his power has won
Shall be put to death & two set on fire,
Who had been unable to curb their tongues.

1.60
Near Italy an Emperor shall be born
Who shall cost the Empire a pretty pence :
They shall ask to what people he is sworn,
Finding him more a butcher than a prince.

1.61
The republic miserable, without hap,
Shall be devastated by a new judge :
Then the wicked pack of exiles comes back,
Forcing the Swabians to break their pledge.

1.62
What great loss alas shall letters suffer
Before the Moon completes her cycle fair :
Fire, massive flooding, plus clueless rulers,
Which it shall take centuries to repair.

1.63
The scourges passed, the world a smaller place :
In inhabited lands a lasting peace :
Safe passage by air, earth, river & sea :
Then the wars starting up again apace.

1.64

De nuict soleil penseront avoir veu,
Quand le pourceau demy homme on verra :
Bruict, chant, bataille, au ciel battre aperceu :
Et bestes brutes à parler l'on orra.

1.65

Enfant sans mains jamais veu si grand foudre :
L'enfant royal au jeu d'œsteuf blessé :
Au puy brisé fulgures allant mouldre,
Trois souz les chaines par le milieu troussés.

1.66

Celuy qui lors portera les nouvelles,
Après un peu il viendra respirer.
Viviers, Tournon, Montferrant & Pradelles,
Gresle & tempestes les fera souspirer.

1.67

La grand famine que je sens approcher,
Souvent tourner, puis estre universelle,
Si grande & longue qu'on viendra arracher
Du bois racine & l'enfant de mamelle.

1.68

O quel horrible & malheureux tourment,
Trois innocens qu'on viendra à livrer :
Poyson suspecte, mal garde, tradiment,
Mis en horreur par bourreaux enyvrés.

1.69

La grand montaigne ronde de sept estades,
Après paix, guerre, faim, inondation,
Roulera loin abismant grans contrades,
Mesmes antiques & grand fondation.

1.70

Pluie, faim, guerre en Perse non cessée,
La foy trop grande trahira le monarque :
Par là finie en Gaule commencée,
Secret augure pour à un estre parque.

1.64

At night they shall believe the sun does shine
When at the half-human pig they get a peek :
Noise, song, battalions battling in the sky
Shall be perceived & brute beasts heard to speak.

1.65

A child sans hands, lightning as never fell :
The royal child hurt in a tennis game :
Gone to grind grain at the lightning-scarred well,
Three shall be wrapped around the waist in chains.

1.66

He who shall then arrive with news to tell
Shall catch his breath again after a time :
At Viviers, Tournon, Monferrand, Pradelles,
Hail & storms shall make them heave quite a sigh.

1.67

The great famine that I sense approaching,
Turning this way & that, ever widespread,
So great, so long they shall end up plucking
Roots from the woods & babes from the breast.

1.68

To what horrible torments subjected,
Three innocents seized & delivered up :
Treachery, lax guarding, poison suspected,
Terrorized by hangmen in their cups.

1.69

The great mountain, seven stades in the round,
After peace, war, famine, inundation,
Shall roll afar, plunge lands into the ground,
With their ancient ruins & vast foundations.

1.70

Rain, famine, war in Persia dragging on,
The king betrayed by those he trusted best :
What there shall end was first begun in Gaul :
Secret warning against undue largesse.

1.71

La tour marine trois fois prise & reprise,
Par Hespaignolz, Barbares, Ligurins :
Marseille & Aix, Arles par ceux de Pise :
Vast, feu, fer, pille Avignon des Thurins.

1.72

Du tout Marseille des habitans changée,
Course & poursuitte jusques au près de Lyon :
Narbon. Tholoze par Bourdeaux outragée,
Tués captifz presque d'un million.

1.73

France à cinq pars par neglect assaillie,
Tunys, Argel esmeuz par Persiens :
Leon., Secille, Barcelonne faillie,
N'aura la classe par les Venitiens.

1.74

Aprés sejour vogueront en Épire,
Le grand secours viendra vers Antioche :
Le noir poil crespe tendra fort à l'Empire,
Barbe d'ærain le roustira en broche.

1.75

Le tyran Sienne occupera Savone :
Le fort gaigné tiendra classe marine :
Les deux armées par la marque d'Anconne :
Par effrayeur le chef s'en examine.

1.76

D'un nom farouche tel proferé sera,
Que les trois seurs auront fato le nom :
Puis grand peuple par langue & fait duira,
Plus que nul autre aura bruit & renom.

1.77

Entre deux mers dressera promontoire,
Que puis mourra par le mords du cheval :
Le sien Neptune pliera voile noire,
Par Calpre & classe auprès de Rocheval.

1.71

The sea fort thrice taken & retaken
By Spain, Liguria & Barbary :
At Marseille, Aix, Arles, Pisan vastation :
Fire, sword, Avignon sacked by Turinese.

1.72

Marseille's population utterly changed,
Flight & pursuit all the way to Lyon :
Narbonne & Toulouse by Bordeaux outraged :
Captives shall be killed, nearly a million.

1.73

Heedless France on five sides shall be assailed,
Tunis, Algiers stirred up by the Persians :
Sicily's Leon., Barcelona failed,
Shall have no help by sea from Venetians.

1.74

After a rest, they'll set sail for Epire,
Near Antioch they'll get a great assist :
Blackcurl shall take the side of the Empire,
Bronzebeard proceed to roast him on a spit.

1.75

Siena's tyrant shall strike Savona :
Its fort seized, he shall lay hold of its fleet :
The two hosts cross the Marches of Ancona :
Fearing for his life, the chief drags his feet.

1.76

He shall be called by the fiercest of names,
That of Fate, as the Three Sisters are known :
Then by word & deed he'll lead a great race,
Surpassing all men in fame & renown.

1.77

Twixt two seas shall the promontory rise
Of him who later by a horse bite dies :
His own Neptune shall then furl his black sail,
Coasting by Gibraltar near Rocheval.

1.78

D'un chef vieillard naistra sens hebeté
Degenerant par savoir & par armes :
Le chef de France par sa sœur redouté :
Champs divisés, concedés aux gendarmes.

1.79

Bazaz, Lectore, Condon, Ausch, & Agine,
Esmeus par loix, querelle & monopole,
Car., Bourd., Toulouze, Bay. mettra en ruine,
Renouveller voulant leur tauropole.

1.80

De la sixiesme claire splendeur celeste
Viendra tonner si fort en la Bourgongne :
Puis naistra monstre de treshideuse beste :
Mars, Avril, May, Juin grand charpin & rongne.

1.81

D'humain trouppeau neuf seront mis à part,
De jugement & conseil separés :
Leur sort sera divisé en depart :
Kappa, Thita, Lambda mors, bannis, esgarés.

1.82

Quand les colomnes de bois grande tremblée
D'Auster conduicte couvertes de rubriche,
Tant vuidera dehors grande assemblée :
Tembler Vienne & le Pays d'Autriche.

1.83

La gent estrange divisera butins,
Saturne en Mars son regard furieux :
Horrible strage aux Tosquans & Latins,
Grecs qui seront à frapper curieux.

1.84

Lune obscurcie aux profondes tenebres,
Son frere pasle de couleur ferrugine :
Le grand caché long temps soubz les latebres,
Tiedera fer dans la plaie sanguine.

1.78

From an aged chief is born a half-wit son,
Degenerate in knowledge & in arms :
France's chief by his sister shall be shunned :
Fields divided, conceded to gendarmes.

1.79

Bazas, Condom, Auch, Agen & Lectoure,
Stirred up by sects & the intrigues of fools,
Shall put to ruin Car., Bord., Bay. & Toulouse,
Wanting to revive their sacrifice of bulls.

1.80

From the sixth celestial splendor so bright
Great thunderclaps shall visit Burgundy :
A hideous beast shall spawn a monstrous sight :
March, April, May, June, blown to smithereens.

1.81

From human flock nine shall be set apart,
All due process & counsel be denied :
Their fate shall be decided from the start :
Kappa, Theta, Lambda : dead, scattered wide.

1.82

When wooden columns with red clay adorned
Tremble in the gusts of the southern wind,
The great assembly shall spill out of doors :
Vienna & all Austria shall cringe.

1.83

The foreigners shall divvy up the spoils
When Saturn against Mars angrily glows :
Tuscans & Latins slaughtered on their soil,
The Greeks eager to weigh in with their blows.

1.84

The moon obscured within the shadows' maze,
Its brother wan, as dull as iron rust :
The lord, having long lurked in his hiding place,
Shall warm his blade within the bloody wound.

1.85

Par la responce de dame roy troublé,
Ambassadeurs mespriseront leur vie :
Le grand ses freres contrefera doublé :
Par deux mourront ire : haine, envie.

1.86

La grande royne quand se verra vaincue,
Fera excès de masculin courage :
Sus cheval, fleuve passera toute nue :
Suite par fer : à soy fera outrage.

1.87

Ennosigée, feu du centre de terre,
Fera trembler au tour de cité neufve :
Deux grands rochiers long temps feront la guerre,
Puis Arethuse rougira nouveau fleuve.

1.88

Le divin mal surprendra le grand prince :
Un peu devant aura femme espousée :
Son bruict, credit à un coup viendra mince,
Conseil mourra pour la teste rasée.

1.89

Tous ceux de Ilerde seront dedans Moselle,
Mettant à mort tous ceux de Loire & Seine :
Secours marin viendra pres d'haute velle,
Quant Hespagnol ouvrira toute veine.

1.90

Bourdeaux, Poitiers au son de la campane,
A grande classe ira jusques à l'Angon :
Contre Gauloys sera leur tramontane,
Quand monstre hydeux naistra près de Orgon.

1.91

Les dieux feront aux humains apparence,
Ce qu'ilz seront auteurs de grand conflict :
Avant ciel veu serain espée & lance,
Que vers main gauche sera plus grand aflict.

1.85

The king troubled by the lady's answer,
The ambassadors shall fear for their lives :
The lord shall fake the hand of both brothers :
Anger, hatred, envy : the two shall die.

1.86

When the mighty queen sees herself subdued,
She shall display more courage than a man :
On horseback she shall cross the river nude :
Armed pursuit : she shall have broken the pact.

1.87

Ennosigaeus, the fire at earth's core,
Shall set the New City all aquake :
Two lords shall go on fighting futile wars :
New stream makes Arethusa blush with shame.

1.88

The prince shall be seized by epilepsy :
His wife, shortly before, he shall have wed :
His reputation shall plummet suddenly,
The counsel be killed by the shaven head.

1.89

Lerida folk shall advance to the Moselle,
Killing everyone from the Loire & Seine :
Help from the sea shall come near Hauteville,
When the Spaniard has opened every vein.

1.90

At the toll of the bell, Bordeaux, Poitiers
Shall march off as an army toward Langon :
Their northern wind shall gust against the Gauls,
When a hideous monster is born near Orgon.

1.91

The gods shall make it clear to mortal eye
That they are the authors of this great war :
Sword & lance shall be seen in the clear sky,
Then toward the left hand disasters galore.

1.92
Souz un la paix par tout sera clamée,
Mais non long temps pille & rebellion :
Par refus ville, terre, & mer entamée :
Mors & captifz le tiers d'un million.

1.93
Terre Italique près des monts tremblera :
Lyon & coq non trop confederés
En lieu de peur l'un l'autre s'aidera :
Sault Castulon & Celtes moderés.

1.94
Au port Selin le tyran mis à mort,
La liberté non pourtant recouvrée :
Le nouveau Mars par vindicte & remort :
Dame par force de frayeur honnorée.

1.95
Devant moustier trouvé enfant besson,
D'heroic sang de moine & vetustisque :
Son bruit par secte, langue & puissance son,
Qu'on dira fort eslevé le vopisque.

1.96
Celuy qu'aura la charge de destruire,
Temples, & sectes, changés par fantasie :
Plus aux rochiers qu'aux vivans viendra nuire,
Par langue ornée d'oreilles ressaisie.

1.97
Ce que fer, flamme n'a sceu parachever,
La douce langue au conseil viendra faire :
Par repos, songe, le Roy fera resver :
Plus l'ennemy en feu, sang militaire.

1.98
Le chef qu'aura conduit peuple infiny,
Loing de son ciel, de meurs & langue estrange :
Cinq mil en Crete et Thessalie finy,
Le chef fuyant sauvé en marine grange.

1.92

Under one, universal peace decreed,
But not for long : plunder & rebellion :
Defiant city stormed by land & sea :
Dead or captured, a third of a million.

1.93

Near the mountains Italic earth shall quake :
The Lion & the Cock, though loosely leagued,
Shall help each other out under the shock :
Castille & Celts content to wait & see.

1.94

The tyrant has been slain at port Selin,
Yet liberty is not thereby restored :
The new Mars seeks war, seething with revenge :
The Lady honored out of fear & force.

1.95

Before a cloister a monk stumbles on
A twin of heroic & ancient race :
His local renown, the power of his tongue
Speak greatly for this sole-surviving twain.

1.96

The one who shall be invited to wipe
Out temples & sects shall change his game :
His bark shall be far louder than his bite,
All ears tethered to his tongue's golden chains.

1.97

What neither fire nor iron could achieve,
Smooth tongue in council shall bring to pass :
A dream shall come to the King in his sleep :
Now his longtime enemy bleeds its last.

1.98

The chief who shall have led armies of men
Far from homes, foreign of custom & speech :
Thessaly, Crete, five thousand of them dead,
Chief fleeing, saved in a grange by the sea.

1.99

Le grand monarque qui fera compagnie,
Avec deux roys unis par amitié :
O quel souspir fera la grand mesgnie :
Enfans Narbon. à l'entour quel pitié!

1.100

Long temps au ciel sera veu gris oiseau,
Auprès de Dole & de Touscane terre,
Tenant au bec un verdoyant rameau :
Mourra tost grand & finera la guerre.

———————

CENTURIE II

2.1

Vers Aquitaine par insults Britanniques,
Et par eux mesmes grandes incursions :
Pluyes, gelées feront terroirs iniques,
Port Selyn fortes fera invasions.

2.2

La teste blue fera la teste blanche,
Autant de mal que France a faict leur bien :
Mort à l'anthene grand pendu sus la branche,
Quand prins des siens le Roy dira combien.

2.3

Pour la chaleur solaire sus la mer
De Negrepont les poissons demis cuits :
Les habitans les viendront entamer,
Quand Rhod. & Gennes leur faudra le biscuit.

2.4

Depuis Monech jusque auprès de Sicile,
Toute la plage demourra desolée :
Il n'y aura fauxbourg, cité, ne ville,
Que par Barbares pillée soit & vollée.

1.99

The great monarch who shall keep company
With two kings united by amity :
O what a sigh his mighty host shall heave :
For the children of Narbonne, what pity!

1.100

For days on end a gray bird shall be seen
In the skies of Tuscany & near Dole,
Holding in its beak a fresh branch of green :
The lord shall soon die & then no more war.

CENTURY II

2.1

Toward Aquitaine the assaults by Britain
On their behalf shall bring great incursions :
Rains & frosts shall render the lands barren,
Port Selin the site of great invasions.

2.2

Blue turban on white turban shall inflict
As much harm as France has done them good :
Dead man on yardarm, great lord hanged on sprit,
King telling how many of his men they took.

2.3

The fish half-cooked by the heat of the sun
Near Negrepont where the locals shall come
Partake of them when they have fully run
Out of hardtack from Genoa & Rhodes.

2.4

From Monaco almost to Sicily
The entire coast remains desolate :
There shall be no suburb, town, or city
The Barbarians shall not pillage & rape.

2.5

Quand dans prison fer & lettre enfermée,
Hors sortira qui puis fera la guerre,
Aura par mer sa classe bien ramée,
Apparoissant près de Latine terre.

2.6

Auprès des portes & dedans deux cités,
Seront deux fleaux : oncques n'aperceu un tel :
Faim, dedans peste, de fer hors gens boutés,
Crier secours au grand Dieu immortel.

2.7

Entre plusieurs aux isles deportés,
L'un estre nay à deux dents en la gorge :
Mourront de faim les arbres esbrotés :
Pour eux neuf Roy nouvel edict leur forge.

2.8

Temples sacrés prime façon Romaine,
Rejecteront les goffes fondements,
Prenant leurs loix premieres & humaines,
Chassant, non tout des sainctz les cultements.

2.9

Neuf ans le regne le maigre en paix tiendra,
Puis il cherra en soif si sanguinaire :
Pour luy grand peuple sans foy & loy mourra,
Tué par un beaucoup plus debonnaire.

2.10

Avant long temps le tout sera rangé :
Nous esperons un siecle bien senestre :
L'estat des marques & des scelz bien changé :
Peu trouveront qu'à son rang vueille estre.

2.11

Le prochain filz de l'aisnier parviendra,
Tant eslevé jusque au regne des fors :
Son aspre gloire un chascun la craindra,
Mais ses enfantz du regne gettés hors.

2.5

When clapped in prison by letter & sword,
He goes free, who shall proceed to wage war,
He shall sail the sea with many an oar,
Making his appearance near the Latin shore.

2.6

Nearby the gates & within two cities
Two scourges shall strike, such as never seen :
Famine, plague within: folk cast out by sword
Cry to the immortal Lord for relief.

2.7

Among all those deported to the isles
One shall be born with two teeth in its throat :
Folk shall die of hunger, trees nibbled clean :
For them the new king issues a new decree.

2.8

The temples, like the early church of Rome,
Shall reject all uncouth foundations,
Making the first & humane laws their own,
Banning most if not all the cults of saints.

2.9

The thin one shall rule for nine years in peace,
Then fall into an immense thirst for blood :
For this lawless one a great people dies,
To be slain by a rival far more good.

2.10

Before too long all things shall be ordained :
We sense a sinister age on its way :
The state of marks & seals shall be most changed :
Few to be found content with their stations.

2.11

The next donkey-driver's son shall succeed,
Having risen all the way to the helm :
One & all shall fear his glorious deeds,
Though his children be cast out of the realm.

2.12

Yeux clos, ouverts d'antique fantasie,
L'habit des seulz seront mis à neant :
Le grand monarque chastier leur frenaisie,
Ravir des temples le tresor par devant.

2.13

Le corps sans ame plus n'estre en sacrifice.
Jour de la mort mise en nativité,
L'esprit divin fera l'ame felice,
Voyant le verbe en son eternité.

2.14

A Tour Jean gardes seront yeulx penetrans,
Descouriront de loing la grand sereine :
Elle & sa suitte au port seront entrant :
Combats poulsez : puissance souveraine.

2.15

Un peu devant monarque trucidé,
Castor, Pollux en nef, astre crinite :
L'erain public par terre & mer vuidé :
Pise, Ast, Ferrare, Turin, Terre interdicte.

2.16

Naples, Palerme, Sicille, Syracuses,
Nouveaux tyrans, fulgures feux celestes :
Force de Londres, Gand, Bruxelles, & Suses,
Grand hecatombe, triomphe faire festes.

2.17

Le camp du temple de la vierge vestale,
Non esloigné d'Elne & monts Pyrenées,
Le grand conduict est caché dans la male :
North gelés fleuves & vignes mastinées.

2.18

Nouvelle pluie subite impetueuse,
Empeschera subit deux exercites :
Pierre ciel, feux faire la mer pierreuse :
La mort de sept terre & marin subites.

2.12

Eyes shut, open as if in ancient trances,
The monks' habits shall be reduced to naught :
The great monarch to chastise their madness,
Who once sacked the temple's precious loot.

2.13

Body without soul shall suffer no more.
Reborn on its day of death, the soul
Shall be made joyous by the Holy Ghost,
Seeing the Word in its eternal whole.

2.14

The guards watchful in the Saint-Jean tower,
Espying his majesty from afar
As his retinue makes its way into port :
Halt quarrels : make way for sovereign power.

2.15

Shortly before the monarch killed shall be,
Bearded star, Castor & Pollux on ship :
Public treasury sacked by land & sea :
Pisa, Ast, Ferrara, Turin, off-limits.

2.16

Naples, Palermo, Sicily's Syracusa,
New tyrants, divine fires, thunderbolts :
A force come from London, Ghent, Brussels, Susa,
Great hecatomb, triumph & feasts galore.

2.17

Across the plain of vestal virgin's church,
Near Elne & the mountainous Pyrenees,
The great one is driven hid in a coach :
To the north, rivers & vines in deep freeze.

2.18

The new rain, so sudden, impetuous,
Suddenly stops two armies in their tracks :
Firestones from the sky pebbling the waters :
Land & sea seven struck by sudden death.

2.19
Nouveaux venus lieu basty sans defence,
Occuper place par lors inhabitable :
Prez, maisons, champs, villes, prendre à plaisance :
Faim, peste, guerre : arpen long labourable.

2.20
Freres & seurs en divers lieux captifz
Se trouveront passer près du monarque :
Les contempler ses rameaux ententifz,
Desplaisant voir menton, front, nez, les marques.

2.21
L'ambassadeur envoyé par biremes,
A my chemin d'incongneuz repoulsés :
De tel renfort viendront quatre triremes :
Cordes & chaines en Negrepont troussés.

2.22
Le camp Asop d'Eurotte partira,
S'adjoignant proche de l'isle submergée :
D'artimon classe phalange pliera,
Nombril du monde plus grand voix subrogée.

2.23
Palais, oyseaux par oyseau dechassé,
Bien tost après le prince, prevenu,
Combien qu'hors fleuve ennemi repoulsé,
Dehors saisi trait d'oyseau soustenu.

2.24
Bestes farouches de faim fleuves tranner :
Plus part du camp encontre Hister sera :
En caige fer le grand fera treisner,
Quand Rin enfant Germain observera.

2.25
La garce estrange trahira forteresse,
Espoir & umbre de plus hault mariage :
Garde deceue, fort. prinse dans la presse :
Loyre, Son., Rosne, Gar. à mort oultrage.

2.19

Newcomers undefended sites shall fill,
Occupy uninhabitable grounds :
Meadows, houses, fields, towns taken at will :
Famine, plague, war : the acres long to plow.

2.20

Brothers & sisters captured here & there
Shall find themselves paraded by the king :
His attentive heirs shall stand there & stare,
Shocked by all the marks on the brow, nose, chin.

2.21

The ambassador dispatched on biremes
Shall be turned back by unknowns halfway :
To his rescue shall come four triremes :
In Negrepont, captives in ropes & chains.

2.22

The Asop force shall leave from Eurotas :
Having arrived near the isle submerged,
The fleet shall furl its sails & call forth
The great voice at the navel of the earth.

2.23

Near palace, one bird chasing off another :
Soon after this, though forewarned by this sight,
And despite the foe's retreat to the river,
The prince shall die surprised by arrow's flight.

2.24

Beasts wild with hunger shall swim the rivers :
Most of the host shall move against Ister :
He'll have the great one dragged in iron cage,
When the child the German Rhine surveys.

2.25

The foreign wench the fortress shall betray,
Hoping to rise in station through marriage :
Garrison tricked, fortress in disarray :
In Loire, Saône, Rhône, Garonne, mortal outrage.

2.26

Pour la faveur que la cité fera
Au grand qui tost perdra champ de bataille,
Fuis le rang Po Thesin versera :
De sang feuz mors noiés de coups de taille.

2.27

Le divin verbe sera du ciel frappé,
Qui ne pourra proceder plus avant :
Du reserant le secret estoupé,
Qu'on marchera par dessus & devant.

2.28

Le penultiesme du surnom du prophete,
Prendra Dial pour son jour & repos :
Loing vaguera par frenetique teste,
Et delivrant un grand peuple d'impos.

2.29

L'Oriental sortira de son siege,
Passer les monts Apennins voir la Gaule :
Transpercera du ciel les eaux & neige,
Et un chascun frappera de sa gaule.

2.30

Un qui les dieux d'Annibal infernaulx,
Fera renaistre, effrayeur des humains :
Oncq'plus d'horreur ne plus pires fourneaux
Qu'avint viendra par Babel aux Romains.

2.31

En Campanie Cassilin sera tant
Qu'on ne verra que d'eaux les champs couverts :
Devant, après, la pluye de long temps :
Hors mis les arbres, rien l'on verra de vert.

2.32

Laict, sang, grenoilles escoudre en Dalmatie,
Conflict donné, peste près de Balenne :
Cry sera grand par toute Esclavonie,
Lors naistra monstre près & dedans Ravenne.

2.26

For the favor the city shall bestow
On the lord who's soon bound to lose the war,
Breaking ranks, Ticino overthrows Po :
A bloodbath, drowned by blows struck by sword.

2.27

The Divine Word shall be struck by lightning,
Bringing its procession to a full stop :
Who dares reveal this shall have his lips sealed,
So they shall just be marching on & off.

2.28

The next to last of the prophet's name
Shall take Joveday as his day of relaxation :
He shall wander far with his frenetic brain,
Delivering a great nation from taxation.

2.29

Man from the East shall sally from his seat,
Crossing all the Apennines to see Gaul :
He shall pass through showers of rain & sleet,
And with his rod he shall strike one & all.

2.30

The one whom Hannibal's infernal gods
Shall cause to be reborn, a bane to man :
Furnaces worse than ever burned this hot
Babylon shall inflict on the Romans.

2.31

In Campania the Cassiline shall so rise
One shall see water where the fields had been :
Before & after, rain without respite :
Save for the trees, nothing green to be seen.

2.32

Milk, blood, frogs showering Dalmatia,
Battle breaking out, plague near Balenna :
A great cry throughout all Slavonia,
Then monster born near & in Ravenna.

2.33
Par le torrent qui descent de Veronne
Par lors qu'au Po guindera son entrée :
Un grand naufrage, & non moins en Garonne
Quant ceux de Gennes marcheront leur contrée.

2.34
L'ire insensée du combat furieux,
Fera à table par freres le fer luire :
Les despartir, mort, blessé, curieux :
Le fier duelle viendra en France nuire.

2.35
Dans deux logis de nuict le feu prendra,
Plusieurs dedans estoufés & rostis :
Près de deux fleuves pour seur il adviendra :
Sol, l'Arq. & Capr. tous seront amortis.

2.36
Du grand Prophete les lettres seront prinses :
Entre les mains du tyrant deviendront :
Frauder son roy seront ses entreprinses,
Mais ses rapines bien tost le troubleront.

2.37
De ce grand nombre que l'on envoyera
Pour secourir dans le fort assiegés,
Peste & famine tous les devorera,
Hors mis septante qui seront profligés.

2.38
Des condamnés sera fait un grand nombre
Quand les monarques seront conciliés,
Mais à l'un deux viendra si malencombre,
Que gueres ensemble ne seront raliés.

2.39
Un an devant le conflict Italique,
Germains, Gaulois, Hespaignolz pour le fort,
Cherra l'escolle maison de republicque,
Ou, hors mis peu, seront suffoqués mors.

2.33
From the torrent that descends from Verona
The boat maneuvers its way to the Po :
A great shipwreck, as bad as in Garonne
When the Genoans march into their home.

2.34
The senseless fury of a feud leading
Brothers to flash their steel over a meal :
A rush to pull them apart, dead, bleeding :
These wanton duels shall harm France a great deal.

2.35
Fire shall break out in two lodgings at night,
Many shall suffocate & roast inside :
This shall occur near two rivers for sure :
Sun in Sag. & Capricorn, all shall die.

2.36
The mighty Prophet's letters interception
Shall place them in the hands of the tyrant :
To defraud the king is his intention,
But his thefts shall soon come back to haunt him.

2.37
Of the great number of those sent away
To rescue those besieged within the fort,
All shall be devoured by famine & plague,
Save the seventy slaughtered for sport.

2.38
A great number shall be condemned to death
When the monarchs are reconciled,
But one of them shall encounter such rebuffs
That their alliance shall not long survive.

2.39
A year before the Italian war,
Germans, Gauls, Spaniards vying for the fort,
A schoolhouse of the republic shall fall,
All, save a few, suffocating to death.

2.40

Un peu après non point longue intervalle,
Par mer & terre sera faict grand tumulte :
Beaucoup plus grande sera pugne navalle,
Feux, animeux, qui plus feront d'insulte.

2.41

La grand'estoille par sept jours bruslera,
Nuée fera deux soleils apparoir :
Le gros mastin toute nuict hurlera,
Quand grand pontife changera de terroir.

2.42

Coqs, chiens & chats de sang seront repeus
Et de la plaie du tyrant trouvé mort,
Au lict d'un autre jambes & bras rompus,
Qui n'avoit peur mourir de cruel mort.

2.43

Durant l'estoille chevelue apparente,
Les trois grans princes seront faits ennemis :
Frappés du ciel paix terre tremulente :
Po, Timbre undans, serpent sus le bort mis.

2.44

L'aigle posée entour de pavillons
Par autre oyseau d'entour sera chassée,
Quand bruit de cymbes, tubes & sonnaillons
Rendront le sens de la dame insensée.

2.45

Trop le ciel pleure l'Androgyn procréé :
Près de ce ciel sang humain respandu :
Par mort trop tarde grand peuple recréé :
Tard & tost vient le secours attendu.

2.46

Après grant trouble humain plus grand s'appreste :
Le grand moteur les siecles renouvelle :
Pluye, sang, laict, famine, fer & peste,
Au ciel veu feu, courant longue estincelle.

2.40

Shortly thereafter, little time in fact,
On land & sea shall be great alarum :
The naval battle greater in impact,
Greek fire inflicting the greatest harm.

2.41

The mighty star shall blaze seven days straight,
Cloud shall cause two suns in the sky to stand :
The hefty mastiff shall howl the night late,
When the great pontiff moves from land to land.

2.42

The cocks, dogs & cats shall feast on the blood
And the wounds of the tyrant who's found dead
In another's bed, his arms & legs crushed,
Who had no fear of dying a cruel death.

2.43

At the appearance of the bearded star,
The three great princes shall turn mortal foes :
Lightning from on high : peace on earth scarred :
Po, Tiber overflow, snakes on the shore.

2.44

Perched here & there on the tents, the eagle
By another bird shall be chased away
When the clamor of cymbals, trumps & bells
Restores the senses of the senseless lady.

2.45

Heaven overweeps the Androgyne's birth :
Much human blood shed near this place on earth :
Death overslow gives a great race new life :
Soon & late the awaited help arrives.

2.46

After major chaos, more on the way :
The mighty Mover renews the ages :
A rain of blood, milk, famine, war & plague,
Fire in the sky, trail of sparks in its wake.

2.47

L'ennemy grand vieil dueil meurt de poison :
Les souverains par infims subjuguez :
Pierres plouvoir : cachés soubz la toison :
Par mort articles en vain sont alleguez.

2.48

La grand copie qui passera les monts,
Saturne en l'Arq. tournant du poisson Mars :
Venins cachés soubz testes de saulmons,
Leur chief pendu à fils de polemars.

2.49

Les conseilliers du premier monopole,
Les conquerants seduits pour la Melite,
Rodes, Bisance pour leurs exposant pole,
Terre faudra les poursuivants de fuite.

2.50

Quand ceux d'Hainault, de Gand & de Bruxelles
Verront à Langres le siege devant mis,
Derrier leurs flancz seront guerres cruelles :
La plaie antique fera pis qu'ennemis.

2.51

Le sang du juste à Londres fera faulte :
Bruslés par fouldres de vint & trois les six :
La dame antique cherra de place haute :
De mesme secte plusieurs seront occis.

2.52

Dans plusieurs nuits la terre tremblera :
Sur le printemps deux effors feront suite :
Corinthe, Ephese aux deux mers nagera :
Guerre s'esmeut par deux vaillans de luite.

2.53

La grande peste de cité maritime
Ne cessera que mort ne soit vengée
Du juste sang par pris damné sans crime :
De la grand dame par feincte n'outraigée.

2.47

The agèd foe grieves & dies of poison :
Sovereigns are subjugated by the plebs :
Stones rain down : people hide beneath the fleece :
At death, items cited for no good reason.

2.48

Mighty host making its way over mountains,
Saturn in Sag., Mars lapsed into Pisces :
Poisons hidden in the heads of psalmons,
Their chief hanged by a noose of wrapping twine.

2.49

The counselors of the oldest of leagues
With nothing but Malta now on their mind,
Leaving Rhodes & Byzantium behind,
Shall lose their land, pursued by enemies.

2.50

When the folk of Ghent, Brussels & Hainaut
Witness the siege that's laid upon Langres,
Fierce combat shall erupt behind their flanks :
Age-old plague harder on them than their foes.

2.51

No blood of the just shall be spilled in London :
Six times twenty-three consumed by lightning :
The ancient dame shall fall from high station :
Many of the same sect shall lose their lives.

2.52

For several nights the earth shall heave & quake :
Come the spring two further shocks shall follow :
Corinth, Ephesus in two seas shall wallow :
Two brave warriors shall enter the fray.

2.53

The mighty plague in the city by the sea
Shall not end until the death is avenged
Of innocent blood unjustly condemned :
The great dame outraged by the knavery.

2.54

Par gent estrange, & de Romains loingtaine
Leur grand cité après eaue fort troublée :
Fille sans main : trop different domaine,
Prins chef, sarreure n'avoir esté riblée.

2.55

Dans le conflict le grand qui peu valloit,
A son dernier fera cas merveilleux :
Pendant qu'Hadrie verra ce qu'il falloit,
Dans le banquet pongnale l'orgueilleux.

2.56

Que peste & glaive n'a peu seu definer
Mort dans le puys, sommet du ciel frappé :
L'abbé mourra quand verra ruiner
Ceux du naufrage, l'escueil voulant grapper.

2.57

Avant conflict le grand mur tombera :
Le grand à mort, mort, trop subite & plainte :
Nay imparfaict : la plus part nagera :
Auprès du fleuve de sang la terre tainte.

2.58

Sans pied ne main dent ayguë & forte,
Par globe au front de porc & laye nay :
Près du portail desloyal se transporte :
Silene luit : petit grand emmené.

2.59

Classe Gauloise par appuy de grand garde,
Du grand Neptune, & ses tridens souldars :
Rongée Provence pour soustenir grand bande,
Plus Mars Narbon par javelotz & dards.

2.60

La foy Punicque en Orient rompue,
Gand. Ind. & Rosne, Loyre & Tag changeront :
Quand du mulet la faim sera repue,
Classe espargie, sang & corps nageront.

2.54

A foreign nation far removed from Rome
Their great city by the sea shall afflict :
A girl sans hand : his fief being opposed,
The chief shall be seized, his locks left unpicked.

2.55

The great lord who did not excel in war
Shall in the end commit a deed most fine :
While Adria tends to its needs, at the feast
He shall stab the one who's bursting with pride.

2.56

He whom neither plague nor sword could lay low
Found dead in the well, thunderstruck from on high :
The abbot shall die when he sees the crew
Shipwrecked on the reef, grasping for their lives.

2.57

Before the battle the great wall shall fall :
The lord's untimely death they shall deplore :
A birth deformed : most swim for it & drown :
Beside the river, the earth stained with gore.

2.58

Sans foot or hand & sharp & strong of tooth,
Born of ram & sow, with a glob for a face :
The traitor sidles toward the gate : the moon
Shines : led away are the small & the great.

2.59

Gallic fleet fortified by great La Garde,
This great Neptune & his trident sailors :
Provence gnawed to the bone to feed the horde :
Many spears & darts harm Narbonne of Mars.

2.60

The Punic pact now broken in the East,
Ganges, Indus, Rhône, Loire, Tagus shall change :
When the mule has no more desire to eat,
Fleet dispersed, blood & bodies on the waves.

2.61

Enge, Tamins, Gironde & la Rochele :
O sang Troien ! Mars au port de la Flesche :
Derrier le fleuve au fort mise l'eschele,
Pointes à feu grand meurtre sus la bresche.

2.62

Mabus puis tost alors mourra, viendra
De gens & bestes une horrible defaite :
Puis tout à coup la vengeance on verra,
Sans main, soif, faim, quand courra la comete.

2.63

Gaulois, Ausone bien peu subjuguera :
Po, Marne & Seine fera Parme tuerie
Qui le grand mur contre eux dressera :
Du moindre au mur le grand perdra la vie.

2.64

Seicher de faim, de soif, gent Genevoise,
Espoir prochain viendra au defaillir :
Sur point tremblante sera loy Gébenoise :
Classe au grand port ne se peut accueillir.

2.65

Le p. arc. enclin grande calamité
Par Hesperie & Insubre fera :
Le feu en nef peste & captivité,
Mercure en l'Arq. Saturne fenera.

2.66

Par grans dangiers le captif eschapé,
Peu de temps grand a fortune changée,
Dans le palais de peuple est attrapé :
Par bon augure la cité est assiegée.

2.67

Le blonde au nez forche viendra commettre
Par le duelle & chassera dehors :
Les exilés dedans fera remettre,
Aux lieux marins commettant les plus fors.

2.61

The Thames swells La Rochelle & the Gironde :
O Trojan blood ! Mars at the port of La Flèche :
Beyond the river, ladder leaned on fort,
Harquebuses wrecking havoc in the breach.

2.62

So Mabus soon shall die & there shall be
A massacre befalling man & beast :
Suddenly the vengeance shall be seen,
Sans hand, thirst, hunger, when the comet streaks.

2.63

Ausonia shall not fully fall to Gaul :
Parma shall slaughter Po & Seine & Marne
And against them shall raise a mighty wall
Where the great one shall be felled by the small.

2.64

The Genevans parched with hunger & thirst,
Their hopes for help looking ever more bleak :
This shall strike fear into the Cévennes sect :
The great port refuses entrance to the fleet.

2.65

Arctic pole shall provoke calamities
Throughout Hesperia and Insubria :
Lightning striking ships, plague & captivity,
Mercury in Sag., Saturn at his scythe.

2.66

Amid great risks the captive breaking free,
A change of fortune soon afflicts the chief,
By his own people in his palace seized :
Fortunately, the city is besieged.

2.67

In a duel the blond one shall come to blows
With the forked nose & throw him out of doors :
He shall invite all the exiles back home,
Committing the strongest to guard the ports.

2.68
De l'aquilon les efforts seront grands :
Sus l'Ocean sera la porte ouverte :
Le regne en l'isle sera reintegrand,
Tremblera Londres par voille descouverte.

2.69
Le roy Gaulois par la Celtique dextre,
Voiant discorde de la grand Monarchiea,
Sus les trois parts fera florir son sceptre,
Contre la cappe de la grand Hierarchie.

2.70
Le dard du ciel fera son estendue :
Mors en parlant : grande execution :
La pierre en l'arbre : la fiere gent rendue,
Brut, humain monstre : purge, expiation.

2.71
Les exilés en Sicile viendront,
Pour delivrer de faim la gent estrange :
Au point du jour les Celtes luy faudront :
La vie demeure : à raison Roy se range.

2.72
Armée Celtique en Italie vexée
De toutes pars, conflict & grande perte :
Romains fuis, ô Gaule repoulsée!
Pres du Thesin, Rubicon, pugne incerte.

2.73
Au lac Fucin de Benac le rivaige
Prins du Leman au port de l'Ogmion :
Nay de trois bras predict bellique image,
Par trois couronnes au grand Endymion.

2.74
De Sens, d'Autun viendront jusques au Rosne
Pour passer outre vers les monts Pyrenées :
La gent sortie de la Marque d'Anconne
Par terre & mer les suivra à grans trainées.

2.68

The northern army shall be great in size,
The door to the Ocean shall open wide :
The throne shall be recovered on the isle,
London tremble when the sails are espied.

2.69

The Gallic king with his Celtic right arm,
Seeing discord in the great Monarchy,
Shall plant his scepter over the three parts,
Against the cope of the great Hierarchy.

2.70

The spear of the sky shall streak far & wide :
Many executed, talking as they die :
Stone striking tree : proud people on its knees :
Man-beast monster born : purge & purify.

2.71

To Sicily the exiles shall make their way
To rescue the foreigners from famine :
Come dawn, by the Celts these shall be betrayed :
Lives are spared, king at last seeing reason.

2.72

Beset from every side in Italy
The Celtic host shall suffer great defeat :
Flee the Romans, O Gaul now in retreat!
Near Ticino, Rubicon, no victory.

2.73

Lake Fucino shall take Lake Garda's shore
As Port'Ercole shall take Lake Leman :
Three-armed child predicts images of war
Three crowns wage against great Endymion.

2.74

From Sens & Autun they shall reach the Rhône
And cross beyond into the Pyrenees :
The folk from the Marches of Ancona
Shall chase them in great leaps by land & sea.

2.75

La voix ouye de l'insolit oyseau
Sur le canon du respiral estage :
Si hault viendra du froment le boisseau,
Que l'homme d'homme sera Antropophage.

2.76

Foudre en Bourgongne fera cas portenteux,
Que par engin oncques ne pourroit faire,
De leur senat sacriste fait boiteux,
Fera sçavoir aux ennemis l'affaire.

2.77

Par arcs, feux, poix, & par feux repoussés,
Cris hurlements sur la minuit ouys :
Dedans sont mis par les rampars cassés :
Par cunicules les traditeurs fuys.

2.78

Le grand Neptune du profond de la mer,
De gent Punique & sang Gaulois meslé :
Les Isles à sang, pour le tardif ramer
Plus luy nuira que l'occult mal celé.

2.79

La barbe crespe & noire par engin
Subjuguera la gent cruelle & fiere :
Le grand CHYREN ostera du longin
Tous les captifs par Seline baniere.

2.80

Après conflict du lesé l'eloquence
Par peu de temps se trame faint repos :
Point l'on admet les grands à delivrance :
Les ennemis sont remis à propos.

2.81

Par feu du ciel la cité presque aduste,
L'urne menace encore Deucalion :
Vexée Sardaigne par la Punique fuste,
Après que Libra lairra son Phaëton.

2.75
The voice of the fabulous bird
Is heard upon the chimney flue :
Wheat bushel's price shall rise so high
That man to man shall become food.

2.76
Thunder in Burgundy, prodigious omen,
Confusion such as craft could never sow :
In their senate the clubfooted sexton
Shall make the affair known to the foes.

2.77
Beaten back by bows, burning pitch & fire,
Toward midnight the sound of howls & screams :
Through the ramparts' breeches they pass in file :
Traitors tunnel underground in retreat.

2.78
This mighty Neptune issued from the sea,
The blood of Gaul crossed with the Punic breed :
Bloodbath on the Isles : his sailing so late
Does him more harm than poorly masked intrigue.

2.79
The beard so black & curly shall by ruse
Subjugate the nation so proud & cruel :
Great CHYREN shall free captives from cesspools
Beneath the banner of the crescent Moon.

2.80
After battle, the losers' eloquence
Weaves a brief moment of pretended truce :
The ransoming of nobles is refused :
Foes to be dealt with according to rules.

2.81
The city almost burned down by lightning,
The Urn threatens another Deucalion :
In Sardinia Punic ships shall be fighting,
After Libra liberates its Phaëthon.

2.82
Par faim la proye fera loup prisonnier,
L'assaillant lors en extreme detresse,
Le nay aiant au devant le dernier,
Le grand n'eschappe au milieu de la presse.

2.83
Le gros traffic du grand Lion changé,
La plus part tourne en pristine ruine :
Proye aux souldars par pille vendengé
Par Jura mont & Sueve bruine.

2.84
Entre Campaigne, Sienne, Flora, Tustie,
Six mois neuf jours ne plovra une goutte :
L'estrange langue en terre Dalmatie
Courira sus, vastant la terre toute.

2.85
Le vieux plain barbe soubs le statut severe,
A Lyon faict dessus l'Aigle Celtique :
Le petit, grant trop outre persevere :
Bruit d'arme au ciel : mer rouge Lygustique.

2.86
Naufrage à classe près d'onde Hadriatique :
La terre esmeue sus l'air en terre mis :
Egypte tremble augment Mahometique :
L'Herault soy rendre à crier est commis.

2.87
Après viendra des extremes contrées
Prince Germain, sus le throsne doré :
La servitude ès feaux rencontrées :
La dame serve, son temps plus n'a duré.

2.88
Le circuit du grand faict ruineux :
Le nom septiesme du cinquiesme sera
D'un tiers plus grand : l'estrange belliqueux
Mouton, Lutece, Aix ne garantira.

2.82
The hungry wolf shall be seized by his prey,
The assailant fall into great disarray,
The monster child be born backwards faced,
The lord unable to flee from the fray.

2.83
The rich trade of great Lyon in decline,
Most return to their penury of old
As troops maraud, plundering left & right,
Down from Jura & Swabia, mist enfolds.

2.84
Campania, Siena, Florence, Tuscany,
For six months nine days not a drop of rain :
Foreign speakers shall rush into the fray
In Dalmatia, laying all the lands to waste.

2.85
The full-bearded old man with laws severe
At Lyon the Celtic Eagle shall best :
The small, great too eager to persevere :
Sword-clang in sky : Ligustic sea blood-red.

2.86
Fleet shipwrecked near the Adriatic sea :
Earth tossed into air, falling back to land :
Egypt trembling at Islam's swift increase :
The herald dispatched, surrender in hand.

2.87
German prince shall later come from regions
Most remote to take up the golden throne :
Bondage remarked among his loyal legions :
As for the lady slave, her days were short.

2.88
The lord shall ride over his foes roughshod :
The seventh name of the fifth one shall stand
One third greater: the warlord from abroad
Shall not spare Paris, Aix his battering ram.

2.89
Du jou seront demis les deux grands maistres :
Leur grand pouvoir se verra augmenté :
La terre neufve sera en ses hauts estres
Au sanguinaire le nombre racompté.

2.90
Par vie & mort changé regne d'Ongrie,
La loy sera plus aspre que service :
Leur grand cité d'urlemens, plaincts & crie :
Castor & Pollux ennemis dans la lice.

2.91
Soleil levant un grand feu l'on verra,
Bruit & clarté vers Aquilon tendants :
Dedans le rond mort & cris l'on orra :
Par glaive, feu, faim, mort les attendants.

2.92
Feu couleur d'or du ciel en terre veu :
Frappé du haut : nay faict cas merveilleux :
Grand meurtre humain : prins du grand le neveu,
Morts d'espectacles eschappé l'orgueilleux.

2.93
Bien près du Tymbre presse la Lybitine :
Un peu devant grand'inondation :
Le chef du nef prins, mis à la sentine :
Chasteau, palais en conflagration.

2.94
GRAND PO grand mal pour Gaulois recevra,
Vaine terreur au maritin Lyon :
Peuple infiny par la mer passera,
Sans eschapper un quart d'un milion.

2.95
Les lieux peuplés seront inhabitables
Pour champs avoir grande division :
Regnes livrés à prudents incapables,
Lors les grands freres mort & dissention.

2.89
The two great masters shall make their way free :
Their great power shall be seen to increase :
They'll count the sums that from new lands accrue
For the bloody prince in his tower rooms.

2.90
Life & death changing Hungary's regime,
The law far harsher than mere loyalty :
Their capital shall ring with howls, pleas, screams :
Castor Pollux in the lists as enemies.

2.91
At dawn a great ball of fire shall appear,
So loud & bright as it rolls to the North :
In its burning globe screams of death they'll hear :
Witnesses dying by fire, hunger, sword.

2.92
A golden flame from sky to earth is seen :
Struck from on high : a newborn babe amazes :
Major massacres : the lord's nephew seized :
Deaths at the theater : the proud one flees.

2.93
Libitina falls hard upon Tiber :
Somewhat before the great inundation :
The ship captain is seized, thrown in the hole :
Castle, palace in conflagration.

2.94
Gaul shall wreak much woe on the MIGHTY PO,
Vain terror seize the Lion of the seas :
Across the waters multitudes shall flee,
Quarter million unable to get free.

2.95
Deserted lands that were once filled with life,
The fields now reapportioned left & right :
Kingdoms handed over to timid fools,
Noble brothers engaged in deadly duels.

2.96

Flambeau ardent au ciel soir sera veu
Près de la fin & principe du Rosne :
Famine, glaive : tard le secours pourveu,
La Perse tourne envahir Macedoine.

2.97

Romain Pontife garde de t'approcher,
De la cité que deux fleuves arrose,
Ton sang viendras au près de là cracher,
Toy & les tiens quand fleurira la rose.

2.98

Celuy du sang resperse le visaige,
De la victime proche sacrifiée,
Tonant en Leo augure par presaige,
Mis estre à mort lors pour la fiancée.

2.99

Terroir Romain qu'interpretoit augure
Par gent Gauloyse par trop sera vexée :
Mais nation Celtique craindra l'heure,
Boreas, classe trop loing l'avoir poussée.

2.100

Dedans les isles si horrible tumulte,
Bien on n'orra qu'une bellique brigue :
Tant grand sera des predateurs l'insulte,
Qu'on se viendra ranger à la grand ligue.

CENTURIE III

3.1

Après combat & bataille navale,
Le grand Neptune à son plus haut befroy :
Rouge adversaire de fraieur viendra pasle
Mettant le grand Ocean en effroy.

2.96

In the night sky a flaming torch espied
Near to the mouth & the source of the Rhône :
Famine & sword : the help late to arrive :
Persia returns to invade Macedone.

2.97

Pontiff of Rome, beware of approaching
The city where the two rivers pool :
You shall come to spit up your blood here,
You & yours, when the rose is in bloom.

2.98

He whose face is spattered by the blood spilled
By the sacrificial victim nearby,
With Jupiter in Leo boding ill,
Shall be put to death for the future bride.

2.99

The Roman lands marked out by the augur
Shall be sorely vexed by the race of Gaul :
But this Celtic nation shall fear the hour
Boreas blows its boats off course with squalls.

2.100

With the islands in such awful uproar,
All one shall hear are the boastings of war :
So great shall the insults of pirates be
One shall cast one's lot with the mighty league.

CENTURY III

3.1

After all the war & naval battle,
The great Neptune risen to his power's height :
The enemy red shall grow pale with fear,
Throw the mighty ocean into affright.

3.2
Le divin verbe donrra à la substance,
Comprins ciel terre, occult au faict mystique :
Corps, ame, esprit ayant toute puissance,
Tant soubz ses piedz comme au siege celique.

3.3
Mars & Mercure & l'argent joint ensemble,
Vers le midy extreme siccité :
Au fond d'Asie on dira terre tremble :
Corinthe, Ephese lors en perplexité.

3.4
Quand seront proches le defaut des lumières,
De l'un à l'autre ne distant grandement,
Froid, siccité, danger vers les frontieres,
Mesme où l'oracle a prins commencement.

3.5
Près loing defaut de deux grands luminaires,
Qui surviendra entre l'Avril & Mars :
O quel cherté ! mais deux grans debonnaires,
Par terre & mer secourront toutes pars.

3.6
Dans temple clos le fouldre y entrera,
Les citadins dedans lors fort grevez :
Chevaux, bœufs, hommes, l'onde mur touchera,
Par faim, soif, sous, les plus foibles arnez.

3.7
Les fugitifs, feu du ciel sus les piques :
Conflict prochain des corbeaux s'esbatans :
De terre on crie aide secours celiques,
Quand près des murs seront les combatans.

3.8
Les Cimbres joints avecques leurs voisins
Depopuler viendront presque l'Espaigne :
Gens amassez, Guienne & Limosins,
Seront en ligue & leur feront compaigne.

3.2

Spread through heaven & earth, the Divine Word
Shall give the substance, veiled in mystery :
A body, spirit, soul, as almighty
Here beneath its feet as on heaven's throne.

3.3

Mars & Mercury & the Moon conjoined,
Extreme drought shall afflict the southern climes :
Earthquakes reported in furthest Asia :
Corinth, Ephesus then in wretched plight.

3.4

When eclipse of sun & moon draws nigh,
With no major interval between each,
Cold & drought & danger at the confines,
Even where the oracle first found speech.

3.5

Near far from the failing of these two great lights
Which shall take place between April & March :
What prices ! But two great ones good & kind
By land & sea shall bring help to all parts.

3.6

The lightning shall crash into the closed church,
Citizens within shall be overwhelmed :
The waters flood horses, cattle, walls, men,
The weakest felled by hunger, mud & thirst.

3.7

As they flee, sky-fire alights on their pikes :
Coming conflict presaged by ravens' flight :
Calls from earth for intervention divine,
When the enemy troops draw into sight.

3.8

Allied with their neighbors, the Cimbrians
Shall unpeople Spain almost to a man :
Folk amassed in Guyenne & Limousin
Shall enter into league & join their band.

3.9

Bourdeaux, Rouan, & la Rochelle joints,
Tiendront autour la grand mer Oceane :
Anglois, Bretons, & les Flamans conjoints,
Les chasseront jusques auprès de Rouane.

3.10

De sang & faim plus grand calamité
Sept fois s'appreste à la marine plage :
Monech de faim, lieu pris, captivité,
Le grand mené croc en ferrée caige.

3.11

Les armes battre au ciel longue saison,
L'arbre au milieu de la cité tombé :
Vermine, rongne, glaive, en face tyson,
Lors le monarque d'Hadrie succombé.

3.12

Par la tumeur d'Heb., Po, Tag., Timbre, & Rosne
Et par l'estang Leman & Aretin :
Les deux grands chefs & citez de Garonne,
Prins mors noyez. Partir humain butin.

3.13

Par fouldre en l'arche or & argent fondu,
Des deux captifs l'un l'autre mangera :
De la cité le plus grand estendu,
Quand submergée la classe nagera.

3.14

Par le rameau du vaillant personnage
De France infime, par le pere infelice :
Honneurs, richesses, travail en son vieil aage,
Pour avoir creu le conseil d'homme nice.

3.15

Cœur, vigueur, gloire le regne changera,
De tous points contre ayant son adversaire :
Lors France enfance par mort subjuguera :
Le grand regent sera lors plus contraire.

3.9
Bordeaux, Rouen & La Rochelle in league
Shall hold the land around the ocean sea :
The English, Bretons & Flemish in league
Shall drive them almost as far as Roanne.

3.10
Blood & famine, major calamity
About to strike the coast a seventh time :
Monaco starved, fort seized, captivity,
Its lord dragged by hook in an iron cage.

3.11
The sword-clash in the sky proceeds apace,
The tree in the city square has fallen :
Vermin, scabies, blade, a torch to the face,
Thus the Adriatic monarch succumbs.

3.12
The swelling of the Eb., Po, Tag., Tib., Rhône
As Arezzo's & Leman's waters roil :
In the two great cities of the Garonne,
Bodies seized, drowned. Dividing human spoils.

3.13
Lightning melting the gold & silver chest,
One of the captives shall the other eat :
The city's strongman shall be laid to rest,
When sailors swim from their sunken fleet.

3.14
From a minor branch of a valiant lord
Of France, from an unlucky father born :
He shall know honors & riches when old,
Though a fool's advice cause him untold woe.

3.15
From courage, strength, glory the realm shall stray,
Enemies converging from every side :
When the king dies, a child France shall betray :
This the mighty regent shall not abide.

3.16

Le prince Anglois Mars à son cœur de ciel,
Voudra poursuivre sa fortune prospere :
Des deux duelles l'un percera le fiel,
Hay de luy, bien-aymé de sa mere.

3.17

Mont Aventine brusler nuict sera veu,
Le ciel obscur tout à un coup en Flandres :
Quand le monarque chassera son nepveu,
Lors gens d'Eglise commettront les esclandres.

3.18

Après la pluye de laict assés longuette,
En plusieurs lieux de Reims le ciel toucher :
O quel conflict de sang près d'eux s'appreste !
Pere & fils Roys n'oseront approcher.

3.19

En Luques sang & laict viendra plouvoir,
Un peu devant changement de preteur :
Grand peste & guerre, faim & soif fera voir,
Loing où mourra leur Prince & grand recteur.

3.20

Par les contrées du grand fleuve Bethique,
Loing d'Iberie au regne de Grenade,
Croix repoussées par gent Mahometique :
Un de Cordube trahira la contrade.

3.21

Au Crustumin par mer Hadriatique,
Apparoistra un horride poisson,
De face humaine, & la fin aquatique,
Qui se prendra dehors de l'ameçon.

3.22

Six jours l'assaut devant cité donné :
Livrée sera forte & aspre bataille :
Trois là rendront & à eux pardonné :
Le reste à feu & à sang, tranche, taille.

3.16

The English prince, Mars at mid-sky his sign,
Shall seek out the fortune he has in store :
One duelist shall pierce the other's spleen,
Hated by him, but by his mother adored.

3.17

The Aventine Hill seen aflame at night,
Above Flanders skies shall suddenly dim :
The monarch then driving out his nephew,
The church people then making quite a din.

3.18

After a somewhat longish rain of milk,
The lightning shall be general over Reims :
Alas, what a bloodbath being prepared !
King's father & son shall not dare advance.

3.19

On Lucca blood & milk down shall rain,
Shortly before the change of the praetor :
A sign of famine & drought, war & plague,
Where death comes to their prince & great rector.

3.20

In the lands of the great Baetic river,
Far from Iberia, in Grenada,
The crosses shall be repulsed by Muslims :
Cordoba shall betray the contrada.

3.21

At Crustumerium near the Adriatic
There shall appear a fish of horrid look,
With a human face & tail aquatic,
Who'll be dragged from the waters by a hook.

3.22

The assault upon the city shall last six days :
A fierce & bitter battle shall be waged :
Three shall give it up & their skins be saved :
No quarter for the rest, all hacked & flayed.

3.23

Si France passes outre mer lygustique,
Tu te verras en isle & mer enclos :
Mahommet contraire, plus mer Hadriatique :
Chevaux & d'asnes tu rongeras les os.

3.24

De l'entreprinse grande confusion,
Perte de gens, thresor innumerable :
Tu n'y dois faire encore extension :
France à mon dire fais que sois racordable.

3.25

Qui au Royaume Navarrois parviendra,
Quand de Sicile et Naples seront joints,
Bigore & Landes par Foyx Loron tiendra,
D'un qui d'Espaigne sera par trop conjoint.

3.26

Des Roys & Princes dresseront simulacres,
Augures creuz eslevez aruspices :
Corne, victime dorée, & d'azur, d'acre,
Interpretez seront les extispices.

3.27

Prince Libyque puissant en Occident,
François d'Arabe viendra tant enflammer,
Sçavans aux lettres fera condescendent,
La langue Arabe en François translater.

3.28

De terre foible & pauvre parentele,
Par bout & paix parviendra dans l'empire :
Long temps regner une jeune femelle,
Qu'oncques en regne n'en survint un si pire.

3.29

Les deux nepveus en divers lieux nourris,
Navale pugne, terre peres tombez,
Viendront si haut eslevez enguerris
Venger l'injure : ennemis succombez.

3.23

France, if you pass beyond the Ligurian sea,
Within isles & seas you shall be enclosed :
Muslim foe, in Adriatic more so :
You shall gnaw at horse & donkey bones.

3.24

The enterprise shall end in confusion,
Great loss of life & treasure beyond price :
Beware of your overextension :
France, just try to remember my advice.

3.25

He who shall take up the throne of Navarre
When Sicily & Naples are allied,
From Oloron, Foix shall hold Landes, Bigorre,
Although very much on the Spanish side.

3.26

Of kings & princes images they'll unfurl,
Haruspices, augurs, their crooks raised high :
Victims' horns, gold, lapis lazuli, pearl,
Entrails to be interpreted for signs.

3.27

A Libyan prince with influence in the West
Shall so inflame François for Arab matters
That in his knowledge of letters he shall abet
The translation of its language into French.

3.28

From a puny land & of poor parentage,
Let into the empire by the back door :
A young female reigning on for ages,
Nothing worse ever witnessed on a throne.

3.29

The two nephews from a different place,
Their fathers fallen in battle at sea,
Shall come, scions of a warrior race,
Avenge the insult : enemy defeat.

3.30
Celuy qu'en luitte & fer au faict bellique,
Aura porté plus grand que luy le pris,
De nuict au lict six luy feront la pique,
Nud sans harnois subit sera surpris.

3.31
Aux champs de Mede, d'Arabe et d'Armenie,
Deux grans copies trois fois s'assembleront :
Près du rivage d'Araxes la mesgnie,
Du grand Solman en terre tomberont.

3.32
Le grand sepulcre du peuple Aquitanique
S'approchera auprès de la Toscane,
Quand Mars sera près du coing Germanique,
Et au terroir de la gent Mantuane.

3.33
En la cité où le loup entrera,
Bien près de là les ennemis seront :
Copie estrange grand pays gastera,
Haults murs & Alpes les amis passeront.

3.34
Quand le deffaut du Soleil lors sera,
Sur le plain jour le monstre sera veu :
Tout autrement on l'interpretera :
Cherté n'a garde : nul n'y aura pourveu.

3.35
Du plus profond de l'Occident d'Europe,
De pauvres gens un jeune enfant naistra :
Qui par sa langue seduira grande trope,
Son bruit au regne d'Orient plus croistra.

3.36
Ensevely non mort apopletique,
Sera trouvé avoir les mains mangées,
Quant la cité damnera l'heretique,
Qu'avoit leurs loix si leur sembloit changées.

3.30
He who in the battle snatched the prize
From a far finer swordsman & fighter
Shall be attacked in bed by six at night,
Naked, unarmed, much taken by surprise.

3.31
On the Median, Arab, Armenian plains
Three times in battle shall two great hosts meet :
Near the banks of the Araxes the main
Of great Süleyman goes down in defeat.

3.32
He who put all Aquitaine in the grave
Shall make his way into the Tuscan lands,
When in Germany Mars prepares his reign
Or the country of the Mantuan clan.

3.33
When the wolf enters through the city gate,
The enemy shall lie quite close at hand :
Foreign army laying waste to the land,
Alpine walls traversed by a friendly state.

3.34
When the eclipse of the sun takes place,
An omen in broad daylight shall be seen :
It shall be interpreted the wrong way :
No one prepared : prices so unforeseen.

3.35
At Europe's farthermost western reaches,
To poor folk a small infant shall be born :
He shall seduce great crowds with his speeches,
His great fame spreading to Orient shores.

3.36
Not dead when buried, just apoplectic,
He shall be found to have his hands all gnawed,
When the city condemns the heretic
Who, so it seemed to them, had changed their laws.

3.37
Avant l'assaut oraison prononcée :
Milan prins d'aigle par embusches deceuz :
Muraille antique par canons enfoncée :
Par feu & sang à mercy peu receus.

3.38
La gent Gauloise & nation estrange,
Outre les monts, morts prins & profligez :
Au mois contraire & proche de vendange,
Par les Seigneurs en accord redigez.

3.39
Les sept en trois seront mis en concorde,
Pour subjuguer des Alpes Apennines :
Mais la tempeste & Ligure couarde,
Les profligent en subites ruines.

3.40
Le grand theatre se viendra redresser,
Le dez geté & les rets ja tendus,
Trop le premier en glaz viendra lasser,
Par arcs prostrais de long temps ja fendus.

3.41
Bossu sera esleu par le conseil,
Plus hideux monstre en terre n'apperceu :
Le coup volant prelat crevera l'œil,
Le traistre au Roy pour fidelle receu.

3.42
L'enfant naistra à deux dents en la gorge,
Pierres en Tuscie par pluye tomberont :
Peu d'ans après ne sera bled ny orge,
Pour saouler ceux qui de faim failliront.

3.43
Gens d'alentour de Tarn, Loth, & Garonne,
Gardez les monts Apennines passer :
Vostre tombeau près de Rome & d'Anconne,
Le noir poil crespe fera trophée dresser.

3.37
Before the assault an exhortation :
Kite seized by Eagle, ambushed by surprise :
Ancient wall crumbling under cannon fire :
Little mercy shown : total devastation.

3.38
The French people & the nation that lies
Beyond the mounts, all dead, captive, done for :
In the month opposite, near harvest time,
The leaders shall urge them into accord.

3.39
The seven as three shall come to agree
To subjugate the mounts of Apennines :
But the storm & Ligurian dastardy
Shall smash them all into smithereens.

3.40
The great theater shall be fitted afresh,
The nets already stretched, dais in place,
Causing the earlier structure to crash,
The old cracked beams breaking under the weight.

3.41
Council elects a hunchback to a seat,
On earth no more hideous monster seen :
The prelate's eye smashed by a blow most fleet,
The traitor believed loyal to the king.

3.42
The child is born with two teeth in its throat,
In Tuscany the stones fall just like rain :
A few years later, no barley, no wheat
To feed those whom hunger renders faint.

3.43
Folk from the vicinity of Tarn, Lot & Garonne,
Beware of passing over the Apennines :
Your tomb shall lie near Ancona & Rome,
The black curlybeard shall raise the trophy.

3.44

Quand l'animal à l'homme domestique,
Après grands peines & sauts viendra parler :
Le fouldre à vierge sera si malefique,
De terre prinse & suspendue en l'air.

3.45

Les cinq estanges entrez dedans le temple
Leur sang viendra la terre prophaner :
Aux Tholousains sera bien dur exemple,
D'un qui viendra ses loix exterminer.

3.46

Le ciel (de Plancus la cité) nous presaige,
Par clers insignes & par estoilles fixes,
Que de son change subit s'aproche l'aage,
Ne pour son bien, ne pour ses malefices.

3.47

Le vieux monarque dechassé de son regne
Aux Orients son secours ira querre :
Pour peur des croix pliera son enseigne,
En Mitylene ira pour port & terre.

3.48

Sept cens captifz estacher rudement,
Pour la moitié meurtrir, donné le sort :
Le proche espoir viendra si promptement,
Mais non si tost qu'une quinzaine mort.

3.49

Regne Gaulois tu seras bien changé :
En lieu estrange est translaté l'empire :
En autres mœurs & loix seras rangé :
Rouan, & Chartres te feront bien du pire.

3.50

La republique de la grande cité,
A grand rigueur ne voudra consentir :
Roy sortir hors par trompette cité,
L'eschelle au mur, la cité repentir.

3.44
When the pet dog rushes up to the man
And after yelps & leaps proceeds to speak :
Lightning having so struck the virgin,
She hangs there in thin air, swept off her feet.

3.45
When the five strangers have entered the church,
Their blood shall profane the holy ground :
Harsh example for the people of Toulouse
Of one who shall come to destroy their laws.

3.46
To us (of Plancus town) the sky presages
By its clear signs & by its fixed stars
The approach of the age of sudden change,
None for the better & none for the worse.

3.47
The agèd monarch driven from his realm
Shall be searching for succor in the East :
Fearing crosses, he shall furl his ensign
And seek a safe haven in Mytilene.

3.48
For the seven hundred captives in chains
Lots shall be drawn to execute the half :
The hoped-for rescue is quick to arrive,
But not before some fifteen are slain.

3.49
You shall change for the worse, kingdom of Gaul :
To a foreign place Empire is transferred :
You shall know other customs, other laws :
Rouen & Chartres shall do you much worse.

3.50
The government of that mighty town,
Too stubborn to withdraw beyond the gates
As so summoned by the king's trumpet call :
The town shall regret this, ladder at wall.

3.51

Paris conjure un grand meurtre commettre,
Bloys le fera sortir en plain effect :
Ceux d'Orleans vouldront leur chef remettre,
Angiers, Troyes, Langres, leur feront un meffait.

3.52

En la campaigne sera si longue pluye,
Et en la Pouille si grande siccité :
Coq verra l'Aigle, l'æsle mal accomplie,
Par Lyon mise sera en extremité.

3.53

Quand le plus grand emportera le pris,
De Nuremberg, d'Auspourg, & ceux de Basle
Par Agrippine le chef Frankfort repris,
Traverseront par Flamans jusques en Gale.

3.54

L'un des plus grans fuira aux Espaignes,
Qu'en longue playe après viendra saigner,
Passant copies par les hautes montaignes,
Devastant tout & puis en paix regner.

3.55

En l'an qu'un œil en France regnera,
La court sera à un bien facheux trouble :
Le grand de Bloys son amy tuera,
Le regne mis en mal & doubte double.

3.56

Montauban, Nismes, Avignon & Besier,
Peste, tonnerre, & gresle à fin de Mars :
De Paris pont, Lyon mur, Montpellier
Depuis six cens & sept vingts & trois pars.

3.57

Sept fois changer verrez gent Britannique,
Tainte en sang en deux cens nonante an,
Franche non point, par apuy Germanique :
Aries doubte son pole Bastarnan.

3.51

Paris plots to commit a great murder,
Blois shall make quite sure that the thing shall play :
Orléans shall want its own chief back in place,
Angers, Troyes, Langres shall make them pay.

3.52

In Campania it shall not stop raining,
In Puglia drought shall be no stranger :
Cock shall see the Eagle waver on wing
And the Lion put him in extreme danger.

3.53

When the strongest lord seizes the prize
That is Nuremberg, Augsburg & Bâle,
Frankfurt's seat retaken by Agrippine,
With Flemish help, they'll cross into Wales.

3.54

One of the noblest lords to Spain shall hie
And shall bleed its veins again & again,
Passing his troops over the mountains high,
Laying waste to all, then in peace to reign.

3.55

The year one eye over all France shall reign,
The court shall find itself quite befuddled :
The lord from Blois shall have killed his friend,
The realm troubled & the fears redoubled.

3.56

At Montauban, Nîmes, Avignon, Béziers,
Plague, thunder & hail at the end of March :
Paris bridge, Lyon wall, Montpellier shall fall,
Six hundred seven plus twenty-three parts.

3.57

Seven times you'll see the British people change,
Stained with blood, in two hundred ninety years,
Not that they'll be free, under German sway :
Bastarnian climes being what Aries fears.

3.58
Auprès du Rin des montaignes Noriques,
Naistra un grand de gent trop tard venu,
Qui defendra SAUROM. & Pannoniques,
Qu'on ne sçaura qu'il sera devenu.

3.59
Barbare empire par le tiers usurpé,
La plus grand part de son sang mettra à mort :
Par mort senile par luy le quart frappé,
Pour peur que sang par le sang ne soit mort.

3.60
Par toute Asie grande proscription,
Mesme en Mysie, Lysie, & Pamphylie :
Sang versera par absolution,
D'un jeune noir remply de felonnie.

3.61
La grande bande & secte crucigere,
Se dressera en Mesopotamie :
Du proche fleuve compaignie legiere,
Que telle loy tiendra pour ennemie.

3.62
Proche del duero par mer Tyrrene close,
Viendra perser les grands monts Pyrenées :
La main plus courte & sa percée gloze,
A Carcassonne conduira ses menées.

3.63
Romain pouvoir sera du tout abas,
Son grand voisin imiter ses vestiges :
Occultes haines civiles & debats,
Retarderont aux bouffons leurs folliges.

3.64
Le chef de Perse remplira grands OLXAΛES,
Classe Trireme contre gent Mahometique,
De Parthe, & Mede, & piller les Cyclades :
Repos long temps au grand port Ionique.

3.58

Near the Rhine & the mountains of Noricum
Shall be born a prince of a line come late,
Who shall so defend SAUROM. & Pannon.
That one shall know nothing about his fate.

3.59

Barbarian empire usurped by the third
Who shall kill a good lot of his own kin :
By him the fourth, an old man, is struck dead,
For fear that close kin do themselves in.

3.60

A great proscription throughout Asia,
Even Mysia, Lysia & Pamphylia :
In expiation one shall shed the blood
Of a most unmerciful young black buck.

3.61

The mighty host & sect of cross-bearers
Shall rise up in Mesopotamia :
Light horse from the next river over
Shall consider this religion its foe.

3.62

Being shut off from the Tyrrhenian Sea,
From the Duero he shall cross the Pyrenees :
Pressed for time & disguising his goal,
He maneuvers his way to Carcassonne.

3.63

The decline of Rome shall be quite profound,
Its great neighbor following down its route :
All the covert hates & civic disputes
Alone hindering the idiocies of clowns.

3.64

Persia's chief shall load up great OLXAΔDES
With Parthians & Medes, a fleet of triremes
Against the Muslims, & sack the Cyclades :
At the great Ionian port they'll be at ease.

3.65
Quand le sepulcre du grand Romain trouvé,
Le jour après sera esleu Pontife :
Du Senat gueres il ne sera prouvé,
Empoisonné son sang au sacré scyphe.

3.66
Le grand Baillif d'Orleans mis à mort,
Sera par un de sang vindicatif :
De mort merite ne mourra, ne par sort,
Des pieds & mains mal le faisoit captif.

3.67
Une nouvelle secte de Philosophes,
Mesprisant mort, or, honneurs & richesses,
Des monts Germains ne seront limitrophes,
A les ensuyvre auront appuy & presses.

3.68
Peuple sans chef d'Espaigne & d'Italie,
Morts profligez dedans le Cherronesse :
Leur duict trahi par legiere folie,
Le sang nager par tout à la traverse.

3.69
Grand exercite conduict par jouvenceau,
Se viendra rendre aux mains des ennemis :
Mais le vieillart nay au demy pourceau,
Fera Chalon & Mascon estre amis.

3.70
La grand Bretaigne comprinse l'Angleterre,
Viendra par eaux si haut à inonder :
La ligue neufve d'Ausonne fera guerre,
Que contre eux mesmes ils se viendront bander.

3.71
Ceux dans les villes de long temps assiegez,
Prendront vigueur, force contre ennemis :
Ceux par dehors mors de faim profligez,
En plus grand faim que jamais seront mis.

3.65

When the mighty Roman's tomb is dug up,
The pope elected the following day :
He shall not be approved by the senate,
His poisoned blood within the sacred cup.

3.66

The great bailiff of Orléans put to death
By someone with much vengeance in his veins :
He shall not die a deserved death nor by chance,
But bound hand & foot, a poor captive man.

3.67

A new sect of philosophers who hold
Death, gold, honors & riches in disdain
Shall extend beyond the German mountains,
Aided by those quick to follow their ways.

3.68

A leaderless people from Italy & Spain
Shall die, slaughtered in the Chersonese :
Their battle plan undone by daft mistakes,
The blood flowing freely through the streets.

3.69

The great army led by the stripling youth
Shall surrender into enemy hands :
But the old man born back at the Half-Swine
Shall make sure Chalon & Mâcon are friends.

3.70

All of Great Britain including England
Shall come to be full flooded by the seas :
In Ausonia, so at war is the new league
They shall ally themselves each against each.

3.71

Those trapped within towns long held under siege
Shall gain vim & vigor against their foes,
While all those left outside, famished & weak,
Shall just starve to death as never before.

3.72
Le bon vieillart tout vif ensevely,
Près du grand fleuve par fausse souspeçon :
Le nouveau vieux de richesse ennobly,
Prins au chemin tout l'or de la rançon.

3.73
Quand dans le regne parviendra le boiteux,
Competiteur aura proche bastard :
Luy & le regne viendront si fort rogneux,
Qu'ains qu'il guerisse son faict sera bien tard.

3.74
Naples, Florence, Favence, & Imole,
Seront en termes de telle fascherie,
Que pour complaire aux malheureux de Nolle,
Plainct d'avoir faict à son chef mocquerie.

3.75
PAV., Verone, Vicence, Sarragousse,
De glaives loings terroirs de sang humides :
Peste si grande viendra à la grand gousse,
Proche secours & bien loing les remedes.

3.76
En Germanie naistront diverses sectes,
S'approchant fort de l'heureux paganisme :
Le cœur captif & petites receptes,
Feront retour à payer le vray disme.

3.77
Le tiers climat sous Aries comprins,
L'an mil sept cens vingt & sept en Octobre :
Le Roy de Perse par ceux d'Egypte prins :
Conflit, mort, perte : à la croix grand opprobre.

3.78
Le chef d'Escosse avec six d'Alemaigne
Par gens de mer Orientaux captifs
Traverseront le Calpre & Espaigne,
Present en Perse au nouveau Roy craintifs.

3.72
The good old man shall be buried alive
By the great river under a cloud of doubt :
The bad old man whom wealth raised to such heights,
The entire ransom of gold seized en route.

3.73
When the lame-footed one ascends the throne,
A bastard kinsman shall play his foe :
He & the kingdom becoming so scabby
That in the end things shall fare most badly.

3.74
Naples, Florence, Faenza & Imola
Shall be widely criticized & deplored,
People complaining they insulted its lord
When rescuing the wretches of Nola.

3.75
PAV., Verona, Vicenza, Saragoss.,
All their lands soaked with the blood of long swords :
A great plague shall strike the Italian coast,
Help at hand but remedies quite remote.

3.76
Germany shall see the birth of divers sects
Quite like the paganism of ancient times :
Conquering hearts & content with small receipts,
They shall return to paying the true tithe.

3.77
In the third clime comprehended by Aries,
October seventeen twenty-seven :
King of Persia seized by the Egyptians :
Battle, death, defeat : the cross most disgraced.

3.78
The Scottish chief with six from Germany,
Captured by Eastern sailors of the sea,
Shall traverse Gibraltar & Spain to be
Gifts offered, scared stiff, to the new Persian king.

3.79

L'ordre fatal sempiternel par chaisne,
Viendra tourner par ordre consequent :
Du port Phocen sera rompue la chaisne,
La cité prinse, l'ennemy quant & quant.

3.80

Du regne Anglois l'indigne dechassé,
Le conseiller par ire mis à feu :
Ses adherans iront si bas tracer,
Que le bastard sera demy receu.

3.81

Le grand criar sans honte audacieux,
Sera esleu gouverneur de l'armée :
La hardiesse de son contentieux :
Le pont rompu, cité de peur pasmée.

3.82

Freins, Antibol, villes autour de Nice,
Seront vastées fer par mer & par terre :
Les sauterelles terre & mer vent propice :
Prins, morts, troussez, pillés sans loy de guerre.

3.83

Les longs cheveux de la Gaule Celtique
Accompaignez d'estranges nations
Mettront captif la gent Aquitanique,
Pour succomber à internitions.

3.84

La grand cité sera bien desolée,
Des habitans un seul n'y demourra :
Mur, sexe, temple, & vierge violée,
Par fer, feu, peste, canon peuple mourra.

3.85

La cité prinse par tromperie & fraude,
Par le moyen d'un beau jeune attrappé :
Assaut donné Roubine près de L'AUDE,
Luy & tous morts pour avoir bien trompé.

3.79

The chain of never-ending destiny
Shall turn by order of catenation :
The Phocaeans' port shall be broken,
The enemy taking the city by and by.

3.80

The weak king driven from the English throne,
General outrage, councilor burned at stake :
His clique shall seek a successor so low
The bastard shall be only half embraced.

3.81

The big loudmouth, so shamelessly bold,
Shall be elected governor of troops :
His rival's daring shall come to the fore :
The bridge down, city quaking in its boots.

3.82

Fréjus, Antibes & the towns around Nice,
Shall be destroyed from land & sea by sword :
Locusts land & sea favorable breeze :
Seized, bound, raped, killed without the rules of war.

3.83

The long-haired warriors of Celtic Gaul
Accompanied by foreign nations
Shall place the folk of Aquitaine in chains
And subject it to extermination.

3.84

The great city shall be quite desolate,
No single inhabitant shall remain :
Its walls & women, churches & nuns raped,
All dying by sword, fire, cannon, plague.

3.85

The city taken by deceit & ruse,
A handsome young man shall have been the dupe :
The attack launched at Robine near the AUDE,
He & everyone killed by the subterfuge.

3.86

Le chef d'Ausonne aux Espaignes ira,
Par mer fera arrest dedans Marseille :
Avant sa mort un long temps languira,
Après sa mort on verra grand merveille.

3.87

Classe Gauloise n'approches de Corseigne,
Moins de Sardaigne tu t'en repentiras :
Trestous mourrez, frustrez de l'aide : groeigne,
Sang nagera : captifve me croiras.

3.88

De Barselonne par mer si grand armée,
Toute Marseille de frayeur tremblera :
Isles saisies de mer ayde fermée,
Ton traditeur en terre nagera.

3.89

En ce temps là sera frustrée Cypres,
De son secours de ceux de mer Egée :
Vieux trucidez, mais par masles & galyphres
Seduict leur Roy, Royne plus outragée.

3.90

Le grand Satyre & Tigre d'Hyrcanie,
Don presenté à ceux de l'Ocean :
Un chef de classe istra de Carmanie,
Qui prendra terre au Tyrren Phocean.

3.91

L'arbre qu'estoit par long temps mort seché,
Dans une nuict viendra à reverdir :
Cron. Roy malade, Prince pied destaché,
Craint d'ennemis fera voile bondir.

3.92

Le monde proche du dernier periode,
Saturne encore tard sera de retour :
Translat empire devers nation Brodde,
L'œil arraché à Narbon par Autour.

3.86
Ausonia's leader shall leave by sea
For Spain with a layover in Marseille :
Before his death a long time shall he ail,
After his death great portent shall be seen.

3.87
Go not near Corsica, O Gallic fleet,
Sardinia even less, this you'll regret :
You shall all die, no help in sight : snouts wet
With blood : once captive, you'll believe me yet.

3.88
The Barcelona armada so great
That all Marseille shall be trembling with fear :
Its islands seized, no hope of help from sea,
He who betrayed you sailing off upstream.

3.89
At that time Cyprus isle shall be deprived
Of the help of those from the Aegean Sea :
The old shall be killed, males' debauchery
Seducing their king, outraging his bride.

3.90
The great Satyr & Hyrcanian Tyger
Shall be offered to those of the Ocean :
The fleet admiral shall leave Carmania
To land in the Tyrrhenian port Phocaean.

3.91
The tree that was dry as death for years
Shall in a single night again grow green :
King chronically ill, prince now free to act,
Feared by foes, his sails snapping in the breeze.

3.92
The world's final age drawing ever close,
Slow Saturn again making a return :
Empire transferred toward the nation of Brodde,
Vulture plucking out the eye at Narbonne.

3.93

Dans Avignon tout le chef de l'empire,
Fera aprest pour Paris desolé :
Tricast tiendra l'Annibalique ire,
Lyon par change sera mal consolé.

3.94

De cinq cens ans plus compte l'on tiendra,
Celuy qu'estoit l'aornement de son temps :
Puis à un coup grande clarté donra,
Que par ce siecle les rendra trescontens.

3.95

La loy Moricque on verra defaillir,
Après une autre beaucoup plus seductive :
Boristhenes premier viendra faillir,
Par dons & langue une plus attractive.

3.96

Chef de Fossan aura gorge coupée,
Par le ducteur du limier & levrier :
Le faict patré par ceux du mont Tarpée,
Saturne en Leo 13. de Fevrier.

3.97

Nouvelle loy terre neufve occuper,
Vers la Syrie Judée, & Palestine :
Le grand empire barbare corruer,
Avant que Phebe son cycle determine.

3.98

Deux royalz freres si fort guerroyeront,
Qu'entre eux sera la guerre si mortelle,
Qu'un chacun places fortes occuperont,
De regne & vie sera leur grand querelle.

3.99

Aux champs herbeux d'Alein & du Varneigue,
Du mont Lebron proche de la Durance,
Camps de deux parts conflict sera si aigue,
Mesopotame defaillira en la France.

3.93

In Avignon the leaders of empire
Shall prepare the ravaging of Paris :
Tricastin shall parry this Hannibal ire,
Lyon poorly consoled by the exchange.

3.94

For five hundred years nobody shall care
About him, the ornament of his age :
Then suddenly he'll cast a brilliant glare,
Most pleasing to the people of that day.

3.95

One shall witness the Moorish creed recede,
Followed by another more seductive :
The Borysthenes shall be the first to cede,
The new one's gifts & tongue more attractive.

3.96

The lord of Fossano's throat shall be cut
By the master of the hunt, the deed be
Done by the men from the Tarpeian Rock :
Saturn in Leo, February thirteen.

3.97

The new creed shall occupy a new land
Toward Syria, Judea & Palestine :
The great barbarian empire shall collapse
Before Phoebe has completed its cycle.

3.98

The two royal brothers shall so wage war
And so fight each other to bitter death
That each shall occupy the other's forts,
Competing for their very life & realm.

3.99

In the green fields of Alleins & Vernègues,
By the Lubéron mounts near the Durance,
The conflict between the two camps so harsh
Mesopotamia shall end here in France.

3.100

Entre Gaulois le dernier honnoré,
D'homme ennemy sera victorieux :
Force & terroir en moment exploré,
D'un coup de traict quand mourra l'envieux.

———————

CENTURIE IV

4.1

Cela du reste de sang non espandu,
Venise quiert secours estre donné :
Après avoir bien long temps attendu,
Cité livrée, au premier corn sonné.

4.2

Par mort la France prendra voyage à faire,
Classe par mer, marcher monts Pyrenées,
Espaigne en trouble, marcher gent militaire :
Des plus grand Dames, en France emmenées.

4.3

D'Arras & Bourges, de Brodes grans enseignes,
Vn plus grand nombre de Gascons batre à pied :
Ceux long du Rosne saigneront les Espaignes
Proche du mont où Sagonte s'assied.

4.4

L'impotent prince faché, plaincts & querelles,
De rapts & pilles, par coqz & par Lybiques :
Grand est par terre, par mer infinies voilles,
Seure Italie sera chassant Celtiques.

4.5

Croix, paix, soubz un accomply divin verbe,
L'Espaigne & Gaule seront unis ensemble :
Grand clade proche, & combat très acerbe,
Cœur si hardy ne sera qui ne tremble.

3.100
Among the Gauls the last among the best
Shall finally have his sworn enemy's head :
His forces & the terrain once assessed,
With a single arrow he'll shoot him dead.

CENTURY IV

4.1
There still being unshed blood that remains,
Venice asks that aid be sent at long last :
Having waited with such quiet patience,
The city yields at the first trumpet blast.

4.2
A death shall drive France into foreign parts,
Its fleet by sea, on foot through Pyrenees :
Spain in disarray, soldiers on the march,
Their finest ladies taken back to France.

4.3
Large regiments from Arras, Bourges & Brodes,
Further mass of Gascons fighting on foot :
Those from Rhône's banks bloody the Spanish troops
Below the mountain where Sagunto broods.

4.4
Enraged, the powerless prince rants & raves
About Libyans & Cocks that sack & loot :
The lord laid low, countless sails upon the waves,
Steadfast Italy driving Celts from its boot.

4.5
Cross in peace under perfect word divine,
Spain & Gaul then together shall unite :
Disaster nigh & conflict most unkind,
No heart so bold as not to quake with fright.

4.6

D'habits nouveaux après faicte la treuve,
Malice tramme & machination :
Premier mourra qui en fera la preuve :
Couleur Venise insidiation.

4.7

Le mineur filz du grand & hay prince,
De lepre aura à vingt ans grande tache :
De dueil sa mere mourra bien triste & mince :
Et il mourra là où tombe chef lache.

4.8

La grand cité d'assaut prompt repentin
Surprins de nuict, gardes interrompus :
Les excubies & veille sainct Quintin,
Trucidés gardes & les pourtails rompus.

4.9

Le chef du camp au milieu de la presse
D'un coup de fleche sera blessé aux cuisses,
Lors que Geneve en larmes et detresse,
Sera trahie par Lozan & Souysses.

4.10

Le jeune prince accuser faulsement,
Mettra en trouble le camp & en querelles :
Meurtry le chef pour le soustenement,
Sceptre apaiser : puis guerir escrouelles.

4.11

Celuy qu'aura gouvert de la grand cappe,
Sera induict à quelque cas patrer :
Les douze rouges viendront souiller la nappe.
Soubz meurtre, meurtre se viendra perpetrer.

4.12

Le camp plus grand de route mis en fuite,
Guaires plus oultre ne sera pourchassé :
Ost recampé, & legion reduicte,
Puis hors des Gaules du tout sera chassé.

4.6

After having discovered the disguise,
Malice, conspiracy, machination :
The first to uncover the clues shall die :
Colors of Venice, dissimulation.

4.7

The youngest son of the prince most hated
Shall at twenty bear a large leper stain :
His mother shall die of grief, sad & wasted :
He shall lie near his coward leader's grave.

4.8

The great city shall be surprised by night
By sudden attack, guards caught in their rounds :
At the vigil of Saint-Quentin & midnight rites,
The guards all be slain & the gates all down.

4.9

The warlord in the midst of the melee
Wounded in the thigh by an arrow's flight :
Geneva in tears & full disarray
By Lausanne & the Swiss shall be betrayed.

4.10

The young prince spouting false accusations,
Throws the camp into chaos & dissension :
Struck in head by a stanchion : then grows calm
And on scrofula lays a healing balm.

4.11

He who shall govern over the great cope
Shall be induced to perpetrate a crime :
The twelve red ones shall stain the altar cloth,
Murder on murder, to the end of time.

4.12

The camp put to flight in the greatest rout
Shall not be further pursued in retreat :
Though troops regroup & legion turn about,
Its complete rout from Gaul shall be a feat.

4.13

De plus grand perte nouvelles raportées,
Le raport fait le camp s'estonnera,
Bandes unies encontre revoltées,
Double phalange grand abandonnera.

4.14

La mort subite du premier personnage
Aura changé & mis un autre au regne :
Tost, tard venu à si haut & bas aage,
Que terre & mer faudra que l'on le craigne.

4.15

D'où pensera faire venir famine,
De là viendra le ressasiement :
L'œil de la mer par avare canine
Pour de l'un l'autre donra huyle, froment.

4.16

La cité franche de liberté fait serve,
Des profligés & resveurs faict asyle :
Le roy changé à eulx non si proterve,
De cent seront devenus plus de mille.

4.17

Changer à Beaune, Nuy, Chalons & Dijon,
Le duc voulant amander la Barrée,
Marchant près fleuve, poisson, bec de plongeon,
Verra la queue : porte sera serrée.

4.18

Des plus lettrés dessus les faits celestes
Seront par princes ignorants reprouvés :
Punis d'Edit, chassés, comme scelestes,
Et mis à mort là où seront trouvés.

4.19

Devant Rouan d'Insubres mis le siege,
Par terre & mer enfermés les passages :
D'Haynault, & Flandres, de Gans & ceux de Liege,
Par dons lænées raviront les rivages.

4.13
More news arriving of greater defeat,
The camp shall greet reports with disbelief :
The troops all agreed to rise in revolt,
The battalion shall abandon its chief.

4.14
The sudden death of the leader shall change
It all & place another one in power :
One come so soon, late, at so young, old age,
That land & sea one shall be bound to cower.

4.15
From where one thought famine would take its lead,
Nourishment shall now instead be received :
The eye of the sea, with dog-toothed greed,
Shall trade oil & wheat for whatever need.

4.16
The frank city, once so free, now enslaved,
Asylum to dreamers & downtrodden :
King softening in their regard & now changed,
From a hundred they shall become thousands.

4.17
Changing route at Beaune, Chalon, Dijon, Nuits,
The duke, out to thrash the Barrois estate,
Walks by the river, sees a fish tail peek
From a diving bird's beak : strait is the gate.

4.18
Among those most versed in lore celestial,
Some by inept princes shall be reproved :
Banned by edicts, hounded like criminals,
Or put to death wherever they dare move.

4.19
Insubria laying siege before Rouen,
All passages by land & sea now blocked :
The men of Hainaut, Flanders, Gand & Liège
Shall lay waste the whole coastline, half-crocked.

4.20

Paix, uberté, long temps lieu louera :
Par tout son regne desert la fleur de lys :
Corps morts d'eau, terre là l'on aportera,
Sperants vain heur d'estre là ensevelis.

4.21

Le changement sera fort difficile,
Cité, province au change gain fera :
Cœur haut, prudent mis chassé l'inhabile,
Mer, terre, peuple son estat changera.

4.22

La grand copie qui sera deschassée
Dans un moment fera besoing au Roy :
La foy promise de loing sera faulcée,
Nud se verra en piteux desarroy.

4.23

La legion dans la marine classe,
Calcide, Magnes soulphre & poix bruslera :
Le long repos de l'asseurée place,
Port Selyn, Hercle feu les consumera.

4.24

Ouy soubs terre saincte dame voix fainte,
Humaine flamme pour divine voir luire :
Fera des seulz de leur sang terre tainte,
Et les saincts temples par les impurs destruire.

4.25

Corps sublimés sans fin à l'œil visibles
Obnubiler viendront par ces raisons
Corps, front comprins, sens, chief & invisibles.
Diminuant les sacrées oraisons.

4.26

Lou grand eyssame se levera d'abelhos,
Que non sauran don te siegen venguddos :
Denuech l'enbousque, lou gach dessous las treilhos :
Ciurad trahido per cinq lengos non nudos.

4.20
There peace & abundance shall find its land,
With the lily growing wild everywhere :
The dead shall be brought in by sea and land,
In the vain hope of being buried there.

4.21
The transformation shall be slow & hard,
But city & province shall make some gains :
Throw the lout out & keep proud, prudent hearts,
Land & sea, people shall change their estates.

4.22
The great host which shall be driven away
Shall soon prove very crucial to the king :
The help promised from afar not coming,
He shall stand there naked, in disarray.

4.23
Chalcis & Magnesia shall shower
The sailors with burning sulfur & tar :
Defended fortresses, exempt from war,
Port Selin, Port'Ercole, consumed by fire.

4.24
Heard below sacred ground, a soul's voice faint,
The divine light captured by this human flame :
Says the ground with blood of monks shall be stained
And the holy churches wrecked by the profane.

4.25
Sublimates without end, clearly visible,
Shall thereby obnubilate the body,
Including brow, head, sense & invisibles,
Thus abbreviating all sacred prayers.

4.26
The swarming bees shall so rise to the sky
That no one shall know from whence they have come :
Ambush at night, watchmen beneath the vines :
City betrayed by five well-whetted tongues.

4.27

Salon, Mansol, Tarascon, de SEX. l'arc,
Où est debout encor la piramide,
Viendront livrer le prince Dannemarc :
Rachat honny au temple d'Artemide.

4.28

Lors que Venus du Sol sera couvert,
Soubs l'esplendeur sera forme occulte :
Mercure au feu les aura descouvert :
Par bruit bellique sera mis à l'insulte.

4.29

Le Sol caché eclipsé par Mercure,
Ne sera mis que pour le ciel second :
De Vulcan Hermes sera faicte pasture,
Sol sera veu pur, rutilant & blond.

4.30

Plus xi. fois ☽. ☉ ne voudra,
Tous augmenté & baissez de degré
Et si bas mis que peu or on coudra :
Qu'après faim, peste, descouvert le secret.

4.31

La Lune au plain de nuict sur le haut mont,
Le nouveau sophe d'un seul cerveau l'a veu :
Par ses disciples estre immortel semond :
Yeux au midy, en seins mains, corps au feu.

4.32

Es lieux & temps chair au poiss. donra lieu :
La loy commune sera faicte au contraire :
Vieux tiendra fort puis osté du milieu :
Le πάντα χοῖνα φιλῶν mis fort arriere.

4.33

Jupiter joinct plus Venus qu'à la Lune,
Apparoissant de plenitude blanche :
Venus cachée souz la blancheur Neptune
De Mars frappée par la gravée branche.

4.27
At Salon, Mausole, Tarascon, arch of SEX.,
There where the pyramid still does rise,
They shall deliver up the Danish prince :
At Artemis temple, what a shameful price.

4.28
When Venus is blotted out by the Sun,
Her form shall be hid beneath its splendor :
Mercury by fire shall have laid them bare :
He shall be battered by the din of war.

4.29
The Sun hidden, by Mercury eclipsed,
Merely taken for a second heaven :
Hermes becoming fodder for Vulcan :
Sun to the eye : pure, rutilant & blond.

4.30
More than xi. times one would not wish
The ☽. ☉ to soar or fall in value
Or priced so low that few would seek for gold :
Plague, famine, then the secret shall be told.

4.31
The moon at midnight on the mountain high,
The new sage gazing, not right in the brain :
He is called by his disciples to eternal life :
Eyes raised, hands on chest, his body in flames.

4.32
In due time & place flesh shall give way to fish :
Everything in fact shall be held in common :
The old one shall hold strong, then made to vanish :
The πάντα χοῖνα φιλῶν soon forgotten.

4.33
Jove more conjoined with Venus than the Moon
Shall display himself in a blaze of white :
Venus hidden in the candor of Neptune
Shall be pestled by Mars's leaden might.

4.34
Le grand mené captif d'estrange terre,
D'or enchainé au Roy CHYREN offert,
Qui dans Ausone, Milan perdra la guerre,
Et tout son ost mis à feu & à fer.

4.35
Le feu estaint, les vierges trahiront
La plus grand part de la bande nouvelle :
Fouldre à fer, lance : les seulz Roy garderont
Etrusque & Corse, de nuict gorge allumelle.

4.36
Les jeux nouveaux en Gaule redressés,
Après victoire de l'Insubre champaigne :
Monts d'Esperie, les grands liés, troussés :
De peur trembler la Romaigne & l'Espaigne.

4.37
Gaulois par saults, monts viendra penetrer,
Occupera le grand lieu de l'Insubre :
Au plus profond son ost fera entrer,
Gennes, Monech pousseront classe rubre.

4.38
Pendant que Duc, Roy, Royne occupera,
Chef Bizantin captif en Samothrace :
Avant l'assault l'un l'autre mangera,
Rebours ferré suyvra du sang la trasse.

4.39
Les Rodiens demanderont secours,
Par le neglet de ses hoyrs delaissée :
L'empire Arabe revalera son cours,
Par Hesperies la cause redressée.

4.40
Les forteresses des assiegés serrés,
Par poudre à feu profondées en abysme,
Les prodixeurs seront touts vifs serrés :
Onc aux sacristes n'advint si piteux scisme.

4.34
The lord of a foreign land, led captive
On a golden chain, gift to King CHYREN,
Who shall lose the Italian war at Milan,
His entire host felled by sword & flame.

4.35
With tapers quenched, the nuns shall scapegoat
The greater part of this new sect : lightning
On lances : king guarded by monks : nighttimes
Etruscan, Corsican, blade to the throat.

4.36
In Gaul the new games shall be refounded
After victory over Milan & Campania :
Near the Hesperian mounts, lords captive & bound :
All Spain shall tremble with fear, plus Romagna.

4.37
Having passed through the defiles of mountains,
Gauls shall occupy the regions of Milan :
Driving their armies deep into its lands,
The red ships fended off by Monech, Gennes.

4.38
While the Duke is distracting King & Queen,
Byzantine chief is seized in Samothrace :
Before battle, each shall the other eat,
The ruthless hound tracking the bloody trace.

4.39
The men of Rhodes shall cry out for more aid,
Their isle disowned by its neglectful lords :
The Arab empire shall lessen its pace,
The common cause given new hope by Spain.

4.40
The barred-up fortresses of the besieged,
Blown by gunpowder into the abysm,
The traitors shall be sawed in half alive :
No priesthood ever endured such a schism.

4.41

Gynique sexe captive par hostage,
Viendra de nuit custodes decevoir :
Le chef du camp deceu par son langage
Lairra à la gente, fera piteux à voyr.

4.42

Geneve & Langres par ceux de Chartres et Dole,
Et par Grenoble captif au Montlimard,
Seyssel, Losanne par fraudulente dole
Les trahiront par or soyxante marc.

4.43

Seront oys au ciel les armes battre :
Celuy an mesme les divins ennemis
Voudront loix sainctes injustement debatre :
Par foudre & guerre bien croyans à mort mis.

4.44

Lous gros de Mende, de Roudés & Millau,
Cahours, Limoges, Castres malo sepmano :
De nuech l'intrado, de Bourdeaux un cailhau,
Par Perigort au toc de la campano.

4.45

Par conflit roy, regne abandonnera,
Le plus grand chef faillira au besoing :
Mors profligés peu en rechapera :
Tous destranchés, un en sera tesmoing.

4.46

Bien defendu le faict par excellence,
Garde toy Tours de ta proche ruine :
Londres & Nantes par Reims fera defense
Ne passer outre au temps de la bruine.

4.47

Le noir farouche quand aura essayé
Sa main sanguine par feu, fer, arcs tendus,
Trestout le peuple sera tant effraié,
Voyr les plus grans par col & pieds pendus.

4.41

One of the fairer sex, captured hostage,
Shall manage to elude her guards at night :
Camp commander, deceived by her language,
Succumbs to the wench, such a sorry sight.

4.42

Geneva, Langres, led captive to Montélimar
By those of Chartres & Grenoble & Dole,
Seyssel & Lausanne, shall defraud them all
With a ruse costing sixty marks in gold.

4.43

The clash of arms shall be heard in the skies :
That very year, the foes of the good Lord
Shall take up unjust arms against holy rites :
True believers struck down by bolts of war.

4.44

For notables of Mende, Rodez, Millau,
Cahors, Limoges, Castres, the week bodes ill :
A night raid by an apostate from Bordeaux,
Throughout Périgord as the bells do toll.

4.45

The conflict shall cause the king to quit the state,
His greatest chief missing in hour of need :
Dead & done for, few manage to escape :
Hacked to pieces : one witness to the deed.

4.46

Well defended as you think you now sit,
Be careful, Tours, of going to the dogs !
To London & Nantes Reims shall interdict
All further passage under cloak of fog !

4.47

When the ferocious black shall have tried
His bloody hand at fire, sword, bended bow,
People everywhere shall be terrified
To see their lords hanged by the neck & toe.

4.48
Planure Ausonne fertile, spacieuse,
Produira taons si trestant sauterelles :
Clarté solaire deviendra nubileuse,
Ronger le tout, grand peste venir d'elles.

4.49
Devant le peuple sang sera respandu,
Que du haut ciel ne viendra esloigner,
Mais d'un long temps ne sera entendu :
L'esprit d'un seul le viendra tesmoigner.

4.50
Libra verra regner les Hesperies,
De ciel & terre tenir la monarchie :
D'Asie forces nul ne verra peries,
Que sept ne tiennent par rang la hierarchie.

4.51
Le duc cupide son ennemi ensuyvre,
Dans entrera empeschant sa phalange :
Hastez à pied si près viendront poursuyvre,
Que la journée conflite près de Gange.

4.52
La cité obsesse aux murs hommes & femmes,
Ennemis hors, le chef prest à soy rendre :
Vent sera fort encontre les gendarmes,
Chassez seront par chaux, poussiere, & cendre.

4.53
Les fugitifs & bannis revoquez,
Peres & fils grands garnissant les hauts puits :
Le cruel pere & les siens suffoquez,
Son fils plus pire submergé dans le puits.

4.54
Du nom qui onques ne fut au Roy Gaulois,
Jamais ne fut un fouldre si craintif :
Tremblant l'Itale, l'Espaigne & les Anglois,
De femmes estranges grandement attentif.

4.48
The Ausonian plain, so fertile & huge,
Shall produce gadflies & hosts of locusts :
The light of the sun shall be overcast :
All things devoured, mighty plagues ensue.

4.49
Before the people he lies there bleeding,
Who far from heaven never did subsist,
But his death throes shall long go unheeded :
One man alone minded to bear witness.

4.50
Libra shall see the Hesperias reign,
And hold kingship over heaven & earth :
No one shall see how Asia's forces wane
Until seven in turn have ruled the Church.

4.51
The duke, keen to pursue his enemy,
Shall fall upon him, blocking his phalange :
Those fleeing on foot shall be so hounded
That the battle shall then be waged near Ganges.

4.52
The city besieged, men, women on walls,
Foe outside, chief ready to surrender :
The wind shall wheel against the attackers,
Driven back by gusts of lime, dust, cinders.

4.53
The fugitives & exiles welcomed back,
Father & son fortifying the high hills :
The cruel father & his men all strangled,
His son, faring far worse, drowned in the well.

4.54
The first of the French kings to bear this name,
No thunderbolt ever so fierce as he :
He struck fear into Italy, England, Spain,
And by foreign ladies was most intrigued.

4.55
Quand la corneille sur tour de brique joincte
Durant sept heures ne fera que crier :
Mort presagée, de sang statue taincte,
Tyran meurtri, aux Dieux peuple prier.

4.56
Après victoire de rabieuse langue,
L'esprit tempré en tranquil & repos :
Victeur sanguin par conflict faict harangue,
Roustir la langue & la chair & les os.

4.57
Ignare envie au grand Roy supportée,
Tiendra propos deffendre les escriptz :
Sa femme non femme par un autre tentée :
Plus double deux ne fort ne criz.

4.58
Soleil ardent dans le gosier coller,
De sang humain arrouser terre Etrusque :
Chef seille d'eaue mener, son fils filer,
Captive dame conduicte en terre Turque.

4.59
Deux assiegez en ardente ferveur,
De soif estaincts pour deux plaines tasses :
Le fort limé, & un vieillart resveur
Aux Genevois de Nira monstra trasses.

4.60
Les sept enfans en hostaige laissés,
Le tiers viendra son enfant trucider :
Deux par son filz seront d'estoc percés,
Gennes, Florence, lors viendra encunder.

4.61
Le vieux mocqué & privé de sa place,
Par l'estrangier qui le subornera :
Mains de son filz mangées devant sa face,
Le frere à Chartres, Orl., Rouan trahyra.

4.55
When the crow shall caw for seven hours
Without cease upon its high brick tower :
A death foretold, statue running with blood,
Tyrant stabbed, people praying to the gods.

4.56
After this rabid tongue has won the war,
The mind is tempted by peace & repose :
His victory harangues a bloody bore,
Roasting his tongue along with flesh & bones.

4.57
The King endures the envy of the snide,
But shall ban all the writings of their scribes :
The bride he took was another man's wife :
More than four of whom shall be gagged and tied.

4.58
Their throats glued shut by the fiery sun,
Human blood shall lave the Etruscan plain :
Pail of water enough to snare the son,
Lady captive embarked to Turkish main.

4.59
Burning with fever two besieged towns rage
For two cups of water to slake their thirst :
The fortress sapped, a dreamer in old age
Tells Geneva how Nira was his first.

4.60
Of seven children who remain hostage,
The third shall come to slaughter his own child :
His son shall pierce two others with his blade,
And then drive Florence & Genoa wild.

4.61
The old one mocked, knocked from his rightful place
By the usurper who comes from afar :
His son's hands eaten before his very face,
Orl., Rouen betrayed by brother at Chartres.

4.62

Un coronnel machine ambition,
Se saisira de la plus grande armée :
Contre son prince fainte invention,
Et descouvert sera soubz la ramée.

4.63

L'armée Celtique contre les montaignars
Qui seront sceuz & prins à la lipée :
Paysants fresz pousseront tost faugnars,
Precipitez tous au fil de l'espée.

4.64

Le deffaillant en habit de bourgeois,
Viendra le Roy tempter de son offence :
Quinze souldartz la pluspart Ustageois,
Vie derniere & chef de sa chevance.

4.65

Au deserteur de la grand forteresse,
Après qu'aura son lieu abandonné :
Son adversaire fera si grand prouesse,
L'Empereur tost mort sera condamné.

4.66

Soubz couleur faincte de sept testes rasées
Seront semés divers explorateurs :
Puys & fontaines de poysons arrousées,
Au fort de Gennes humains devorateurs.

4.67

L'an que Saturne & Mars esgaulx combust,
L'air fort seiché longue trajection :
Par feux secretz, d'ardeur grand lieu adust,
Peu pluye, vent chault, guerres, incursions.

4.68

En l'an bien proche esloigné de Venus,
Les deux plus grans de l'Asie & d'Afrique
Du Ryn & Hister qu'on dira sont venus,
Crys, pleurs à Malte & costé ligustique.

4.62

An ambitious colonel contrives & schemes
To seize full commandment of all the troops :
Against the prince a stratagem he weaves,
And ends up discovered beneath the leaves.

4.63

French troops shall fall upon the mountain folk,
Hunt them all down & seize them while they sup :
Fresh recruits shall smash their presses of oak,
Sword blade shall fell them all & cut them up.

4.64

The weakling gussied up in townsman's clothes
Shall tempt the King with a shady scheme :
Fifteen fighting men, outlaws for the most,
One last life, then master of his demesne.

4.65

Against the deserter of the great fort,
After he has abandoned its defense :
His enemy shall fight him with such sport,
The Emperor shall doom him to early death.

4.66

Seven spies disguised as seven friars
Shall be dispersed through the town in advance :
Poison sprinkled in the wells & fountains,
At Genoa's fort, man devouring man.

4.67

Saturn & Mars equidistant to Sun,
The scorched air, the comet's great trajection :
Entire regions gone up in secret flames,
The rain scarce, the wind hot, wars, incursions.

4.68

Not far away from Venus some year soon,
Asia's & Africa's two great hosts
Shall meet those from the Rhine & the Danube :
Shrieks, tears on Malta, Ligurian coast.

4.69
La cité grande les exilés tiendront,
Les citadins morts, meurtris & chassés :
Ceulx d'Aquilée à Parme promettront,
Monstrer l'entrée par les lieux non trassés.

4.70
Bien contiguë des grans monts Pyrenées,
Un contre l'aigle grand copie addresser :
Ouvertes veines, forces exterminées,
Que jusque à Pau le chef viendra chasser.

4.71
En lieu d'espouse les filles trucidées,
Meurtre à grand faulte ne sera superstite :
Dedans le puys vestales inondées,
L'espouse estaincte par hauste d'Aconite.

4.72
Les Artomiques par Agen & Lectore,
A sainct Felix feront leur parlement :
Ceulx de Basas viendront à la mal'heure,
Saisir Condon & Marsan promptement.

4.73
Le nepveu grand par forces prouvera,
Le pache fait du cœur pusillanime :
Ferrare & Ast le Duc esprouvera,
Par lors qu'au soir sera le pantomime.

4.74
Du lac Lyman & ceux de Brannovices,
Tous assemblez contre ceux d'Aquitaine :
Germains beaucoup encore plus Souisses,
Seront defaictz avecques ceux du Maine.

4.75
Prest à combatre fera defection,
Chef adversaire obtiendra la victoire :
L'arrieregarde fera defension,
Les defaillans morts au blanc territoire.

4.69

The great town taken by those it banished,
Its citizens killed, maimed & put to flight :
Aquileia then shall promise Parma
To show it a way back in, on the sly.

4.70

At the very rim of the Pyrenees,
One shall throw his troops against the Eagle :
Bloodshed, the whole army in smithereens,
As far as Pau he shall pursue the chief.

4.71

The daughters slaughtered in lieu of the wife
Who shall not survive this murder most vile :
The virgin girls shall be drowned in the well,
The wife shall be poisoned by aconite.

4.72

Arecomicians via Agen & Lectoure
At Saint-Félix their parliament shall convoke :
Those from Bazas, arriving out of nowhere,
Take Condom & Marsan at a single stroke.

4.73

The noble nephew shall put to the test
The pact that was just a cowardly game :
The Duke shall probe Ferrara & Asti,
One evening while the mime is onstage.

4.74

Those from Lake Leman & Brunnovices
Shall unite against those of Aquitaine :
Many Germans & a great more Swiss
Shall be defeated with those from Maine.

4.75

About to join the fray, he shall vanish :
The enemy general shall win the fight :
The rear guard shall rally to the defense,
The weak dying on the field of the white.

4.76
Les Nictobriges par ceux de Perigort,
Seront vexez tenant jusques au Rosne :
L'associé de Gascons & Bigort,
Trahir le temple, le prestre estant au prosne.

4.77
SELIN monarque l'Italie pacifique,
Regnes unis Roy chrestien du monde :
Mourant voudra coucher en terre blesique
Après pyrates avoir chassé de l'onde.

4.78
La grande armée de la pugne civile,
Pour de nuict Parme à l'estrange trouvée :
Septanteneuf meurtris dedans la ville,
Les estrangiers passez tous à l'espée.

4.79
Sang Royal fuis, Monhurt, Mas, Eguillon,
Remplis seront de Bourdelois les landes :
Navarre, Bygorre poinctes & eguillons,
Profondz de faim vorer de liege glandes.

4.80
Près du grand fleuve, grand fosse, terre egeste,
En quinze pars sera l'eau divisée :
La cité prinse, feu, sang, cris, conflict mettre,
Et la plus part concerne au collisée.

4.81
Pont on fera promptement de nacelles,
Passer l'armée du grand prince Belgique :
Dans profondrés & non loing de Brucelles,
Outre passés, detrenchés sept à picque.

4.82
Amas s'approche venant d'Esclavonie,
L'Olestant vieux cité ruynera :
Fort desolée verra sa Romanie,
Puis la grand flamme estaindre ne sçaura.

4.76
The Nictobriges by those from Périgord
Shall be hounded all the way to the Rhône :
An ally of the Gascons & Bigorre
Betrays the church before the sermon's done.

4.77
SELIN monarch, Italy now at peace,
A single world ruled by a Christian king :
At Blois he would repose at his decease,
Having swept all the pirates from the seas.

4.78
The mighty army of this civil war,
Found at night in Parma on foreign soil :
Seventy-nine are slaughtered in the town,
Every single stranger put to the sword.

4.79
Flee Monhurt, Mas, Eguillon, O royal blood,
The Landes shall be aswarm with Bordelais :
Points & spurs throughout Navarre & Bigorre:
So starved they'll eat the acorns of the cork.

4.80
Near great river, great conduit feeds the land,
Water divided into fifteen spouts :
The city seized, fire, blood, shrieks, war at hand :
Most of them in the arena, hiding out.

4.81
They shall promptly link boats into a bridge
To pass the troops of the great Belgian prince :
Not far from Brussels, they shall all fall in :
Seven get across, to be hacked to bits.

4.82
The horde approaches from Slavonia,
The ancient Vandal the city shall maim :
Laid to waste he shall see Romania,
Nor know how to extinguish the flames.

4.83

Combat nocturne le vaillant capitaine,
Vaincu fuyra, peu de gens profligé :
Son peuple esmeu, sedition non vaine,
Son propre filz le tiendra assiegé.

4.84

Un grand d'Auxerre mourra bien miserable,
Chassé de ceux qui soubz luy ont esté :
Serré de chaines, auprès d'un rude cable,
En l'an que Mars, Venus, & Sol mis en esté.

4.85

Le charbon blanc du noir sera chassé,
Prisonnier faict mené au tombereau :
More Chameau sus piedz entrelassez,
Lors le puisné sillera l'aubereau.

4.86

L'an que Saturne en eau sera conjoinct,
Avecques Sol, le Roy fort & puissant :
A Reims & Aix sera receu & oingt,
Après conquestes meurtrira innocens.

4.87

Un filz du Roy tant de langues aprins,
A son aisné au regne different :
Son pere beau au plus grand filz comprins
Fera perir principal adherant.

4.88

Le grand Antoine du nom de faict sordide
De Phthyriase à son dernier rongé :
Un qui de plomb voudra estre cupide,
Passant le port d'esleu sera plongé.

4.89

Trente de Londres secret conjureront,
Contre leur Roy sur le pont l'entreprinse :
Luy, satalites la mort degousteront,
Un Roy esleu blonde, natif de Frize.

4.83

Brave captain, routed in the night melee,
Shall flee, incurring minor casualties :
His people dismayed, a mutinous scheme :
His very own son holds him under siege.

4.84

An Auxerre lord shall meet his wretched end,
Driven away by those who served him once :
Bound up in thick rope, then enwrapped in chains,
At summer junction of Mars, Venus, Sun.

4.85

The black coal follows on the white coal's heels,
Captive carted off in backseat of a tumbrel :
The Moorish Camel, hobbled at its feet :
The younger son the falcon's eyes shall seel.

4.86

When Saturn is in water-sign conjoined
With the Sun, the King is strong & potent :
Received at Reims & Aix, then anointed,
His wars won, he shall kill the innocent.

4.87

A royal son, learnèd in many tongues,
So different from his elder in the realm :
His father-in-law, urged on by older son,
Shall go after his main supporter's head.

4.88

Great Antoine by name, & the lousy fact
Of phthiriasis eating him up with crabs :
One who shall just simply lust after lead,
The port passed, the elector drowns him dead.

4.89

Thirty of London shall secretly scheme
Against their King, plot transpiring at sea :
He & his acolytes on death shall feast :
Fair-haired King elected, native of Fries.

4.90
Les deux copies aux murs ne pourront joindre,
Dans cest instant trembler Milan, Ticin :
Faim, soif, doubtance si fort les viendra poindre,
Chair, pain, ne vivres n'auront un seul boucin.

4.91
Au duc Gaulois contrainct battre au duelle,
La nef Mellele Monech n'approchera :
Tort accusé, prison perpetuelle,
Son fils regner avant mort taschera.

4.92
Teste tranchée du vaillant capitaine,
Sera gettée devant son adversaire :
Son corps pendu de sa classe à l'antenne,
Confus fuira par rames à vent contraire.

4.93
Un serpent veu proche du lict royal,
Sera par dame, nuict chiens n'abayeront :
Lors naistre en France un prince tant royal,
Du ciel venu tous les princes verront.

4.94
Les deux grans freres seront chassez d'Espaigne,
L'aisné vaincu sous les monts Pyrenées :
Rougir mer, Rosne sang Leman d'Alemaigne,
Narbon., Blyterre, d'Agath. contaminées.

4.95
Le regne à deux laissé bien peu tiendront,
Trois ans sept moys passés feront la guerre :
Les deux vestales contre rebelleront,
Victor puis nay en Armonique terre.

4.96
La sœur aisnée de l'isle Britannique,
Quinze ans devant le frere aura naissance :
Par son promis moyennant verrifique,
Succedera au regne de balance.

4.90
The armies shall not join up at the walls,
Milan & Pavia quaking with fright :
Hunger, thirst, doubt shall so pierce them withal,
Of bread or rations not a single bite.

4.91
The Gallic duke compelled to fight a duel,
Mellila's ship shan't reach Monaco's shore :
Wrongly accused, condemned to life in jail,
Before he dies, his son shall strive to rule.

4.92
The valiant captain's dissevered head
Before his adversary shall be thrown :
His body strung up on the yard, his fleet
Aghast, against the wind, away shall row.

4.93
Near her royal bed the lady apprehends
A snake : not a dog shall bark that night :
Then in France a prince of such royal line
Is born princes greet him as a godsend.

4.94
Two brothers shall be driven out of Spain,
The elder defeated by the Pyrenees :
Sea red, Rhône, Leman bloodied by Germany,
Agde contaminating Narbonne, Béziers.

4.95
The two shall briefly occupy the throne
Left to them, three years seven months of war :
The two vestals shall rise up in revolt,
The later-born, victor on Breton shore.

4.96
The elder sister of the British Isle,
Born some fifteen years before her brother :
Through her betrothed, should this be verified,
She shall succeed to the reign of Libra.

4.97

L'an que Mercure, Mars, Venus, retrograde,
Du grand Monarque la ligne ne faillit :
Esleu du peuple Lusitan près d'Almade,
Qu'en paix & regne viendra fort envieillir.

4.98

Les Albanois passeront dedans Rome,
Moyennant Langres de miples affublés :
Marquis & Duc ne pardonner à homme,
Feu, sang, morbilles, point d'eau, faillir les bledz.

4.99

L'aisné vaillant de la fille du Roy,
Repoussera si profond les Celtiques :
Qu'il mettra foudres, combien en tel arroy,
Peu & loing puis profond és Hesperiques.

4.100

De feu celeste au Royal edifice,
Quand la lumiere de Mars defaillira :
Sept mois grand guerre, mort gent de malefice,
Rouen, Evreux au Roy ne faillira.

CENTURIE V

5.1

Avant venue de ruine Celtique,
Dedans le temple deux parlementeront :
Poignard au cœur, d'un monté au coursier & picque,
Sans faire bruit le grand enterreront.

5.2

Seps conjurés au banquet feront luire,
Contre les trois le fer, hors de navire :
L'un les deux classes au grand fera conduire,
Quant par le mail Denier au front luy tire.

4.97

Mercury, Mars, Venus retrograding,
That year the Monarch's line without failing :
Elected by Portuguese near Cádiz,
One who shall reign into old age in peace.

4.98

The troops of Alba into Rome shall fare,
Langres shall not be half-attacked for naught :
Marquis & Duke no living soul shall spare :
Fire, blood, smallpox & crop-destroying drought.

4.99

The King's daughter's most valiant elder son
Shall drive the Celts so deep into retreat,
He'll hurl his bolts down on everyone,
Near, far, then deep into the Hesperides.

4.100

Fire from on high falls upon the palace
When the light of Mars begins to grow pale :
Seven months of war, folk killed by malice,
But Rouen, Évreux the King shall not fail.

CENTURY V

5.1

Before the ruin of the Celts does start,
Two shall come to terms within the church :
Horseman stabs pike & dagger in the heart,
The great one buried, not a sound is heard.

5.2

Seven plotters at the banquet, their swords
Shall flash against three who have come ashore :
Two fleets to lead shall be given the lord,
Who for a pittance gets shot in the gourd.

5.3

Le successeur de la Duché viendra,
Beaucoup plus outre que la mer de Tosqane :
Gauloise branche la Florence tiendra,
Dans son giron d'accord nautique Rane.

5.4

Le gros mastin de cité deschassé,
Sera fasché de l'estrange alliance,
Après aux champs avoir le cerf chassé,
Le loup & l'Ours se donront defiance.

5.5

Souz ombre faincte d'oster de servitute,
Peuple & cité l'usurpera luy mesme :
Pire fera par fraux de jeune pute,
Livré au champ lisant le faux proesme.

5.6

Au roy l'Augur sur le chef la main mettre,
Viendra prier pour la paix Italique :
A la main gauche viendra changer le sceptre
De Roy viendra Empereur pacifique.

5.7

Du Triumvir seront trouvez les os,
Cherchant profond thresor ænigmatique :
Ceux d'alentour ne seront en repos,
De concaver marbre & plomb metallique.

5.8

Sera laissé le feu vif, mort cachée,
Dedans les globes horrible espouventable,
De nuict à classe cité en poudre laschée,
La cité à feu, l'ennemy favorable.

5.9

Jusques au fonds la grand arq demolue,
Par chef captif, l'amy anticipé :
Naistra de dame front face chevelue,
Lors par astuce Duc à mort attrape.

5.3

The Duchy's next successor shall advance
Well beyond the shores of the Tuscan sea :
The Gallic branch shall firmly land Florence
In its lap, to which Sea-Frog shall agree.

5.4

Chased away from the city, the great cur
Shall snarl & bark at the strange alliance :
Having hunted the stag across the fields,
Wolf & bear shall face off in defiance.

5.5

Pretending to reduce their servitude,
He shall usurp the city & its folk :
What's worse, lying like a young prostitute,
He'll read a false proem, imposing his yoke.

5.6

Laying his hand on the head of the King,
The Augur shall pray for Italic peace :
He'll transfer the scepter to his left hand,
Transformed from King to Emperor of Peace.

5.7

The bones of the Triumvir shall be found
While seeking cryptic treasures of the dead :
No peace for those who lie in nearby ground
When they go digging for marble & lead.

5.8

The lately living hidden, dead, away
In heaps, a most unimaginable woe :
City reduced to ash at night, they say,
Its burned remains serving its former foe.

5.9

The mighty jail to the ground shall be razed
By the friend awaited by captive chief :
A child born with hair all over its face :
A trick then traps the Duke into his death.

5.10

Un chef Celtique dans le conflict blessé,
Auprès de cave voyant siens mort abbatre :
De sang & playes & d'ennemis pressé,
Et secouru par incognus de quatre.

5.11

Mer par solaires seure ne passera,
Ceux de Venus tiendront toute l'Afrique :
Leur regne plus Saturne n'occupera,
Et changera la part Asiatique.

5.12

Auprès du lac Leman sera conduite,
Par garse estrange cité voulant trahir :
Avant son meurtre à Auspourg la grand suitte
Et ceux du Rhyn la viendront invahir.

5.13

Par grand fureur le Roy Romain Belgique
Vexer vouldra par phalange barbare :
Fureur grinsseant chassera gent Lybique
Despuis Pannons jusques Hercules bare.

5.14

Saturne & Mars en Leo Espagne captive,
Par chef Lybique au conflict attrapé,
Proche de Malthe, & Rhodes prinse vive,
Et Romain sceptre sera par coq frappé.

5.15

En navigant captif prins grand pontife,
Grans apretz faillir les clercz tumultuez :
Second esleu absent son bien debife,
Son favory bastard à mort tué.

5.16

A son hault pris plus la lerme sabée,
D'humaine chair par mort en cendre mettre :
A l'isle Pharos par croisars perturbée,
Alors qu'à Rodes paroistra dur espectre.

5.10

A Celtic chief who was hurt in the war,
Seeing his own troops struck dead near the cave,
Hard pressed by foes, drowning in blood & gore,
By four who are unknown to him is saved.

5.11

No longer shall Solars safely cross the sea,
Those of Venus all Africa shall hold :
Saturn shall cease to occupy their seat,
And all Asia Minor shall be transformed.

5.12

The treasonous city shall be induced
To Lake Leman by a foreign maid :
Before her murder, a flight to Augsburg
Which the Rhinelanders shall then invade.

5.13

The Roman Belgian king in a passion
Shall wish to harry the Barbary host :
He'll furiously hound the Libyans
From Pannonia to Gibraltar's coast.

5.14

Saturn & Mars in Leo, captive Spain,
Seized by the Libyans in time of war,
Taken alive near to Malta & Rhodes,
The cock striking out at the Roman sword.

5.15

The pope made captive while on the high seas,
The priests up in arms, great plans gone awry :
The next-elect, absent from his damaged see,
His bastard favorite shall be doomed to die.

5.16

Tears of Saba shall no more soar in price
To reduce human flesh to ash at death :
Crusaders shall make raids on Pharos isle,
While a tough old ghost appears on Rhodes.

5.17
De nuict passant le roy près d'une Andronne,
Celuy de Cipres & principal guette :
Le roy failli la main fuict long du Rosne,
Les conjurés l'iront à mort mettre.

5.18
De dueil mourra l'infelix profligé,
Celebrera son vitrix l'hecatombe :
Pristine loy franc edict redigé,
Le mur & Prince au septiesme jour tombe.

5.19
Le grand Royal d'or, d'ærain augmenté,
Rompu la pache, par jeune ouverte guerre :
Peuple affligé par un chef lamenté,
De sang barbare sera couverte terre.

5.20
Delà les Alpes grand armée passera,
Un peu devant naistra monstre vapin :
Prodigieux & subit tournera,
Le grand Tosquan à son lieu plus propin.

5.21
Par le trespas du monarque latin,
Ceux qu'il aura par regne secouruz :
Le feu luyra, divisé le butin,
La mort publique aux hardis incoruz.

5.22
Avant qu'à Rome grand aye rendu l'ame,
Effrayeur grande à l'armée estrangiere :
Par Esquadrons, l'embusche près de Parme,
Puis les deux rouges ensemble feront chere.

5.23
Les deux contens seront unis ensemble,
Quand la plupart à Mars seront conjoinct :
Le grand d'Affrique en effraieur & tremble :
Duumvirat par la classe desjoinct.

5.17
As the king winds down the alley at night,
The main ruler of Cyprus he'll espy :
The king mistaken, troops flee down the Rhône,
Conspirators then deciding he'll die.

5.18
The wretch laid so low he shall die of grief,
His victrix shall then celebrate his fall :
Fresh set of laws, drawing up of decrees :
The seventh day both Prince & wall shall fall.

5.19
The great golden sovereign, debased by bronze,
The truce broken, a mere youth declares war :
The chief taking the people as his pawns,
The earth covered with barbarian gore.

5.20
A mighty army through the Alps shall march
Just before the ravening monster's born :
Suddenly, miraculously the arch-
Tuscan shall withdraw to his nearby home.

5.21
Upon the passing of the Latin king,
Those for whom he provided in the realm :
The loot shall be divided, the fire singe,
Public death incurred by courageous men.

5.22
Before the lord of Rome gives up the ghost
Terror shall reign among the foreign host :
Near Parma his squadrons shall strike them dead,
The two red ones then meeting to break bread.

5.23
The two rivals shall then come to unite
When most of the stars with Mars are conjoined :
The African lord shall tremble with fright
When at sea the duumvirate's disjoined.

5.24
Le regne & loy souz Venus eslevé,
Saturne aura sus Jupiter empire :
La loy & regne par le Soleil levé,
Par Saturnins endurera le pire.

5.25
Le prince Arabe Mars, Sol, Venus, Lyon,
Regne d'Eglise par mer succombera :
Devers la Perse bien près d'un million,
Bisance, Egypte, ver. serp. invadera.

5.26
La gent esclave par un heurt martial,
Viendra en haut degré tant eslevée :
Changeront prince, naistre un provincial,
Passer la mer, copie aux monts levée.

5.27
Par feu & armes non loing de la marnegro,
Viendra de Perse occuper Trebizonde :
Trembler Pharos, Methelin, Sol alegro,
De sang Arabe d'Adrie couverte l'onde.

5.28
Le bras pendu & la jambe liée,
Visaige pasle au seing poignard caché :
Trois qui seront jurez de la meslée,
Au grand de Gennes sera le fer lasché.

5.29
La liberté ne sera recouvrée,
L'occupera noir fier, vilain inique :
Quand la matiere du pont sera ouvrée,
D'Hister, Venise faschée la republique.

5.30
Tout à l'entour de la grande cité,
Seront soldats logez par champs & villes :
Donner l'assaut Paris, Rome incité,
Sur le pont lors sera faicte grand pille.

5.24
When law & power 'neath Venus are raised,
Saturn over Jupiter shall hold sway :
When law & power by the Sun are raised,
The Saturnine shall greatly make them pay.

5.25
The Arab Prince, Mars, Sun, Venus, Lion :
By the sea shall all Christendom succumb :
Out there in Persia more than a million :
The snake shall invade Egypt, Byzantium.

5.26
The slavish race by the fortunes of war
Shall be raised up to an immense degree :
They shall change their king for one country-born
Who'll lead his mountain troops across the sea.

5.27
By fire & arms not far from Mar Negro,
The Persians shall occupy Trebizond :
Pharos, Mytilene quake, Sol allegro :
The Adriatic swims with Arab blood.

5.28
Hung by the arms & with his legs in chains,
Face pale, hiding a dagger by his side :
Three shall swear allegiance to the scheme,
Genoa's lord be run through by a blade.

5.29
Liberty shall be forever lost, stalled
By that unjust proud black lowborn menace :
When the matter of the bridge is resolved,
Ister shall vex the republic of Venice.

5.30
All around the great city there shall be
Troops billeted in every field & town :
Rome inciting them to strike at Paris,
Upon the sea great pillage shall abound.

5.31

Par terre Attique chef de la sapience,
Qui de présent est la rose du monde :
Pont ruiné & sa grand preeminence,
Sera subdite & naufrage des undes.

5.32

Où tout bon est, tout bien Soleil & Lune,
Est abondant : sa ruine approche :
Du ciel s'advance varier ta fortune,
En mesme estat que la septiesme roche.

5.33

Des principaux de cité rebellée,
Qui tiendront fort pour liberté ravoir :
Detrencher masles, infelice meslée,
Crys, hurlemens à Nantes piteux voir.

5.34

Du plus profond de l'occident Anglois :
Où est le chef de l'isle Britannique :
Entrera classe dans Gyronde par Bloys,
Par vin & sel, feux cachez aux barriques.

5.35

Par cité franche de la grand mer Saline
Qui porte encores à l'estomach la pierre :
Angloise classe viendra soubs la bruine
Un rameau prendre, du grand ouverte guerre.

5.36

De sœur le frere par simulte faintise,
Viendra mesler rosée en myneral :
Sur la placente donne à vieille tardifve,
Meurt, le goustant sera simple & rural.

5.37

Trois cents seront d'un vouloir & accord,
Que pour venir au bout de leur attaincte :
Vingts mois après tous & records,
Leur Roy trahi simulant haine faincte.

5.31
That Attic land, first & foremost in science,
And the rose of the world to this very day :
The sea shall ruin its preeminence,
It shall be submerged & drowned in the waves.

5.32
Where all goes well, there go the Sun & Moon,
Things are booming : things are doomed to ruin :
Your fortune varies with the sky above,
In the same estate as the seventh stone.

5.33
The major actors in the town's rebellion,
Who most want to have their liberty back :
The angry mob shall go after these men :
Shouts, screams at Nantes : one's completely aghast.

5.34
From the furthest west of the British Isles,
There where the English king does reside :
At Blois' behest, fleet shall invade Gironde :
Not wine & salt, but fires in casks do hide.

5.35
To the free city off the great Seline sea
Which still bears the name of rock at its core :
Under cover of fog an English fleet
Shall come seize the branch : the lord declares war.

5.36
Duping his sister the brother shall brew
The dew with a little dose of mineral :
She'll die of the cake given to the slow
Old crone, to be tasted by some yokel.

5.37
Three hundred shall be of one mind & will
To achieve the object of their long wait :
Twenty months later they shall all recall
Betraying their king while hiding their hate.

5.38
Ce grand monarque qu'au mort succedera,
Donnera vie illicite & lubrique,
Par nonchalance à tous concedera,
Qu'à la parfin faudra la loy Salique.

5.39
Du vray rameau de fleur de lys issu,
Mis & logé heritier d'Hetrurie :
Son sang antique de longue main tissu,
Fera Florence florir en l'armoirie.

5.40
Le sang royal sera si tresmeslé,
Contraints seront Gaulois de l'Hesperie :
On attendra que terme soit coulé,
Et que memoire de la voix soit perie.

5.41
Nay souz les umbres & journée nocturne
Sera en regne & bonté souveraine :
Fera renaistre son sang de l'antique urne,
Renouvellant siecle d'or pour l'ærain.

5.42
Mars eslevé en son plus haut befroy,
Fera retraire les Allobrox de France :
La gent Lombarde fera si grand effroy,
A ceux de l'Aigle comprins souz la balance.

5.43
La grande ruine des sacrez ne s'esloigne,
Provence, Naples, Sicille, Seez & Ponce :
En Germanie, au Rhin & à Cologne,
Vexez à mort par tous ceux de Magonce.

5.44
Par mer le rouge sera prins de pyrates,
La paix sera par son moyen troublée :
L'iré & l'avare commettra par fainct acte,
Au grand Pontife sera l'armée doublée.

5.38

This mighty king, successor to the throne,
Shall live a life illicit & lubricious,
Nonchalantly giving in to all & one :
Salic law in the end more judicious.

5.39

Born of the true branch of the fleur-de-lis,
Then set in place as heir to Tuscany :
Her ancient blood woven on ancient loom
Shall make the crest of Florence burst with blooms.

5.40

The royal blood shall much commingled be,
The Gauls be forced to quit Hesperides :
One shall wait until the term has passed
And that the voice vanish from memory.

5.41

Born in shadows & day as dark as night,
With sovereign benevolence he shall rule :
From the ancient urn he'll refresh his line,
Remake the age of bronze an age of gold.

5.42

Mars now exalted to his apogee
Shall drive from France the Allobroges line :
Terrorized by the folk of Lombardy,
The Eagle's troops there under Libra's sign.

5.43

The clergy's great ruin lies near ahead,
Provence, Naples, Sicily, Sées & Pons :
In Germany, at the Rhine & Cologne,
All those of Mainz shall hound them to death.

5.44

At sea the red one is seized by pirates,
The state of peace thereby greatly troubled :
The ploy shall provoke avarice & ire,
The great Pontiff shall his army double.

5.45

Le grand Empire sera tost desolé,
Et translaté près d'arduenne silve :
Les deux bastardz par l'aisné decollé,
Et regnera Aenobarb. nez de milve.

5.46

Par chapeaux rouges querelles & nouveaux scismes,
Quand on aura eslu le Sabinois :
On produira contre luy grans sophismes,
Et sera Rome lesée par Albanois.

5.47

Le grand Arabe marchera bien avant,
Trahy sera par les Bisantinois :
L'antique Rodes luy viendra au devant,
Et plus grand mal par austre Pannonois.

5.48

Après la grande affliction du sceptre,
Deux ennemis par eux seront defaictz :
Classe d'Affrique aux Pannons viendra naistre,
Par mer & terre seront horribles faictz.

5.49

Nul de l'Espaigne mais de l'antique France,
Ne sera esleu pour le tremblant nacelle,
A l'ennemy sera faicte fiance,
Qui dans son regne sera peste cruelle.

5.50

L'an que les freres du lys seront en aage,
L'un d'eux tiendra la grande Romanie :
Trembler les monts, ouvert Latin passage,
Pache macher, contre fort d'Armenie.

5.51

La gent de Dace, d'Angleterre & Polonne
Et de Boesme feront nouvelle ligue :
Pour passer outre d'Hercules la Colonne,
Barcins, Tyrrens dresser cruelle brigue.

5.45
The mighty Empire shall be soon wrecked
And transferred to the woods of the Ardennes :
The elder shall cut off the two bastards' heads
And the hawk-nosed Ahenobarbus reign.

5.46
Cardinals feuding, creating schisms
When the Sabine shall have been elected :
He shall be the victim of great sophisms,
And Rome by Alba be disrespected.

5.47
The mighty Arab shall make his way,
But be by the Byzantines betrayed :
Ancient Rhodes rushing to oppose him,
The Pannonian inflicting greater pain.

5.48
After the mighty king is overthrown,
They shall send down two foes into defeat :
Pannonians beset by the Afric fleet,
On land & sea what horrors to be seen.

5.49
Never from Spain but one from ancient France
Shall be elected the wavering barque to helm :
With the enemy they shall try their chances,
Who shall prove a most cruel plague to his realm.

5.50
The year the French brothers shall come of age,
One of them shall rule great Romania :
Hills shall quake the Latin road once engaged :
A pact to attack the chief of Armenia.

5.51
Those of Dacia, England & Poland
And Bohemia shall join into league :
To pass beyond the Pillars of Hercules,
Those of Tyre & Barcino cruelly scheme.

5.52

Un Roy sera qui donra l'opposite,
Les exilez eslevez sur le regne :
De sang nager la gent caste hyppolite,
Et florira long temps soubs telle enseigne.

5.53

La loy du Sol, & Venus contendus,
Appropriant l'esprit de prophetie :
Ne l'un ne l'autre ne seront entendus,
Par Sol tiendra la loy du grand Messie.

5.54

Du pont Euxine, & la grand Tartarie,
Un roy sera qui viendra voir la Gaule :
Transpercera Alans & l'Armenie,
Et dans Bisance lairra sanglante Gaule.

5.55

De la felice Arabie contrade,
Naistra puissant de loy Mahometique :
Vexer l'Espaigne, conquester la Grenade,
Et plus par mer à la gent Lygustique.

5.56

Par le trespas du tresvieillart pontife,
Sera esleu le Romain de bon aage :
Qu'il sera dict que le siege debiffe,
Et long tiendra & de picquant ouvrage.

5.57

Istra du mont Gaulsier & Aventin,
Qui par le trou advertira l'armée :
Entre deux rocs sera prins le butin,
De SEXT. Mansol faillir la renommée.

5.58

De l'aqueduct d'Uticense, Gardoing,
Par la forest & mont inaccessible :
En my du pont sera tasché au poing,
Le chef Nemans qui tant sera terrible.

5.52

There shall be a King who turns contrary,
Favoring exiles over his own regime :
Aswim in blood, the pure & ordinary :
Long shall he flourish under this sign.

5.53

The creeds of Sol & Venus shall disagree,
Each borrowing the spirit of prophecy,
Each deaf to what the other has begun :
The great Messiah shall rule through the Sun.

5.54

From beyond the Black Sea & great Tartary,
There shall come a King to look upon Gaul :
He shall pierce through Armenia & Alany,
And within Byzance plant his bloody rod.

5.55

In Arabia Felix, fair contrada,
Shall be born a strongman of Muslim creed :
To vex Spain & to conquer Grenada,
And invade Liguria from the sea.

5.56

When the Pope dies who was far too old,
They shall elect a Roman ripe of age :
Of him shall be said he tatters the throne,
So long and prickly shall be his reign.

5.57

Down from the Aventine & Mount Gaussier
He'll warn the troops having spied through the hole :
Between two rocks they'll fall upon their prey :
So fades the fame of Saint-Paul-de-Mausole.

5.58

By the aqueduct of Uzès, Gardon,
Over inaccessible woods & hills :
At midbridge he shall be punched in the throat,
That chief from Nîmes who would do them such ill.

5.59

Au chef Anglois à Nimes trop sejour,
Devers l'Espaigne au secours Aenobarbe :
Plusieurs mourront par Mars ouvert ce jour,
Quant en Artois faillir estoille en barbe.

5.60

Par teste rase viendra bien mal eslire,
Plus que sa charge ne porte passera :
Si grand fureur & raige fera dire,
Qu'à feu & sang tout sexe trenchera.

5.61

L'enfant du grand n'estant à sa naissance,
Subjuguera les hauts mont Apennis :
Fera trembler tous ceux de la balance
Et des monts feux jusques à mont Senis.

5.62

Sur les rouchers sang on verra pleuvoir,
Sol Orient, Saturne Occidental :
Près d'Orgon guerre, à Rome grand mal voir,
Nefs parfondrées & prins le Tridental.

5.63

De vaine emprise l'honneur indue plaincte,
Galliotz errans par latins froit, faim, vagues :
Non loing du Tymbre de sang la terre taincte
Et sur humains seront diverses plagues.

5.64

Les assemblés par repos du grand nombre,
Par terre & mer conseil contremandé :
Près de l'Ausonne Gennes, Nice de l'ombre,
Par champs & villes le chef contrebandé.

5.65

Subit venu l'effrayeur sera grande,
Des principaux de l'affaire cachés :
Et dame en braise plus ne sera en veue.
Ce peu à peu seront les grands faschés.

5.59
English chief overstays his days at Nîmes
En route to help Ahenobarbus in Spain :
Many shall die in the war that starts that day
A bearded star shoots over the Artois plain.

5.60
The friars shall cause him to miscalculate,
He won't manage under a load this dire :
His tongue shall run with such rants & raves
All sects shall be consigned to blood & fire.

5.61
His child unborn, the great one shall lay low
The great mountains of the Apennines :
He'll strike fear into those beneath Libra,
From Mount Cenis to the Pyrenees.

5.62
One shall see blood rain down upon the rocks,
Sun in the East, Saturn in the West :
War in Orgon, Rome gone to the dogs,
Ships capsized, Tridental under arrest.

5.63
Honorable failures, undue complaints,
Boats tossed in Latin seas, cold, hunger, waves :
Not far from Tiber, land with blood is stained,
And mankind afflicted with divers plagues.

5.64
To calm the most of those there assembled,
They'll countermand the attack by land & sea :
Near autumn Genoa, Nice dissemble :
Through town & field the insurgent chief.

5.65
Major fright when he bursts onto the scene,
The various culprits shall go scot-free :
The more the lady in flames is perceived,
The more enraged all their lordships shall be.

5.66

Soubz les antiques edifices vestaux,
Non esloignez d'aqueduct ruyné :
De Sol & Lune sont les luisans metaulx,
Ardante lampe Trajan d'or buriné.

5.67

Quand chef Perouse n'osera sa tunique
Sens au couvert tout nud s'expolier :
Seront prins sept faict Aristocratique,
Le pere & filz mors par poincte au colier.

5.68

Dans le Danube & du Rhin viendra boire,
Le grand Chameau ne s'en repentira :
Trembler du Rosne & plus fort ceux de Loire,
Et près des Alpes coq le ruinera.

5.69

Plus ne sera le grand en faux sommeil,
L'inquietude viendra prendre repoz :
Dresser phalange d'or, azur, & vermeil,
Juguer Affrique la ronger jusques oz.

5.70

Des regions subjectes à la Balance,
Feront troubler les monts par grande guerre :
Captifz tout sexe deu & toute Bisance
Qu'on criera à l'aube terre à terre.

5.71

Par la fureur d'un qui attendra l'eau,
Par la grand raige tout l'exercite esmeu :
Chargé des nobles à dix & sept bateaulx,
Au long du Rosne, tard messagier venu.

5.72

Pour le plaisir d'edict voluptueux,
On meslera la poyson dans l'aloy :
Venus sera en cours si vertueux,
Qu'obfusquera du Soleil tout à loy.

5.66
Near the ancient buildings of the vestals,
Not that far from the ruined aqueduct :
Of Sun & Moon the glittering metals,
The engravèd lamp of the golden goat.

5.67
When the Perugian chief no longer dares
Strip off his tunic & stand there chest bared :
Seven seized, nobles behind the affair,
Spiked collar killing both father & heir.

5.68
Coming to drink of the Danube & Rhine,
The mighty Camel no remorse shall show :
The folk of the Rhône & Loire affrighted :
Near the Alps the Cock shall lay him low.

5.69
The great lord shall safely lay down his head,
His uneasy dreams now at last consoled :
He'll array his troops in gold, blue, red,
Conquer Africa, gnaw it to the bone.

5.70
Among the lands subjected to Libra,
They'll assail the mountains with mighty war :
All holy sects, all Byzance now unmanned,
Each dawn they shall cry out from land to land.

5.71
Seized with mighty rage to reach the water,
All the troops are furious to move on :
Seventeen boats loaded up with nobles,
Messenger coming late along the Rhône.

5.72
The pleasure of an edict this worldly
Shall cause the faith to be mixed with poison :
So virtuous shall the course of Venus be
It shall cloud the quality of the Sun.

5.73

Persecutée sera de Dieu l'Eglise,
Et les sainctz temples seront expoliez :
L'enfant la mere mettra nud en chemise,
Seront Arabes aux Polons raliez.

5.74

De sang Troyen naistra cœur Germanique
Qu'il deviendra en si haute puissance :
Hors chassera gent estrange Arabique,
Tournant l'Eglise en pristine preeminence.

5.75

Montera haut sur le lieu plus à dextre,
Demourra assis sur le pierre quarrée :
Vers le midy posé à la senestre,
Baston tortu en main, bouche serrée.

5.76

En lieu libre tendra son pavillon,
Et ne voudra en citez prendre place :
Aix, Carpen., l'isle volce, mont Cavaillon,
Par tous ses lieux abolira sa trasse.

5.77

Tous les degrez d'honneur Ecclesiastique,
Seront changez en dial quirinal :
En Martial quirinal flaminique,
Un Roy de France le rendra vulcanal.

5.78

Les deux unis ne tiendront longuement,
Et dans treze ans au Barbare Satrappe :
Aux deux costez feront tel perdement,
Qu'un benyra le Barqué & sa cappe.

5.79

Par sacrée pompe viendra baisser les aisles,
Par la venue du grand legislateur :
Humble haulsera, vexera les rebelles,
Naistra sur terre aucun æmulateur.

5.73

The Church of God shall be much oppressed
And the holy Temples roundly looted :
The child shall send its mother out half-dressed,
Polonians & Arabs in cahoots.

5.74

Of Trojan blood shall be born a German great
Who shall attain a power so storied
He'll drive out the alien Arab race,
Restoring the Church to its former glory.

5.75

High over the realm, to the right inclining,
He shall be seated on the squarish rock :
Toward the south, now on the left reclining,
Mouth shut, his hand grasping a twisted crook.

5.76

In the open country he shall pitch his camp,
In no town shall he want to show his face :
Carpentras, Cavaillon, Vaucluse or Aix,
Razing his trace in every single place.

5.77

All the ranks of ecclesiastic honor
Shall turn into Jupiter Quirinal,
Into Mars Quirinal sacerdotal,
With a French king then turning Vulcanal.

5.78

The two shall not be allies thirteen years
Or so against the Barbarian satrap :
On either side such losses they shall bear
That blessèd shall be the barque & its cope.

5.79

The wings of sacred pomp shall be clipped
Once the great legislator arrives :
He'll raise the lowly, vex insurrectionists :
Never on earth shall be born his like.

5.80

L'Ogmion grande Bisance approchera,
Chassée sera la barbarique ligue :
Des deux loix l'une l'estinique lachera,
Barbare & franche en perpetuelle brigue.

5.81

L'oiseau royal sur la cité solaire,
Sept mois devant fera nocturne augure :
Mur d'Orient cherra, tonnerre, esclaire,
Sept jours aux portes les ennemis à l'heure.

5.82

Au conclud pache hors de la forteresse,
Ne sortira celuy en desespoir mis :
Quand ceux d'Arbois, de Langres, contre Bresse,
Auront mont Dolle, bouscade d'ennemis.

5.83

Ceux qui auront entreprins subvertir,
Nompareil regne, puissant & invincible :
Feront par fraude, nuictz trois advertir,
Quand le plus grand à table lira Bible.

5.84

Naistra du gouphre & cité immesurée,
Nay de parents obscurs & tenebreux :
Qui la puissance du grand roy reverée,
Voudra destruire par Rouan & Evreux.

5.85

Par les Sueves & lieux circonvoisins,
Seront en guerre pour cause des nuées :
Gambes marin, locustes & cousins,
Du Leman sautes seront bien desnuées.

5.86

Par les deux testes, & trois bras separés,
La cité grande par eaux sera vexée :
Des grands d'entre eux par exil esgarés,
Par teste Perse Bisance fort pressée.

5.80
Upon Byzance Ogmion shall advance,
Finishing off the Barbarian league :
Of the two creeds, the heathen shall be smashed,
Between Barbarian & French no surcease.

5.81
Above the solar city, the royal bird,
Nocturnal omen, seven months before :
Thunder & lightning, the Eastern wall sheared,
Seven days to the hour, foe at the door.

5.82
He shall not venture out from the fortress,
Pact once signed, fallen into great despair :
When those from Arbois & Langres near Bresse
Ambush their foes in the hills near to Dole.

5.83
Those who have undertaken to subvert
That peerless realm, puissant, invincible :
Under dark of night three they shall alert,
As the chief at his table reads the Bible.

5.84
From the abyss & city without end,
Born of parents obscure & tenebrous :
The power of that king most reverend
He would destroy at Rouen & Évreux.

5.85
Swabia & its surrounding neighbors
Shall go to war to defend the latest rage :
Locusts & mosquitoes in naval ports,
The pastures of Leman lying ravaged.

5.86
By two turbans & three separate arms,
The great city shall be attacked by sea :
Its exiled leaders now scattered abroad,
By blue-turbaned Byzantium much harried.

5.87

L'an que Saturne sera hors de servage,
Au franc terroir sera d'eau inundé :
De sang Troyen sera son mariage,
Et serra seur d'Espaignols circundé.

5.88

Sur le sablon par un hideux deluge,
Des autres mers trouvé monstre marin :
Proche du lieu sera faict un refuge,
Tenant Savone esclave de Turin.

5.89

Dedans Hongrie par Boheme, Navarre,
Et par banniere fainctes seditions :
Par fleurs de lys pays pourtant la barre,
Contre Orleans fera esmotions.

5.90

Dans les Cyclades, en Perinthe Larisse,
Et dedans Sparte tout le Peloponesse :
Si grand famine, peste par faux connisse,
Neuf mois tiendra & tout le Cherronesse.

5.91

Au grand marché qu'on dict des mensongiers,
Du tout Torrent & champ Athenien :
Seront surprins par les chevaux legiers,
Par Albanois Mars, Leo, Sat. un versien.

5.92

Après le siege tenu dix & sept ans,
Cinq changeront en tel revolu terme :
Puis sera l'un esleu de mesme temps,
Qui des Romains ne sera trop conforme.

5.93

Soubs le terroir du rond globe lunaire,
Lors que sera dominateur Mercure :
L'Isle d'Escosse fera un luminaire,
Qui les Anglois mettra à desconfiture.

5.87

The year Saturn ceases to be bondsman,
The Frankish land shall experience floods :
It shall make a marriage with Trojan blood,
And be safe, surrounded by the Spaniards.

5.88

Upon the sands after horrid deluge
A sea monster from other seas is found :
Near to that place they'll create a refuge
That shall hold Savona slave to Turin.

5.89

Within Hungary devious seditions
By Bohemia, Navarre and that banner :
Bearing the fleur-de-lis crossed by a bar
Against Orléans he'll stir up emotions.

5.90

In Perinthus, Larissa, Cyclades,
In Sparta & all the Peloponnese,
The traitor shall inflict famine & plague,
Nine months of it, throughout the Chersonese.

5.91

At what is called the marketplace of lies,
By the river of Athens & its plain :
By Albanian light horse they'll be surprised,
Mars, Leo, Saturn in Aquarius.

5.92

After seventeen years holding the seat,
Five shall change within this same lapse of time :
One shall be elected concurrently
Who shall not quite toe the Roman line.

5.93

Beneath the realm of the round lunar globe,
When Mercury exercises his sway :
A shining star from the isle of Scotland
Shall throw the English into disarray.

5.94

Translatera en la grand Germanie,
Brabant & Flandres, Gand, Bruges, & Bolongne :
La traifve faincte, le grand duc d'Armenie,
Asaillira Vienne & la Cologne.

5.95

Nautique rame invitera les umbres,
Du grand Empire lors viendra conciter :
La mer Aegée des lignes les encombres,
Empeschant l'onde Tyrrene de floter.

5.96

Sur le milieu du grand monde la rose,
Pour nouveaux faicts sang public espandu :
A dire vray on aura bouche close,
Lors au besoing viendra tard l'attendu.

5.97

Le nay difforme par horreur suffoqué,
Dans la cité du grand Roy habitable :
L'edict severe des captifs revoqué,
Gresle & tonnerre, Condon inestimable.

5.98

A quarante huict degré climaterique,
A fin de Cancer, si grande seicheresse :
Poisson en mer, fleuve, lac, cuit hectique,
Bearn, Biggore par feu ciel en detresse.

5.99

Milan, Ferrare, Turin, & Aquilleye,
Capue, Brundis vexés par gent Celtique :
Par le Lyon & phalange aquilée
Quand Rome aura le chef vieux Britannique.

5.100

Le boutefeu par son feu atrapé,
De feu du ciel à Carcas. & Cominge :
Foix, Aux, Mazeres, haut viellart eschappé,
Par ceux de Hasse, des Saxons & Turinge.

5.94
He shall shift toward greater Germania
Brabant & Flanders, Ghent, Bruges, Boulogne :
Feigning truce, the grand Duke of Armenia
Shall fall upon Vienna & Cologne.

5.95
The Sea-Frog shall welcome in the shades,
Then unsettle the Empire far & wide :
With driftwood he'll load the Aegean Sea,
Blocking the flow of the Tyrrhenian tide.

5.96
The rose at the core of the greater world,
New allegations civic bloodshed feed :
One's mouth shall be closed, if the truth be told,
The awaited one late in time of need.

5.97
In horror they smother the deformed babe
Born in the city of the mighty King :
The severe edict on captives erased,
Hail & thunder, Condom a priceless thing.

5.98
At forty-eight degrees of latitude,
At the end of Cancer a drought so dry :
Scrawny fish in river, lake, sea are stewed,
And Béarn & Bigorre scorched by lightning.

5.99
Milan, Ferrara, Aquileia, Turin,
Capua, Brindisi, vexed by the Celts :
By the Lion & aquiline legions
When an old Britannic chief shall rule Rome.

5.100
The arsonist hoisted by his own flame,
Sky-fire falling on Carcas. & Comminges :
Foix, Auch, Mazères, an old noble escapes
Among Hessians, Saxons, Thuringians.

CENTURIE VI

6.1

Autour des monts Pyrenées grans amas
De gent estrange secourir roy nouveau :
Près de Garonne du grand temple de Mas,
Un Romain chef le craindra dedans l'eau.

6.2

En l'an cinq cens octante plus & moins,
On attendra le siecle bien estrange :
En l'an sept cens & trois cieux en tesmoings,
Que plusieurs regnes un à cinq feront change.

6.3

Fleuve qu'esprouve le nouveau nay Celtique,
Sera en grande de l'Empire discorde :
Le jeune prince par gent ecclesiastique,
Ostera sceptre coronal de concorde.

6.4

Le Celtiq fleuve changera de rivaige,
Plus ne tiendra la cité d'Agripine :
Tout transmué ormis le vieil langaige,
Saturne, Leo, Mars, Cancer en rapine.

6.5

Si grand famine par unde pestifere,
Par pluye longue le long du polle arctique :
Samarobryn cent lieux de l'hemisphere,
Vivront sans loy, exempt de pollitique.

6.6

Apparoistra vers le Septentrion,
Non loin de Cancer l'estoille chevelue :
Suze, Sienne, Boece, Eretrion,
Mourra de Rome grand, la nuict disperue.

6.7

Norneigre & Dace, & l'isle Britannique,
Par les unis freres seront vexées :
Le chef Romain issu de sang Gallique,
Et les copies aux foretz repoulsées.

CENTURY VI

6.1
Around the Pyrenees a mighty throng
Of foreign troops come to the new king's aid :
Near the great church of Mas on the Garonne,
In the waters a Roman chief afraid.

6.2
In the year fifteen eighty more or less,
One shall expect an age that's very strange :
In seventeen three, heavens as witness,
Many of the realms, one to five, shall change.

6.3
The stream that tests the Celtic king at birth
Shall in the course of Empire know discord :
The young prince guided by those of the Church,
Shall shed the royal scepter of concord.

6.4
The Celtic stream shall change its very shores,
Agrippine's city go down in defeat :
All but the ancient tongue shall be transformed,
Saturn, Leo, Mars, Cancer in retreat.

6.5
Such famine brought on by such waves of plague,
By endless rain along the arctic pole :
At Samarobryn for a hundred leagues,
They shall live without creed or civic rule.

6.6
There shall appear toward the Septentrion,
Not far from Cancer, the star with the beard :
Susa, Siena, Boeotia, Eretrion :
Rome's lord shall die the night it disappears.

6.7
Norneigre & Dacia & the British isle
Shall be vexed by brothers in alliance :
The Roman chief issued of Gallic blood
Chased back to the woods with all of his troops.

6.8
Ceux qui estoient en regne pour sçavoir,
Au Royal change deviendront apouvris :
Uns exilez sans appuy, or, n'avoir,
Lettrez & lettres ne seront à grand prix.

6.9
Aux sacrez temples seront faicts escandales,
Comptez seront par honneurs & louanges
D'un que l'on grave d'argent d'or les medalles,
La fin sera en tormens bien estranges.

6.10
Un peu de temps les temples des couleurs
De blanc & noir des deux entremeslée :
Rouges & jaunes leur embleront les leurs,
Sang, terre, peste, faim, feu, d'eau affolée.

6.11
Des sept rameaux à trois seront reduicts,
Les plus aisnez seront surprins par mort,
Fratricider les deux seront seduicts,
Les conjurez en dormans seront morts.

6.12
Dresser copies pour monter à l'Empire,
Du Vatican le sang Royal tiendra :
Flamans, Anglois, Espaigne avec Aspire,
Contre l'Itale & France contendra.

6.13
Un dubieux ne viendra loing du regne,
La plus grand part le voudra soustenir :
Un Capitole ne voudra point qu'il regne,
Sa grande charge ne pourra maintenir.

6.14
Loing de sa terre Roy perdra la bataille,
Prompt eschappé poursuivy suivant prins,
Ignare prins soubs la dorée maille,
Soubs fainct habit & l'ennemy surprins.

6.8

Those in the realm esteemed for their learning
Shall grow poor with the change of the regime :
Some exiled, forlorn, without a farthing,
Scholars & letters to be held quite cheap.

6.9

In holy churches scandals shall be seen
That shall be counted honors fit for praise :
For whom gold & silver coins are engraved,
Amid strange torments he shall end his days.

6.10

For a while the churches shall still remain
White & black, a melding of both these hues :
Reds & yellows shall then steal these away :
Blood, land, plague, famine, fire, mad deluge.

6.11

Seven branches shall be reduced to three,
Death shall take the eldest ones by surprise :
Two shall be seduced into fratricide,
The conspirators in their sleep shall die.

6.12

Armies raised to march into the Empire,
The Vatican's royal blood shall hold firm :
Flanders, England, Spain as well as Aspire
Against France & Italy now shall turn.

6.13

A dubious one shall nearly come to reign,
The majority shall lend him its acclaim :
A Capitol not wanting him to reign,
His charge he'll be unable to maintain.

6.14

Far from his land, the King suffers defeat,
Quickly escaping, pursued & then seized :
Unaware that the gold mail hides this prize,
The foe is much surprised by the disguise.

6.15

Dessoubs la tombe sera trouvé le Prince,
Qu'aura le pris par dessus Nuremberg :
L'Espaignol Roy en Capricorne mince,
Fainct & trahy par le grand Vvitemberg.

6.16

Ce que ravy sera du jeune Milve,
Par les Normans de France et Picardie :
Les noirs du temple du lieu de Negrisilve
Feront aulberge & feu de Lombardie.

6.17

Après les limes bruslez les asiniers,
Contraints seront changer habits divers :
Les Saturnins bruslez par les meusniers,
Hors la pluspart qui ne sera convers.

6.18

Par les phisiques le grand Roy delaissé,
Par sort non art de l'Ebrieu est en vie,
Luy & son genre au regne hault poussé,
Grace donnée à gent qui Christ envie.

6.19

La vraye flamme engloutira la dame,
Que voudra mettre les Innocens à feu :
Près de l'assaut l'exercite s'enflamme,
Quand dans Seville monstre en bœuf sera veu.

6.20

L'union faincte sera peu de durée,
Des uns changés, reformés la plupart :
Dans les vaisseaux sera gent endurée,
Lors aura Rome un nouveau liepart.

6.21

Quant ceux du polle arctiq unis ensemble,
En Orient grand effraieur & crainte :
Esleu nouveau, soustenu le grand temple,
Rodes, Bisance de sang Barbare taincte.

6.15

Beneath the tombstone they shall find the Prince
Who shall have triumphed over Nuremberg :
The Spanish King, when Capricorn is thin,
Shall be betrayed by the lord of Wittenberg.

6.16

What shall be plundered from the youthful Milve
By the French of Normandy & Picardy :
The black monks of the land of Negresilve
Shall make the inn & hearth of Lombardy.

6.17

After penances the priests shall be burned,
Obliged to change their various habits :
Millers shall burn the Saturnines alive,
Except the majority of converts.

6.18

The King abandoned by his physicians,
Fate, not the Hebrew's art, has saved his life :
Heights of power reached by him & his kin :
Forgiveness to all those who yearn for Christ.

6.19

The lady shall be burned by the true flame
That would roast all Innocents in hell :
The army on fire before the campaign,
When a monster bull is seen in Seville.

6.20

The sham alliance shall not long endure,
Some are transformed but the most are reformed :
The ships filled with troops hard-bitten & dour,
And a new leopard ruling over Rome.

6.21

Once all those of the northern climes unite,
Great fear & terror shall reign in the East :
A new election, the Church set aright,
Rhodes, Byzance by Barbary blood be stained.

6.22

Dedans la terre du grand temple celique,
Nepveu à Londres par paix faincte meurtry :
La barque alors deviendra scismatique,
Liberté faincte sera au corn & cry.

6.23

D'esprit de regne munismes descriées,
Et seront peuples esmeuz contre leur Roy :
Paix, faict nouveau, sainctes lois empirées,
Rapis onc fut en si tresdur arroy.

6.24

Mars & le sceptre se trouvera conjoinct,
Dessoubz Cancer calamiteuse guerre :
Un peu après sera nouveau Roy oingt,
Qui par long temps pacifiera la terre.

6.25

Par Mars contraire sera la monarchie,
Du grand pescheur en trouble ruyneux :
Jeune noir rouge prendra la hierarchie,
Les proditeurs iront jour bruyneux.

6.26

Quatre ans le siege quelque peu bien tiendra,
Un surviendra libidineux de vie :
Ravenne & Pyse, Veronne soustiendront,
Pour eslever la croix de Pape en vie.

6.27

Dedans les isles de cinq fleuves à un,
Par le croissant du grand Chyren Selin :
Par les bruynes de l'aer fureur de l'un,
Six eschappés, cachés fardeaux de lyn.

6.28

Le grand Celtique entrera dedans Rome,
Menant amas d'exilés & bannis :
Le grand pasteur mettra à mort tout homme,
Qui pour le coq estoient aux Alpes unys.

6.22

Within the land of the heavenly church,
At London, nephew wounded, peace a sham :
The barque then shall completely split apart,
Sham liberty shouted throughout the land.

6.23

The coin of the realm shall be much descried
And peoples incited against their King :
Peace, novelties, holy laws in decline,
Never before did Rapis feel this sting.

6.24

When Mars & Jupiter come to conjoin
Under Cancer, most calamitous war :
Shortly thereafter, new King anointed,
Who shall bring a lasting peace to the world.

6.25

Fending off Mars the holy monarchy
Of the fisherman shall go to the dogs :
A young black, red shall seize the hierarchy :
Treacherous deeds under a pall of fog.

6.26

Four years he'll have a hold over the see,
One shall succeed who'll live a life of lust :
Ravenna, Pisa, Verona shall increase
The Pope's desire to campaign for the cross.

6.27

In the isles where five streams flow into one,
'Neath the lunar crescent of Chyren Selin :
In the misted air one flies into a rage :
Hid in bundles of flax, six shall escape.

6.28

The mighty Celt shall enter into Rome
With a throng of the exiled & banished :
The Pope shall put to death every man
United against the Cock in the Alps.

6.29
La vefve saincte entendant les nouvelles,
De ses rameaux mis en perplex & trouble :
Qui sera duict appaiser les querelles,
Par son pourchas des razes fera comble.

6.30
Par l'apparence de faincte saincteté,
Sera trahy aux ennemis le siege :
Nuict qu'on cuidoit dormir en seureté,
Près de Brabant marcheront ceux du Liege.

6.31
Roy trouvera ce qu'il desiroit tant,
Quand le Prelat sera reprins à tort :
Responce au duc le rendra malcontent,
Qui dans Milan mettra plusieurs à mort.

6.32
Par trahysons de verges à mort battu,
Prins surmonté sera par son desordre :
Conseil frivole au grand captif sentu,
Nez par fureur quant Berich viendra mordre.

6.33
Sa main derniere par Alus sanguinaire,
Ne se pourra par la mer guarentir :
Entre deux fleuves craindre main militaire,
Le noir, l'ireux le fera repentir.

6.34
De feu volant la machination,
Viendra troubler au grand chef assiegez :
Dedans sera telle sedition,
Qu'en desespoir seront les profligez.

6.35
Près de Trion, & proche à blanche laine,
Aries, Taurus, Cancer, Leo, la Vierge,
Mars, Jupiter, le Sol ardra grand plaine,
Bois & citez, lettres cachez au cierge.

6.29

The saintly widow hearing the reports
About the persecution of her heirs :
She'll be induced to put an end to wars,
And pursue the monks to their very lairs.

6.30

Feigning an appearance of sanctity,
He shall betray the see to the enemy :
Just as one thought it was safe to sleep,
Near Brabant, one hears Liège's marching feet.

6.31

The King shall discover what he so desired,
When the Prelate is blamed by mistake :
His reply to the duke shall raise his ire,
Who in Milan shall send many to the stake.

6.32

Charged with treason, pummeled to death by sticks,
Captured at the very height of his woes :
Trifling assurance to the great captive,
When mad Berich comes to bite off his nose.

6.33

Bloodied by Alus, his remaining force
Shall be unable to retreat by the sea :
An army is feared between the two streams :
Black & wrathful, he shall inspire remorse.

6.34

Of flying fire such the machination
That the great chief shall be struck by terror :
Within there shall be so much sedition
That the besieged are driven to despair.

6.35

Near Trion, not far from the white-wooled Ram,
Taurus, Cancer, Leo, Virgo, Aries,
Mars, Jupiter: the Sun shall scorch the plain,
The woods & cities : letters sealed with wax.

6.36
Ne bien ne mal par bataille terrestre,
Ne parviendra aux confins de Perouse :
Rebeller Pise, Florence voir mal estre,
Roy nuict blessé sur mulet à noire house.

6.37
L'œuvre ancienne se parachevera,
Du toict cherra sur le grand mal ruyne :
Innocent faict mort on accusera :
Nocent caiché taillis à la bruyne.

6.38
Aux profligez de paix les ennemis,
Après avoir l'Italie superée :
Noir sanguinaire rouge sera commis,
Feu, sang verser, eaue de sang coulorée.

6.39
L'enfant du regne par paternelle prinse,
Expolié sera pour delivrer :
Auprès du lac Trasimen l'azur prinse,
La troupe hostaige pour trop fort s'enyvrer.

6.40
Grand de Magonce pour grande soif estaindre,
Sera privé de sa grand dignité :
Ceux de Cologne si fort le viendront plaindre,
Que le grand groppe au Ryn sera getté.

6.41
Le second chef du regne d'Annemarc,
Par ceux de Frise et l'isle Britannique,
Fera despendre plus de cent mille marc,
Vain exploicter voyage en Italique.

6.42
A l'Ogmyon sera laissé le regne,
Du grand Selin qui plus sera de faict :
Par les Itales estendra son enseigne,
Regi sera par prudent contrefaict.

6.36

For good or for ill the land army's troops
Shall reach the outskirts of Perugia :
Pisa shall revolt, Florence know much woe :
King hurt night on mule in black gaiter boots.

6.37

The ancient work shall be fulfilled in time :
The roof shall come crashing down on the lord :
An innocent blamed for the mortal crime,
The culprit hiding in the misty grove.

6.38

Enemies of peace to the vanquished,
Their conquest of Italy once assured :
The bloody black, red one shall commit this :
Fire, bloodshed, rivers running red with gore.

6.39

His father captured, the child of the realm
Shall be despoiled & held for ransom :
The Blues shall be seized near Trasimen,
The troops taken hostage, stinking drunk.

6.40

The lord of Mainz, having overdrunk his fill,
Shall lose all dignity, the tipsy swine :
Cologne so complains about the imbecile
That his butt shall be thrown into the Rhine.

6.41

The second chief of the realm of Denmark
Shall ask the Frisians & the British isles
To spend more than a hundred thousand marks
To fund his futile Italian trip in style.

6.42

To Ogmion shall devolve the kingdom
Of the great Selin whose deeds he'll improve :
Through Italy he'll extend its ensign,
Governed by guile & singular prudence.

6.43

Long temps sera sans estre habitée,
Où Signe et Marne autour vient arrouser :
De la Tamise & martiaux tentée,
Deceuz les gardes en cuidant repouser.

6.44

De nuict par Nantes Lyris apparoistra,
Des artz marins susciteront la pluye :
Arabiq goulfe grand classe parfondra,
Un monstre en Saxe naistra d'ours & truye.

6.45

Le gouverneur du regne bien sçavant,
Ne consentir voulant au faict Royal :
Mellite classe par le contraire vent,
Le remettra à son plus desloyal.

6.46

Un juste sera en exil renvoyé,
Par pestilence aux confins de Nonseggle :
Responce au rouge le fera desvoyé,
Roy retirant à la Rane & à l'aigle.

6.47

Entre deux monts les deux grans assemblés
Delaisseront leur simulte secrette :
Brucelle & Dolle par Langres acablés
Pour à Malignes executer leur peste.

6.48

La saincteté trop faincte & seductive,
Accompaignée d'une langue diserte,
La cité vieille & Parme trop hastive,
Florence & Sienne rendront plus deserte.

6.49

De la partie de Mammer grand pontife,
Subjuguera les confins du Dannube :
Chasser les croix par fer raffe ne riffe,
Captifz, or, bagues plus de cent mille rubes.

6.43

The land shall long remain without a soul
That's watered by the rivers Seine & Marne :
The Thames armies shall take it as their goal :
No guard should think he could lay down his arms.

6.44

By night near to Nantes shall the rainbow beam,
Spells cast on the sea bringing rain somehow :
Fleet sunk in the Arab gulf : a monster seen
In Saxony, born of a bear & sow.

6.45

The most learnèd governor of the land,
Unwilling to bow to the king's command :
Malta's fleet, stalled by the contrary winds,
Makes him an even more disloyal man.

6.46

A just one into exile shall be sent,
With plague around the confines of Nonseggle :
His reply to the red means he's misled,
King withdrawing before the Frog & Eagle.

6.47

The two lords assembled between two mounts
Shall put aside their well-concealed hate :
Brussels & Dole by Langres so hounded
That at Malines they shall inflict their plague.

6.48

With their sham & seductive sanctity,
Attended by their arts of fluency,
To Florence, Siena they shall lay waste,
The old city & Parma prone to haste.

6.49

The great pontiff of the party of Mammer
Shall conquer the confines of the Danube :
By hook or by crook a crusade he'll prepare :
Captives, gold, rings, hundred thousand rubies.

6.50
Dedans le puys seront trouvés les oz,
Sera l'incest commis par la maratre :
L'estat changé, on querra bruict et loz,
Et aura Mars ascendant pour son astre.

6.51
Peuple assemblé, voir nouveau expectacle,
Princes & Roys par plusieurs assistans :
Pilliers faillir, murs : mais comme miracle,
Le Roy sauvé & trente des instans.

6.52
En lieu du grand qui sera condemné,
De prison hors son amy en sa place :
L'espoir Troyen en six moys joinct, mort nay
Le Sol à l'urne seront prins fleuves en glace.

6.53
Le grand Prelat Celtique à Roy suspect,
De nuict par cours sortira hors du regne :
Par duc fertile à son grand Roy, Bretaigne,
Bisance à Cipres & Tunes insuspect.

6.54
Au poinct du jour au second chant du coq,
Ceulx de Tunes, de Fez, & de Bugie :
Par les Arabes captif le Roy Maroq,
L'an mil six cens & sept, de Liturgie.

6.55
Au chalmé Duc, en arrachant l'esponce,
Voile Arabesque voir, subit descouverte :
Tripolis, Chio, & ceux de Trapesonce,
Duc prins, Marnegro & sa cité deserte.

6.56
La crainte armée de l'ennemy Narbon,
Effrayera si fort les Hesperiques :
Parpignan vuide par l'aveugle darbon,
Lors Barcelon par mer donra les piques.

6.50

The bones shall be found within the pit,
The stepmother incest shall commit :
The state once changed, they'll seek fame & praise
And Mars ascending shall rule its fate.

6.51

People assembled to see the new show,
Bystanders including princes & kings :
Pillars, walls fall : miraculously though,
The King & thirty spectators come through.

6.52

To replace the lord who shall be condemned,
His friend released from prison shall agree :
Child stillborn, six months of Trojan hopes end :
Sun in Aquarius, all the rivers freeze.

6.53

The Celtic prelate suspect to the King
Shall quit the realm by night undetected :
By a duke fertile to his British king,
Byzance by Cyprus, Tunis unsuspected.

6.54

At daybreak after the cock's second crow,
Those of Tunis, of Fez & of Bougie :
The Arabs the Moroccan King shall hold,
Sixteen oh seven of the liturgy.

6.55

Diving for sponges in the noonday sun,
The Duke suddenly sees the Arab fleet :
Tripolis, Chios, those of Trebizond :
His city emptied, Duke seized by Black Sea.

6.56

The much-feared army of the Narbonne foe
Shall cause the Hesperians sudden fright :
Perpignan be emptied by the blind mole,
Barcelona by sea shall start the fight.

6.57
Celuy qu'estoit bien avant dans le regne,
Ayant chef rouge proche à la hierarchie :
Aspre & cruel, & se fera tant craindre,
Succedera à sacré monarchie.

6.58
Entre les deux monarques esloignez,
Lors que le Sol par Selin clair perdue :
Simulte grande entre deux indignez,
Qu'aux Isles & Sienne la liberté rendue.

6.59
Dame en fureur par rage d'adultere,
Viendra à son Prince conjurer nom de dire :
Mais bref congneu sera le vitupere,
Que seront mis dix & sept à martire.

6.60
Le Prince hors de son terroir Celtique,
Sera trahy, deceu par interprete :
Rouan, Rochelle par ceux de l'Armorique
Au port de Blave deceus par moyne & prebstre.

6.61
Le grand tappis plié ne monstrera,
Fors qu'à demy la pluspart de l'histoire :
Chassé du regne loing aspre apparoistra
Qu'au faict bellique chascun le viendra croire.

6.62
Trop tard tous deux les fleurs seront perdues,
Contre la loy serment ne voudra faire :
Des ligueurs forces par gallots confondues,
Savone, Albingue par Monech grand martyre.

6.63
La dame seule au regne demeurée,
L'unic estaint premier au lict d'honneur :
Sept ans sera de douleur explorée,
Puis longue vie au regne par grand heur.

6.57
He whose temporal power was quite clear,
With a red chief close to the hierarchy :
Harsh & cruel & inspiring so much fear,
He shall take over the sacred monarchy.

6.58
Between the two monarchs who are estranged,
When the sunlight is eclipsed by the moon :
Such rivalry between these two enraged
That Siena & the Isles are let loose.

6.59
The lady enraged having been betrayed
Asks her prince to say no to her rival :
Once the dispute becomes a public shame,
Seventeen shall be denied survival.

6.60
Out of his Celtic lands the prince shall be
Betrayed by his interpreter in chief :
Rouen, Rochelle deceived by Brittany,
The port of Blaye duped by monk & priest.

6.61
The great folded tapestry shall not show
More than half of the celebrated tale :
Routed from the realm, so fierce shall he grow,
All shall think him quite the warrior male.

6.62
Both come too late, the flowers shall be lost,
Loath to swear an oath against the creed :
The rebel foes by the French staved off :
Savona, Albenga by Monech shall bleed.

6.63
The lady left alone upon the throne,
Who welcomed the first & only to bed :
Seven years shall she be aggrieved & mourn,
Then a long & fortunate reign instead.

6.64
On ne tiendra pache aucune arrestée,
Tous recevans iront par tromperie :
De paix & tresve, terre & mer protestée,
Par Barcelone classe prins d'industrie.

6.65
Gris & bureau, demie ouverte guerre,
De nuict seront assaillis & pillez :
Le bureau prins passera par la serre,
Son temple ouvert deux au plastre grillez.

6.66
Au fondement de la nouvelle secte,
Seront les oz du grand Romain trouvés :
Sepulcre en marbre apparoistra couverte,
Terre trembler en Avril, Mai enfouetz.

6.67
Au grand Empire parviendra tout un aultre
Bonté distant plus de felicité :
Regi par un issu non loing du peaultre,
Corruer regnes, grande infelicité.

6.68
Lors que souldartz fureur seditieuse,
Contre leur chef feront de nuict fer luire :
Ennemy d'Albe soit par main furieuse,
Lors vexer Rome & principaux seduire.

6.69
La pitié grande sera sans loing tarder,
Ceux qui donnoient seront contrains de prendre,
Nudz, affamez, de froit, soif, soy bander,
Les monts passer commettant grand esclandre.

6.70
Au chef du monde le grand Chyren sera,
Plus oultre après aymé, craint, redoubté :
Son bruit & loz les cieux surpassera,
Et du seul tiltre victeur fort contenté.

6.64

Not a single treaty guaranteed,
The credulous all taken for a ride :
Land & sea echoing with truce & peace,
The fleet taking Barcelona by guile.

6.65

War half-declared between the gray and brown,
Attacked & then plundered during the night :
The captured brown one into dungeon thrown,
Two terra-cotta figures in his shrine.

6.66

At the founding of the sect deemed so new,
They shall dig up the great Roman's remains :
The marble-clad tomb shall come into view :
Earthquake in April, burial in May.

6.67

A stranger shall make imperial news,
Further from goodness than felicity :
Ruled by one born not far from the stews,
When kingdoms collapse, great the misery.

6.68

When soldiers in their seditious rage
Flash their swords at night against their chief :
Alba attacked, the troops on a rampage,
Then vexing Rome & duping its elite.

6.69

Great succor shall soon be on its way,
Those who gave shall be constrained to take :
Naked, starved, thirsty, cold, as an army
They shall cross the mountains, wreaking havoc.

6.70

Lord of the world the great Chyren shall be,
Plus ultra left behind, much loved & feared :
His fame & praise shall outsurpass the skies,
Well pleased to be the sole victor revered.

6.71
Quand on viendra le grand roy parenter
Avant qu'il ait du tout l'ame rendue :
Celuy qui moins le viendra lamenter,
Par lyons, d'aigles, croix, couronne vendue.

6.72
Par fureur faincte d'esmotion divine,
Sera la femme de grand fort violée :
Juges voulans damner telle doctrine,
Victime au peuple ignorant imolée.

6.73
En cité grande un moyne & artisan,
Près de la porte logés & aux murailles :
Contre Modène secret, caue disant,
Trahis pour faire souz couleur d'espousailles.

6.74
La deschassée au regne tournera,
Ses ennemis trouvés des conjurés :
Plus que jamais son temps triomphera,
Trois & septante à mort trop asseurés.

6.75
Le grand pilot par Roy sera mandé,
Laisser la classe pour plus haut lieu attaindre :
Sept ans après sera contrebandé.
Barbare armée viendra Venise craindre.

6.76
La cité antique d'antenorée forge,
Plus ne pouvant le tyran supporter :
Le manchet sainct au temple couper gorge,
Les siens le peuple à mort viendra bouter.

6.77
Par la victoire du deceu faudulente,
Deux classes une, la revolte Germaine :
Le chef meurtry, & son filz dans la tente,
Florence, Imole pourchassés dans Romaine.

6.71

When to the great king they'll pay their respects
Before he has even drawn his last breath :
To him who shall have the least cause to mourn
Shall lion, eagles sell the cross & crown.

6.72

In a feigned frenzy of possession divine,
The woman is violated by the lord :
The judges wanting to damn such doctrines,
The victim is immolated by the mob.

6.73

A friar & artisan sneak into town,
Near the walls & gate take up their lodgings :
Plotting against Modena, keeping mum,
Betrayed, claiming they're there for a wedding.

6.74

She who was banished shall return to power,
Revealed the victim of conspiracy :
More than ever she'll know her finest hour :
Certain death for all the seventy-three.

6.75

The King shall command the mighty pilot
To leave the navy for a higher post :
Seven years later he'll be put to rout :
Venice shall fear the Barbarian host.

6.76

The ancient town founded by Antenor
Shall no longer tolerate the tyrant :
In the church they shall slash the cripple's throat,
While the citizens bump off his henchman.

6.77

Deceived by the victory most fraudulent,
Winner taking all, revolt in Germania :
The chief wounded & his son in the tent :
Florence, Imola chased into Romagna.

6.78
Crier victoire du grand Selin croissant,
Par les Romains sera l'Aigle clamé,
Ticcin, Milan, & Gennes n'y consent,
Puis par eux mesmes Basil grand reclamé.

6.79
Près du Tesin les habitans de Loyre,
Garonne & Saonne, Seine, Tarn, & Gironde :
Outre les monts dresseront promontoire,
Conflict donné Po granci, submergé onde.

6.80
De Fez le regne parviendra à ceux d'Europe.
Feu leur cité, & lame trenchera :
Le grand d'Asie terre & mer à grand troupe,
Que bleux pers, croix, à mort dechassera.

6.81
Pleurs, crys & plaincts, hurlement, effraieur,
Cœur inhumain, cruel, noir, & transy :
Leman, les isles de Gennes les majeurs,
Sang espancher, frofaim, à nul mercy.

6.82
Par les desers de lieu, libre, & farouche,
Viendra errer nepveu du grand Pontife :
Assommé à sept avecques lourde souche,
Par ceux qu'après occuperont le cyphe.

6.83
Celuy qu'aura tant d'honneur & caresses,
A son entrée de la Gaule Belgique :
Un temps après fera tant de rudesses,
Et sera contre à la fleur tant bellique.

6.84
Celuy qu'en Sparte Claude ne peut regner,
Il fera tant par voye seductive :
Que du court l'on le fera araigner,
Que contre Roy fera sa perspective.

6.78
Victorious over great Crescent Selene,
He shall be acclaimed by Romans as Eagle :
Pavia, Milan, Genoa disagree,
Then decide to demand their own Basil.

6.79
Near the Ticino, people from the Seine,
Garonne & Saone, Loire & Tarn & Gironde
Beyond the mountains shall a bridgehead gain :
The battle erupts: Po swollen, flood zone.

6.80
The realm of Fez into Europe shall spread,
Burning its cities, slashing with the sword :
Land & sea, the horde of the Asian lord,
Blue turbans most, shall hunt the cross to death.

6.81
Tears, shrieks & moans, vociferation, fright,
Inhuman heart, cruel, & blacker than stone :
In Leman and Genoa's greater isles,
Bloodshed, no wheat to eat, no mercy shown.

6.82
Through the wilderness & the forest thick
Shall wander the nephew of the Pontiff :
Murdered by seven with a candlestick,
Who shall proceed to seize the chalice.

6.83
He who shall be a great celebrity
Upon his entry into Belgic Gaul
Shall soon thereafter most ungracious be,
With much hostility toward the flower.

6.84
He who's too lame over Sparta to reign
Shall find his way through guile & much deceit :
But sooner or later he'll be arraigned,
For he shall have the King within his sights.

6.85
La grand cité de Tharse par Gaulois
Sera destruite, captifz tous à Turban :
Secours par mer du grand Portugalois,
Premier d'esté le jour du sacre Urban.

6.86
Le grand Prelat un jour après son songe,
Interpreté au rebours de son sens :
De la Gascoigne luy surviendra un monge,
Qui fera eslire le grand Prelat de Sens.

6.87
L'election faicte dedans Frankfort,
N'aura nul lieu Milan s'opposera :
Le sien plus proche semblera si grand fort
Que outre le Rhyn es mareschz chassera.

6.88
Un regne grand demourra desolé,
Auprès del Hebro se feront assemblées :
Monts Pyrennées le rendront consolé,
Lors que dans May feront terres tremblées.

6.89
Entre deux cymbes piedz & mains estachés,
De miel face oingt & de laict substanté :
Guespes & mouches, fitine amour fachés.
Poccilateur faucer, Cyphe tempté.

6.90
L'honnissement puant abhominable
Après le faict sera felicité,
Grand excusé pour n'estre favorable,
Qu'à paix Neptune ne sera incité.

6.91
Du conducteur de la guerre navale,
Rouge effrené, severe horrible grippe,
Captif eschappe de l'aisné dans la basle :
Quand il naistra du grand un filz Agrippe.

6.85

The town of Tarsus by the Gauls shall be
Destroyed, all those in turbans led away :
Help by sea supplied by the Portuguese,
At summer's eve & on St. Urban's Day.

6.86

The day after the Prelate dreams a dream,
Interpreted in its opposite sense :
A Gascon monk shall appear in a gleam,
Meaning he's elected Prelate of Sens.

6.87

The election that was held in Frankfurt
Shall not apply : Milan not so inclined :
His closest kin shall seem such a strong threat
He'll drive him into the bogs beyond the Rhine.

6.88

A mighty kingdom ever desolate,
Near to the Ebro shall be their conclave :
The Pyrenees shall provide him solace,
When the lands all quake in the month of May.

6.89

Between two jugs, his hands & feet tied up,
Face smeared with a mix of milk & honey,
The faithless lover, pricked by wasps & flies,
Throat parched, not a drop to drink in the cup.

6.90

A foul abominable rank disgrace
After which he shall be roundly praised :
The lord excused who averted his face
Lest Neptune be moved to sue for peace.

6.91

The commander of the naval force,
Flushed & fierce, now harshly settles the score :
Captive escapes his elder in a bale,
When an Agrippan son is born to the lord.

6.92

Prince de beauté tant venuste,
Au chef menée, le second faict trahy :
La cité au glaive de poudre, face aduste,
Par trop grand meurtre le chef du roy hay.

6.93

Prelat avare d'ambition trompé,
Rien ne sera que trop viendra cuider :
Ses messagiers, & luy bien attrapé,
Tout au rebours voir qui le bois fendroit.

6.94

Un Roy iré sera aux sedifragues,
Quant interdicts seront harnois de guerre :
La poison taincte au succre par les fragues
Par eaux meurtris mors, disant serre, serre.

6.95

Par detracteur calumnie à puynay,
Quant istront faicts enormes & martiaux :
La moindre part dubieuse à l'aisnay,
Et tost au regne seront faicts partiaux.

6.96

Grande cité à soldartz abandonnée,
Onques ny eust mortel tumult si proche :
O quelle hideuse calamité s'approche,
Fors une offence n'y sera pardonnée.

6.97

Cinq & quarante degrés ciel bruslera,
Feu approcher de la grand cité neufve,
Instant grand flamme esparse sautera,
Quant on voudra des Normans faire preuve.

6.98

Ruyné aux Volques de peur si fort terribles,
Leur grand cité taincte, faict pestilent :
Piller Sol, Lune & violer leurs temples :
Et les deux fleuves rougir de sang coulant.

6.92
The prince of such great beauty & power
Brought to the chief, betrayed a second time :
Town put to the sword, face burned by powder,
The king hating the chief for all his crimes.

6.93
Greedy bishop, so duped by ambition,
As to believe it all without a clue :
He & his envoys now in submission :
A woodsman would take quite a different view.

6.94
A King raging at wreckers of the see,
When arms of war are put under the ban :
Poison tainting the sugared strawberries :
Dunked in water, dying, shouting "Close Ranks!"

6.95
A liar shall defame the younger prince
When his feats of war cause stupefaction :
His elder is denied all preference,
And soon the whole realm falls into factions.

6.96
The great city to soldiers is abandoned,
Never was deadly tumult so close by :
Oh, what hideous disaster comes nigh,
Not a single offense shall be pardoned.

6.97
The sky shall burn at forty-five degrees,
The great new city threatened by the fire :
The flames leaping here & there suddenly
As they seek to deal with the Normans' ire.

6.98
Ruin to the Volcae, fearsome to behold,
Their great city tainted, with plague aflood :
Their churches sacked, seized their silver & gold,
And both their rivers running red with blood.

6.99

L'ennemy docte se tournera confus,
Grand camp malade, & defaict par embusches,
Monts Pyrennées & Pœnus luy seront faicts refus,
Proche du fleuve descouvrant antiques oruches.

6.100

Legis Cantio Contra Ineptos Criticos.

Quos legent hosce versus mature censunto,
Profanum vulgus, et inscium ne attrestato :
Omnesque Astrologi, Blenni, Barbari procul sunto,
Qui aliter facit is rite, sacer esto.

CENTURIE VII

7.1

L'arc du thresor par Achilles deceu,
Aux procréés sceu la quadrangulaire :
Au faict Royal le comment sera sceu,
Corps veu pendu au veu du populaire.

7.2

Par Mars ouvert Arles ne donra guerre,
De nuict seront les soldartz estonnés :
Noir, blanc à l'inde dissimulés en terre,
Souz la faincte umbre traistres verez & sonnés.

7.3

Après de France la victoire navale,
Les Barchinons, Saillinons, les Phocens,
Lierre d'or, l'enclume serré dedans la basle,
Ceux de Ptolon au fraud seront concens.

7.4

Le duc de Langres assiegé dedans Dolle,
Accompaigné d'Ostun & Lyonnois :
Geneve, Auspour, joincts ceux de Mirandole,
Passer les monts contre les Anconnois.

6.99

The learnèd foe shall turn around, confused,
His troops ailing, by ambushes undone :
The Pyrenees & Pennines to him refused :
Near the river unearthing ancient stones.

6.100

Incantation of the Law Against Inept Critics.

Let those who read these lines consider them with care,
Let the profane & vulgar herd keep to the side :
Astrologers, Fools & Barbarians, beware,
May he who defies be cursed by the sacred rites.

CENTURY VII

7.1

The treasure arch by Achilles concealed,
Descendants shall the panel recognize :
The how & why of the royal decree,
Corpses hanging before the public's eyes.

7.2

War once declared, Arles shall refuse to fight,
The soldiers shall all be surprised at night :
Black, white, hid in the ground Indian-style,
Out of the faint dark, traitors in profile.

7.3

After the victory of France at sea,
The Barchinons, Salians, Phocaeans :
Golden ivy, anvil wrapped in a bale,
Those of Ptolon shall aid in the deceit.

7.4

The duke of Langres besieged at Dole,
With those from Ostun & the Lyon region:
Geneva, Augsburg, those of Mirandole
Shall cross the mounts against Ancona's legion.

7.5
Vin sur la table en sera respandu,
Le tiers n'aura celle qu'il pretendoit :
Deux fois du noir de Parme descendu,
Perouse à Pize fera ce qu'il cuidoit.

7.6
Naples, Palerme, & toute la Secille,
Par main barbare sera inhabitée,
Corsicq, Salerne & de Sardeigne l'isle,
Faim, peste, guerre fin de maux intemptée.

7.7
Sur le combat des grans chevaux legiers,
On criera le grand croissant confond :
De nuict tuer, monts, habits de bergiers,
Abismes rouges dans le fossé profond.

7.8
Flora fuis, fuis le plus proche Romain,
Au fesulan sera conflict donné :
Sang espandu les plus grans prins à main,
Temple ne sexe ne sera pardonné.

7.9
Dame à l'absence de son grand capitaine,
Sera priée d'amours du Viceroy :
Faincte promesse & malheureuse estraine,
Entre les mains du grand prince Barrois.

7.10
Par le grand prince limitrophe du Mans,
Preux & vaillant chef de grand exercite :
Par mer & terre de Gallotz & Normans,
Calpre passer, Barcelone pillé isle.

7.11
L'enfant Royal contemnera la mere,
Oeil, piedz blessés, rude, inobeissant :
Nouvelle à dame estrange & bien amere,
Seront tués des siens plus de cinq cens.

7.5
Over the table the wine shall be spilled,
The third shall not have the lady he desired :
From the black of Parma descended twice,
Perugia shall do to Pisa what it wills.

7.6
Naples, Palermo & all Sicily
Shall be occupied by Barbarian hand :
Salerno, Corsica & Sardinia,
Famine, plague, endless ills throughout the land.

7.7
After the light cavalry's swift success,
They shall proclaim the great crescent vanquished :
Night combat, mountains, & as shepherds dressed,
Red abysses in the depths of the ditch.

7.8
Flee Flora, flee the nearest one from Rome,
At Fiesole shall the war be declared :
Blood shall be shed, the mighty overcome,
Neither church nor sect shall from this be spared.

7.9
A lady, her great captain now absent,
Shall be loved by the Viceroy from afar :
A promise feigned, an unlucky present,
In the grasp of the great prince from Bar.

7.10
For the great prince who rules nearby Le Mans,
Leading his army with courage & style :
On land & sea of the French & Normans,
Pass Gibraltar, loot Barcelona's isle.

7.11
His mother shall despise the royal child,
Coarse, disobedient, bad feet, bad eye :
For the lady a sad & strange surprise :
More than five hundred of her men shall die.

7.12

Le grand puisné fera fin de la guerre,
Aux dieux assemble les excusés :
Cahors, Moissac iront long de la serre,
Reffus Lectore, les Agenois razés.

7.13

De la cité marine & tributaire,
La teste raze prendra la satrapie :
Chasser sordide qui puis sera contraire,
Par quatorze ans tiendra la tyrannie.

7.14

Faux exposer viendra topographie,
Seront les cruches des monuments ouvertes :
Pulluler secte, faincte philosophie,
Pour blanches, noires, & pour antiques vertes.

7.15

Devant cité de l'Insubre contrée,
Sept ans sera le siege devant mis :
Le tresgrand Roy y fera son entrée,
Cité, puis libre hors de ses ennemis.

7.16

Entrée profonde par la grand Royne faicte
Rendra le lieu puissant inaccessible :
L'armée des trois lyons sera deffaite,
Faisant dedans cas hideux & terrible.

7.17

Le prince rare de pitié & clemence,
Viendra changer par mort grand cognoissance :
Par grand repos le regne travaillé,
Lors que le grand tost sera estrillé.

7.18

Les assiégés couloureront leurs paches,
Sept jours après feront cruelle issue :
Dans repoulsés, feu, sang, sept mis à l'hache,
Dame captive qu'avoit la paix tissue.

7.12

The younger born shall put an end to war,
And recommend the pardoned to the gods :
Moissac shall flee his clutches, & Cahors :
Lectoure repulsed, Agen reduced to sod.

7.13

Of the maritime tributary city
The shaved head shall seize the satrapy,
Expel the rat, his future enemy,
For fourteen years exercise tyranny.

7.14

The scythe shall expose the topography,
Earthen pots revealed at the ancient sites :
Sects pullulate, & sham philosophy :
New mistaken for old, & black for white.

7.15

To the city of the Insubrian plain
For seven long years a siege they shall lay :
The mighty King shall enter it one day,
Free the city, chase its enemies away.

7.16

The mighty gate erected by the Queen,
The site impregnable, thus fortified :
The army of three lions shall know defeat :
Hideous & horrific scene inside.

7.17

The rare pity & mercy of this king
Whose death shall transform simply everything :
In times of great peace, the realm at ill ease,
When the lord goes down to major defeat.

7.18

The besieged shall paint the truce their own hue,
Seven days later they'll counterattack :
Fire, blood, seven hacked to death, driven back :
The lady captured who had wove the truce.

7.19

Le fort Nicene ne sera combatu,
Vaincu sera par rutilant metal :
Son faict sera un long temps debatu,
Aux citadins estrange espouvantal.

7.20

Ambassadeurs de la Toscane langue,
Avril & May Alpes & mer passer :
Celuy de veau expoussera l'harangue,
Vie Gauloise ne venant effacer.

7.21

Par pestilente inimitié Volsicque,
Dissimulée chassera le tyrant :
Au pont de Sorgues se fera la traffique,
De mettre à mort luy & son adherant.

7.22

Les citoyens de Mesopotamie,
Yrés encontre amis de Tarracone,
Jeux, ritz, banquetz, toute gent endormie,
Vicaire au Rosne, prins cité, ceux d'Ausone.

7.23

Le Royal sceptre sera contrainct de prendre,
Ce que ses predecesseurs avoient engaigé :
Puis que l'aneau on fera mal entendre,
Lors qu'on viendra le palays saccager.

7.24

L'ensevely sortyra du tombeau,
Fera de chaines lier le fort du pont :
Empoysonné avec œuf de barbeau,
Grand de Lorraine par le Marquis du Pont.

7.25

Par guerre longue, l'exercite expuiser,
Que pour souldartz ne trouveront pecune :
Lieu d'or, d'argent, cuir on viendra cuser,
Gaulois ærain, signe croissant de Lune.

7.19

There shall be no fight for the fort of Nice,
It shall fall to the dazzling gleam of gold :
Its fate shall long be open to surmise,
Citizens thinking it a strange scarecrow.

7.20

Ambassadors of the tongue of Tuscany
Shall pass the Alps & sea in April, May :
He of Vaud shall expose the colloquy,
Lest life in Gaul be completely erased.

7.21

Dissimulated pestilential hate
Shall chase the tyrant from the Volcae land :
At the bridge of Sorgues the pact shall be made
To put the man to death & his henchman.

7.22

The citizens of Mesopotamia,
Incensed at their friends in Tarragona :
Games, rituals, feasts, one & all asleep :
Vicar at Rhône, city seized, Ausonia.

7.23

The royal scepter he'll be forced to take,
Like his predecessors changing status :
Then with the ring they shall prevaricate,
When they proceed to plunder the palace.

7.24

He who was buried shall step from the tomb
And wrap the strongman of the bridge in chains :
Marquis du Pont shall proceed to poison
With barbel roe the great lord of Lorraine.

7.25

By endless warring the army is spent,
No money to pay the various platoons :
Instead of gold, silver, leather they'll mint :
Gallic bronze, the sign of the crescent Moon.

7.26
Fustes & gallées autour de sept navires,
Sera livrée une mortelle guerre :
Chef de Madric recevra coup de vires,
Deux eschapées & cinq menées à terre.

7.27
Au cainct de Vast la grand cavalerie,
Proche à Ferrage empeschée au bagaige :
Promt à Turin feront tel volerie,
Que dans le fort raviront leur hostaige.

7.28
Le capitaine conduira grande proye,
Sur la montaigne des ennemis plus proche :
Environné, par feu fera tel voye,
Tous eschappez or trente mis en broche.

7.29
Le grand duc d'Albe se viendra rebeller
A ses grans peres fera le tradiment :
Le grand de Guise le viendra debeller,
Captif mené & dressé monument.

7.30
Le sac s'approche, feu, grand sang espandu,
Po, grand au fleuve, aux bouviers l'entreprise,
De Gennes, Nice, après long attendu,
Foussan, Turin, à Savillan la prinse.

7.31
De Languedoc, & Guienne plus de dix,
Mille voudront les Alpes repasser :
Grans Allobroges marcher contre Brundis,
Aquin & Bresse les viendront recasser.

7.32
Du mont Royal naistra d'une casane,
Qui cave et compte viendra tyranniser,
Dresser copie de la marche Millane,
Favene, Flora d'or & gents espuiser.

7.26
Caravels & galleons out to thrash
Seven ships, fighting them to the last man :
The Madrid chief receiving several shafts :
Two shall escape & five be towed to land.

7.27
The immense cavalry near Vasto's fort
By Ferrajo shall cut off the supplies :
At Turino they'll plunder with such sport
That from the fort their hostage they shall hie.

7.28
The captain shall capture many a prey
In the mountains, the enemy in sight :
Surrounded, by fire he shall make his way :
All shall escape, save thirty burned alive.

7.29
Duke of Alba shall rise in rebellion,
Betraying his forefathers before him :
The great duke of Guise shall overwhelm him,
Take him prisoner & set up his tomb.

7.30
The sack at hand, fire everywhere, bloodshed,
Po, waters rising, & herdsman displeased :
From Genoa, Nice, waiting without end,
Fossano, Turin, at Savigliano seized.

7.31
From Languedoc & Guyenne more than ten
Thousand shall want to cross over the Alps :
Against Brindisi Allobrogian men
Shall march, repulsed by Aquino, Brescia.

7.32
From Mount Royal shall be born on a farm
One who shall tyrannize vault & account :
He'll raise an army from the Milanese march,
Drain men & gold from Fayence & Florence.

7.33
Par fraude, regne, forces expolier,
La classe obsesse, passages à l'espie :
Deux fainctz amys se viendront rallier,
Esveiller hayne de long temps assoupie.

7.34
En grand regret sera la gent Gauloise,
Cœur vain, legier, croira temerité :
Pain, sel, ne vin, eaue, venin ne cervoise,
Plus grand captif, faim, froit, necessité.

7.35
La grande pesche viendra plaindre, plorer,
D'avoir esleu, trompés seront en l'aage :
Guiere avec eux ne voudra demourer,
Deçeu sera par ceux de son langaige.

7.36
Dieu, le ciel, tout le divin verbe à l'unde,
Pourté par rouges sept razes à Bizance :
Contre les oingz trois cens de Trebisconde,
Deux loix mettront, & horreur, puis credence.

7.37
Dix envoyés, chef de nef mettre à mort,
D'un averty, en classe guerre ouverte :
Confusion, chef, l'un se picque & mord,
Leryn, Stecades, nefz cap dedans la nerte.

7.38
L'aisné Royal sur coursier voltigeant,
Picquer viendra, si rudement courir :
Gueulle, lipée, pied sans l'estrein pleigeant,
Trainé, tiré, horriblement mourir.

7.39
Le conducteur de l'armée Françoise,
Cuidant perdre le principal phalange :
Par sus pavé de lavaigne & d'ardoise,
Soy parfondra par Gennes gent estrange.

7.33

The forces of the kingdom sapped by fraud,
The army besieged, under surveillance :
Two pretend friends shall form themselves a squad
To awaken hatreds long in abeyance.

7.34

The French shall be bereft of all good cheer,
Lightheartedness shall be held to be foolish :
No bread, salt, wine, water, medicines, beer :
Their noblest captive : hunger, cold, anguish.

7.35

The great fishery shall protest & lament
The election : time shall prove them wrong :
He shall not choose to remain among them,
Disappointed by those who speak his tongue.

7.36

Good lord, the Divine Word is out at sea,
Borne by seven tonsured reds to Byzance :
Against Trebizond's three hundred devotees,
Shall pass two laws: horror, then faith at last.

7.37

Ten sent to put the ship captain to death,
The fleet at war, one shall give him warning :
Confusion, captain : one then stabbed to death :
Off Lérins, Hyères : ships, cape in the gloaming.

7.38

The eldest prince on his galloping steed,
Spurring it on until it pants for breath :
Mouth swollen by bit, his foot coming free
From stirrup, dragged to a horrible death.

7.39

The leader of the fighting force of France,
Fearing the loss of his main formation :
Advancing over the pavement of slate,
Through Genoa shall pour the alien nation.

7.40
Dedans tonneaux hors oingz d'huille & gresse,
Seront vingt un devant le port fermés
Au second guet par mort feront prouesse :
Gaigner les portes & du guet assommés.

7.41
Les oz des piedz & des mains enserrés,
Par bruit maison longtemps inhabitée :
Seront par songes concavant deterrés,
Maison salubre & sans bruyt habitée.

7.42
Deux de poison saisiz nouveau venuz,
Dans la cuisine du grand Prince verser :
Par le souillard tous deux au faict congneuz,
Prins qui cuidoit de mort l'aisné vexer.

7.40

Hidden in casks smeared tight with grease & oil,
Before the port twenty-one shall be sealed :
At second watch unto the death they'll toil,
Gaining the gates & by the watch be killed.

7.41

Hand & foot bones clapped into creaking chains,
House long abandoned because of these sounds :
Dug out by dreams, they shall all flit away :
House now healthful again, its loud guests gone.

7.42

Two unknowns seized in the prince's kitchen
In the act of pouring out some poison :
The scullion shall catch them in their deed :
The one who thought to kill the prince is seized.

To the Most Invincible, Most Powerful, and Most Christian Henri King of France the Second; Michel Nostradamus his most humble, most obedient servant & subject, Victory & Felicity.

With that sovereign respect which I have experienced, O most Christian & victorious King, ever since my long-obscured face has presented itself before the deity of Your Immeasurable Majesty, ever since then have I remained perpetually dazzled, never ceasing to honor & worthily venerate that day when I first presented myself before a Majesty so unique & so humane.

Now, searching for some occasion whereby I might manifest my goodness & openness of heart, so that I might thereby amply extend my gratitude to Your Most Serene Majesty.

Now, seeing that to declare this by my deeds was impossible, combined with my singular desire to be transported from my all too protracted darkness & obscurity & suddenly be illumined before the face of the sovereign Eye & Prime Monarch of the World, I was therefore long in doubt to whom I should dedicate these three Centuries of my remaining Prophecies that round off the thousand, & having long meditated this act of such rash audacity, I have ventured to address Your Majesty, not daunted like those mentioned by that most eminent author Plutarch (in his Life of Lycurgus), who were so astounded by the cost of the offerings & gifts brought as sacrifices to the temples of the immortal gods of those times that, fearing the expense, they dared not present themselves at the temples.

This notwithstanding, seeing your Royal Splendor to be accompanied by such incomparable humanity, I have ventured an address to you, not as to those Kings of Persia whom it was absolutely forbidden to stand before, much less approach.

But it is to a Prince most prudent & wise that I have dedicated my nocturnal & prophetic computations, composed out of natural instinct &

accompanied by poetic furor rather than according to the rules of poetry, & most of them composed in accord with Astronomical calculations corresponding to the years, months & weeks of the regions, countries, & most of the towns & cities of all Europe, including Africa & a portion of Asia, as these regions change & approach their various latitudes, & all this composed in a natural manner: someone who might do well to wipe his nose could retort that their rhythm is as facile as their meaning is difficult.

That, O Most Humane King, is because most of these prophetic quatrains are so knotty that people cannot make their way through them, much less interpret them, nonetheless, wanting to set out in writing the years, towns, cities, regions where most of them will occur, especially those of the year 1585 & of the year 1606, reckoning from the present time, which is the fourteenth of March 1557, & extending far beyond the advent of the beginning of the seventh millennium (as carefully worked out by computation), when, insofar as my astronomic calculations & other knowledge manage to reach that far, the adversaries of Jesus Christ & his Church shall become legion, all of which has been composed & calculated in days & hours carefully chosen & set out as accurately as I could.

And all of this when *Minerva was free & well-disposed*, by calculating almost as many of the events of future times as of ages past, comprehending the present & what everywhere over the course of time shall come to be recognized as the future, precisely as is written, with nothing superfluous added, although some might say: *As for the future, the truth cannot entirely be determined.*

It is true, Sire, by that natural instinct of mine which was bequeathed to me by my ancestors, not intending to prophesy but adjusting & according this natural instinct with my lengthy computations, & emptying my soul, mind & heart of all care, worry & disquiet through mental calm & tranquillity.

All of which was brought into accord & foretold *by means of the bronze tripod.*

Although there are many who would attribute to me what is as much mine as it is nothing of the kind, for Eternal God alone (who is the thorough examiner of human hearts, holy, just & merciful) is the true judge of this & to whom I pray that he defend me from the calumny of wicked men who, in their own slanderous fashion, would likewise also want to inquire how all your most venerable ancestors among the Kings of France cured people of scrofula, while those of other nations cured snake bites, & yet others had a certain instinct for the divinatory arts, & other examples too long to recount here.

Notwithstanding those in whom the malignity of the evil spirit shall be apprehended over the course of time after my earthly extinction, my writings shall fare better than during my own lifetime, even if I have made errors in my computation of ages or prove unable to please all persons.

May it please your more than Imperial Majesty to forgive me, for I protest before God & his Saints that I do not claim to put anything into writing in the present epistle which might go against the true Catholic faith, devising my Astronomic calculations to the best of my ability: for the extent of time of our ancestors is such (deferring to the correction of sounder judgment) that Adam the first man preceded Noah by about a thousand two hundred years (not reckoning by such Gentile calculations as Varro committed to writing, but solely by the Holy Scriptures, & according to my feeble understanding of my own Astronomic calculations).

About a thousand eighty years after Noah & the universal flood came Abraham who, according to some, was a masterful Astrologer, the first inventor of the Chaldean alphabet: after him came Moses some five hundred fifteen or sixteen years later, & between his time & that of David some five hundred seventy years elapsed.

Then, between the time of David & the time of our savior & redeemer Jesus Christ, born of the unique virgin, one thousand three hundred fifty years elapsed (according to some chronographers): some may object that this calculation cannot be true, because it differs from that of Eusebius.

And from the time of human redemption until the loathsome blandishments of the Saracens there were six hundred twenty-one years or thereabouts, from which one can easily adduce the amount of time gone by, if my computations hold good for all nations, for everything has been calculated according to the movements of the heavens, combined with the emotions, handed down to me by my ancestors, which come over me at certain forsaken hours.

But the danger of these times requires, O Most Serene King, that such secret events be expressed only in enigmatic terms which however have only one sense & single meaning, with no ambiguity or amphibiological calculation thrown in: but rather under a cloud of obscurity, with a natural infusion approximating the phrasing of one of the thousand & two Prophets who have existed since the creation of the world, according to the computations & Punic Chronicle of Joel: *I will pour out my spirit upon all flesh; & your sons & your daughters shall prophesy.*

But such prophecy proceeded from the mouth of the Holy Ghost who was the sovereign & eternal power, in conjunction with the celestial bodies, & some of this prophetic company predicted great & marvelous happenings: as concerns me here, I would never claim such a title, never, please God, I readily admit that everything proceeds from God, & I render Him thanks, honor & everlasting praise, without having adulterated it with anything that might have proceeded from *prophetic utterance*, but *from God, from nature*, & most of this accompanied by the movement of the heavens, much like seeing in a flaming mirror (as with clouded vision) those immense events (so sad & prodigious) & calamities that now begin to draw nigh on account of the ruling religious factions.

These shall befall, first, the temples of God, then, second, those who depend on the land, who shall fall into such decline, together with a thousand other calamities, which shall come to be known to occur in due time.

For God shall look upon the long-barren Great Lady, who thereupon shall produce two principal children: but she being at risk, the girl-child to whom she shall have given birth shall, by the foolhardiness of her age, be in danger of dying in her eighteenth year, & shall be unable to live beyond her thirty-sixth year, so that Great Lady shall leave behind three males & one female, & two of these shall not have had the same father, & among the three brothers there shall be such differences, but then they shall be so reunited & so in accord that the third & fourth parts of Europe shall tremble: the youngest in age shall sustain & augment the Christian monarchy: sects elevated & suddenly repressed, Arabs retreating, Kingdoms united, new Laws promulgated: among the other children, the oldest one shall rule the land whose escutcheon is furious crowned Lions, their paws on the intrepid coat of arms.

The second in age, accompanied by the Latins, shall launch a distant campaign, until a second furious & trembling path shall be beaten to the Mount of Jove, descending from which he shall drive up into the Pyrenees which shall not, however, be transferred to the ancient crown, & there shall be a third human bloodbath & for a long time war shall not occur during Lent.

And the daughter shall be married off for the preservation of the Christian Church, with her lord falling into the paganism of the new infidels, she shall have two daughters, one in matrimony, one out of it, confirmed by the Catholic Church.

And the other one, to her great confusion & belated remorse, shall decide to ruin her, & there shall be three regions due to the extreme differences among the leagues, that is to say, Romania, Germany, Spain, which shall create divers sects by military means, starting from the 50th & 52nd degrees of latitude & all the distant religions paying homage to the regions of Europe north of the 48th parallel, the latter who shall be the first to quake in foolish fear, then the Westerners, the Southerners & Easterners shall tremble in their turn, their power such that what they bring about through concord & union shall prove to be insuperable by military conquest.

They shall be equal in nature, but most different in faith.

After this, the Barren Lady, greater in power than the second one, shall be received by two nations, by the first one rendered stubborn by him who was once all-powerful, by the second, & by the third which shall extend its forces toward the perimeter of Eastern Europe, toward the already slaughtered & subdued Pannonia, & shall by sea spread its sway to Adriatic Sicily with its Myrmidons & thoroughly battered Germans, & the Barbarian sect shall be mightily afflicted & chased away by all the Latins.

Then the great Empire of the Antichrist shall commence in Attila, &

Xerxes shall descend upon the earth with a great & innumerable host, such that the coming of the Holy Ghost, proceeding from the 48th degree, shall undergo transmigration, chasing out the abomination of the Antichrist, making war on the prince who is the great vicar of Jesus Christ, & against his church, & his reign shall be *for a time & to the end of time,*

& this shall be preceded by a solar eclipse more dark & gloomy than any between the creation of the world & the death & passion of Jesus Christ, or from that time to now,

& it shall be in the month of October that some great translation shall take place, such that one shall think that the gravity of the earth has lost its natural movement & that it is to be plunged into an abyss of perpetual darkness & during the previous spring & thereafter there shall be extreme changes, transformations of kingdoms, with great earthquakes & with the sprouting up of the New Babylon, that wretched daughter, augmented by the abomination of the first holocaust,

& this shall last for only seventy-three years, seven months, then there shall burgeon from that branch which has for long lain barren, proceeding from the fiftieth degree, one who shall renew the whole Christian Church.

And great peace & union & concord shall be established between children who turn their faces away from each other, separated by different kingdoms, & such a peace shall be made that the promoter & sustainer of military factions shall remain chained in the deepest pit by the various religious movements, & the Kingdom of the Rabid One, playing the sage, shall be united.

And the countries, towns, cities, realms & provinces which shall have abandoned their original ways in order to gain liberty (only to find themselves more ensnared), shall be secretly grieved by the loss of their freedom & their perfect religion, & shall start striking out to the left, then return to the right,

& reestablishing their long-abandoned holiness with their original scriptures, so that the great dog, the huge mastiff shall then go forth & destroy everything, even that which has previously been perpetuated, & the temples shall be rebuilt as in ancient times, & the priesthood shall be restored to its former state, & shall start whoring & luxuriating & committing countless crimes.

And at the eve of another desolation, when she shall have attained her highest & most sublime dignity, military potentates & their forces shall rise up against her, & her two swords shall be removed & only her banners shall remain, & from the crooked path that so attracts them, these forces shall be placed back on the straight path by the people, unwilling to submit themselves to those of the opposite extreme with their wrists cocked, touching ground, spurring things on until from a branch of that long-barren Lady shall be born one who shall deliver all the nations from their meek & willing enslavement, placing himself under the protection of Mars, robbing Jupiter of all his honors & dignities, for the sake of that free city set up & located in another narrow Mesopotamia.

And the chief & governor shall be cast out from the middle & hung up high, ignorant of the conspiracy mounted against him with the help of the second Thrasybulus, who shall have been plotting all this for some time,

& all the shameful impurities & abominations shall be laid to the charge & consigned to the shadows of the veiled light, which shall cease toward the end of the overthrow of his regime, & the chiefs of the Church shall fall short of the love of God, & several of them shall renounce the true faith, & of the three sects, the middle one shall be allowed by its members to fall somewhat into decline.

The first shall spread throughout Europe, most of Africa shall be exterminated by the third, profiting from those poor in spirit whom madmen shall encourage into extravagance & luxury, & corrupt.

The common people shall rise up in support, chase out the backers of the legislators, & from the way realms shall have been weakened by the Easterners, it shall seem that God the Creator has loosed Satan from the prisons of hell to give birth to the great Dog & Dogam, who shall create such an abominable breach within the Churches that neither the reds nor the whites (being without eyes or hands) shall know what to make of it, & their power shall be taken from them.

Then more persecutions shall be visited upon the Church than ever before.

Meanwhile, there shall arise a plague so great that more than two-thirds of the earth shall be wiped out.

So much so that it shall be impossible to ascertain the true owners of fields & houses, & the weeds in the city streets shall rise higher than the knees.

And the clergy shall be completely wiped out & the warlords shall usurp all the revenues from the City of the Sun, from Malta & the Isles of Hyères, & the great chain of the port which takes its name from the sea-calf shall be opened.

And the beaches shall see a new invasion from the sea, hoping to deliver the Sierra Morena from its first recapture by the Muslims.

And all their assaults shall not be in vain, & the place which was once the abode of Abraham shall fall to the blows of those who hold the Jovialists in veneration.

And this very city of Ashem shall be surrounded & assailed from all sides by a most powerful host.

And the Westerners shall weaken their great fleets at sea, & great desolation shall be visited on this kingdom, & its grandest cities shall be emptied of people & those who enter into them shall be subject to the wrathful vengeance of God.

And the sepulcher, long an object of immense veneration, shall remain there in the open, under clear skies, visible to the eyes of heaven, the Sun, & the Moon, & the holy place shall be converted into a stable for herds large & small, & put to profane uses.

O what calamitous afflictions shall befall women with child at this time, & then shall the principal Eastern chief be vanquished by the Northerners & the Westerners & most of his people, stirred up, shall be put to death, overwhelmed & the rest put to flight, & his children by several women shall be imprisoned, & then shall be fulfilled the prophecy of the Royal Prophet: *That he hear the groaning of the prisoners & deliver the children of those doomed to die,*

what mighty oppression shall then be visited upon the Princes & Governors of kingdoms, especially those maritime & Eastern ones whose tongues are commingled with all the others (the tongues of the Latins & the Arabs, through communication with the Punic), & all these Kings shall be chased off, overthrown, exterminated,

not at all because of any action on the part of the forces of the Kings of the North, or because of the drawing near of our own age through the three secretly united in their search for death, plotting ambushes against each other,

& the renewal of this triumvirate shall last seven years, & the renown of their religion shall spread through the world, & the sacrifice of the Holy & Immaculate Host shall be maintained,

& then the Lords of the North (two in number) shall be victorious over the Easterners, & such a great noise & tumult of war shall they make that all the East shall tremble in fear of these brothers (although not brothers) of the North.

And because, Sire, in this address I am presenting these predictions almost confusedly, both in respect to when they shall take place & to the amount of time which shall elapse before they occur, which conforms very little (if at all) with that which has been set forth above, yet it was determined by astronomy & other means (including the Holy Scriptures), which can in no way fail, & had I wanted to give a date to each quartile, this could be done: but would not be agreeable to all, still less were I to interpret them, at least until, Sire, Your Majesty had fully authorized me to do so, lest slanderers be provided the occasion to nip at me.

However, counting the years from the creation of the world until the birth of Noah, there passed one thousand five hundred & six years, & from the birth of Noah to the completion of the Ark, at the approach of the universal deluge, there passed six hundred years (whether the years were solar or lunar or a mixture of the two, though I maintain that the Holy Scriptures hold them to be solar).

And at the end of these six hundred, Noah entered the Ark to be saved from the flood, & this flood was universal on earth, & lasted one year & two months.

And from the end of the flood to the birth of Abraham there passed two hundred ninety-five years.

And from the birth of Abraham to the birth of Isaac there passed one hundred years.

And from Isaac to Jacob, sixty years, & from the time he entered Egypt until he left there passed one hundred thirty years.

And from the entry of Jacob into Egypt until he left it there passed four hundred thirty years.

And from the exodus from Egypt until the building of the temple by Solomon in the fourth year of his reign there passed four hundred eighty (or fourscore) years.

And from the building of the temple to the birth of Jesus Christ, according to the calculations of the sacred writings, there passed four hundred ninety years.

Thus, according to my calculations (gathered from sacred scriptures), this all comes to about four thousand one hundred seventy-three years & eight months, more or less.

But given the diversity of sects, from the time of Jesus Christ to now, I shall say nothing, & having calculated & computed the present prophecies, all according to the order of the chain which contains its own revolution, all according to astronomical doctrine & natural instinct, & after a while, finding the time when Saturn shall go retrograde beginning on the seventh of the month of April until August 25, Jupiter on June 14 until October 7, Mars from April 17 to June 22, Venus from April 9 to May 22, Mercury from February 3 to February 27.

And after that, from June 1 to June 24, & from September 25 to October 16, Saturn in Capricorn, Jupiter in Aquarius, Mars in Scorpio, Venus in Pisces, Mercury for a month in Capricorn, Aquarius & Pisces, the Moon in Aquarius, the Dragon's head in Libra:

its tail in the opposite sign following a conjunction of Jupiter with Mercury, with a quartile aspect between Mars & Mercury, & the head of the Dragon alongside a conjunction of the Sun with Jupiter, the year shall be peaceful without any eclipse whatsoever, & it shall mark the commencement of everything that shall endure,

& beginning with that year the Christian Church shall be persecuted more fiercely than it ever was in Africa, & this shall last until the year seventeen ninety-two, which shall be considered the beginning of a new age:

after this the Roman people shall begin to reestablish itself & to chase off certain dark shadows, recovering a bit of its original brilliance, but not without great divisions & continual upheavals.

Thereafter Venice shall with great force & power raise its wings very high, not short of the might of ancient Rome, & at that time great ships from Byzantium, allied with the Ligurians, & with the support of the Northern powers, shall somehow prevent the two Cretans from keeping their promises.

The arks built by the Warriors of ancient times shall sail in company through Neptune's waves, & in the Adriatic there shall be mighty discord, what was united shall be torn asunder, to a mere house shall be reduced that which was (& is) a major city, including the Pampotania & Mesopotamia of Europe on the forty-fifth parallel & others on the forty-first, forty-second & thirty-seventh,

& at that time, & in these countries, the power of Hell shall set against the Church of Jesus Christ the power of the enemies of its creed, which shall be the second Antichrist, who shall persecute this Church & its true Vicar, by the means of the power of the temporal Kings, who in their ignorance shall be seduced by tongues that shall cut more deeply than any sword in a madman's hands:

the said reign of the Antichrist shall last only to the death of him who was born at the beginning of the age, & of the other one in the city of Plancus, accompanied by the elected ruler of Modona Fulcy, by Ferrara, supported by the Ligurians of the Adriatic, & the proximity of greater Sicily.

Then the Gallic Ogmion shall pass the Mountain of Jove, accompanied by such a vast host that the Empire of his great law shall extend very far, & at that time & for some times thereafter the blood of the Innocents shall be shed profusely by villains of middling station, then, because of great floods, the memory of the things contained in such documents shall suffer an incalculable loss, even the memory of writing: this shall befall the People of the North by the will of God, & Satan shall be bound again.

And universal peace shall be established among mankind, & the Church of Jesus Christ shall be delivered from tribulation, however much the Philistines might want to meld the honey of their malice with their pestilent seduction,

& this shall come to pass near the seventh millennium, when the sanctuary of Jesus Christ shall no longer be trampled underfoot by the infidels from the North, the world approaching a mighty conflagration, although according to my calculations in my Prophecies the course of time runs much further.

In the Epistle that several years ago I dedicated to my son César Nostradamus, I declared a number of points fairy openly, without making predictions.

But here, O Sire, are contained many great & marvelous events which those who come after shall see,

& during the period of these Astrological calculations, devised in accordance with the sacred writings, the persecution of the clergy shall find its origin in the power of the Northern Kings, allied with the Easterners,

& this persecution shall last eleven years (or somewhat less), whereupon the chief Northern King shall fall,

& at the end of these years, his Southern ally shall intensify the persecution for three years, thanks to the seductive apostasy of one who shall hold absolute power within the Church Militant,

& the holy people of God who observe his law, & all the religious orders, shall be fiercely persecuted & afflicted, so much so that the blood of the true church people shall flow far & wide,

& one of the horrible temporal Kings shall be covered with great praise by his followers for having spilled more of the blood of innocent church people than anyone could spill of wine,

& this King shall commit incredible crimes against the Church, & blood shall flow in the public streets & temples, like water after a violent rain, & the nearby rivers shall run red with blood, as shall the seas in the wake of another naval battle, causing one King to say to another: *The sea blushed red with warring ships.*

Then during the same year & those following there shall ensue a most horrible plague, all the more stupendous because of the famine which shall precede it, & there shall be tribulations throughout the Latin nations greater than any that have occurred since the foundation of the Christian Church, leaving traces in various regions of Spain.

Thereupon the third King of the North, hearing the laments of the people of his principal domain, shall raise a mighty army, & crossing the straits once traversed by his ancestors recent & remote, shall restore almost everything to its former state,

& the great vicar of the cope shall be restored to his original state, but abandoned of all comfort & company, he shall return to find the Holy of Holies destroyed by paganism, & the old & new Testaments thrown out & burned,

& thereafter the Antichrist shall be the Prince of Hell, & again (for the last time) all the Kingdoms of Christianity & those of the infidels shall tremble for the space of twenty-five years, & there shall be even more terrible wars & battles, & towns, cities, castles & all the other buildings shall be burned, sacked, & destroyed with great shedding of virgin blood, wives & widows raped, suckling babes dashed & shattered against city walls, & so many evils shall be committed through the influence of Satan, Prince of Hell, that almost the entire world shall find itself undone & abandoned,

& before these events a number of fabulous birds shall cry out *Huy huy* in midair & then swiftly vanish,

& after this has gone on for a long time, there shall be a virtual renewal of another reign of Saturn, or Age of Gold,

& God, hearing the afflictions of his people, shall order Satan to be bound & thrown deep into the pit of the bottomless abyss,

& then a universal peace shall commence between God & man, & Satan shall remain bound for about the space of a thousand years, & turning all his might against the power of the Church, shall then return unleashed.

That all these figures accurately adapt the Sacred Scriptures to visible celestial bodies, namely, Saturn, Jupiter, Mars & others conjoined, as might be seen at more length by applying various quartiles.

I could have gone more deeply into my calculations, & adapted the ones to the others.

But seeing, O Most Serene King, that some given to censure shall raise difficulties, & that this shall cause me to withdraw my pen for the sake of my nocturnal repose,

Many events, most powerful of Kings, of the most astounding sort, are to transpire soon, but we neither can nor will include them all in this your epistle, but in order to comprehend certain horrible facts, a few must be set forth, even though your generosity & humanity toward all men are so great, as is your divine piety, that you alone seem worthy of the great title of the Most Christian King, to whom the highest authority in all religion should be deferred.

But I shall only beseech you, O most merciful King, by this singular & prudent humanity of yours, to hearken rather to the desire of my heart, & the sovereign diligence with which I have sought to obey your Most Serene Majesty, ever since my eyes came so near to your solar splendor, yet only inasmuch as the grandeur of my labors might achieve or deserve it. From Salon this 27th June, fifteen hundred and fifty-eight.

Written by Michael Nostradamus
Of Salon de Craux
In Provence.

CENTURIE VIII

8.1
PAU, NAY, LORON plus feu qu'à sang sera.
Laude nager, fuir grand aux surrez.
Les agassas entree refusera.
Pampon, Durance les tiendra enserrez.

8.2
Condon & Aux & autour de Mirande
Je voy du ciel feu qui les environne.
Sol Mars conjoint au Lyon puis marmande
Fouldre, grand gresle, mur tombe dans Garonne.

8.3
Au fort chasteau de Viglanne & Resviers
Sera serré le puisnay de Nancy :
Dedans Turin seront ards les premiers,
Lors que de dueil Lyon sera transy.

8.4
Dedans Monech le coq sera receu,
Le Cardinal de France apparoistra
Par Logarion Romain sera deceu
Foiblesse à l'aigle, & force au coq naistra.

8.5
Apparoistra temple luisant orné,
La lampe & cierge à Borne & Breteuil.
Pour la lucerne le canton destorné,
Quand on verra le grand coq au cercueil.

8.6
Clarté fulgure à Lyon apparante
Luysant, print Malte subit sera estainte,
Sardon, Mauris traitera decepvante,
Geneve à Londes à coq trahyson fainte.

8.7
Verceil, Milan donra intelligence,
Dedans Tycin sera faite la paye.
Courir par Siene eau, sang, feu par Florence.
Unique choir d'hault en bas faisant maye.

CENTURY VIII

8.1

More fire than blood at OLORON, PAU, NAY :
Lord swims Aude & escapes to nearby streams :
To all magpies shall entrance be gainsaid :
Pompon, Durance shall keep them well besieged.

8.2

Condom & Auch & all around Mirande,
I see the sky-fire that's surrounding them :
Sun, Mars in Leo, & then at Marmande
Hail, lightning : wall falling into Garonne.

8.3

In the fortress of Viglanne & Resviers
Shall Nancy's younger prince be locked & barred :
In Turin the first shall be put to fire,
Lyon taking its mourning very hard.

8.4

In Monaco the cock shall be received,
The Cardinal of France shall soon step forth :
By Ogmion shall the Roman be deceived,
The eagle weaken & the cock gain force.

8.5

At Bornel, Breteuil, lamps & candles bright,
He'll appear in church ornate & shining,
Every canton turning to glimpse that light,
To see the great cock in coffin reclining.

8.6

A blazing light at Lyon shall be seen,
Then, Malta seized, be extinguished again :
Sardinia the Moors shall treat with deceit :
Genoa at sea : to cock, treason feigned.

8.7

Through Vercelli, Milan the news shall transpire :
Ticino is where the wound shall be made :
Florence floods Siena with blood, water, fire :
Maying, the one & only falls from grace.

8.8
Pres de linterne dans de tonnes fermez,
Chivaz fera pour l'aigle la menee,
L'esleu cassé luy ses gens enfermez,
Dedans Turin rapt espouse emmenee.

8.9
Pendant que l'aigle & le coq à Savone
Seront unis Mer Levant & Ongrie,
L'armee à Naples, Palerne, Marque d'Ancone
Rome, Venise par Barb' horrible crie.

8.10
Puanteur grande sortira de Lausanne,
Qu'on ne saura l'origine du fait,
Lon mettra hors toute la gent loingtaine
Feu veu au ciel, peuple estranger deffait.

8.11
Peuple infiny paroistra à Vicence
Sans force feu brusler la Basilique
Pres de Lunage deffait grand de Valence,
Lors que Venise par more prendra pique.

8.12
Apparoistra aupres de Buffalorre
L'hault & procere entré dedans Milan
L'Abbé de Foix avec ceux de saint Morre
Feront la forbe abillez en vilan.

8.13
Le croisé frere par amour effrenee
Fera par Praytus Bellerophon mourir,
Classe à mil ans la femme forcenee
Beu le breuvage, tous deux apres perir.

8.14
Le grand credit d'or, d'argent l'abondance
Fera aveugler par libide l'honneur
Sera cogneu d'adultere l'offence,
Qui parviendra à son grand deshonneur.

8.8

Near Cisterna in barrels sealed up tight,
For the eagle Chivas shall plot the move :
His troops besieged, elected one in flight :
At Turin wife taken by force, removed.

8.9

While cock & eagle fight for Savona,
The Levant Sea & Hungary shall unite :
Troops at Palermo, Naples, Ancona :
Rome, Venice filled with horrid Barbar cries.

8.10

From Lausanne such a strong stench shall arise
That no one shall know from where it has come :
Aliens expelled, fire seen in the skies :
All the foreign people shall be undone.

8.11

Multitudes shall appear at Vicenza,
Set fire to the Basilica without force :
Near Lunigiana falls the lord Valenza,
While Venice shall be harassed by the Moors.

8.12

He shall appear near to Buffalora
Who entered Milan so high & mighty :
The abbot of Foix with those of St. Maur
Dressed as peasants shall commit treachery.

8.13

The crusader monk, his head turned by love,
Shall like Proetus make Bellerophon die :
Troops at Milan : the woman come unstrung :
The potion drunk, the two shall then expire.

8.14

The mass of silver, the great credit of gold,
Shall cause honor to be blinded by greed :
Once the crime of debasing coin is known,
It shall bring him great dishonor indeed.

8.15
Vers Aquilon grand efforts par hommasse
Presque l'Europe & l'univers vexer,
Les deux eclypses mettra en telle chasse,
Et aux Pannons vie & mort renforcer.

8.16
Au lieu que HIERON feit sa nef fabriquer,
Si grand deluge sera & si subite,
Qu'on n'aura lieu ne terres s'atacquer
L'onde monter Fesulan Olympique.

8.17
Les bien aisez subit seront desmis
Par les trois freres le monde mis en trouble,
Cité marine saisiront ennemis,
Faim, feu, sang, peste, & de maux le double.

8.18
De Flora issue de sa mort sera cause,
Un temps devant par jeusne & vieille bueyre
Par les trois lys luy feront telle pause,
Par son fruit sauve comme chair crue mueyre.

8.19
A soustenir la grand cappe troublee,
Pour l'esclaircir les rouges marcheront,
De mort famille sera presque accablee.
Les rouges rouges le rouge assomeront.

8.20
Le faux messaige par election fainte
Courir par urben, rompue pache arreste,
Voix acheptees, de sang chapelle tainte,
Et à un autre l'empire contraicte.

8.21
Au port de Agde trois fustes entreront
Portant l'infect non foy & pestilence
Passant le pont mil milles embleront,
Et le pont rompre à tierce resistance.

8.15

A mannish northern female's great actions
Shall vex Europe & well-nigh all Creation :
She shall put two eclipses to the flight,
Bolster Pannonia through death & life.

8.16

In the place HIERON built his famous ship,
Such a sudden & mighty flood there'll be
That there'll be no more land at which to grip :
Waves shall climb Olympian Fiesole.

8.17

The well-to-do shall quickly be dethroned,
By the three brothers the world shall be troubled :
The city of the sea be seized by foes,
Famine, fire, blood, plague, & all ills redoubled.

8.18

From Flora come, his early death she'll cause
With a drink that young & old did once imbibe :
By the three lilies they'll give him much pause,
Through her untouched fruit like flesh thought ripe.

8.19

To support the great cope in his troubles sore
The reds shall work to put things right instead :
His family shall find itself at death's door :
The reddest reds killing his redness dead.

8.20

The election fixed, false rumors shall flood
The city: snapped, the pact no longer stands :
Votes bought, the holy chapel stained with blood,
The empire transferred to another's hands.

8.21

Into the port of Agde three foists shall sail,
Bringing foul heresy & pestilence :
From across the sea they'll steal thousands away,
And break through the thrice-resistant bridge.

8.22
Gorsan, Narbonne, par le sel advertir
Tucham, la grace Parpignan trahye,
La ville rouge n'y vouldra consentir.
Par haulte vol drap gris vie faillie.

8.23
Lettres trouvees de la royne les coffres,
Point de subscrit sans aucun nom d'hauteur
Par la police seront cachez les offres.
Qu'on ne scaura qui sera l'amateur.

8.24
Le lieutenant à l'entree de l'huys,
Assomera le grand de Parpignan,
En se cuidant saulver à Montpertuis.
Sera deceu bastard de Lusignan.

8.25
Coeur de l'amant ouvert d'amour fertive
Dans le ruysseau fera ravyr la Dame,
Le demy mal contrefera lassive,
Le pere à deux privera corps de l'ame.

8.26
De Caton es trouves en Barsellonne,
Mys descouvers lieu terrouers & ruyne,
Le grand qui tient ne tient vouldra Pamplonne.
Par l'abbage de Monserrat bruyne.

8.27
La voye auxelle l'une sur l'autre fornix
Du muy deser hor mis brave & genest,
L'escript d'empereur le fenix
Veu en celuy ce qu'à nul autre n'est.

8.28
Les simulachres d'or & d'argent enflez,
Qu'apres le rapt au lac furent gettez
Au descouvert estaincts tous & troublez.
Au marbre escript presciptz intergetez.

8.22

Coursan, Narbonne admonished about salt,
Prosperous Tuchan, Perpignan betrayed :
The red city shall refuse to comply :
The good life gone while the gray banner waves.

8.23

Letters are found inside the queen's coffers,
No signature, no name of the author :
The police shall hide the secret offers :
No one shall know who shall be the lover.

8.24

The lieutenant standing by the gate
Shall put to death the lord of Perpignan :
Thinking Montpertuis a safe haven,
He'll be deceived, the bastard of Lusignan.

8.25

The lover's heart rent by a furtive love,
He shall ravish the Lady in the shoals :
The hussy shall half protest too much,
Father shall strike both bodies from their souls.

8.26

Traces of Cato found in Barcelona,
Discovered in a place of awe & ruin :
The lord without holdings wants Pamplona :
The abbey of Montserrat lies in gloom.

8.27

By the aqueduct with its arch on arch,
Le Muy deserted save darnel & broom :
The inscription of the phoenix Emperor :
Seeing in this what no one else presumes.

8.28

The idols tricked out with silver & gold
Which after the sack were thrown in the lake,
When found, shall all be dimmed & dulled :
Marble inscriptions, scattered, out of date.

8.29

Au quart pillier lon sacre à Saturne.
Par tremblant terre & deluge fendu
Soubz l'edifice Saturnin trouvee urne,
D'or Capion ravy & puis rendu.

8.30

Dedans Tholoze non loing de Belvezer
Faisant un puy loing, palais d'espectacle
Tresor trouvé un chacun ira vexer,
Et en deux locz tout & pres del vasacle.

8.31

Premier grand fruit le prince de Pesquiere
Mais puis viendra bien & cruel malin,
Dedans Venise perdra sa gloire fiere
Et mys à mal par plus joyue Celin.

8.32

Garde toy roy Gaulois de ton nepveu
Qui fera tant que ton unique filz.
Sera meurtry à Venus faisant voeu,
Accompaigné de nuict que trois & six.

8.33

Le grand naistra de Veronne & Vincence,
Qui portera un surnom bien indigne.
Qui à Venise vouldra faire vengeance
Luy mesme prins homme du guet & signe.

8.34

Apres victoire du Lyon au Lyon
Sus la montaigne de JURA Secatombe
Delues & brodes septieme million
Lyon, Ulme à Mausol mort & tombe.

8.35

Dedans l'entree de Garonne & Bayse
Et la forest non loing de Damazan
Du marsaves gelees, puis gresle & bize
Dordonnois gelle par erreur de mezan.

8.29

At the fourth column long sacred to Saturn,
By flood & earthquake split & upturned :
Beneath the Saturnine pile is found the urn
Of gold looted by Caepio, then returned.

8.30

Not far from the Belvedere in Toulouse,
Digging a ditch for a palais des spectacles :
A treasure's found that shall deeply confuse,
In two places quite close to the Bazacle.

8.31

Pescara's prince shall bear good fruit at first,
But then a cruel bastard he shall become :
At Venice his fine glory shall be burst,
And be threatened by the younger Selin.

8.32

Beware, O French king, of your own cousin,
Who shall act much as if your only son :
While making vows to Venus he'll be smitten,
Consorting at night after a mere nine months.

8.33

At Verona or Vicenza born the lord
Who shall bear a nickname that is most vile :
Who on Venice would wish to sow discord,
Yet shall be captured by a watchman's sign.

8.34

One Lion having crushed the other Lion,
Hecatomb on the JURA mountains :
Drowned & charred some seven million,
Lion scourged, killed at the mausoleum.

8.35

Where the Baïse flows into the Garonne,
And in the forest near to Damazan :
Frozen marshes, then hail & north wind strong :
Dordogne freezes, getting the month all wrong.

8.36

Sera commis conte oingdre aduché
De Saulne & sainct Aulbin & Bell'oeuvre
Paver de marbre de tours loing espluché
Non Bleteram resister & chef d'oeuvre.

8.37

La forteresse aupres de la Tamise
Cherra par lors le Roy dedans serré,
Aupres du pont sera veu en chemise
Un devant mort, puis dans le fort barré.

8.38

Le Roy de Bloys dans Avignon regner
Une autre foys le peuple emonopolle,
Dedans le Rosne par murs fera baigner
Jusques à cinq le dernier pres de Nolle.

8.39

Qu'aura esté par prince Bizantin,
Sera tollu par prince de Tholoze.
La foy de Foix par le chief Tholentin,
Luy faillira ne refusant l'espouse.

8.40

Le sang du Juste par Taurer la daurade,
Pour se venger contre les Saturnins
Au nouveau lac plongeront la maynade,
Puis marcheront contre les Albanins.

8.41

Esleu sera Renad ne sonnant mot,
Faisant le saint public vivant pain d'orge,
Tyrannizer apres tant à un cop,
Mettant à pied des plus grans sus la gorge.

8.42

Par avarice, par force & violence
Viendra vexer les siens chiefz d'Orleans,
Pres saint Memire assault & resistance,
Mort dans sa tante diront qu'il dort leans.

8.36
County to duchy connection is planned
Via Saulne & Saint-Aubin & Bell'Oeuvre,
Paved with marble from far-off towers grabbed :
The Bletterans name resists: a chef d'oeuvre.

8.37
The great tower by the river Tamise
Shall fall just when the King is locked within :
Near the bridge he shall be seen in chemise :
One dead out front, then barred inside again.

8.38
The King of Blois shall reign in Avignon,
Monopolize the land with single rule :
Over the walls so they'll bathe in the Rhône
Some five he'll throw, the latter toward Yule.

8.39
To him who stood with the Byzantine prince
Toulouse's prince no courtesy denies :
By the trust of Foix he'll not be convinced,
That Toulouse prince, yet not refuse the bride.

8.40
The blood of the Just for Dorade & Taur,
To take revenge against the Saturnines :
They'll cast the whole crew into the new pool,
Then shall march off against the Albanines.

8.41
The Fox shall be elected, bite his tongue,
Play the saint, publicly live on barley bread :
Then suddenly a tyrant he'll become,
His foot at the throat of powerful men.

8.42
By avarice, by force & violence,
In confusion his Orléans chiefs he'll keep :
Near Saint-Memire, assault & resistance,
So dead in his tent they'll say he's asleep.

8.43

Par le decide de deux choses bastars
Nepveu du sang occupera le regne
Dedans lectoyre seront les coups de dars
Nepveu par peur pleira l'enseigne.

8.44

Le procrée naturel dogmion,
De sept à neuf du chemin destorner
A roy de longue & amy aumi hom,
Doit à Navarre fort de PAU prosterner.

8.45

La main escharpe & la jambe bandee,
Longs puis nay de Calais portera
Au mot du guet la mort sera tardee,
Puis dans le temple à Pasques saignera.

8.46

Pol mensolee mourra trois lieuës du rosne,
Fuis les deux prochains tarasc destrois :
Car Mars fera le plus horrible trosne,
De coq & d'aigle de France freres trois.

8.47

Lac Trasmenien portera tesmoignage,
Des conjurez sarez dedans Perouse,
Un despolle contrefera le sage,
Tuant Tedesq de sterne & minuse.

8.48

Saturne en Cancer, Jupiter avec Mars,
Dedans Fevrier Chaldondon salvaterre.
Sault Castallon assailly de trois pars,
Pres de Verbiesque conflit mortelle guerre.

8.49

Satur. au beuf jove en l'eau, Mars en fleiche,
Six de Fevrier mortalité donra,
Ceux de Tardaigne à Bruge si grand breche,
Qu'à Ponteroso chef Barbarin mourra.

8.43
Through the demise of two misbegot things,
The monarch's nephew shall the kingdom hold :
Within Lectoure then shall the spearpoints ring :
Fearful, the nephew shall his banner fold.

8.44
The natural offspring of Ogmion
Shall rout some seven to nine lines of troops
From their routes &, friend of the demi-man,
In Navarre shall soon make PAU's fort bow down.

8.45
The younger son of Calais shall long display
His bandaged leg, his hand in sling for show :
On watch's word the death shall be delayed,
Then in the church at Easter blood shall flow.

8.46
He'll die at Pol-Mausole, three leagues from Rhône :
Flee both, not far from the Tarascon strait :
For Mars shall sit upon his awful throne :
Cock vs. eagle, three French brothers wait.

8.47
The Transmenian lake sends the message
About the plotters holed up in Pérouse :
A despot shall play the role of a sage,
Killing the Teuton, hacking him askew.

8.48
Saturn in Cancer, Jupiter with Mars,
Calends of February, Salvatierra :
Passes of Castille assailed from three parts :
Near Briviesca war & mortal terror.

8.49
Saturn in Bull, Jove in Water Carrier,
Mars in Archer, Feb. six, everything dies :
Catalans at Bruges shall break such barrier
That at Ponterosso Barb. chief shall die.

8.50
La pestilence l'entour de Capadille,
Un autre faim pres de Sagont s'appreste :
Le chevalier bastard de bon senille,
Au grand de Thunes fera trancher la teste.

8.51
Le Bizantin faisant oblation,
Apres avoir Cordube à soy reprinse :
Son chemin long repos pamplation,
Mer passant proy par la Colongna prinse.

8.52
Le roy de Bloys dans Avignon regner,
D'amboise & seme viendra le long de Lyndre
Ongle à Poitiers sainctes aesles ruiner
Devant Boni.

8.53
Dedans Bolongne vouldra laver ses fautes,
Il ne pourra au temple du soleil,
Il volera faisant choses si haultes
En hierarchie n'en fut oncq un pareil.

8.54
Soubz la colleur du traicte mariage,
Fait magnanime par grand Chyren selin,
Quintin, Arras, recouvrez au voyage
D'espaignolz fait second banc macelin.

8.55
Entre deux fleuves se verra enserré,
Tonneaux & caques unis à passer outre,
Huict pontz rompus chef à tant enferré
Enfans parfaictz sont jugutez en coultre.

8.56
La bande foible le tertre occupera
Ceux du hault lieu feront horribles crys,
Le gros troppeau d'estre coin troublera,
Tombe pres D.nebro descouvers les escris.

8.50
Pestilence falls all about Capellades,
Near Sagunto, famine raises its head :
Misbegotten knight of the king so aged
Shall take the Tunis lord & him behead.

8.51
The Byzantine shall make oblations,
Once he's taken Cordoba for his sake :
At journey's end, long rest, pampination :
Passing through the Pillars their prey they'll take.

8.52
In Avignon the king of Blois shall reign,
From Amboise he'll swarm up the Indre :
Poitiers uncle shall clip his sacred wings
Before Bonny

8.53
At Bologna he'd like to wash his sins,
Impossible at the church of the sun :
He'll soar so high, his deeds such linchpins :
Never did the clergy see such a man.

8.54
Beneath the cover of a marriage pact,
Great Selin Chyren's magnanimous act :
Quentin, Arras recovered in his path :
Worse than a butcher's plank that Spanish clash.

8.55
Between two rivers shall find himself trapped,
Barrels & casks lashed in order to pass :
Eight bridges down, the chief grievously stabbed,
Noblemen's children with their throats all slashed.

8.56
The weakest flank shall occupy the heights
And there create a fierce hullabaloo :
The main force shall attack toward the right :
Near Ebro they'll find writings on a tomb.

8.57
De souldat simple parviendra en empire,
De robe courte parviendra à la longue
Vaillant aux armes en eglise ou plus pyre,
Vexer les prestres comme l'eau fait l'esponge.

8.58
Regne en querelle aux freres divisé,
Prendre les armes & le nom Britannique
Tiltre Anglican sera tard advisé,
Surprins de nuict mener à l'air Gallique.

8.59
Par deux fois hault, par deux fois mis à bas
L'orient aussi l'occident foyblira
Son adversaire apres plusieurs combats,
Par mer chassé au besoing faillira.

8.60
Premier en Gaule, premier en Romanie,
Par mer & terre aux Angloys & Parys
Merveilleux faitz par celle grand mesnie
Violant terax perdra le NORLARIS.

8.61
Jamais par le decouvrement du jour
Ne parviendra au signe sceptrifere
Que tous ses sieges ne soyent en sejour,
Portant au coq don du TAG amifere.

8.62
Lors qu'on verra expiler le saint temple,
Plus grand du rosne leurs sacrez prophaner
Par eux naistra pestilence si ample,
Roy fuit injuste ne fera condamner.

8.63
Quant l'adultere blessé sans coup aura
Meurdry la femme & le filz par despit,
Femme assoumee l'enfant estranglera:
Huit captifz prins, s'estouffer sans respit.

8.57

From simple soldier he shall race to power,
From short tunic to long robe he shall lunge :
Most valiant in arms, though at his worst hour
Shall pursue priests as water does a sponge.

8.58

The realm in strife, twixt brothers divided,
They'll take up arms & vie for Britain's name :
The term Anglican later provided :
Seized by night: dancing to the Gallic tune.

8.59

Twice shall it rise, & twice be brought low,
The East like the West ever growing weak :
After full many battles shall its foe,
Pursued by sea, founder in time of need.

8.60

First in Gaul & first in Romania,
By land & sea vs. the English & Paris,
This mighty host with such marvelous deeds :
Violent monster shall lose NOLARIS.

8.61

Never by the slow dawning of the day
Shall he attain a scepter-bearing post,
Until all the sees have been vacated
And cock offered the gift of an armed host.

8.62

When they see the holy church laid to waste,
The great one of the Rhône, its rites profaned,
Through them shall arise such enormous plagues,
He'll not condemn the unjust, King astray.

8.63

The adulterer, wounded without a blow,
Shall murder his wife & son out of spite :
His wife knocked senseless, his child he shall choke :
Eight captives seized, smothered without respite.

8.64

Dedans les Isles les enfans transportez,
Les deux de sept seront en desespoir,
Ceux du terrouer en seront supportez,
Nom pelle prins des ligues fuy l'espoir.

8.65

Le vieux frustré du principal espoir,
Il parviendra au chef de son empire:
Vingt mois tiendra le regne à grand pouvoir,
Tiran, cruel en delaissant un pire.

8.66

Quand l'escriture D.M. trouvee,
Et cave antique à lampe descouverte,
Loy, Roy, & Prince Ulpian esprouvee,
Pavillon Royne & Duc sous la couverte.

8.67

PAR. CAR. NERSAF, à ruine grand discorde,
Ne l'un ne l'autre n'aura election,
Nersaf du peuple aura amour & concorde,
Ferrare, Collonne grande protection.

8.68

Vieux Cardinal par le jeusne deceu,
Hors de sa charge se verra desarmé,
Arles ne monstres double soit aperceu,
Et Liquiduct & le Prince embausmé.

8.69

Aupres du jeune le vieux ange baisser,
Et le viendra surmonter à la fin :
Dis ans esgaux au plus vieux rabaisser,
De trois deux l'un l'huitiesme seraphin.

8.70

Il entrera vilain, meschant, infame
Tyrannisant la Mesopotamie,
Tous amys fait d'adulterine d'ame.
Tertre horrible noir de phisonomie.

8.64

Toward the Isles the children transported,
Two out of seven shall be in despair :
The locals shall thereby be supported,
Nompelle taken, the leagues seem not to care.

8.65

Frustrated in his fondest ambitions,
The old one shall reach the heights of power :
Twenty months he'll hold on to his station,
A tyrant cruel, leading to far worse hours.

8.66

When the inscription D.M. shall be found,
And ancient vault by lamplight discovered,
Ulpian law, prince, king shall then redound :
The Duke & his Queen under tent cover.

8.67

PAR., CAR., NERSAF, great ruin & discord,
Nor one nor other shall find election :
The folk of Nersaf shall want love, concord,
Ferrara, Colonna great protection.

8.68

Old cardinal by the younger deceived,
Stripped of his post, he shall appear disarmed :
Arles, show not that the double be perceived,
Neither Liqueduct nor the prince embalmed.

8.69

The agèd angel bows before the young
But shall overmaster him in the end :
Ten years his equal, he'll not be outdone :
One of the three two & eighth seraphim.

8.70

Wicked & vile he shall make his entry
And tyrannize Mesopotamia :
All friends made by the adulterous lady,
Dire monster, black of physiognomy.

8.71
Croistra le nombre si grand des astronomes
Chassez, bannis & livres censurez,
L'an mil six cens & sept par sacre glomes
Que nul aux sacres ne seront asseurez.

8.72
Champ Perusin o l'enorme deffaite
Et le conflit tout au pres de Ravenne,
Passage sacre lors qu'on fera la feste,
Vainqueur vaincu cheval manger la venne.

8.73
Soldat Barbare le grand Roy frappera,
Injustement non eslongné de mort,
L'avare mere du fait cause sera
Conjurateur & regne en grand remort.

8.74
En tetre neufve bien avant Roy entré
Pendant subges luy viendront faire acueil,
Sa perfidie aura tel recontré
Qu'aux citadins lieu de feste & recueil.

8.75
Le pere & filz seront meurdris ensemble
Le prefecteur dedans son pavillon
La mere à Tours du filz ventre aura enfle.
Caiche verdure de feuilles papillon.

8.76
Plus Macelin que roy en Angleterre
Lieu obscur nay par force aura l'empire :
Lasche sans foy, sans loy saignera terre,
Son temps s'approche si pres que je souspire.

8.77
L'antechrist trois bien tost annichilez,
Vingt & sept ans sang durera sa guerre,
Les heretiques mortz, captifs, exilez,
Sang corps humain eau rogie gresler terre.

8.71

So great the number of astronomers,
They'll be hounded, banned, & their books censored
In sixteen oh seven by church councils,
So that none shall feel their safety assured.

8.72

On Perugia's field O what huge defeat,
And so close to Ravenna what affray :
The clergy trampled during a feastday :
The victor's horse the loser's oats shall eat.

8.73

Barbarian soldier shall strike the King
Almost to death for reasons hard to say :
Ambitious mother standing in the wings,
The schemer & the realm shall rue the day.

8.74

Long before the King enters the new land,
While subjects come to extend their greetings,
His perfidy shall be so out of hand,
Citizens shall celebrate their fleecing.

8.75

Father & son together shall be done
In by the count within his pavilion :
The mother at Tours, heavy with a son,
Hides like a butterfly in leaves of green.

8.76

More a butcher than any English king,
Born obscure, to power by force he'll rise :
Faithless, lawless, he shall bleed the land dry,
His time so fast approaching that I sigh.

8.77

The Antichrist, three soon annihilated,
His war shall last seven & twenty years :
Heretics dead, captured, expatriated :
Blood, corpses : on earth a red hail of tears.

8.78

Un Bragamas avec la langue torte
Viendra des dieux [rompre] le sanctuaire,
Aux heretiques il ouvrira la porte
En suscitant l'eglise militaire.

8.79

Qui par fer pere perdra nay de Nonnaire,
De Gorgon sur la sera sang perfetant
En terre estrange fera si tout de taire,
Qui bruslera luy mesme & son entant.

8.80

Des innocens le sang de vefve & vierge.
Tant de maulx faitz par moyen se grand Roge
Saintz simulachres trempez en ardant cierge
De frayeur crainte ne verra nul que boge.

8.81

Le neuf empire en desolation,
Sera changé du pole aquilonaire.
De la Sicile viendra l'esmotion
Troubler l'emprise à Philip tributaire.

8.82

Ronge long, sec faisant du bon valet,
A la parfin n'aura que son congie
Poignant poyson & lettres au collet
Sera saisi eschappé en dangie.

8.83

Le plus grand voile hors du port de Zara,
Pres de Bisance fera son entreprinse,
D'ennemy perte & l'amy ne sera
Le tiers à deux fera grand pille & prinse.

8.84

Paterne orra de la Sicile crie,
Tous les aprests du goulphre de Trieste,
Qui s'entendra jusque à la trinacrie.
De tant de voiles fuy, fuy l'horrible peste.

8.78

A soldier of fortune with twisty tongue
Shall do the gods' sanctuary great wrong :
To the heretics he'll open the door,
And so stir up the church to holy war.

8.79

He shall kill his whoreson father by sword,
Thereby giving new issue to Gorgon's blood :
In foreign parts to silence he'll be sworn,
He who shall burn himself & his own son.

8.80

Blood of innocents, virgins & widows :
So much pain inflicted by the Great Red :
Holy icons dipped in flaming tallow :
None shall be seen to move, for fear & dread.

8.81

The new empire shall know desolation,
Buffeted by those from the northern climes :
From Sicily the upsurge of emotion
Shall exasperate Philip's enterprise.

8.82

Tall, dry, pinched, playing the faithful servant,
In the end he shall only be dismissed :
Vial of poison & letters as pendants
On his neck, he shall pay for what he risked.

8.83

The biggest fleet that Zara ever saw
Shall maneuver toward the port of Byzance,
Holding neither friend nor foe in awe :
A third shall fall upon both & smash them.

8.84

Paternò shall hear the cry of Sicilia,
Preparations in the gulf of Trieste
Shall soon extend as far as Trinacria :
Flee from this fleet, flee this horrific pest.

8.85
Entre Bayonne & à saint Jean de Lux
Sera posé de Mars le promottoire
Aux Hanix d'Aquillon Nanar hostera lux
Puis suffocqué au lict sans adjutoire.

8.86
Par Arnani tholoser ville franque,
Bande infinie par le mont Adrian,
Passe riviere, Hurin par pont la planque
Bayonne entrer tous Bihoro criant.

8.87
Mort conspiree viendra en plein effect,
Charge donnee & voiage de mort,
Esleu, crée, receu par siens deffait.
Sang d'innocence devant soy par remort.

8.88
Dans la Sardeigne un noble Roy viendra.
Que ne tiendra que trois ans le royaume,
Plusieurs coulleurs avec soy conjoindra,
Luy mesmes apres soin someil marrit scome.

8.89
Pour ne tumber entre mains de son oncle,
Qui ses enfans par regner trucidez,
Orant au peuple mettant pied sur Peloncle
Mort & traisné entre chevaulx bardez.

8.90
Quand des croisez un trouvé de sens trouble
En lieu du sacre verra un boeuf cornu
Par vierge porc son lieu lors sera comble,
Par roy plus ordre ne sera soustenu.

8.91
Frymy les champs des Rodanes entrees
Ou les croysez seront presque unys,
Les deux brassieres en pisces rencontrees
Et un grand nombre par deluge punis.

8.85
Between Bayonne & port Saint-Jean-de-Luz
Mars shall reach its extremity & head :
To northern allies Navarre shall light refuse,
Who shall die smothered, helpless in his bed.

8.86
Through Ernani, Villafranca, Tolosa,
Over Adrian mounts the mighty host flows :
They cross river on planks laid over boats,
Enter Bayonne, all shouting "Bichoro!"

8.87
The death plot put into execution,
The charges stick & the voyage to death :
Undone by those behind his election,
Innocent blood inspiring repentance.

8.88
Into Sardinia shall come a noble King,
His reign no more than three years in number :
Several colors to his aid he shall bring :
After taunts, his cares afflict his slumbers.

8.89
Not to fall into the hands of his uncle
Who slaughtered his children to reach the throne,
Pleading with the plebs, foot on Peloncle,
He dies, & is dragged along by barded horse.

8.90
When one of the crusaders goes berserk
And sees a horned ox in the holy church,
The pig shall take over the virgin's place
And the king no longer maintain his base.

8.91
Among fields crowded with folk from the Rhône,
Where crusaders shall almost be as one,
The two braziers into Pisces shall come,
And a great number be punished by flood.

8.92
Loin hors du regne mis en hazard voiage
Grand ost duyra pour soy l'occupera,
Le roy tiendra les siens captif ostage
A son retour tout pays pillera.

8.93
Sept moys sans plus obtiendra prelature
Par son deces grand scisme fera naistre :
Sept moys tiendra un autre la preture
Pres de Venise paix union renaistre.

8.94
Devant le lac ou plus cher fut getté
De sept mois, & son host desconfit
Seront Hyspans par Albannois gastez
Par delay perte en donnant le conflict.

8.95
Le seducteur sera mis en la fosse,
Et estaché jusques à quelque temps,
Le clerc uny le chef avec sa crosse
Pycante droite attraira les contens.

8.96
La synagogue sterile sans nul fruit
Sera receu entre les infideles
De Babylon la fille du porsuit
Misere & triste luy trenchera les aisles.

8.97
Aux fins du VAR changer le pompotans,
Pres du rivage les trois beaux enfans naistre.
Ruyne au peuple par aage competans
Regne au pays changer plus voir croistre.

8.98
Des gens d'eglise sang sera espandu,
Comme de l'eau en si grande abondance :
Et d'un long temps ne sera restanché
Ve Ve au clerc ruyne & doleance.

8.92

Far from the realm on perilous voyage,
The king shall lead his host, their faith confirm,
Hold all of his own prisoners hostage,
Then sack the whole land upon his return.

8.93

Seven months, no more, shall last his prelacy :
A great schism shall arise at his decease :
Seven months shall another know sovereignty :
Near Venice peace & union find release.

8.94

Before the lake in which his dearest was cast
At seven months, down on its luck his host :
Spaniards by Alba's troops are overmastered :
He who hesitates to attack is lost.

8.95

Into the pit the seducer shall be thrown
And be bound & tied a while for sheer sport :
Clerk & lord with crosier standing alone,
Who, laying to the right, shall draw support.

8.96

The barren, fruitless synagogue of yore
Shall find welcome among the infidels :
The sad daughter of the victims of Babylon
Shall have her wretched wings clipped quite well.

8.97

At the limits of the VAR power shall change,
Near its banks three fine children shall be born :
Ruin to the people when they come of age,
So altering the realm it shall grow no more.

8.98

The blood of churchmen shall be freely shed
Like the gush of water in inundation
And for a long time shall it spill unchecked :
Woe to the clergy, ruin & lamentation.

8.99

Par la puissance des trois rois temporelz,
En autre lieu sera mis le saint siege :
Où la substance de l'esprit corporel,
Sera remys & receu pour vray siege.

8.100

Pour l'abondance de larme respandue
Du hault en bas par le bas au plus hault
Trop grande foy par ieu vie perdue,
De soif mourir par habondant deffault.

CENTURIE IX

9.1

Dans la maison du traducteur de Bourc
Seront les lettres trouvees sus la table,
Bourgne, roux, blanc, chanu tiendra de cours,
Qui changera au nouveau connestable.

9.2

Du hault du mont Aventin voix ouye,
Vuydez vuydez de tous les deux costez,
Du sang des rouges sera l'ire assomye,
D'Arimin Prato, Columna debotez.

9.3

La magna vaqua à Ravenne grand trouble,
Conduitz par quinze enserrez à Fornase
A Romme naistre deux monstres à teste double
Sang, feu, deluge, les plus grands à l'espase.

9.4

L'an ensuyvant descouvertz par deluge,
Deux chefs esleuz le premier ne tiendra
De fuyr umbre à l'un d'eux le refuge,
Saccagee case qui premier maintiendra.

8.99

By power of the three temporal kings,
They shall change the site of the Holy See :
Where the corporal substance of the spirit
Shall be restored & received as the true seat.

8.100

Through excess of tears so easily wrung
From high to low, from low to high above,
Lives lost in the gullible play of faith :
To die of thirst from surfeit of mistake.

CENTURY IX

9.1

In the house of the translator of Bourg,
The letters shall be found on the table :
One-eyed, red hair grizzled, he'll hold the course,
All which shall change with the new constable.

9.2

From the Aventine Hill a voice on high :
Be gone, be gone, all of you, on both sides :
The blood of the red ones shall appease the ire :
From Rimini, Prato, the Colonna drive.

9.3

The magna vaqua, the trouble in Ravenna,
Fifteen locked up in Fornase try to cope :
Two doubled-headed monsters born in Rome :
Blood, fire, flood, leaders swinging by the rope.

9.4

The following year, revealed by the deluge,
Two chiefs elected, the first shall not hold :
Fleeing the dark, one of them seeks refuge,
House plundered, into which the first one stole.

9.5
Tiers doit du pied au premier semblera.
A un nouveau monarque de bas hault
Qui Pyse & Lucques Tyran occupera
Du precedant corriger le deffault.

9.6
Par la Guyenne infinité d'Anglois
Occuperont par nom d'Anglaquitaine
De Languedoc Ispalme Bourdeloys.
Qu'ilz nommeront apres Barboxitaine.

9.7
Qui ouvrira le monument trouvé,
Et ne viendra le serrer promptement.
Mal lui viendra & ne pourra prouvé,
Si mieux doit estre roy Breton ou Normand.

9.8
Puisnay Roy fait son pere mettre à mort,
Apres conflit de mort tres inhoneste :
Escrit trouvé soubson donra remort,
Quand loup chassé pose sus la couchette.

9.9
Quand lampe ardente de feu inextinguible
Sera trouvé au temple des Vestales,
Enfant trouvé feu, eau passant par trible :
Perir eau Nymes, Tholose cheoir les halles.

9.10
Moyne moynesse d'enfant mort exposé,
Mourir par ourse & ravy par verrier.
Par Fois & Pamyes le camp sera posé
Contre Tholose Carcas dresser forrier.

9.11
Le juste à tort à mort lon viendra mettre
Publiquement, & du millieu estaint :
Si grande peste en ce lieu viendra naistre,
Que les jugeans fouyr seront constraint.

9.5

He shall seem a mere third toe to the first,
A new monarch of such tiny stature,
Playing the tyrant to Pisa & Lucca :
Small corrective to his predecessor.

9.6

Anglos by droves shall occupy Guyenne
And then dub it Anglaquitania :
From Languedoc, Lapalme to Bordelais :
Which they shall then name Barboccitania.

9.7

He who opens up the newly found trove
And cannot immediately close the thing,
Evil shall befall him, nor can one prove
What's better, a Breton or Norman king.

9.8

The younger son, now King, shall kill his sire
After deadly conflict full of deceit :
Suspicious letter found remorse inspires,
When hunted wolf assumes his bed of ease.

9.9

When the ever-burning lamp is unearthed
Within the Temple of Diana's walls :
Flame found by a child, working with a sieve :
Floods destroy Nîmes, Toulouse's market halls.

9.10

Child of monk & nun left exposed to die,
Killed by a she-bear, dragged off by a boar :
Near Foix & Pamiers shall the army lie,
The scouts of Carcas. at Toulouse's door.

9.11

The just man shall unjustly be condemned
To public death & quite extinguished be :
In this place shall such pestilence ascend
That all the judges shall be forced to flee.

9.12

Le tant d'argent de Diane & Mercure
Les simulachres au lac seront trouvez,
Le figulier cherchant argille neufve
Luy & les siens d'or seront abbrevez.

9.13

Les exilez autour de la Soulongne
Conduis de nuit pour marcher à Lauxois,
Deux de Modene truculent de Bologne,
Mys descouvers par feu de Burançoys.

9.14

Mys en planure chaulderons d'infecteurs,
Vin, miel & huyle, & bastis sur forneaulx
Seront plongez sans mal dit mal facteurs
Sept. fum extaint au canon des borneaux.

9.15

Pres de Parpan les rouges detenus,
Ceux du milieu parfondrez menez loing :
Trois mis en pieces & cinq mal soustenus,
Pour le Seigneur & Prelat de Bourgoing.

9.16

De castel Franco sortira l'assemblee,
L'ambassadeur non plaisant fera scisme :
Ceux de Ribiere seront en la meslée,
Et au grand goulphre desnier ont l'entrée.

9.17

Le tiers premier pys que ne feit Neron,
Vuidez vaillant que sang humain respandre :
R'edifier fera le forneron,
Siecle d'or, mort, nouveau roy grand esclandre.

9.18

Le lys Dauffois portera dans Nansy
Jusques en Flandres electeur de l'empire,
Neufve obturee au grand Montmorency,
Hors lieux provez delivre a clere peyre.

9.12

A potter digging away for fresh clay
Shall unearth silver likenesses untold
Of Hermes & Diana in the lake :
He & his ilk shall have their fill of gold.

9.13

The exiles in the region of Sologne
Shall be marched off by night toward Auxois :
Two from Modena by fierce Bologna
Shall be caught by the fire of Burançoys.

9.14

Dyers' cauldrons shall be set up on the plain,
Filled with wine, honey, oil, placed over fires :
Into these shall be plunged seven without blame,
Boiled until the last wisp of smoke expires.

9.15

Near Perpignan the red ones are detained,
Those in the middle ruined & led away :
Three hacked apart & five barely sustained,
For the Lord & Prelate of Burgundy.

9.16

From Castelfranco troops shall make forays,
The irksome envoy shall go his separate way :
Those of the coast shall leap into the fray,
And deny entry to the mighty bay.

9.17

Worse than Nero shall the third first behave,
How much valiant human blood a waste :
The furnace shall again be set in place,
Golden age gone, the new King an outrage.

9.18

Dauphiné's lily shall dispatch to Nancy,
Flanders-bound, the Elector of the Empire :
More jail time for the great Montmorency,
Far from known paths, thrown upon flaming pyre.

9.19

Dans le millieu de la forest Mayenne,
Sol au lyon la fouldre tombera,
Le grand bastard yssu du gran du Maine,
Ce jour fougeres pointe en sang entrera.

9.20

De nuict viendra par la forest de Reines,
Deux pars vaultorte Herne la pierre blanche,
Le moyne noir en gris dedans Varennes
Esleu cap. cause tempeste feu, sang tranche.

9.21

Au temple hault de Bloys sacre Solonne,
Nuict pont de Loyre, prelat, roy pernicant
Curseur victoire aux maretz de la lone
Dou prelature de blancs à bormeant.

9.22

Roy & sa court au lieu de langue halbe,
Dedans le temple vis à vis du palais
Dans le jardin Duc de Mantor & d'Albe,
Albe & Mantor poignard langue & palais.

9.23

Puisnay jouant au fresch dessouz la tonne,
Le hault du toict du milieu sur la teste,
Le pere roy au temple saint Solonne,
Sacrifiant sacrera fum de feste.

9.24

Sur le palais au rochier des fenestres
Seront ravis les deux petits royaux,
Passer aurelle Luthece Denis cloistres,
Nonain, mallods avaller verts noyaulx.

9.25

Passant les pontz venir pres des rosiers,
Tard arrivé plustost qu'il cuydera,
Viendront les noves espaignolz à Besiers,
Qui icelle chasse emprinse cassera.

9.19
In the midst of the forest of Mayenne,
With Sun in Leo, lightning shall descend :
The bastard issue of the lord of Maine
Shall that day at Fougères be stabbed to death.

9.20
He shall come by night through the woods of Reines,
Two via Pierre Blanche, Herne, & Vaultorte,
The black monk all in gray within Varennes,
Elected cap. causes storm, fire, blood, sword.

9.21
Near Blois' towering church of Saint-Solenne,
Night, Loire bridge, prelate, king doing the kill :
News of victory carried to marshes of Olonne
Whence prelacy of the whites abominable.

9.22
King & court in the place where tongues are run,
Inside the church vis-à-vis the palace :
Dukes of Mantua & Alba in the garden :
Former stabs latter in tongue & palate.

9.23
The younger son at play beneath the vault,
The roof collapsing squarely on his head :
The king his father at Saint-Solenne
During mass shall sanctify the incense.

9.24
From the windows of the palace balcony
Shall be snatched the two little royal kids :
To Orléans, Paris, abbey of Saint-Denis,
Where wicked nuns swallow down the green pits.

9.25
Crossing bridges to hasten toward Rosiers,
Sooner than he thought he shall arrive :
The new Spaniards have their eye on Béziers,
Their enterprise thwarted by his swift drive.

9.26
Nice sortie sur nom des letres aspres,
La grande cappe fera present non sien,
Proche de vultry aux murs de vertes capres
Apres plombin le vent à bon essien.

9.27
De bois la garde vent cloz rond pont sera,
Hault le receu frappera le Daulphin,
Le vieux teccon bois unis passera,
Passant plus oultre du duc le droit confin.

9.28
Voille Symacle port Massiliolique,
Dans Venise port marcher aux Pannons :
Partir du goulfre & sinus Illirique,
Vast à Socile, Ligurs coups de canons.

9.29
Lors que celuy qu'à nul ne donne lieu,
Abandonner vouldra lieu prins non prins :
Feu nef par saignes, bitument à Charlieu,
Seront Quintin Balez reprins.

9.30
Au port de POULA et de saint Nicolas,
Perir Normande au goulfre Phanaticque,
Cap. de Bisance rues crier helas,
Secors de Gaddes & du grand Philipique.

9.31
Le tremblement de terre à Mortara,
Cassich saint George à demy perfondrez,
Paix assoupie, la guerre esveillera,
Dans temple à Pasques absysmes enfondrez.

9.32
De fin porphire profond collon trouvee
Dessoubz la laze escriptz capitolin :
Os poil retors Romain force prouvee,
Classe agiter au port de Methelin.

9.26
Nice leaving its name in bitter letters,
The Pope shall make an unwarranted gift :
Near Voltri with its walls of green capers :
After Piombino, the breeze good & stiff.

9.27
Palace of wood, covered bridge against winds,
The honored guest shall tap the young Dauphin :
The old operator then boards his fleet
And sails away, beyond the duke's demesne.

9.28
The allied fleet in the ports of Marseille
And Venice to march on Pannonia :
They'll sail from the gulf & Illyrian bay
To rape Sicily, bombard Liguria.

9.29
When he who is unrivaled near & far
Decides to cede a place but half-taken :
Fire, ship, swamp, Charlieu, hot tar,
Saint-Quentin, Calais shall be retaken.

9.30
At the port of PULA & Saint Nicholas,
Normans shall perish in Phanatic Bay :
Cap. Byzance's streets full of screams alas,
Saved by Cádiz & the Philippine great.

9.31
All around Mortara the earth shall quake,
St. George Caltagirone half laid waste :
Peace now slumbering, war shall again awake :
In church at Easter the abyss agape.

9.32
A porphyry column found buried deep,
Beneath its base, writings capitoline :
Rome shall overpower the scraggly beards,
Fleet riled up in the port of Mytilene.

9.33

Hercule Roy de Romme & d'Annemarc,
De Gaule trois Guion surnommé,
Trembler l'Itale & l'unde de sainct Marc
Premier sur tous monarque renommé.

9.34

Le part soluz mary sera mittré,
Retour conflict passera sur le thuille :
Par cinq cens un trahyr sera tiltré,
Narbon & Saulce par coutaux avons d'huille.

9.35

Et Ferdinand blonde sera descorte,
Quitter la fleur suyvre le Macedon.
Au grand besoing defaillira sa routte,
Et marchera contre le Myrmidon.

9.36

Un grand Roy prins entre les mains d'un Joyne,
Non loing de Pasque confusion coup cultre :
Perpet. captifs temps que fouldre en la husne,
Lors que trois freres se blesseront & murtre.

9.37

Pont & molins en Decembre versez,
En si haut lieu montera la Garonne :
Murs, edifices, Tholose renversez,
Qu'on ne sçaura son lieu autant matronne.

9.38

L'entree de Blaye par Rochelle & l'Anglois,
Passera outre le grand Aemathien,
Non loing d'Agen attendra le Gaulois,
Secours Narbonne deceu par entretien.

9.39

En Arbissel à Veront & Carcari,
De nuict conduitz pour Savonne atrapper,
Le vifz Gascon Turbi, & la Scerry
Derrier mur vieux & neuf palais gripper.

9.33
King of Rome & Denmark Hercules shall be,
And surnamed leader of tripartite Gaul :
Italy trembles as do St. Mark's seas :
He'll be renowned as monarch over all.

9.34
The mitered one furious at the breach of faith,
War swirls up again among roofs of tile :
By five hundred the treacherous one is blamed,
At Narbonne & Salces, we'll have oil for knives.

9.35
Ferdinand, escorting the fair-haired one,
Shall quit the flower to follow Macedon :
In his hour of need he shall swerve off course,
And end up marching against the Myrmidon.

9.36
A great King in the clutches of a youth,
Near Easter much confusion, flash of knives :
Lightning striking topmast, captives for life,
When three brothers each other kill & wound.

9.37
Bridge & mills in December overturned,
So high shall crest the flooding Garonne :
Walls, buildings all throughout Toulouse upturned,
Destroyed beyond recall, like the Matronne.

9.38
The English entry at Rochelle & Blaye
Shall pass well beyond the Macedonian :
Not far from Agen the Gaul shall wait :
Fed up with parlays, he'll seek Narbonne's aid.

9.39
At Albisola, Veront, Carcari,
To entrap Savona, a night sortie :
Brisk Gascon at Turbie, & La Scerry
New palace behind old wall shall besiege.

9.40

Pres de Quintin dans la forest bourlis,
Dans l'abbaye seront Flamens ranches,
Les deux puisnais de coups my estourdis
Suitte oppressee & garde tous aches.

9.41

Le grand Chyren soy saisir d'Avignon,
De Romme letres en miel plein d'amertume
Letre ambassade partir de Chanignon,
Carpentras pris par duc noir rouge plume.

9.42

De Barsellonne, de Gennes & Venise,
De la Secille peste Monet unis,
Contre Barbare classe prendront la vise,
Barbar, poulse bien loing jusqu'à Thunis.

9.43

Proche à descendre l'armee Crucigere
Sera guettee par les Ismaëlites
De tous cottez batus par nef Raviere,
Prompt assaillis de dix galeres eslites.

9.44

Migres, migre de Genesve trestous
Saturne d'or en fer se changera,
Le contre RAYPOZ exterminera tous,
Avant l'a ruent le ciel signes fera.

9.45

Ne sera soul jamais de demander,
Grand Mendosus obtiendra son empire
Loing de la cour fera contremander,
Pymond, Picard, Paris, Tyron le pire.

9.46

Vuydez, fuyez de Tholose les rouges
Du sacrifice faire expiation,
Le chef du mal dessouz l'umbre des courges
Mort estrangler carne omination.

9.40

Near Saint-Quentin, deep in the Bourlon woods,
In the abbey Flemings shall be cut dead :
The two younger brothers knocked for a loop,
Their train hard pressed & their guard hacked to shreds.

9.41

The great Chyren shall go seize Avignon,
From Rome honeyed acrimonious letters :
Diplomatic word sent from Chanignon,
Carpentras seized by black duke with red feather.

9.42

Plague from Barcelona, Genoa, Venice
And Sicily to Monaco shall race :
Against the Barbar fleet they'll take their aim,
And back to Tunis chase Barbar away.

9.43

Ready to land, the Crusader army
Shall be ambushed by the Ishmaelites :
Marauding ships beset them on all sides,
Ten elite galleys take them by surprise.

9.44

Flee, flee, O Geneva, every last one,
Saturn's gold for iron shall be exchanged :
RAYPOZ shall wipe out all opposition,
Before his advent, the sky's signs shall change.

9.45

Nothing satisfying his immense demands,
Great Mendosus shall acquire full control :
Far from court, he'll issue countermands,
Bad for Piedmont, Paris, Picard, Tyrron.

9.46

Be gone, flee from the red ones of Toulouse,
Perform your sacrificial expiation :
The evil lord, in the shadow of the gourds,
Lies strangled, foretold by haruspication.

9.47

Les soulz signes d'indigne delivrance,
Et de la multe auront contre advis,
Change monarque mis en perille pence,
Serrez en caige se verront vis à vis.

9.48

La grand cité d'occean maritime,
Environee de maretz en cristal:
Dans le solstice hiemal & la prime,
Sera temptee de vent espouvantal.

9.49

Gand & Bruceles marcheront contre Envers
Senat de Londres mettront à mort leur roy
Le sel & vin luy seront à l'envers,
Pour eux avoir le regne en desarroy.

9.50

Mandosus tost viendra à son hault regne
Mettant arriere un peu de Norlaris:
Le rouge blaisme, le masle à l'interregne,
Le jeune crainte & frayeur Barbaris.

9.51

Contre les rouges sectes se banderont,
Feu, eau, fer, corde par paix se minera,
Au point mourir ceux qui machineront,
Fors un que monde sur tout ruynera.

9.52

La paix s'approche d'un costé, & la guerre
Oncques ne feut la poursuitte si grande,
Plaindre homme, femme, sang innocent par terre
Et ce sera de France à toute bande.

9.53

Le Neron jeune dans les trois cheminees
Fera de paiges vifz pour ardoir getter
Heureux qui loing sera de telz menees,
Trois de son sang le feront mort guetter.

9.47

The signers of the disgraceful treaty
Shall find the people otherwise inclined :
Changing kings can cost a pretty penny :
Shut in a cage, they shall see eye to eye.

9.48

The great maritime city of the sea
Surrounded by marshes of crystal rime
At the winter solstice & in springtime
Shall by gale-force winds buffeted be.

9.49

Ghent & Brussels shall march against Antwerp,
The senate of London its king shall slay :
Wine & salt contribute to his reverse,
Thus throwing the realm into disarray.

9.50

Mandosus taking power on a grand scale
Shall grab a goodly part of Norlaris :
The pale red one, the interregnum's male,
So young, so fearful of the Barbaries.

9.51

The sects shall all conspire against the reds :
Fire, flood, sword, rope by peace are laid to rest :
The intriguers shall all end up near dead,
Save one who'll bring the world down upon our heads.

9.52

Peace nigh on one side, but never was war
Pursued with such unparalleled vengeance :
Pity all the men & women, the gore
Of innocents spilled throughout all of France.

9.53

The youthful Nero three fires shall fashion
In which to cremate his page boys alive :
Happy he who lives far from such cruel times,
Ambushed to death by three of his kinsmen.

9.54

Arrivera au port de Corsibonne,
Pres de Ravenne qui pillera la dame,
En mer profonde legat de la Vlisbonne
Souz roc cachez raviront septante ames.

9.55

L'horrible guerre qu'en l'occident s'apreste
L'an ensuivant viendra la pestilence,
Si fort horrible que jeune, vieulx, ne beste,
Sang, feu, Mercure, Mars, Jupiter en France.

9.56

Camp pres de Noudam passera Goussan ville
Et a Maiotes laissera son enseigne,
Convertira en instant plus de mille,
Cherchant les deux remettre en chaine & legne.

9.57

Au lieu de DRUX un Roy reposera
Et cherchera loy changeant d'Anatheme,
Pendant le ciel si tres fort tonnera,
Portee neufve Roy tuera soy mesme.

9.58

Au costé gauche a l'endroit de Vitry
Seront guettez les trois rouges de France,
Tous assoumez rouge, noir non murdry,
Par les Bretons remis en asseurance.

9.59

A la Ferté prendra la Vidame
Nicol tenu rouge qu'avoit produit la vie.
La grand Loyse naistra que fera clame.
Donnant Bourgongne à Bretons par envie.

9.60

Conflict Barbar en la Cornere noire.
Sang espandu trembler la d'Almatie,
Grand Ismaël mettra son promontoire
Ranes trembler secours Lusitanie.

9.54
At Porto Corsini near Ravenna,
Shall arrive the despoiler of the lady :
Far out at sea, the legate of Lisboa :
Hidden in the rocks, they'll kidnap seventy.

9.55
Dreadful war in the offing in the west :
The following year expect pestilence
So great nor young nor old nor beast is exempt :
Blood, fire, Mercury, Mars, Jupiter in France.

9.56
Past Goussonville, Houdan the army rides,
To display its standard at Maiotes :
Thousands converted in the blink of an eye,
Seeking to chain the two to the pyre post.

9.57
In the place of DRUX a King shall find rest
And try to redress the curse upon his head :
Meanwhile the sky rumbles loud overhead :
After new brood, King kills himself instead.

9.58
To the left of the place known as Vitry
They'll lie in ambush for the three reds of France :
The reds all die, the black one goes scot-free,
And the Bretons regain their assurance.

9.59
At La Ferté the Vidame he shall seize,
Nicholas, red-robed, who had sired a kid,
The newborn Louise with her hearty screams :
Burgundy ceded to Bretons on a whim.

9.60
Barbarians at war in black headdress,
Bloodshed affrighting all Dalmatia :
Mighty Ishmael reaping swift success,
Frightened frogs seek help from Lusitania.

9.61

La pille faite à la coste marine,
In cita nova & parentz amenez
Plusieurs de Malte par le fait de Messine,
Estroit serrez seront mal guerdonnez.

9.62

Au grand de Cheramon agora
Seront croisez par ranc tous attachez,
Le pertinax Oppi, & Mandragora,
Raugon d'Octobre le tiers seront laschez.

9.63

Plainctes & pleurs crys & grands urlemens
Pres de Narbon à Bayonne & en Foix
O quel horrible calamitz changemens,
Avant que Mars revolue quelques foys.

9.64

L'Aemathion passer montz Pyrennees,
En Mars Narbon ne fera resistance,
Par mer & terre fera si grand menee.
Cap. n'ayant terre seure pour demeurance.

9.65

Dedans le coing de luna viendra rendre,
Ou sera prins & mys en terre estrange,
Les fruitz immeurs seront à grand esclandre
Grand vitupere à l'un grande louange.

9.66

Paix, union sera & changement,
Estatz, offices bas hault, & hault bien bas,
Dresser voiage le fruict premier torment,
Guerre cesser, civil proces debatz.

9.67

Du hault des montz à l'entour de Lizer
Port à la roche Valen, cent assemblez
De chasteau neuf pierre late en donzere,
Contre le crest Romans foy assemblez.

9.61
Pillaged shall be the shores along the sea :
To Cittanova & its like are sent
Many Maltese by Messina's decree
And clapped into chains, a poor recompense.

9.62
For the lord of Cheramon's marketplace
Crusaders shall be chained by their degree :
For long-working opium & mandrake,
An October ransom shall set a third free.

9.63
Wailings & tears & great howlings & screams
At Bayonne & Foix & near to Narbonne :
O what dread changes & calamities
Before Mars has completed several rounds.

9.64
The Macedonian crosses the Pyrenees,
In March Narbonne offers no resistance :
So quick shall he bound over land & sea,
Cap. shall find no safe place of residence.

9.65
Into a corner of Luna he'll amble
Where he'll be seized & sent to foreign land :
The unripe fruits subject to great scandal,
Blame heaped on one, praise on the other hand.

9.66
Peace, unity shall reign, yet many a change :
Estates, offices : high fall, low are raised :
First fruit of turmoil, travel tough to arrange :
War over : civil suits, public debates.

9.67
From the mountain heights around the Isère,
At Valence rock, one hundred assembled :
From Châteauneuf, Pierrelatte & Donzère,
Against Crest, Romans, in faith assembled.

9.68
Du mont Aymar sera noble obscurcie,
Le mal viendra au joinct de sonne & rosne
Dans bois caichez soldatz jour de Lucie,
Qui ne fut onc un si horrible throsne.

9.69
Sur le mont de Bailly & la Bresle
Seront caichez de Grenoble les fiers,
Oultre Lyon, Vien. eulx si grande gresle,
Languoult en terre n'en restera un tiers.

9.70
Harnois trenchant dans les flambeaux cachez
Dedans Lyon le jour du Sacrement
Ceux de Vienne seront trestout hachez
Par les cantons Latins Mascon ne ment.

9.71
Aux lieux sacrez animaux veu à trixe,
Avec celuy qui n'osera le jour :
A Carcassonne pour disgrace propice,
Sera posé pour plus ample sejour.

9.72
Encor seront les saincts temples pollus,
Et expillez par Senat Tholassain,
Saturne deux trois cicles revollus,
Dans Avril, May, gens de nouveau levain.

9.73
Dans Fois entrez Roy ceiulee Turbao,
Et regnera moins revolu Saturne
Roy Turban blanc Bizance cœur ban
Sol Mars, Mercure pres la hurne.

9.74
Dans la cité de Fertsod homicide,
Fait & fait multe beuf arant ne macter,
Retour encores aux honneurs d'Artemide,
Et à Vulcan corps morts sepulturer.

9.68

Dimmed is Montélimar's most noble light :
The disaster shall strike where Saône meets Rhône :
On Lucy's day troops in woods hid from sight :
Never was there so horrible a throne.

9.69

On the mounts of Sain-Bel & L'Arbresle,
The pride of Grenoble shall hide away :
Beyond Lyon, Vienne, a storm of hail,
Locusts in fields : a mere third remains.

9.70

Within the torches sharp swords shall be hid,
In Lyon on the day of Sacrament :
Those of Vienne shall all be cut to shreds :
By Latin cantons Mâcon doesn't fib.

9.71

Hairy beasts shall be seen in holy places,
With him who shall not dare to face the day :
At Carcassonne suitable for disgrace,
He shall be set for a more ample stay.

9.72

Again the holy churches shall be defiled
And plundered by the Toulousan Senate :
Saturn having completed two three cycles,
In April, May, folk of a new leaven.

9.73

Into Foix shall enter the blue-turbaned King
And reign less than one of Saturn's turns :
White-turbaned king Byzance heart shall convince,
Sun, Mars & Mercury within the Urn.

9.74

In the city of Fertsod most murderous,
Where plow-ox risks sacrifice on altar,
They'll return to the worship of Artemis,
And bury their dead in Vulcan's honor.

9.75
De l'Ambraxie & du pays de Thrace,
Peuple par mer mal & secours Gaulois,
Perpetuelle en Provence la trace,
Avec vestiges de leur coustume & loix.

9.76
Avec le noir Rapax & sanguinaire
Yssue du peaultre de l'inhumain Neron,
Emmy deux fleuves main gauche militaire,
Sera murtry par Joyne chaulveron.

9.77
Le regne prins le Roy conviera,
La dame prinse à mort jurez à sort,
La vie à Royne fils on desniera,
Et la pellix au fort de la consort.

9.78
La dame Greque de beauté laydique,
Heureuse faicte de procs innumerable,
Hors translatee au regne Hispanique,
Captive prinse mourir mort miserable.

9.79
Le chef de classe par fraude stratageme,
Fera timides sortir de leurs galleres,
Sortis murtris chef renieur de cresme,
Puis par l'embusche luy rendront les saleres.

9.80
Le Duc voudra les siens exterminer,
Envoyera les plus forts lieux estranges,
Par tyrannie Pize & Luc ruiner,
Puis les Barbares sans vin feront vendanges.

9.81
Le Roy rusé entendra ses embusches
De trois quartiers ennemis assaillir,
Un nombre estrange larmes de coqueluches
Viendra Lemprin du traducteur faillir.

9.75

From Ambracia & the country of Thrace,
Seafarers, a boon & bane to the Gauls :
In Provence so everlasting their trace,
With vestiges of their customs & laws.

9.76

With the rapacious & bloodthirsty black,
Brothel-spawn of the inhuman Nero :
Between two rivers, on army's left flank,
He shall be murdered by the young bald one.

9.77

The realm seized, the King shall invite them by,
His lady seized, condemned to death by lot :
The life of the Queen's son they shall deny,
The wife with the mistress sharing the fort.

9.78

The damsel Greek, lovelier than Lais,
In dalliance with suitors without end,
Shall be transported to Hispanic climes,
Taken captive & die a wretched death.

9.79

The admiral by trickery & deceit
Shall coax the timid to quit their galleys :
Badly bruised by this chrism-denying chief,
They'll ambush him, paying back his salary.

9.80

The Duke, wanting to wipe out all his kin,
Shall dispatch the strongest to foreign climes :
As tyrant he shall do Pisa, Lucca in :
Then the Barbarian harvest without wine.

9.81

The wily King intends by ambushes
To assail his enemy on three sides :
A strange amount of tears from coqueluches :
Translator shall fail in his enterprise.

9.82

Par le deluge & pestilence forte
La cité grande de long temps assiegee,
La sentinelle & garde de main morte,
Subite prinse, mais de nul oultragee.

9.83

Sol vingt de taurus si fort terre trembler,
Le grand theatre rempli ruinera,
L'air, ciel & terre obscurcir & troubler,
Lors l'infidelle Dieu & sainctz voguera.

9.84

Roy exposé parfaira l'hecatombe,
Apres avoir trouvé son origine,
Torrent ouvrir de marbre & plomb la tombe
D'un grand Romain d'enseigne Medusine.

9.85

Passer Guienne, Languedoc & le Rosne,
D'Agen tenens de Marmande & la Roole
D'ouvrir par foy par roy Phocen tiendra son trosne
Conflit aupres saint Pol de Manseole.

9.86

Du bourg Lareyne parviendront droit à Chartres
Et feront pres du pont Authoni panse,
Sept pour la paix cautelleux comme martres
Feront entree d'armee à Paris clause.

9.87

Par la forest du Touphon essartee,
Par hermitage sera posé le temple,
Le duc d'Estampes par sa ruse inventee,
Du Mont Lehori prelat donra exemple.

9.88

Calais, Arras secours à Theroanne,
Paix & semblant simulera lescoutte,
Soulde d'Alabrox descendre par Roanne
Destornay peuple qui deffera la routte.

9.82

With floods & plagues raging throughout the land,
The mighty city shall be long besieged :
The watch & sentries strangled by bare hand,
Its fall sudden, but by none mistreated.

9.83

Sun in Taurus at twenty, a quake so great
A crowded theater shall come tumbling down :
The sky, air & earth shall darken & frown,
The infidel calling on his God & saints.

9.84

The King shall reenact the hecatomb,
Having discovered its original trace :
The flood unearths the lead & marble tomb
Of a great Roman with Medusan face.

9.85

To pass Guyenne, Languedoc & the Rhône,
From Agen holding Marmande & La Réole :
By hook by crook Phocaean lord holds the throne :
There'll be fighting near Saint-Paul-de-Mausole.

9.86

From Bourg-la-Reine to Chartres they shall come
And near Pont d'Antony shall seek repose :
Seven proposing peace, sly as martens,
Shall penetrate Paris though it be closed.

9.87

In the Torfou woods, off the beaten path,
Near the hermitage a church they'll erect :
By this wily ruse shall the Duke d'Estampes
The prelate of Montlhéry disrespect.

9.88

Calais, Arras, succor to Thérouanne,
All's fair & well according to the lookout :
Savoy soldiers descending by Roanne,
Deterring those who would end the rout.

9.89

Sept ans sera Philip. fortune prospere,
Rabaissera des Arabes l'effaict,
Puis son mydi perplex rebors affaire
Jeusne ognyon abysmera son fort.

9.90

Un capitaine de la grand Germanie
Se viendra rendre par simulé secours
Un Roy des roys ayde de Pannonie,
Que sa revolte fera de sang grand cours.

9.91

L'horrible peste Perynte & Nicopolle,
Le Chersonnez tiendra & Marceloyne,
La Thessalie vastera l'Amphipolle,
Mal incogneu & le refus d'Anthoine.

9.92

Le Roy vouldra dans cité neufve entrer
Par ennemys expunger lon viendra
Captif libere faulx dire & perpetrer,
Roy dehors estre, loin d'ennemys tiendra.

9.93

Les ennemis du fort bien eslongnez,
Par chariots conduict le bastion,
Par sur les murs de Bourges esgrongnez,
Quand Hercules battra l'Haemathion.

9.94

Faibles galleres seront unies ensemble,
Ennemis faux le plus fort en rampart :
Faible assaillies Vratislave tremble,
Lubecq & Mysne tiendront barbare part.

9.95

Le nouveau faict conduyra l'exercite,
Proche apamé jusques au pres du rivage,
Tendant secour de Milannoile eslite,
Duc yeux privé à Milan fer de cage.

9.89
Fortune shall favor Philip seven years,
He shall put the Arabs back in their place :
Then down south he shall suffer a reverse :
A young Ogmion his power shall erase.

9.90
A captain of greater Germania
Shall pretend to deliver to the King
Of Kings the support of Pannonia,
His revolt achieving massive bleeding.

9.91
A plague on Perinthus, Nicopolis,
Chersonese & all of Macedony,
Ravaging Thessaly, Amphipolis :
Unknown evil, denied by Anthony.

9.92
Into the new city the King would go,
So they've agreed to capture the enemy :
They lie to one freed from captivity,
The King staying outside, far from the foe.

9.93
Far from enemy fortifications,
They move up wagons to the bastion :
Atop Bourges' crumbling crenellations,
When Hercules defeats the Macedon.

9.94
The weakest fleets shall make common cause,
Treacherous foes over ramparts shall preside :
The weak assailed, Bratislava shall pause :
Lübeck & Meissen on the Muslim side.

9.95
The newly appointed shall lead his men
Near the riverbank, almost disengaged :
Aid tendered by the elite of Milan,
Where blinded Duke sits in an iron cage.

9.96

Dans cité entrer exercit desniee,
Duc entrera par persuasion,
Aux foibles portes clam armee amenee,
Mettront feu, mort de sang effusion.

9.97

De mer copies en trois parts divisees,
A la seconde de vivres failleront,
Desesperez cherchant champs Helisees,
Premiers en breche entrez victoire auront.

9.98

Les affligez par faute d'un seul taint,
Contremenant à partie opposite,
Aux Lygonnois mandera que contraint
Seront de rendre le grand chef de Molite.

9.99

Vent Aquilon fera partir le siege,
Par murs geter cendres, chauls, & pousiere,
Par pluye apres qui leur fera bien piege,
Dernier secours encontre leur frontiere.

9.100

Navalle pugne nuit sera superee,
Le feu aux naves à l'Occident ruine :
Rubriche neufve la grand nef coloree,
Ire a vaincu, & victoire en bruine.

CENTURIE X

10.1

A L'ennemy l'ennemy foy promise
Ne se tiendra, les captifs retenus :
Prins preme mort & le reste en chemise,
Damné le reste pour estre soustenus.

9.96

The army denied access to the city,
The Duke shall use subterfuge instead :
Led to its weakest gates in secrecy,
The troops shall torch it, cause untold bloodshed.

9.97

The forces of the sea split into three,
The second fleet shall run out of supplies,
Looking in vain for the Elysian Fields :
Victory to the first to enter the breach.

9.98

Stained by a single one's dishonesty,
They'll break their word to the opposite side :
He'll tell the people of Lyon they'll be
Forced to surrender the chief of Molite.

9.99

The north wind shall cause the siege to be raised,
Ash, lime & dust they'll shower from the walls :
The rain thereafter shall cause great dismay,
Their last chance to bring the siege to a stall.

9.100

Night shall overtake the battle at sea,
Fire shall devastate the Western ships :
Newly ruddled red shall the galleon be :
Merciless defeat : victors in the mist.

CENTURY X

10.1

The promise made enemy to enemy
Shall not hold, the prisoners not exchanged :
One captive near death, the rest in chemise,
All the others damned for being sustained.

10.2

Voille gallere voil de nef cachera,
La grande classe viendra sortir la moindre
Dix naves proches le torneront poulser,
Grande vaincue unies à soy joindre.

10.3

En apres cinq troupeau ne mettra hors un
Fuytif pour Penelon l'ashera,
Faulx murmurer secours venir par lors,
Le chef le siege lors habandonnera.

10.4

Sus la minuict conducteur de l'armee
Se saulvera, subit esvanouy,
Sept ans apres la fame non blasmee,
A son retour ne dira oncq ouy.

10.5

Albi & Castres feront nouvelle ligue,
Neuf Arriens Lisbon & Portugues,
Carcas, Tholosse consumeront leur brigue
Quand chief neuf monstre de Lauragues.

10.6

Sardon Nemans si hault desborderont,
Qu'on cuidera Deucalion renaistre,
Dans le collosse la plus part fuyront,
Vesta sepulchre feu estaint apparoistre.

10.7

Le grand conflit qu'on appreste à Nancy.
L'aemathien dira tout je soubmetz,
L'Isle Britanne par vin, sel en solcy,
Hem. mi deux Phi. long temps ne tiendra Metz.

10.8

Index & poulse parfondera le front
De Senegalia le Conte a son filz propre
La Myrnarmee par plusieurs de prinfront
Trois dans sept jours blesses mors.

10.2

The galley's sails shall hide the ship from sight,
The mighty fleet shall be revealed as weak :
Some ten nearby ships shall put it to flight,
Allies absorbing the great vanquished fleet.

10.3

He'll not lead forth his flock for the next five :
A fugitive for all his pains he'll free :
False rumors of help to come shall soon thrive :
The mighty chief shall then forsake the see.

10.4

At midnight the leader of the army
Shall save his skin, vanishing suddenly :
Seven years later, his fame still intact,
He'll deny all knowledge of it, once back.

10.5

Albi & Castres shall form a new league
With the new Arrianus, Portuguese :
Carcas., Toulouse shall perfect their intrigue :
The new chief, a monster from Lauraguès.

10.6

At Nîmes the Gardon's waters shall so rise
They'll think Deucalion's returning :
Into the coliseum most shall fly,
Extinct flame in Vesta's tomb now burning.

10.7

When at Nancy the great war gets under way,
Macedon shall say, "All under my sway" :
While Britain worries about salt & wine,
Twixt two Phi. Metz shan't resist a long time.

10.8

With his index finger & thumb the Count
Of Senigallia shall moisten his son's brow :
Many slay his Myrmidons right away,
Three wounded to death in seven days.

10.9

De Castillon figuieres jour de brune,
De feme infame naistra souverain prince
Surnom de chausses perhume luy posthume,
Onc Roy ne feut si pire en sa province.

10.10

Tasche de murdre enormes adulteres,
Grand ennemy de tout le genre humain
Que sera pires qu'ayeulx, oncles, ne peres
En fer, feu, eau, sanguin & inhumain.

10.11

Dessoubz Jonchere du dangereux passage
Fera passer le posthume sa bande,
Les monts Pyrens passer hors son bagaige
De Parpignam courira duc à tende.

10.12

Esleu en Pape, d'esleu sera mocqué,
Subit soudain esmeu prompt & timide,
Par trop bon doulx à mourir provocqué,
Crainte estainte la nuit de sa mort guide.

10.13

Soulz la pasture d'animaux ruminant
Par eux conduicts au ventre herbipolique
Soldatz caichez les armes bruit menant,
Non loing temptez de cite Antipolique.

10.14

Urnel Vaucile sans conseil de soy mesmes
Hardit timide par crainte prins vaincu,
Accompaigné de plusieurs putains blesmes
A Barcelonne aux chartreux convaincu.

10.15

Pere duc vieux d'ans & de soif chargé,
Au jour extreme filz desniant les guiere
Dedans le puis vif mort viendra plongé,
Senat au fil la mort longue & legiere.

10.9
Of a Castile carter, one misty night,
A wanton whore shall bear a sovereign prince :
Dropped trou shall be his nickname when he dies :
No King this bad ever ruled his province.

10.10
With murder stained & vast fornications,
A great enemy of the human race,
Worse than all previous generations,
By sword, fire, flood, bloody & inhumane.

10.11
Below Junquera's perilous passage
The posthumous one shall direct his band :
He'll cross the Pyrenees without baggage,
From Perpignan the duke hastens to Tende.

10.12
Elected Pope, soon mocked as Pope-elect,
Suddenly tense, suddenly full of fear :
Too sweet-tempered & thus provoked to death,
But quite fearless the night his end draws near.

10.13
Beneath the fodder of all the cattle
They brought to overgraze this grassy town,
The soldiers hide, bringing sound of battle,
Tempted by Antipolis further down.

10.14
Urnel Vaucile, humble vacillator,
Bold, timid, overcome by fear, captured :
Accompanied by several painted whores,
He converts at Barcelona's Chartreux.

10.15
To the agèd duke so consumed with thirst,
About to die, the son denies a single drop,
Hangs him on a rope, half-alive, head first,
In a pit where death takes too long to stop.

10.16

Heureux au regne de France, heureux de vie
Ignorant sang mort fureur & rapine,
Par non flateurs sera mys en envie,
Roy desrobé trop de foy en cuisine.

10.17

La royne Ergaste voiant sa fille blesme,
Par un regret dans l'estomach encloz,
Crys lamentables seront lors d'Angolesme,
Et au germain mariage fort clos.

10.18

Le ranc Lorrain fera place à Vendosme,
Le hault mys bas & le bas mys en hault,
Le filz d'Hamon sera esleu dans Rome
Et les deux grands seront mys en deffault.

10.19

Jour que sera par royne saluee,
Le jour apres le salut, la priere,
Le compte fait raison & valbuee,
Par avant humble oncques ne feut si fiere.

10.20

Tous les amys qu'auront tenu party,
Pour rude en lettres mys mort & saccagé,
Biens publiez par fixe grand neanty,
Onc Romain peuple ne feut tant outragé.

10.21

Par le despit du Roy soustenant moindre,
Sera meurdry luy presentant les bagues,
Le pere au filz voulant noblesse poindre
Fait comme à Perse jadis feirent les Magues.

10.22

Pour ne vouloir consentir au divorce,
Qui puis apres sera cogneu indigne,
Le roy des Isles sera chassé par force
Mis à son lieu que de roy n'aura signe.

10.16

Happy to reign over France, happy to live
Ignorant of blood, death, frenzy, rapine,
Envied by those with no flattery to give,
A King withdrawn, food his favorite pastime.

10.17

The scheming queen who sees her daughter wan,
Gnawed by a regret that in her belly grows,
Shall hear loud laments come from Angoulême,
But shall a German marriage most oppose.

10.18

The house of Lorraine shall give way to Vendôme,
The low are raised high, the high are cast low :
Hamon's son shall be elected in Rome,
The two lords finding the going quite slow.

10.19

One day she's warmly greeted by the queen,
The next day it's about salvation, prayer :
A reasonable summary of the scene :
She who was once humble now puts on airs.

10.20

All the friends belonging to his crowd
Killed & sacked for his rude-lettered sake :
Beautiful public works razed to the ground,
The Roman people never this outraged.

10.21

The spiteful King, partial to the lesser one,
Shall have him murdered who offers him rings :
Father, to impress nobility on son,
Acts like those ancient Persian Magi kings.

10.22

Unwilling to consent to a divorce
Which afterward might be deemed unseemly,
The king of the Isles shall be forced to flee :
Instead, a king whom no mark does endorse.

10.23

Au peuple ingrat faictes les remonstrances,
Par lors l'armee se saisira d'Antibe,
Dans l'arc Monech feront les doleances,
Et à Frejus l'un l'autre prendra ribe.

10.24

Le captif prince aux Italles vaincu
Passera Gennes par mer jusqu'à Marseille,
Par grand effort des forens survaincu
Sauf coup de feu barril liqueur d'abeille.

10.25

Par Nebro ouvrir de Brisanne passage,
Bien eslongnez el tago fara muestra,
Dans Pelligouxe sera commis l'outrage
De la grand dame assise sur l'orchestra.

10.26

Le successeur vengera son beau frere,
Occuper regne souz umbre de vengeance,
Occis ostacle son sang mort vitupere,
Long temps Bretaigne tiendra avec la France.

10.27

Par le cinquieme & un grand Hercules
Viendront le temple ouvrir de main bellique,
Un Clement, Jule & Ascans recules,
Lespe, clef, aigle, n'eurent onc si grand picque.

10.28

Second & tiers qui font prime musicque
Sera par Roy en honneur sublimee,
Par grasse & maigre presque demy eticque
Raport de Venus faulx randra deprimee.

10.29

De Pol MANSOL dans caverne caprine
Caché & prins extrait hors par la barbe,
Captif mené comme beste mastine
Par Begourdans amenee pres de Tarbe.

10.23

Having much harangued its ungrateful plebs,
The army shall proceed to seize Antibes :
Further grievances at Monaco's fort,
At Fréjus they'll squabble over the shore.

10.24

The captive prince, vanquished in Italy,
Via Genoa to Marseille shall flee :
To foreign might he shall lose the battle,
Save an explosion in a honey barrel.

10.25

From Ebro, passage opened to Pézenas,
Far from where el Tago fara muestra :
From Pelligouxe, an insult against a
Grand lady seated on the orchestra.

10.26

The heir avenges his brother-in-law,
Grabbing power in the dark of vengeance :
The hostage blames his death on his in-laws :
Brittany shall remain loyal to France.

10.27

By him, the fifth & mighty Hercules,
The hand of war the church shall open wide :
Never such strife twixt eagle, sword, & keys :
Clement, Julius Ascanius, steps aside.

10.28

The second & third who prime music make
Shall be most honored by the King's largesse :
Through thick & thin, half-emaciated,
False talk of Love making him most depressed.

10.29

In a goat cave near Saint-Paul-de-MAUSOLE,
Hidden & then caught, hauled out by his beard,
Then dragged off like an old dog on a rope
Toward Tarbes by some people from Bigorre.

10.30

Nepveu & sang du sainct nouveau venu,
Par le surnom soustient arcs & couvert
Seront chassez mis a mort chassez nu,
En rouge & noir convertiront leur vert.

10.31

Le saint empire viendra en Germanie,
Ismaelites trouveront lieux ouverts.
Anes vouldront aussi la Carmanie,
Les soustenens de terre tous couverts.

10.32

Le grand empire chacun an devoir estre
Un sur les autres le viendra obtenir,
Mais peu de temps sera son regne & estre,
Deux ans aux naves se pourra soustenir.

10.33

La faction cruelle à robbe longue,
Viendra cacher souz les pointus poignars
Saisir Florence le duc & lieu diphlongue
Sa descouverte par immeurs & flangnards.

10.34

Gauloys qu'empire par guerre occupera
Par son beau frere mineur sera trahy,
Par cheval rude voltigeant traynera
Du fait le frere long temps sera hay.

10.35

Pusnay royal flagrand d'ardant libide,
Pour se jouyr de cousine germaine,
Habit de femme au temple d'Arthemide:
Allant murdry par incognue du Maine.

10.36

Apres le Roy du soucq guerres parlant,
L'isle Harmotique le tiendra à mepris,
Quelques ans bons rongeant un & pillant
Par tyrranie à l'isle changeant pris.

10.30

Blood nephew of the newly proclaimed saint,
His surname shall support arches & beams :
They'll be expelled, killed, chased away naked :
Into red & black they'll convert their green.

10.31

Holy Empire shall come to Germania,
Ishmaelites shall find the world an open place :
Asses have high hopes too for Carmania,
But their supporters are all in the grave.

10.32

Everyone member of the great empire,
But one shall obtain power over his peers :
His life & reign shall last but a brief while,
His ships sustaining him for two short years.

10.33

The cruel faction in its trailing gowns
Disguises sharp daggers hid in breeches :
Duke seizes Florence & the diphthong town,
Quite a surprise to young fops & leeches.

10.34

The Frenchman who the empire shall invade
By his young brother-in-law is betrayed :
Dragged along by a wild curveting horse,
For which the brother shall be long abhorred.

10.35

The younger prince, fired by flagrant desire,
Lusting for the joys of his first cousin,
At Diana's temple in female attire
Is murdered by an unknown girl from Maine.

10.36

When the King of Souks starts talking of war,
The Harmotic Isle shall hold him in contempt,
A good few years of predation & plunder
Having revised the Isle's esteem for tyrants.

10.37

Lassemblee grande pres du lac de Borget,
Se ralieront pres de Montmelian,
Marchans plus oultre pensifz feront proget
Chambry, Moriane combat sainct Julian.

10.38

Amour alegre non loing pose le siege,
Au sainct barbar seront les garnisons,
Ursins Hadrie pour Gaulois feront plaige,
Pour peur rendus de l'armee aux Grisons.

10.39

Premier fils vefve malheureux mariage,
Sans nuls enfans deux Isles en discord,
Avant dixhuict incompetant eage,
De l'autre pres plus bas sera l'accord.

10.40

Le jeune nay au regne Britannique,
Qu'aura le pere mourant recommandé,
Iceluy mort LONOLE donra topique,
Et à son fils le regne demandé.

10.41

En la frontiere de Caussade & Charlus,
Non guieres loing du fonds de la vallee,
De ville Franche musicque à son de luths,
Environnez combouls & grand myttee.

10.42

Le regne humain d'Anglique geniture,
Fera son regne paix union tenir,
Captive guerre demy de sa closture,
Long temps la paix leur fera maintenir.

10.43

Le trop bon temps trop de bonté royalle:
Fais & deffais prompt subit negligence,
Legier croira faux d'espouse loyalle,
Luy mis à mort par sa benevolence.

10.37

They shall gather in force near Lake Bourget
In a great assembly toward Montmélian :
Pondering their plan, war they'll undertake
On Chambéry, Maurienne, Saint-Julien.

10.38

Easy love lays his siege on them not far,
Garrisons encamped at Santa Barbara :
Orsini & Adria shall pledge for the Gauls,
Lest they be delivered to the Swiss guards.

10.39

First son, widower of luckless marriage,
Without issue, the two Isles in discord :
Before he turns eighteen, not yet of age,
They'll marry off the next & younger lord.

10.40

The young prince born to the British throne,
Whom his dying father did recommend :
At the latter's death, quarrels in LONOLE,
Bringing the young son's kingdom to its end.

10.41

At the frontier of Caussade & Caylus
Not all that distant from the valley floor :
From Villefranche the music of the lute,
Enveloped by cymbals & grand viol.

10.42

The humane reign of English descent
Shall keep the realm in calm & unity :
War half-captive, shut well within the fence,
He'll maintain peace in perpetuity.

10.43

Too many good times, too much royal bounty
Promptly granted & withdrawn, negligence :
Too quick to doubt his wife's integrity,
Put to death for his very benevolence.

10.44

Par lors qu'un Roy sera contre les siens,
Natif de Bloys subjuguera Ligures :
Mammel, Cordube & les Dalmatiens,
Des sept puis l'ombre à Roy estrennes & lemures.

10.45

Lombre du regne de Navarre non vray,
Fera la vie de sort illegitime :
La veu promis incertain de Cambray,
Roy Orleans donra mur legitime.

10.46

Vie sort mort de L'OR vilaine indigne,
Sera de Saxe non nouveau electeur :
De Brunsuic mandra d'amour signe,
Faux le rendant au peuple seducteur.

10.47

De Bourze ville à la dame Guyrlande,
L'on mettra sus par la trahison faicte,
Le grand prelat de Leon par Formande,
Faux pellerins & ravisseurs defaicte.

10.48

Du plus profond de l'Espaigne enseigne,
Sortant du bout & des fins de l'Europe,
Troubles passant aupres du pont de Laigne,
Sera deffaicte par bandes sa grand troppe.

10.49

Jardin du monde au pres de cité neufve,
Dans le chemin des montaignes cavees,
Sera saisi & plongé dans la Cuve,
Beuvant par force eaux soulfre envenimees.

10.50

La Meuse au jour terre de Luxembourg,
Descouvrira Saturne & trois en lurne,
Montaigne & pleine, ville, cité & bourg,
Lorrain deluge trahison par grand hurne.

10.44

A King having gone against his own folk,
A native of Blois conquers the Ligurians,
Memel, Cordoba & the Dalmatians :
Seven seized, King shadowed by omens & ghosts.

10.45

The Kingdom of Navarre's false shadow
Shall make of his life a fate unlawful :
The vow made in Cambrai fallen fallow,
Orléans King erects a wall most lawful.

10.46

His life, death, fate owed to GOLD, that low slut,
He'll not be new Elector of Saxony :
From Brunswick he shall send false signs of love,
Making himself popular by perfidy.

10.47

At Burgos, at Our Lady of Garlands,
They'll deal harshly with the acts of treason :
The great prelate of León at Formande,
Undone by ravishers & fake pilgrims.

10.48

Banners from the most far-flung parts of Spain,
From Europe's furthest reaches they shall stream :
Troubles crossing near the bridge of Laigne,
A small band its mighty army shall defeat.

10.49

Near the new city, garden to the world,
On the road to mountains filled with hollows,
He'll be seized & into the Vat be hurled,
Sulfur-poisoned waters forced to swallow.

10.50

The Meuse around the lands of Luxembourg
Shall find Saturn & three more in the urn :
Mountain & plain, town, city & burg,
Flood in Lorraine, betrayed by the great urn.

10.51

Des lieux plus bas du pays de Lorraine,
Seront des basses Allemaignes unis,
Par ceux du siege Picards, Normans, du Maisne,
Et aux cantons ce seront reunis.

10.52

Au lieu où LAYE & Scelde se marient,
Seront les nopces de long temps maniees,
Au lieu d'Anvers où la crappe charient,
Jeune vieillesse consorte intaminee.

10.53

Les trois pellices de loing s'entrebatron,
La plus grand moindre demeurera à l'escoute :
Le grand Selin n'en sera plus patron,
Le nommera feu pelte blanche routte.

10.54

Nee en ce monde par concubine fertive,
A deux hault mise par les tristes nouvelles,
Entre ennemis sera prinse captive,
Et amené à Malings & Bruxelles.

10.55

Les malheureuses nopces celebreront,
En grande joye, mais la fin malheureuse :
Mary & mere nore desdaigneront,
Le Phybe mort, & nore plus piteuse.

10.56

Prelat royal son baissant trop tiré,
Grand fleux de sang sortira par sa bouche,
Le regne Anglicque par regne respiré,
Long temps mort vif en Tunys comme souche.

10.57

Le sublevé ne cognoistra son sceptre,
Les enfans jeunes des plus grands honnira :
Oncques ne fut en plus ord cruel estre,
Pour leurs espouses à mort noir bannira.

10.51

Some of the most nether lands of Lorraine
Shall be united with the low Germans :
The sees of Picardy, Normandy, Maine,
All joined together with the Swiss cantons.

10.52

Where the LEIE & Schelde come to marry,
The nuptial rites shall have long been arranged :
At the place in Antwerp where chaff is carried,
The old man leaves his young wife undebased.

10.53

The three mistresses shall squabble from afar,
The first keeping an ear out for the last :
The great Selin shall no longer rule her heart,
Lame buckler she'll call him, shooter of blanks.

10.54

Born to this world by a furtive concubine,
Raised high at age two by all the sad news,
She shall be taken captive by her foes,
And led away to Brussels & Malines.

10.55

They'll celebrate the ill-starred wedding vows
With great joy, but the end is unforeseen :
Husband & mother scorn the daughter-in-law,
Her Phoebus dead, all the more to be pitied.

10.56

The royal prelate bowing down too deep,
From his mouth a gush of blood shall stream :
The kingdom of England saved by a queen :
Long dead in Tunis, now alive to breed.

10.57

The upstart shall be ignorant of rule,
He'll shame the children of the noblest men :
Never was there one more filthy & cruel :
As for the wives, he'll send them to black death.

10.58
Au temps du deuil que le selin monarque,
Guerroyera le jeune Aemathien :
Gaule bransler perecliter la barque,
Tenter Phossens au Ponant entretien.

10.59
Dedans Lyon vingt cinq d'une alaine,
Cinq citoyens Germains, Bressans, Latins,
Par dessous noble conduiront longue traine,
Et descouvers par abbois de mastins.

10.60
Je pleure Nisse, Mannego, Pize, Gennes,
Savone, Sienne, Capue, Modene, Malte :
Le dessus sang & glaive par estrennnes,
Feu, trembler terre, eau, malheureuse nolte.

10.61
Betta, Vienne, Emorre, Sacarbance,
Voudront livrer aux Barbares Pannone :
Par picque & feu, enorme violance,
Les conjurez descouvers par matrone.

10.62
Pres de Sorbin pour assaillir Ongrie,
L'heroult de Bude les viendra advertir :
Chef Bizantin, Sallon de Sclavonie,
A loy d'Arabes les viendra convertir.

10.63
Cydron, Raguse, la cité au sainct Hieron,
Reverdira le medicant secours,
Mort fils de Roy par mort de deux heron,
L'Arabe Ongrie feront un mesme cours.

10.64
Pleure Milan, pleure Luqes, Florance,
Que ton grand Duc sur le char montera,
Changer le siege pres de Venise s'advance,
Lors que Colomne à Rome changera.

10.58

In time of mourning the Selene monarch
Shall declare war on the new Macedon,
Who'll shake up Gaul & capsize Peter's barque,
Tempt Marseille to accept the western dawn.

10.59

Within Lyon twenty-five do conspire,
Five Germans, Bressans, Latins among them :
Under a nobleman's eye, all in a file,
But the barking of dogs discovers them.

10.60

I weep for Nice, Monaco, Pisa, Genoa,
Savona, Siena, Capua, Modena, Malta :
Upon you sword & blood as gifts shall fall :
Fire, earthquake, flood, unhappy Nolita.

10.61

Betta, Vienna, Emorra, Scarabantia,
Would cede the Barbarians Pannonia :
By pike & fire the violence hits home :
The plotters discovered by an old crone.

10.62

To assail Hungary near Sorbia
The herald of Buda them shall alert :
Byzantine chief, Salona of Slavonia,
To the Arabic law them shall convert.

10.63

Cydonia, Ragusa, the city of St. Jerome,
Shall flourish again by salutary force :
King's son dead by the deaths of two heroes :
Arab Hungary shall take the same course.

10.64

Weep Milan, weep Lucca, & weep Florence,
When your grand Duke gets up upon his horse
And to lift the siege near Venice advances,
When the Colonnas meet their fate in Rome.

10.65

O vaste Romme ta ruyne s'approche,
Non de tes murs de ton sang & sustance :
L'aspre par lettres fera si horrible coche,
Fer poinctu mis à tous jusques au manche.

10.66

Le chef de Londres par regne l'Americh,
L'isle d'Escosse tempiera par gellee :
Roy Reb auront un si faux antechrist,
Que les mettra trestous dans la meslee.

10.67

Le tremblement si fort au mois de May,
Saturne, Caper, Jupiter, Mercure au beuf :
Venus aussi Cancer, Mars, en Nonnay,
Tombera gresle lors plus grosse qu'un euf.

10.68

L'armee de mer devant cité tiendra.
Puis partira sans faire longue alee,
Citoyens grande proye en terre prendra,
Retourner classe reprendre grand emblee.

10.69

Le fait luysant de neuf vieux eslevé
Seront si grand par midi aquilon,
De sa seur propre grandes alles levé.
Fuyant murdry au buysson d'ambellon.

10.70

L'œil par object fera telle excroissance,
Tant & ardante que tumbera la neige,
Champ arrousé viendra en descroissance,
Que le primat succumbera à Rege.

10.71

La terre & l'air gelleront si grand eau,
Lors qu'on viendra pour jeudi venerer,
Ce qui sera jamais ne feut si beau,
Des quatre pars le viendront honnorer.

10.65

O mighty Rome, your ruin does approach,
Not your walls, but your blood & living parts :
The rough-lettered one shall make such a notch,
His sharp sword driving deep into your heart.

10.66

The chief of London by American reign,
On the isle of Scotland frost holding sway :
In Reb King they'll have an antichrist so false
He'll drag every single one into the fray.

10.67

So great the earthquake in the month of May,
Saturn in Goat, Jove, Mercury in Bull,
And Venus, Mars in Crab, at Annonay :
Bigger than eggs, hailstones by the handful.

10.68

Before the port the pirate ships shall stand,
Then hoist sail without going a great ways :
Many citizens shall be seized on land :
The fleet returning, they'll pillage away.

10.69

The bright deeds of the old man new-inspired
Shall soar on the south wind & Aquilon,
And on his sister's wings rise yet higher :
Fleeing, slain in the thicket of Ambellon.

10.70

The object shall so cause the eye to swell
And burn, much like the falling of snow :
With rain on fields discomfort is dispelled,
When the primate succumbs at Reggio.

10.71

Earth & air shall freeze an enormous sea
When Thursday they shall come to venerate :
Never so fair was that which shall never be :
From the four corners they'll come celebrate.

10.72

L'an mil neuf cens nonante neuf sept mois
Du ciel viendra un grand Roy deffraieur
Resusciter le grand Roy d'Angolmois.
Avant apres Mars regner par bon heur.

10.73

Le temps present avecques le passé
Sera jugé par grand Jovialiste,
Le monde tard luy sera lassé,
Et desloial par le clergé juriste.

10.74

Au revolu du grand nombre septiesme
Apparoistra au temps Jeux d'Hacatombe,
Non esloigné du grand eage milliesme,
Que les entres sortiront de leur tombe.

10.75

Tant attendu ne reviendra jamais
Dedans l'Europe, en Asie apparoistra
Un de la ligue yssu du grand Hermes,
Et sur tous roys des orientz croistra.

10.76

Le grand senat discernera la pompe,
A l'un qu'apres sera vaincu chassé,
Ses adherans seront à son de trompe,
Biens publiez ennemys deschassez.

10.77

Trente adherans de l'ordre des quyretres
Bannys leurs biens donnez ses adversaires,
Tous leurs bienfais seront pour desmerites
Classe espargie delivrez aux corsaires.

10.78

Subite joye en subite tristesse
Sera à Romme aux graces embrassees
Dueil, cris, pleurs, larm. sang excellant liesse
Contraires bandes surprinses & troussees.

10.72

The year nineteen ninety-nine, seventh month,
The sky shall send a great King to defray
And restore the great King from Angoumois :
Before, after March, blessèd be his reign.

10.73

Time present together with time past
Shall be judged by the great Jovialist :
But the world shall tire of him at last,
Betrayed by the clergy's legalists.

10.74

The mighty number seven, its course run,
Shall appear at the Games of the Hecatomb,
Not that far from the great millennium,
When the buried shall rise from their tombs.

10.75

Long awaited, he shall never come again
To Europe, but in Asia shall appear,
One who from mighty Hermes does descend,
Of all the eastern kings the most revered.

10.76

The great senate a triumph shall bestow
On one they'll later overthrow & banish :
As to his followers, while the trumpet blows,
Their assets sold, enemies made to vanish.

10.77

Three members of the order of Quirites
Banished, all their goods given to their foes,
All their good deeds adding up to zero :
Fleet dispersed, surrendered to the pirates.

10.78

Sudden joy turning to sudden sadness
At the Rome of the embracing graces :
Grief, cries, tears, blood, then exceeding gladness :
Enemy bands surprised & placed in traces.

10.79

Les vieux chemins seront tous embelys,
Lon passera à Memphis somentrée,
Le grand Mercure d'Hercules fleur de lys
Faisant trembler terre, mer & contree.

10.80

Au regne grand du grand regne regnant,
Par force d'armes les grands portes d'arain
Fera ouvrir le roy & duc joignant,
Port demoly nef à fons jour serain.

10.81

Mys tresor temple citadins Hesperiques
Dans iceluy retiré en secret lieu,
Le temple ouvrir les liens fameliques.
Reprens ravys proye horrible au milieu.

10.82

Cris, pleurs, larmes viendront avec coteaux
Semblant fouyr donront dernier assault
Lentour parques planter profons plateaux,
Vifs repoulsez & meurdrys de prinsault.

10.83

De batailler ne sera donné signe,
Du parc seront contraint de sortir hors
De Gand lentour sera cogneu l'ensigne,
Qui fera mettre de tous les siens à mors.

10.84

La naturelle à si hault hault non bas
Le tard retour fera martis contens,
Le Recloing ne sera sans debatz
En empliant & perdant tout son temps.

10.85

Le vieil tribung au point de la trehemide
Sera pressee captif ne deslivrer,
Le veuil non veuil le mal parlant timide
Par legitime à ses amys livrer.

10.79

The old roads all repaired, they shall now lead
To a place that like ancient Memphis stands,
The mercurial Gallic Hercules
Inspiring dread on earth, sea & every land.

10.80

When over the realm the regent now reigns,
By force of arms the gates of bronze he'll tear
Open, king & duke coming to his aid :
Port demolished, ships sunk, the skies clear.

10.81

Treasure hid in temple by Hesperians,
Deposited in its most secret part :
Temple broken open by famished men,
Seized, plundered : gruesome spoils at its heart.

10.82

With the knives shall come many moans, tears, cries :
Seeking to flee, they'll mount a last assault :
They'll surround them with pales & platforms high :
Quickly repulsed & killed dead on the spot.

10.83

No sign to commence the battle being made,
They shall be forced to venture beyond their pales :
All around Ghent the colors are displayed
Of him who'll kill them all without avail.

10.84

The lord's bastard girl, not low but so high,
Her late return making the aggrieved content :
The reunion shall not be without dissent,
Occupying & wasting all her time.

10.85

The agèd tribune, his nerves badly frayed,
To free the prisoner shall be hard pressed :
Shilly-shallying, stammering, afraid
To hand him back by law to his friends.

10.86

Comme un gryphon viendra le roy d'Europe
Accompaigné de ceux d'Aquilon,
De rouges & blancz conduira grand troppe
Et yront contre le roy de Babilon.

10.87

Grand roy viendra prendre port pres de Nisse
Le grand empire de la mort si enfera
Aux Antipolles posera son genisse,
Par mer la Pille tout esvanoira.

10.88

Piedz & Cheval à la seconde veille
Feront entree vastient tout par la mer,
Dedans le poil entrera de Marseille,
Pleurs, crys, & sang, onc nul temps si amer.

10.89

De brique en marbre seront les murs reduits
Sept & cinquante annees pacifiques,
Joie aux humains renové Laqueduict,
Santé, grandz fruict joye & temps melifiques.

10.90

Cent foys mourra le tyran inhumain.
Mys à son lieu scavant & debonnaire,
Tout le senat sera dessoubz sa main,
Faché sera par malin themeraire.

10.91

Clergé Romain l'an mil six cens & neuf,
Au chef de l'an feras election
D'un gris & noir de la Compagne yssu,
Qui onc ne feut si maling.

10.92

Devant le pere l'enfant sera tué:
Le pere apres entre cordes de jonc,
Genevois peuple sera esvertué,
Gisant le chief au milieu comme un tronc.

10.86
Like a griffin the King of Europe shall come,
Accompanied by forces from the North :
An army of reds & whites he'll lead forth
To go against the King of Babylon.

10.87
A mighty king shall seize a port near Nice
And spreading death over the empire sweep :
He shall lay aside his broom at Antibes
And with his spoils vanish into the sea.

10.88
At second watch shall horse & foot alike
Force an entry, plundering from the sea :
Within the port of Marseille they shall strike :
Tears, shrieks, blood : times this bitter never seen.

10.89
In marble shall the walls of brick now rise,
Seven & fifty years of lasting peace,
Aqueducts restored, joy to all mankind,
Health, abundant fruit, blissful honeyed times.

10.90
A hundred times shall the cruel tyrant die :
In his place, a learnèd man of good counsel,
The entire senate under his guide,
But soon harassed by a reckless scoundrel.

10.91
Roman clergy, in the year sixteen nine,
At new year's you shall hold an election :
A gray & black monk of the Campania line,
No one quite like him in dereliction.

10.92
They'll kill the child before its father's eyes,
Then they'll tie the father up like a dog :
The Genevans shall heave weary sighs,
Their leader lying dead there like a log.

10.93
La barque neufve recevra les voyages,
Là & aupres transfereront l'empire,
Beaucaire, Arles retiendront les hostages,
Pres deux colomnes trouvees de porphire.

10.94
De Nismes, d'Arles, & Vienne contemner,
N'obey tout à l'edict Hespericque:
Aux labouriez pour le grand condamner,
Six eschappez en habit seraphicque.

10.95
Dans les Espaignes viendra Roy trespuissant,
Par mer & terre subjugant or midy,
Ce mal fera rabaissant le croissant,
Baisser les aesles à ceux du vendredy.

10.96
Religion du nom des mers vaincra,
Contre la secte fils Adaluncatif,
Secte obstinee deploree craindra,
Des deux blessez par Aleph & Aleph.

10.97
Triremes pleines tout aage captif,
Temps bon à mal, le doux pour amertume :
Proye à Barbares trop tost seront hastifs,
Cupid de veoir plaindre au vent la plume.

10.98
La splendeur claire à pucelle joyeuse,
Ne luyra plus long temps sera sans sel :
Avec marchans, ruffiens loups odieuse,
Tous peste mele monstre universel.

10.99
La fin le loup, le lyon, beuf, & l'asne,
Timide dama seront avec mastins,
Plus ne cherra à eux la douce manne,
Plus vigilance & custode aux mastins.

10.93
The new barque embarks on many voyages,
What with the empire transferred here & there :
At Arles, Beaucaire they'll hold the hostages
Near two columns of porphyry found there.

10.94
Scorn pours from Arles & Vienne & Nîmes,
On those who resist Hesperia's decrees :
To torture they'll condemn them in their name :
Disguised as Franciscans, some six escape.

10.95
Greater Spain shall see a King most mighty
Subjugate southern gold by land & sea :
He'll beat down the crescent, inflict misery,
Clip the wings of those who worship Fridays.

10.96
Victory of the faith with the sea's name
Over the heirs of Adaluncatif :
This stubborn, lamented sect shall be afraid
Of the two wounded by Aleph & Alif.

10.97
Triremes packed with captives of all ages
The forecast good for evil, sweet for gall :
Prey to the Barbarians, in too much haste
To see which way the wind makes feather fall.

10.98
That brilliance that the virgin's joy provides
Shall shine no more : long dearth of salt & spice :
With merchants, ruffians, wolves of loathsome stripe,
Helter-skelter, monsters on every side.

10.99
In the end, the wolf, ox, ass & lion
And timid deer shall lie down with the dogs :
No more need for sweet manna to pour down,
No more need to defend the house with dogs.

10.100

Le grand empire sera par Angleterre,
Le pempotam des ans plus de trois cens :
Grandes copies passer par mer & terre,
Les Lusitains n'en seront pas contens.

10.100

By England shall great empire see the day,
More than three hundred years' powerful sway :
To the great discomfort of the Portuguese,
Its great forces shall sweep over land & sea.

Appendix: Five Hundred Years of Reading the *Prophecies*

For close to five centuries, people have linked Nostradamus's quatrains to historical events. Some of the quatrains have lain dormant for decades before suddenly coming into view. Others have surfaced repeatedly. All have lent themselves to private rumination and public conversations. The "truth" of the quatrains matters less than their continued ability to captivate minds and generate new meanings.

From the late Renaissance until the seventeenth century, most readers of the *Prophecies* were literate elites, familiar with poetry and history, awed by wondrous happenings, and eager to make sense of change and conflicts and catastrophes. The death of the French king Henri II after a joust in 1559 was one such calamity. Members of the court and others turned first to Nostradamus's almanacs and prognostications and uncovered, among other suggestive phrases, a verse declaring "The Great One to be no more." At some point (we do not know precisely when, but it was years after the king's death), contemporaries also opened the book and pondered quatrain 1.35:

The young lion shall overcome the old	Le lyon jeune le vieux surmontera,
On the field of battle in single duel :	En champ bellique par singulier duelle :
He'll put out his eyes in his cage of gold,	Dans caige d'or les yeux luy crevera,
Winner taking all, then a death most cruel.	Deux classes une, puis mourir, mort cruelle.

The jousters both had lions as their emblems. Henri was the old one; the count whose lance gouged the king's eye was the young one. The "cage of gold" stood for the king's gilded helmet. Some commentators suggested that the "*deux classes*" in the fourth verse denoted his two wounds, above and below the eye. A death most cruel, indeed—and easier to understand and perhaps accept if it was part of an underlying design rather than a random event.

This quatrain has become a touchstone in the posterity of Nostradamus, a prediction that has served as proof of his prophetic gifts. Other quatrains also assumed significance in the sixteenth century. In 1560, the Venetian ambassador to France wrote in a diplomatic dispatch that quatrain 10.39 had predicted the demise of Henri's successor, the teenage

François II. The fourth verse presumably referred to François' recent marriage to Mary, Queen of Scots:

First son, widower of luckless marriage,	Premier fils vefve malheureux mariage,
Without issue, the two Isles in discord :	Sans nuls enfans deux Isles en discord,
Before he turns eighteen, not yet of age,	Avant dixhuict incompetant eage,
They'll marry off the next & younger lord.	De l'autre pres plus bas sera l'accord.

Following François' death, France fell into years of intermittent conflict between Catholics and Protestants. As chaos reigned, some Frenchmen looked to different authorities, including Nostradamus, for guidance or insight into the next conflagration. In the late 1580s, a high-ranking official and an eminent lawyer exchanged letters about quatrain 3.55:

The year one eye over all France shall reign,	En l'an qu'un œil en France regnera,
The court shall find itself quite befuddled :	La court sera à un bien facheux trouble :
The lord from Blois shall have killed his friend,	Le grand de Bloys son amy tuera,
The realm troubled & the fears redoubled.	Le regne mis en mal & doubte double.

The official and the lawyer could not be sure what this meant, but both entertained the idea that these "magnificent verses" had predicted the recent assassination, on the king's orders, of the ultra-Catholic Duke of Guise. The eye in the first verse referred to the monarch's desire to oversee all happenings in France. The third verse seemed all too clear (the Duke was killed in Blois), and the fourth promised more trouble ahead. By the mid-1590s, some contemporaries took on the public mantle of Nostradamian interpreter and promised to divulge the quatrains' hidden meanings. First among them was Nostradamus's secretary, Jean-Aimé de Chavigny, who depicted his master as a true prophet (rather than a mere astrologer) and promised to serve his king and his readers by illuminating France's recent past. Among the quatrains he elucidated was 6.70:

Lord of the world the great Chyren shall be,	Au chef du monde le grand Chyren sera,
Plus ultra left behind, much loved & feared :	Plus oultre après aymé, craint, redoubté :
His fame & praise shall outsurpass the skies,	Son bruit & loz les cieux surpassera,
Well pleased to be the sole victor revered.	Et du seul tiltre victeur fort contenté.

After positing that "the great Chyren" referred to Henri II (interpreters found droves of anagrams in the *Prophecies*), Chavigny concluded that the quatrain described the coronation of a king of unequaled fame. Like most interpreters, Chavigny picked freely from Nostradamus's ten Centuries, jumping from one to the next. Nostradamus had never claimed, after all, that the quatrains depicted events in chronological order. While Chavigny cautiously peered into the future, he was more comfortable relating quatrains to recent events. This pattern, too, would repeat itself: confirmation proved soothing in uncertain times.

During the seventeenth century, the quatrains continued to channel the forces that shaped and transformed European politics. Some people inquired about papal deaths and elections. In 1609, various Romans and Parisians turned to 10.91:

Roman clergy, in the year sixteen nine,	Clergé Romain l'an mil six cens & neuf,
At new year's you shall hold an election :	Au chef de l'an feras election
A gray & black monk of the Campania line,	D'un gris & noir de la Compagne yssu,
No one quite like him in dereliction.	Qui onc ne feut si maling.

This was one of only nine explicit dates in the *Prophecies*. The current pope, Paul V, had another twelve years to live—no papal deaths or elections in 1609—but other readers turned to Nostradamus to understand the demise of rulers. A year later, quatrain 7.17 seemed to have announced the assassination of French king Henri IV by a Catholic zealot:

The rare pity & mercy of this king	Le prince rare de pitié & clemence,
Whose death shall transform simply everything :	Viendra changer par mort grand cognoissance :
In times of great peace, the realm at ill ease,	Par grand repos le regne travaillé,
When the lord goes down to major defeat.	Lors que le grand tost sera estrillé.

Still others sought to anticipate the outcome of military operations, such as the English siege of the fortress of the city of Saint-Martin-de-Ré, on the island of Ré, off the western coast of France, in 1627. Quatrain 3.71 spelled it out:

Those trapped within isles long held under siege	Ceux dans les isles de long temps assiegez,
Shall gain vim & vigor against their foes,	Prendront vigueur, force contre ennemis :
While all those left outside, famished & weak,	Ceux par dehors mors de faim profligez,
Shall just starve to death as never before.	En plus grand faim que jamais seront mis.

This is the version of quatrain 3.71 that appeared in seventeenth-century editions of the *Prophecies* (slightly different from the present book's, as explained in the notes). A French pamphleteer told the English that "the great prophet Nostradamus had warned us of your arrival. Your designs are not secret enough for the Heavens to ignore them or for the stars to keep them from astrologers."

The quatrains had enough legitimacy to serve as ammunition in high-stakes political battles and propaganda wars. When they did not supply the desired outcome, or did not do so clearly enough, polemicists might simply pen new ones. Many seventeenth-century editions of the *Prophecies* quietly inserted two new quatrains at the end of the seventh Century. The content of these two quatrains varied, but the political intent was always transparent. In 1649, in the midst of the French antimonarchical revolt known as the Fronde, a pamphleteer attributed the following to Nostradamus:

When Innocent shall hold the place of Peter,	Quant Innocent tiendra le lieu de Pierre,
The Sicilian Nizaram shall see himself	Le Nizaram Cicilien se verra
In great honors, but after that shall fall	En grands honneurs, mais après il cherra
Into the quagmire of a civil war.	Dans le bourbier d'une civille guerre.

The first verse referred to the pontificate of Pope Innocent X; the second to the Italian-born Cardinal Mazarin ("Nizaram" being an anagram), principal minister of the young Louis XIV. God, one commentator explained, would maintain Cardinal Mazarin in a mire following the war he had caused. This was not the last time people would ponder forged quatrains.

Under the reign of Louis XIV (1643–1715), commentators and sycophants continued to tap Nostradamus to make sense of their world, act upon current events, imbue them with wonder, or ingratiate themselves to the king. In 1697, for instance, quatrain 7.10 was seen as a prediction of the French siege of Barcelona:

For the great prince who rules nearby Le Mans,	Par le grand prince limitrophe du Mans,
Leading his army with courage & style :	Preux & vaillant chef de grand exercite :
On land & sea of the French & Normans,	Par mer & terre de Gallotz & Normans,
Pass Gibraltar, loot Barcelona's isle.	Calpre passer, Barcelone pillé isle.

A few years later, the author of a book entitled *The Key to Nostradamus* concluded from quatrain 1.92 that the Peace of Ryswick, which had ended the Nine Years' War in 1697, would prove short-lived. France, however, would be spared further misfortune:

Under one, universal peace decreed,	Sous un la paix par tout sera clamée,
But not for long : plunder & rebellion :	Mais non long temps pille & rebellion :
Defiant city stormed by land & sea :	Par refus ville, terre, & mer entamée :
Dead or captured, a third of a million.	Mors & captifz le tiers d'un million.

If any country had cause for concern, this commentator added, it was Great Britain. Quatrain 2.68 said so clearly:

The northern army shall be great in size,	De l'aquilon les efforts seront grands :
The door to the Ocean shall open wide :	Sus l'Occean sera la porte ouverte :
The throne shall be recovered on the isle,	Le regne en l'isle sera reintegrand,
London tremble when the sails are espied.	Tremblera Londres par voille descouverte.

Few quatrains have been interpreted more often or linked to more events over the decades. In 1744, for instance, the Parisian lawyer Edmond Barbier wrote in his diary that the northern army in the first verse denoted the French fleet, which had sailed out to engage British warships near Toulon. If Nostradamus was to be believed, Barbier wrote, they would triumph (they did).

While the *Prophecies* retained a special allure in France, their posterity extended to neighboring countries. Individual quatrains circulated in Great Britain long before the first full translation of 1672. With its revolutions and regicides, its natural calamities and mighty wars, Great Britain witnessed an astrological and prophetic outpouring in the seventeenth century, and Nostradamus found a home across the Channel. First came the civil war and the beheading of King Charles I in 1649. The famed astrologer William Lilly, who sided with Parliament, declared that kings would never again rule over England. How could one doubt it when Nostradamus had predicted the regicide? Here it was in quatrain 9.49:

Ghent & Brussels shall march against Antwerp,	Gand & Bruceles marcheront contre Envers
The senate of London its king shall slay :	Senat de Londres mettront à mort leur roy
Wine & salt contribute to his reverse,	Le sel & vin luy seront à l'envers,
Thus throwing the realm into disarray.	Pour eux avoir le regne en desarroy.

The quatrain's second verse received considerable attention following Charles's execution. Supporters of the king read it as a comment on what one of them called "the shameful and cruel demise of the King of England." A few years later, contemporaries pointed to quatrain 10.22 as evidence of Oliver Cromwell's usurpation and tyranny:

Unwilling to consent to a divorce	Pour ne vouloir consentir au divorce,
Which afterward might be deemed unseemly,	Qui puis apres sera cogneu indigne,
The king of the Isles shall be forced to flee :	Le roy des Isles sera chassé par force
Instead, a king whom no mark does endorse.	Mis à son lieu que de roy n'aura signe.

The quatrains remained in the public eye following the demise of the Protectorate in 1659 and the restoration of the monarchy. In 1665, a plague epidemic killed thousands in London—perhaps one-fifth of the city's population. The *Prophecies* had long been linked to such natural calamities, and they remained so at this time, with politics in the mix. Quatrain 2.53 came under scrutiny:

The mighty plague in the city by the sea	La grande peste de cité maritime
Shall not end until the death is avenged	Ne cessera que mort ne soit vengée
Of innocent blood unjustly condemned :	De juste sang par pris damné sans crime :
The great dame outraged by the knavery.	De la grand dame par feincte n'outraigée.

Theophilus de Garencières, who had not only translated the *Prophecies* into English in 1672 but also provided commentaries, explained that the quatrain had foretold the epidemic and explained its causes. In his reading of these verses, the plague would not end until Charles had been avenged. The king (or *juste sang*, which he translated as "just blood") had been condemned without committing a crime while the sumptuous Cathedral of St. Paul ("the great dame") had been "polluted and made a stable by those prophane wretches." These were Garencières's own words.

The plague was followed by the devastating Great Fire of London, which lasted three days in 1666 and destroyed much of the medieval quarter. The pertinent quatrain (2.51) circulated in popular almanacs and created a stir at posh dinner parties:

No blood of the just shall be spilled in London :	Le sang du juste à Londres fera faulte :
Six times twenty-three consumed by lightning :	Bruslés par fouldres de vint & trois les six :
The ancient dame shall fall from high station :	La dame antique cherra de place haute :
Many of the same sect shall lose their lives.	De mesme secte plusieurs seront occis.

Three times twenty (*vint & trois*) added to six (*les six*) came out to sixty-six, the year 1666. The "dame" referred again to St. Paul's. The last verse, however, posed difficulties. While some believed that the members of the "same sect" were worshippers of the Sun and the planets, Garencières insisted that the verse denoted the many churches involved in "the same woeful conflagration." It was all about divine punishment and expiation—an apocalyptic strand that resonated in seventeenth-century Britain and would grow more preeminent in later readings of the *Prophecies*. By this time, some Britons were also mulling over the very suggestive quatrain 3.57:

Seven times you'll see the British people change,	Sept fois changer verrez gent Britannique,
Stained with blood, in two hundred ninety years,	Tainte en sang en deux cens nonante an,
Not that they'll be free, under German sway :	Franche non point, par apuy Germanique :
Bastarnian climes being what Aries fears.	Aries doubte son pole Bastarnan.

The quatrain seemed to encompass all the upheavals afflicting Great Britain. Commentators tried to tabulate how many such "changes" had already occurred and how many lay in store. This quatrain resurfaced in 1845, a momentous date for Great Britain if one added 1555 and the 290 years mentioned in the second verse. *Fraser's Magazine for Town and Country* discussed the matter at length before declaring, perhaps tongue-in-cheek, that "we hope it bodes no evil." The year 1845 witnessed a catastrophic bridge collapse in Great Yarmouth and the loss of Sir John Franklin's expedition to the Northwest Passage, not to mention the start of the Great Famine in Ireland.

Back in the seventeenth century, the Fronde, the plague, and the Fire of London had set precedents. When they anticipated or encountered turmoil, residents of France and England and other European countries kept turning to the *Prophecies*, which now seemed ancient, mysterious, and reputable. To be sure, the quatrains faded from view during the eighteenth century: reason, science, and worldly decorum did not grant them a place at the table. But they never disappeared altogether. In France, the rapid ascent and collapse of Scottish financier John Law's Banque Générale drew attention to quatrain 1.53 around 1720:

Alas one shall see a great nation bleed	Las qu'on verra grand peuple tourmenté,
And the holy law & all of Christendom	Et la Loy saincte en totale ruine
Reduced to utter ruin by other creeds,	Par autres loix toute Chrestienté,
Each time a new gold, silver mine is found.	Quand d'or, d'argent trouvé nouvelle mine.

The lure of gold and silver (which Law promised to deliver through his scheme in Louisiana) was indeed making France bleed. Meanwhile, Italians paid attention to quatrain 3.35 in the early 1730s:

At Europe's farthermost western reaches,	Du plus profond de l'Occident d'Europe,
To poor folk a small infant shall be born :	De pauvres gens un jeune enfant naistra :
He shall seduce great crowds with his speeches,	Qui par sa langue seduira grande trope,
His great fame spreading to Orient shores.	Son bruit au regne d'Orient plus croistra.

Here was a prediction about the birth of an infant, born of Philip V of Spain, who would attain great fame. In Tuscany, where the duke Gian Gastone de' Medici was childless, some concluded that the infant would eventually rule the Grand Duchy.

Someone had altered the original French in small but pivotal ways in order to make the quatrain more pertinent. In the second verse, *De pauves gens un jeune enfant naistra* became *De doubles noces un jeune enfant naîtra* (From a double marriage a small infant shall be born)—a reference to Philip's second marriage. In the third verse, *Qui par sa langue seduira* became *Qui vers le Po mènera grande troupe* (who would bring a large army to the Po). Nostradamus's international score lent itself to regional variations.

Then came the French Revolution. In the midst of this modern revolution, with its breathless pace of change and its mounting violence, people turned to the *Prophecies* to gain a grip on time and politics and events that were at once wondrous and sinister. Some revolutionaries pointed early on to quatrain 2.10:

Before too long all things shall be ordained :	Avant long temps le tout sera rangé :
We sense a sinister age on its way :	Nous esperons un siecle bien senestre :
The state of marks & seals shall be most changed :	L'estat des marques & des scelz bien changé :
Few to be found content with their stations.	Peu trouveront qu'à son rang vueille estre.

The quatrain referenced prerevolutionary discontent and promised that unrest would end soon. Opponents, in contrast, marshaled quatrains such as 3.50:

The government of that mighty town,	La republique de la grande cité,
Too stubborn to withdraw beyond the gates	A grand rigueur ne voudra consentir :
As so summoned by the king's trumpet call :	Roy sortir hors par trompette cité,
The town shall regret this, ladder at wall.	L'eschelle au mur, la cité repentir.

Paris would free the king (*Roy sortir*) and repent for its sacrilegious behavior (*la cité repentir*). Partisans and enemies of the Revolution alike drew solace or legitimacy from the *Prophecies*.

Both sides were likewise struck by this line in the *Prophecies*' Epistle to Henri II:

Beginning with that [unidentified] year the Christian Church shall be persecuted more fiercely than it ever was in Africa, & this shall last until the year seventeen ninety-two, which shall be considered the beginning of a new age.	Commençant icelle annee sera faite plus grande persecution à l'eglise Chretienne que n'a eté faite en Afrique, & durera cette icy jusques l'an mil sept cens nonante deux que l'on cuydera etre une renovation de siecle.

This seemed to confirm the French Revolution's adversarial relationship with the Church, the Civil Constitution of the Clergy (which allowed the state to name clerics and required priests to swear allegiance to the Revolution), and the advent of a republic in 1792. Some revolutionaries saw this prediction as an endorsement of recent changes and a promise that France was freeing itself from religious superstition. Others understood it differently. According to Nostradamus, they said, the persecution of Catholics would come to an end during this "new age." Pamphlets and newspapers parsed the passage. A revolutionary club posted it outside its door for a week, so that citizens could make up their own minds. In Great Britain, too, people paid attention.

During the nineteenth century, Nostradamus hence became the prophet who had predicted the French Revolution. Journalists and others linked dozens of quatrains to the National Assembly, the decapitation of Louis XVI, and other revolutionary milestones. Again and again, they returned to quatrain 9.20, which had ostensibly predicted the royal family's botched attempt to flee Paris, disguised as commoners, on June 21, 1791:

He shall come by night through the woods of Reines,	De nuict viendra par la forest de Reines,
Two via Pierre Blanche, Herne, & Vaultorte,	Deux pars vaultorte Herne la pierre blanche,
The black monk all in gray within Varennes,	Le moyne noir en gris dedans Varennes
Elected cap. causes storm, fire, blood, sword.	Esleu cap. cause tempeste feu, sang tranche.

Commentators proposed that the royal party had traveled east along a roundabout route (*vaultorte*) and crossed the forest of Rennes-en-Grenouilles (spelled "Raines" in earlier times). "*Herne*" might even be an anagram of *reine* (queen), with the *h* standing in for an *i*. Marie Antoinette wore white clothes, and, according to some reports, her hair turned that same color following her arrest. The third verse introduced the king, wearing an iron gray coat and a round slouch hat that made him resemble a Franciscan monk. It was in the village of Varennes that the royal party was detained after being recognized. As a constitutional monarch, Louis XVI was indeed an "elected Capet," a member of the dynasty that had acceded to the French throne in the tenth century. "Blood, sword" required little comment.

Nor did the widely circulated quatrains that pertained to Napoléon Bonaparte, the Corsican who had risen through the ranks in the 1790s, achieved resounding victories, become consul, and then ruled France and swathes of Europe as emperor until 1815. A new generation turned to Nostradamus for evidence of the emperor's mythic nature, confirmation of his rise or fall, and insight into what lay ahead for the ruler and his country. Supporters of Napoléon were partial to quatrain 8.57:

From simple soldier he shall race to power,	De souldat simple parviendra en empire,
From short tunic to long robe he shall lunge :	De robe courte parviendra à la longue
Most valiant in arms, though at his worst hour	Vaillant aux armes en eglise ou plus pyre,
Shall pursue priests as water does a sponge.	Vexer les prestres comme l'eau fait l'esponge.

The quatrain recapped the rise of a lowly born but valiant leader who had ruled supreme and purified the French church. Further evidence of his achievements was detected in quatrain 2.29:

Man from the East shall sally from his seat,	L'Oriental sortira de son siege,
Crossing all the Apennines to see Gaul :	Passer les monts Apennins voir la Gaule :
He shall pass through showers of rain & sleet,	Transpercera du ciel les eaux & neige,
And with his rod he shall strike one & all.	En un chascun frappera de sa gaule.

The "man from the East" was the Corsican general who, depending on the interpretation, had either vanquished the elements and traversed the Alps (rain and sleet) or else left Egypt to seize power in Paris. A final quatrain (1.60) contained a much-quoted verse about the emperor's birth and three others that could be marshaled against him:

Near Italy an Emperor shall be born	Un Empereur naistra près d'Italie,
Who shall cost the Empire a pretty pence :	Qui à l'Empire sera vendu bien cher :
They shall ask to what people he is sworn,	Diront avec quelz gens il se ralie,
Finding him more a butcher than a prince.	Qu'on trouvera moins prince que boucher.

The association with Napoléon buoyed the Nostradamus phenomenon throughout the nineteenth century. There were new and cheaper editions of the *Prophecies* for a broader readership, interpretations and translations, and all kinds of articles in magazines and daily newspapers. Europeans from all social classes now read about Nostradamus in columns, editorials, dispatches from foreign correspondents, historical features, wire copy, and the innumerable short items that filled up newspaper columns. As in the past, some quatrains resonated in a single country alone while others traveled across borders. Nostradamus could promise favorable resolutions and at the same time feed a mood of despair.

In 1854, London's *New Monthly Magazine* played with the idea that 8.59 promised victory in the Crimean War:

Twice shall it rise, & twice be brought low,	Par deux fois hault, par deux fois mis à bas
The East like the West ever growing weak :	L'orient aussi l'occident foyblira
After full many battles shall its foe,	Son adversaire apres plusieurs combats,
Pursued by sea, founder in time of need.	Par mer chassé au besoing faillira.

During the Franco-Prussian War of 1870, the *Hamburger Nachrichten* (seen as the mouthpiece of Prussian leader Otto von Bismarck) was delighted with quatrain 10.30:

Blood nephew of the newly proclaimed saint,	Nepveu & sang du sainct nouveau venu,
His surname shall support arches & beams :	Par le surnom soustient arcs & couvert
They'll be expelled, killed, chased away naked :	Seront chassez mis a mort chassez nu,
Into red & black they'll convert their green.	En rouge & noir convertiront leur vert.

Napoléon I was the saint mentioned in the first verse, and French emperor Napoléon III was his nephew. The former had gone down in defeat, and the latter would follow soon enough. The last verse was more mysterious, but the interpreter offered a symbolic reading of the green, the red, and the black: "their hope will be turned into blood and mourning."

It certainly seemed that way in France, where Prussian troops were fast advancing toward Paris. Citizens grew alarmed by quatrain 3.84:

The great city shall be quite desolate,	La grand cité sera bien desolée,
No single inhabitant shall remain :	Des habitans un seul n'y demourra :
Its walls & women, churches & nuns raped,	Mur, sexe, temple, & vierge violée,
All dying by sword, fire, cannon, plague.	Par fer, feu, peste, canon peuple mourra.

In this apocalyptic climate, one Frenchwoman told the *New York Times* that she had memorized long passages of the *Prophecies* and could no longer fall asleep at night without dreading a catastrophe. Others read the book and found intimations of a reckoning for a nation that had abandoned tradition and monarchy in favor of illegitimate rulers and modern commerce. The anti-Semitic demagogue Edouard Drumont thus began with the destruction of Paris in 3.84—a necessary step toward purification and regeneration. He then moved to 1.32, which confirmed the demise of Napoléon III and announced the arrival of a savior monarch. This mythic royal figure, which had resurfaced repeatedly since the Renaissance, would now draw France out of its morass and restore the country's moral purity and majesty:

The empire shall soon find itself retired	Le grand empire sera tost translaté,
Into a small place which shall fast expand :	En lieu petit, qui bien tost viendra croistre :
A tiny space within a narrow shire	Lieu bien infime d'exiguë comté,
In midst of which his scepter he shall plant.	Où au milieu viendra poser son sceptre.

Turn-of-the-century anxieties about vertiginous progress, national decline, or political corruption also led people toward gloomy quatrains. While French journalists found confirmation of the 1910 Paris flood (in 4.80), British readers insisted that quatrain 3.16 announced a social revolution in the British Isles, the destruction of London, and the martyrdom of the Prince of Wales, who would die while fighting Socialists and foreign foes:

The English prince, Mars at mid-sky his sign,	Le prince Anglois Mars à son cœur de ciel,
Shall seek out the fortune he has in store :	Voudra poursuivre sa fortune prospere :
One duelist shall pierce the other's spleen,	De deux duelles l'un percera le fiel,
Hated by him, but by his mother adored.	Hay de luy, bien-aymé de sa mere.

Unimaginable destruction came in 1914, of course, and commentators continued to uncover pertinent verses in the *Prophecies*. In France, some reinterpreted quatrain 3.84, which still lingered in collective memory, to announce the country's final days. Others detected a merrier future in quatrain 10.89:

In marble shall the walls of brick now rise,	De brique en marbre seront les murs reduits
Seven & fifty years of lasting peace,	Sept & cinquante annees pacifiques,
Aqueducts restored, joy to all mankind,	Joie aux humains renové Laqueduict,
Health, abundant fruit, blissful honeyed times.	Santé, grandz fruict joye & temps melifique.

Peace would resurface from the ruins (*murs reduits*); people would once again learn to enjoy life; and the next fifty-seven years would prove as sweet as honey. In Germany, meanwhile, newspapers returned to quatrain 2.68, of eighteenth-century fame, and anticipated a naval victory over England ("London tremble when the sails are espied").

This did not pan out, but Nostradamus was not discredited for long. By the late 1930s, a wave of Nostramania hit the West. As astrologers and palm readers grew increasingly popular, ever more books and articles linked quatrains to ongoing turbulence. Quatrain 9.16, for instance, seemed to foretell Franco's victory in the Spanish civil war:

From Castelfranco troops shall make forays,	De castel Franco sortira l'assemblee,
The irksome envoy shall go his separate way :	L'ambassadeur non plaisant fera scisme :
Those of the coast shall leap into the fray,	Ceux de Ribiere seront en la meslée,
And deny entry to the mighty bay.	Et au grand goulphre desnier ont l'entrée.

Most Europeans inquired about the looming war. Hitler's annexations and invasions, his march into Poland, and the British and French declarations of war in September 1939 darkened the mood. In France, some proposed that quatrain 2.9 had foretold the rise and fall of the barbaric German chancellor (the "thin one"):

The thin one shall rule for nine years in peace,	Neuf ans le regne le maigre en paix tiendra,
Then fall into an immense thirst for blood :	Puis il cherra en soif si sanguinaire :
For this lawless one a great people dies,	Pour luy grand peuple sans foy & loy mourra,
To be slain by a rival far more good.	Tué par un beaucoup plus debonnaire.

The most quoted quatrain about Hitler, however, was 2.24:

Beasts wild with hunger shall swim the rivers :	Bestes farouches de faim fleuves tranner :
Most of the host shall move against Ister :	Plus part du camp encontre Hister sera :
He'll have the great one dragged in iron cage,	En caige fer le grand fera treisner,
When the child the German Rhine surveys.	Quand Rin enfant Germain observera.

"Ister" ("Hister" in the old French, formerly spelled "Hifter") most probably referred to the Danube River. In the nineteenth century, French commentators had presented it as an anagram of "Thiers," the name of a leading politician. In the late 1930s it became Hitler, whose wild beasts were poised to attack. Some concluded from the last two verses that the dictator would end up in a cage. What an appealing prospect, mused one Parisian journal in October 1939: Hitler's cage would be rolled down the Champs-Elysées and placed before the Tomb of the Unknown Soldier, under the Arc de Triomphe. There, the French, English, and Polish leaders would make the dictator kneel and beg for forgiveness. Such interpretations gained traction in the United States, where countless books and articles now drew attention to the quatrains. Nostradamus had surfaced there in earlier decades, but only during World War II did he become a household name. American newspapers reported that Hitler was terrorized by quatrain 2.24 and the prospect of ending up in a cage.

German commentators did not link "Hister" to Hitler, but some Nazi leaders paid attention to Nostradamus. A 1921 book by Carl Loog, a postal official who claimed to have discovered the numerological key to the *Prophecies*, went through several editions in the 1930s. Hitler himself owned a copy. Among the quatrains Loog highlighted was the famous 3.57, with its seven changes afflicting the British people. The Bastarnians in the fourth verse, he explained, designated Germanic tribes who had once occupied the lands granted to Poland after World War I. Loog added that the 290-year countdown had begun in 1649 and would thus end in 1939: "Nostradamus evidently wants to explain that 1939 will go hand in hand with the last and greatest English crisis and a crisis for the reconstituted country of Poland."

By 1939, another quatrain came to the attention of Propaganda Minister Joseph Goebbels. It was 5.94:

He shall shift toward greater Germania	Translatera en la grand Germanie,
Brabant & Flanders, Ghent, Bruges, Boulogne :	Brabant & Flandres, Gand, Bruges, & Bolongne :
Feigning truce, the grand Duke of Armenia	La traifve faincte, le grand duc d'Armenie,
Shall fall upon Vienna & Cologne.	Asaillira Vienne & la Cologne.

The "grand Duke" was the chief of the German tribe of the Cherusci—in other words, the Führer of Gross Deutschland who had sent armed warriors into the Rhineland (including Cologne) and then Vienna. Brabant and Flanders were next for Greater Germania. Goebbels ordered agents to spread the rumor that 5.94 predicted the temporary occupation of France and a thousand-year Nazi empire. In the spring of 1940, German planes prepared the invasion of Belgium, Holland, and France by dropping thousands of leaflets about this and other quatrains. The goal was to sow panic and weaken the resolve of civilian populations.

In the United States, interest in Nostradamus intensified after the German invasion of the Soviet Union and Deputy Führer Rudolf Hess's flight to Scotland in 1941. Wire services linked this bizarre event to quatrain 9.90, which told of a German officer pretending to submit himself:

A captain of greater Germania	Un capitaine de la grand Germanie
Shall pretend to deliver to the King	Se viendra rendre par simulé secours
Of Kings the support of Pannonia,	Un Roy des roys ayde de Pannonie,
His revolt achieving massive bleeding.	Que sa revolte fera de sang grand cours.

U.S. propaganda, too, gravitated toward the quatrains, especially in the short features (standard fare in movie theaters) that MGM devoted to Nostradamus. By 1944, the studio was focusing on quatrain 3.96:

The lord of Fossano's throat shall be cut	Chef de Fossan aura gorge coupée,
By the master of the hunt, the deed be	Par le ducteur du limier & levrier :
Done by the men from the Tarpeian Rock :	Le faict patré par ceux du mont Tarpée,
Saturn in Leo, February thirteen.	Saturne en Leo 13. de Fevrier.

The "*Chef de Fossan*" was Hitler, born in the thirteenth degree in the sign of Leo. The master of the hunt (the *limier*) was Hermann Göring, commander of the German air force, while *leurier,* or rather *levrier* (the greyhound), designated Heinrich Himmler, chief of the SS. According to Nostradamus, the leader of the bloodhounds or the leader of the greyhounds would cut Hitler's throat. It was not clear which one it would be—and, frankly, this hardly mattered as long as the deed was done.

Interest in Nostradamus waned at war's end, a by-product of prophetic fatigue and hope in a new postwar era, but the atomic age and the cold war soon generated their own anxieties. During the 1950s, Western media and publishers found intimations of both in the *Prophecies.* One could for instance discern the atomic bombings of Hiroshima and Nagasaki in quatrain 2.91:

At dawn a great ball of fire shall appear,	Soleil levant un grand feu l'on verra,
So loud & bright as it rolls to the North :	Bruit & clarté vers Aquilon tendants :
In its burning globe screams of death they'll hear :	Dedans le rond mort & cris l'on orra :
Witnesses dying by fire, hunger, sword.	Par glaive, feu, faim, mort les attendants.

In 1947 the author of the widely read *Complete Prophecies of Nostradamus,* one Henry C. Roberts, pondered the advent of atomic power via quatrain 9.44:

Flee, flee, O Geneva, every last one,	Migres, migre de Genesve trestous
Saturn's gold for iron shall be exchanged :	Saturne d'or en fer se changera,
RAYPOZ shall wipe out all opposition,	Le contre RAYPOZ exterminera tous,
Before his advent, the sky's signs shall change.	Avant l'a ruent le ciel signes fera.

Though Roberts did not explain what "RAYPOZ" meant, he concluded that Nostradamus warned "with terrifying finality . . . of the eventual destruction of our civilization by means of the release of atomic energy." The last verse held out one last chance of controlling human destiny, however. Roberts tapped the mix of foreboding and hope that had underlain readings of the *Prophecies* for centuries.

Nostradamus's predilection for colors made him a natural guide to the cold war. After all, quatrain 8.19 promised that

The reds shall work to put things right instead   Pour l'esclaircir les rouges marcheront

And quatrain 3.1:

The enemy red shall grow pale with fear   Rouge adversaire de fraieur viendra pasle

Red could plausibly denote all kinds of things during the Renaissance, including the robes worn by leading magistrates. The adjective's meaning had shifted over time, but it retained its suggestive power.

Readers thus uncovered political forces such as Communism in the quatrains. But they also found leaders and celebrities galore—each one triggering a new burst of interest in Nostradamus. In 1963, a *Chicago Tribune* columnist suggested that quatrain 8.97 had predicted that three brothers would take over the government:

At the limits of the VAR power shall change,	Aux fins du VAR changer le pompotans,
Near its banks three fine children shall be born :	Pres du rivage les trois beaux enfans naistre.
Ruin to the people when they come of age,	Ruyne au peuple par aage competans
So altering the realm it shall grow no more.	Regne au pays changer plus voir croistre.

It was of course the Kennedys. The columnist devoted little attention to the dire third verse, but in the 1970s and 1980s interpreters claimed that quatrain 1.26 described the assassinations of John F. and Robert Kennedy:

During daytime a great clap of lightning,	Le grand du fouldre tumbe d'heure diurne,
Ill omen from the bearer of tidings :	Mal est predict par porteur postulaire :
The following portent falling at night :	Suivant presaige tumbe d'heure nocturne,
Conflict in Reims, London, Tuscan blight.	Conflit Reims, Londres, Etrusque pestifere.

The president was shot down by a sudden thunderbolt in broad daylight, and his brother died in the early morning. The second verse referred to the many warnings and threats that both men had received during their terms. The last verse outlined the international repercussions of their deaths. In this quatrain, as in so many others, the individual and the collective come together.

In the early 1980s, it was French Socialist François Mitterrand and Pope John Paul II who turned Nostradamus into a global bestseller. A French pharmaceutical executive named Jean-Charles de Fontbrune had used philology and computer analysis to provide a new book-length interpretation of the *Prophecies*. His most striking commentary surrounded quatrain 2.97:

Pontiff of Rome, beware of approaching	Romain Pontife garde de t'approcher,
The city where the two rivers pool :	De la cité que deux fleuves arrose,
You shall come to spit up your blood here,	Ton sang viendras au près de là cracher,
You & yours, when the rose is in bloom.	Toy & les tiens quand fleurira la rose.

The pope's blood would flow once the French Left gained power. The rose mentioned in the fourth verse—symbol of the French Socialist Party—was indeed in bloom following Mitterrand's election as president in May 1981. Three days later came the assassination attempt on the pope. The quatrain appeared to announce other attacks, perhaps in Lyons, where two rivers come together (the Rhône and Saône). Less than two decades later, the death of Princess Diana drew attention to the second verse of quatrain 2.28:

The next to last of the prophet's name	Le penultiesme du surnom du prophete,
Shall take Joveday as his day of relaxation :	Prendra Dial pour son jour & repos :
He shall wander far with his frenetic brain,	Loing vaguera par frenetique teste,
Delivering a great nation from taxation.	Et delivrant un grand peuple d'impos.

Many editions of the *Prophecies* refer to "Diane" in the second verse. This was probably a misprint for *Dial*, which comes from the Latin *dialis*: relating to Jupiter, i.e., to Thursday. In 1997, however, the reference to Diane alone mattered.

By then, interest in Nostradamus revolved once again around natural catastrophes and new geopolitical threats. In a 1981 docudrama called *The Man Who Saw Tomorrow*, Orson Welles started a small panic in southern California by declaring that quatrain 10.67 foretold an earthquake and the destruction of Los Angeles:

So great the earthquake in the month of May,	Le tremblement si fort au mois de May,
Saturn in Goat, Jove, Mercury in Bull,	Saturne, Caper, Jupiter, Mercure au beuf :
And Venus, Mars in Crab, at Annonay :	Venus aussi Cancer, Mars, en Nonnay,
Bigger than eggs, hailstones by the handful.	Tombera gresle lors plus grosse qu'un euf.

Welles explained that the astrological configuration described in the second and third verses would next occur in Los Angeles in 1988. The earthquake did take place, but a year later and in northern California. The prediction had come close enough for some people.

Meanwhile, perceptions of geopolitical threats in the West were shifting from Soviet nuclear missiles to Muslims and Arabs. Nostradamus himself had lived during an era that looked at the Turkish empire with a mix of awe and trepidation. During the Renaissance, many readers of the *Prophecies* had been obsessed with this menace. The same was true in the twentieth century. In 1907, for instance, New York's *Metropolitan Magazine* found evidence of "yellow perils" in quatrain 6.80:

The realm of Fez into Europe shall spread,	De Fez le regne parviendra à ceux d'Europe.
Burning its cities, slashing with the sword :	Feu leur cité, & lame trenchera :
Land & sea, the horde of the Asian lord,	Le grand d'Asie terre & mer à grand troupe,
Blue turbans most, shall hunt the cross to death.	Que bleux pers, croix, à mort dechassera.

These anxieties have grown yet more acute in recent decades. Quatrain 2.29, which had surfaced during the Napoleonic era, now warned about the "Great Invasion of the Orient" and the Ayatollah Khomeini, the "man from the East" who was imposing Muslim orthodoxy on Iran. Similarly, readers linked quatrain 6.33 to the Gulf War and the defeat of Saddam Hussein:

Bloodied by Alus, his remaining force	Sa main derniere par Alus sanguinaire,
Shall be unable to retreat by the sea :	Ne se pourra par la mer guarentir :
An army is feared between the two streams :	Entre deux fleuves craindre main militaire,
Black & wrathful, he shall inspire remorse.	Le noir, l'ireux le fera repentir.

Around the turn of the millennium, such disquiet melded with apocalyptic fears to associate Nostradamus with a series of real and imagined crises. A quatrain about 1999 (10.72) had loomed in the West for more than a century, announcing world revolution, social upheaval, or religious reckoning. It now grew ubiquitous:

The year nineteen ninety-nine, seventh month,	L'an mil neuf cens nonante neuf sept mois
The sky shall send a great King to defray	Du ciel viendra un grand Roy deffraieur
And restore the great King from Angoumois :	Resusciter le grand Roy d'Angolmois.
Before, after March, blessed be his reign.	Avant apres Mars regner par bon heur.

The first verse seemed to signal the lunar and total solar eclipses that would occur that summer. The second verse was linked to a "great King of Terror," a *grand Roy d'effrayeur*, who causes dismay or fright. But the original verse initially mentioned a *grand Roy deffraieur*: in other words, a king who defrays. An apostrophe had mysteriously surfaced decades after publication and has remained in place ever since. The last verses have lent themselves to different readings, from an airborne attack on Paris to the fall of a Soviet space probe to the appearance of a savior figure.

This quatrain traveled around the globe—Nostradamian globalization in full swing—and reemerged partially days after 9/11. A verse attributed to Nostradamus shot across the Internet and brought the *Prophecies* to the top of best-seller lists in the United States and Europe and beyond: "From the sky will come a great King of Terror." Quatrain 1.87 became equally omnipresent online:

Ennosigaeus, the fire at earth's core,	Ennosigée, feu du centre de terre,
Shall set the New City all aquake :	Fera trembler au tour de cité neufve :
Two lords shall go on fighting futile wars :	Deux grands rochiers long temps feront la guerre,
New stream makes Arethusa blush with shame.	Puis Arethuse rougira nouveau fleuve.

Here were the fire in the new city and the battle between lords—the clash of Eastern and Western civilizations that, many believed, had broken out over the Manhattan skyline.

Nostradamus's presence on the Internet, where quatrains are easily taken out of context and adorned with long interpretative disquisitions, may reflect a historical evolution. People's relationship with the verses may grow less direct and tactile as they read isolated quatrains or Nostradamian exegetes rather than the full *Prophecies*. One may sneer at these interpreters and even relegate the verses to what the nineteenth-century journalist Charles Mackay called "extraordinary popular delusions." But let us also appreciate the remarkable posterity of a book that has kept on sprouting new verses, new stories, and new ways of grappling with a world that is both bereft of meaning and overflowing with it. Besides yielding insights about prophecy and poetics, the *Prophecies* also provide a history of confirmation and anticipation, a history of interpretation and propaganda, and a history of the anxieties and aspirations that successive generations have projected onto cryptic verses. There is always another quatrain around the corner, promising to explain what seems unexplainable. In this respect, too, the book must be seen as extraordinary, though not only for the reasons that Mackay had put forward.

STÉPHANE GERSON

Notes

In preparing these notes I have drawn on, among other sources, Edgar Leoni, *Nostradamus and His Prophecies* (1961); Pierre Brind'Amour, *Nostradamus astrophile* (1993) and *Les premières centuries, ou Prophéties* (1996); Peter Lemesurier, *The Nostradamus Encyclopedia* (1997) and *The Illustrated Prophecies* (2003); Roger Prévost, *Nostradamus: Le mythe et la réalité* (1999); Bruno Petey-Girard, ed., *Les Prophéties* (2003); and Denis Crouzet, *Nostradamus: Une médicine des âmes à la Renaissance* (2011). I have cross-referenced the quatrains to provide a sense of the intricate internal echoes—or synapses—that pull the poem together.

RICHARD SIEBURTH

PREFACE TO CÉSAR

Following the example of Eugène Bareste's 1840 edition of the *Prophecies*, most editors of Nostradamus have divided his preface to the 1555 edition, originally printed as a single unparagraphed block of prose, into numbered sections. To facilitate its reading, I have instead broken the text into paragraphs, following Nostradamus's original punctuation and the overall cadences of his prose. All the passages in italics are in Latin in the original. Biblical citations are taken from the King James Version.

César Nostradame my son: César Nostradamus, born December 18, 1553, was fourteen months old at this point; his father was fifty-one.

Only those who are inspired: From Giovanni Pontano's Italian translation of Pseudo-Ptolemy's *Centiloquium*, first aphorism.

unfortunate events that were to take place throughout the world: Translated from Savonarola's *Compendium revelationum* (1495), contained in the *Mirabilis liber* of 1522—whose compendium of prophecies was an important source for Nostradamus.

Give not that which is holy unto the dogs: Matthew 7:6, from Savonarola.

thou hast hid these things from the wise & prudent: Matthew 11:25, echoing Savonarola.

as do the rays of the sun whose influence works upon bodies both elementary & non-elementary: Entire passage translated from Petrus

Crinitus, *De honesta disciplina* (1543)—another major sourcebook for Nostradamus—here confusing the plural gods of the original with the singular God of Christianity.

It is not for you to know the times: Acts 1:7.

For those divine works which are totally absolute: Translated from Crinitus, *De honesta disciplina*.

For he that is now called a Prophet was beforetime called Seer: I Samuel 9:9, after Savonarola.

For the secrets of God are inscrutable: This and the preceding paragraph translate Savonarola.

things can be known through the Herculean trances of epilepsy: The French reads "par comitiale agitation Hiraclinne." *Le mal comitial* (*morbus comitialis* in Latin) was a term for epilepsy, from which Hercules (according to Hippocrates and Galen) was said to suffer. Cornelius Agrippa had also linked epilepsy to prophetic possession.

the voice heard at the hem by means of the slender flame: Cf. the introductory quatrain 1.2.

all things are naked & opened &c: Hebrews 4:13.

I can err, fail, be deceived: A Latin dictum also quoted in Nostradamus's letters.

from now to the year 3797: The year 3797 would fall nine thousand years after the creation of the world in 5204 B.C.E.

Some might well raise their brows: This and the following two paragraphs are loosely adapted from Savonarola.

the world of letters shall undergo such a massive & incomparable collapse: Cf. quatrain 1.62.

the reign of Saturn shall return: This entire passage is inspired by Richard Roussat's *Livre de l'estat et mutation des temps* (1550): "As for the present work and treatise, it will be divided into four parts: the first will show the conjunction marking the End of the World and Last Times . . . which shall take place after a period of seven thousand years. . . . The second part will demonstrate the end of the world through the movement and rule of the seven planets that are called wandering stars, each of which governs the world for the space of 354 years and four months. . . . Next Mars was in control, up to 6732 years and four months for the third time; and finally the Moon, which governs at present, took over its rule, which it should maintain until the year 7086 [i.e., 1887 C.E.]; and the Sun after it until the year 7441 [i.e., 2242 C.E.]." It was apparently by adding this latter date (2242) to the date of the publication of the first installment of his prophecies (1555) that Nostradamus in this preface to his son César arrives at the date 3797 for the fulfillment of his prophecies. As for the return of Saturn, Nostradamus follows Roussat's claim that seven archangels governing seven celestial bodies will successively reign over seven periods of 354 years and four months.

which shall not vary from age to age: from Roussat.

Mohammedan dreamings: Pontano's commentary on the first aphorism of Pseudo-Ptolemy's *Centiloquium* speaks of the *Mahometani* as a species of prophets.

Then will I visit their transgression with the rod: Psalms 89:32, via Savonarola.

I will not pity, nor spare, nor have mercy, but destroy them: Jeremiah 13:14 and Ezekiel 6:11, via Savonarola.

but when ignorance is cast aside: From Andrea Alciato's *Emblemata* (1531).

CENTURY I

1.1 **Being seated:** From Iamblichus's description of Apollo's oracle at Delphi in *De mysteriis Aegyptiorum*, reprinted by Petrus Crinitus in his *De honesta disciplina* (1543) and discussed by Cornelius Agrippa in *De occulta philosophia* (1510). "The prophetess at Delphi . . . being seated in the inner shrine on a bronze seat having three or four legs . . . would expose herself to the divine spirit, whence she was illuminated with a ray of divine fire."

1.2 **Wand in hand:** From Iamblichus's account of the ancient oracle of Didymus at Branchidai in Asia Minor: "The female oracle at Branchus . . . either holds a wand in her hand or dips her feet or the hem of her robe in the water . . . or inhales some of the vapor arising from the water . . . and in this way is filled with a divine light . . . and predicts what is to come . . . the god becomes externally present . . . and the prophetess . . . is inspired." The term "BRANCHES" (often the case with capitalized words in Nostradamus) suggests a pun on the shape of the sibyl's tripod.

1.4 **the fisher's barque:** The Church of Rome.

1.5 **Carcas.:** Carcassonne.

1.6 **The eye:** Here, as elsewhere (e.g., 3.55), the hieroglyph for a king or prince. From Nostradamus's translation of Horapollo. **Brescia:** Town in Lombardy, occupied by the French between 1512 and 1550? **Turin:** Capital of Savoy, occupied by the armies of François I in 1536. **Vercelli:** Town in the Piedmont captured by the French in 1553.

1.7 **fourteen of a sect:** Prévost identifies these as the fourteen reformers of Meaux who were executed by François I in 1540, the leader of the plot ("the Redhead") being the bishop of Oloron.

1.8 **City of the Sun:** Perhaps Rhodes (formerly dedicated to the sun god Helios). More likely, Rome. **Adria:** Metonym for Venice.

1.9   **Punic:** Includes the Phoenicians and Carthaginians—and, more broadly, the Muslims of North Africa and the Middle East. May allude to the Turkish fleet's victorious attack on Malta in the summer of 1551. Cf. 2.30.

1.10 **iron cage:** In his *Mémoires*, Philippe de Commynes notes that Louis XI invented these cages in the fifteenth century. Cf. 2.24; 3.10.

1.11 **Leon.:** Possibly Leontini in Sicily (today's Lentini).

1.14 **the enslaved:** Usually read as referring to the Protestants of his day, here singing of their martyrdom in prison.

1.16 **Scythe:** From Richard Roussat's *Livre de l'estat et mutation des temps* (1550): "Then Saturn [the scythe] and Jupiter [the tin] shall be conjoined in Sagittarius. . . . Saturn, in the Fire Sign, shall be raised and exalted at its apogee. . . . Whereby pestilence, famine, and all kinds of corruptions, both of body and possessions, shall abound during this Cycle."

1.17 **the rainbow:** From Roussat: "The Venerable Bede (no less) states that Iris (that is to say the Rainbow, or Bow of Peace) shall in no wise be seen for the space of forty years. . . ."

1.18 **Phocaean port:** Marseille. As a result of François I's temporary alliance with the Ottomans, their fleets were allowed to anchor in the ports of Toulon and Marseille during the winter of 1543. Cf. 2.5; 2.59.

1.19 **Trojan blood:** Usually refers to French royal blood (cf. 2.61), but here appears to allude to the ancient Romans. A conflation of episodes from Julius Obsequens's *Book of Prodigies* and Plutarch's "Life of Marius" evoking the flight of this Roman general.

1.20 **Tents shall be pitched:** In the winter of 1543/44, the fields surrounding Toulon had been transformed into a vast tent camp for Muslim troops. Cf. 1.18.

1.21 **the deep white clay:** Phenomenon apparently observable at the Fontaine de Vaucluse. Crouzet sees an allegory extrapolated from Psalm 18 ("The Lord is my rock").

1.24 **Cremo. & Mant.:** Cremona and Mantua, in Lombardy, Italy.

1.25 **Shepherd as demigod:** Jesus Christ?   **the moon completes its full cycle:** I.e., in 1887. According to Roussat, the reign of the Moon had begun in 1533—a date believed by many evangelicals to mark the return of Christ, as presaged by the great comet of 1532. See also the note to 1.48.

1.27 **the hidden treasure:** Cf. 9.7 and Matthew 13:44.

1.28 **Tower of Bouc:** Tower erected in the twelfth century on the Mediterranean coast at Port-de-Bouc, attacked by Barbary pirates in 1536 and overlooking the Turkish fleet's anchorage in the winter of 1543 (cf. 1.18).

1.31 **king of Spain:** Charles V, king of Castile. The eagle was the symbol of the Holy Roman Empire; the cock, that of the Kingdom of France.

1.32 **The empire shall soon find itself retired:** Allusion to the Avignon papacy, 1309–78?

1.35 **The young lion shall overcome the old:** Legend has it that this celebrated quatrain, published in 1555, successfully prophesied the death of King Henri II, who died on July 10, 1559, after a joust in which the lance of the Count of Montgomery, Captain of the Scottish Guard, penetrated his headgear and pierced his right eye and temple. Both combatants used lions as their emblems. But Henri II (the supposed "old lion"), then age forty, was probably only six months older than his adversary. It was not until 1614 that this interpretation appeared in print (in César de Nostredame's *Histoire et chronique de Provence*).

1.39 **note in packet left unread:** May refract Suetonius's account of the assassination of Julius Caesar.

1.40 **A change in coins:** After returning to France from four years of captivity in Egypt, Louis IX in 1263 issued an edict reforming the currency.

1.42 **the Gnostic rite:** Brind'Amour's emendation of the first printing, "rite gotique" (i.e., gothic rite). According to Psellus, as quoted in Petrus Crinitus's *De honesta disciplina*, the Gnostics of yore used to "gather on the evening of the Passion of Our Savior and . . . having put out the lights, copulate promiscuously with their sisters or with their daughters . . . reckoning that this would facilitate the entry of the demons."

1.44 **Honey . . . wax:** Honey is traditonally associated with the mellifluous Word of God, wax with earthly existence.

1.45 **The bane of sects:** Alludes to the contemporary oppression of the Protestants.   **The beast is brought onstage:** Étienne Jodelle's *Cléopâtre captive*, the first modern attempt to imitate ancient tragedy, was performed before the court of Henri II in 1553. In honor of the play's success, Jodelle's friends, the Pléiade poets Ronsard and Baïf, organized a ceremony in which a goat garlanded with flowers was presented to the author in a revival of the pagan rites of Dionysus.

1.46 **Auch . . . Lectoure:** Towns in the Gers, southwestern France. Cf. 8.2.

1.47 **Days shall be as long as weeks:** Parody of the Prophecy of the Tiburtine Sibyl recorded in the *Mirabilis liber* in which, as a result of the arrival of the Antichrist, "years shall be shortened like months, months like weeks, weeks like days, and days like hours." The long-windedness of the Calvinist sermons from Geneva on Lake Leman will produce exactly the opposite effect.

1.48 **Now that the Moon for twenty years has reigned:** According to Roussat, the current reign of Moon had begun in 1533, with the lunar cycle coming to completion in 1887; the following cycle, that of the Sun, would in turn be completed in 2242. In the preface dedicated to his son César, Nostradamus arrives at the date 3797 for the final fulfillment of his prophecies by presumably adding 1555 (the date of publication of the first edition) to 2242 (the end of the solar cycle). Cf. 1.25.

1.50 **water's triplicity:** According to Roussat, the period of "aquatic triplicity" (which assured the reign of the three zodiacal signs of Cancer, Scorpio, and Pisces) began in 1402 and foreboded the coming of the Antichrist, who would celebrate Thursday (the day of Jupiter) as his sabbath. Cf. 10.71.

1.51 **Saturn & Jove at the head of Aries:** Dated as 1702 by Roussat.

1.52 **In Scorpio the two wicked ones:** The conjunction of Saturn and Mars in Scorpio could refer, according to the prophetic calendar, to either August 1572 or October–November 1600.   **The grand seigneur:** In the sixteenth century, the French term *grand seigneur* frequently designated the Ottoman sultan. Sultan Selim died in 1520, the same year Martin Luther was excommunicated by the pope. Charles V (the "new king") was crowned Holy Roman Emperor the previous year.   **the Septentrion:** The North.

1.53 **Each time a new gold, silver mine is found:** By the Spanish conquistadors?

1.54 **Ten revolutions:** Predicted by Roussat to occur toward 1789–91.   **the mobile sign:** Aries, Cancer, Libra, or Capricorn.

1.57 **Great Discord:** The allegorical figure of Discord is taken from Petrus Crinitus's *De honesta disciplina*, who borrows it from Petronius's *Satiricon*.

1.58 **born with two heads:** César de Nostredame suggested this might allude to the birth of a two-headed child at Sénas (near Salon) on January 31, 1554. **Aquileia . . . Turin . . . Ferrara:** Cities of northern Italy. Cf. 2.15 and 5.99.

1.62 **Before the moon completes its cycle:** Cf. 1.48.

1.64 **the half-human pig:** From Julius Obsequens's *Book of Prodigies*—as are the other marvels in this quatrain.

1.65 **The royal child:** May refer to the death of the dauphin François in 1536 after having fallen ill during a game of tennis.

1.66 **Viviers . . . Pradelles:** Towns in the Ardèche, Haute-Loire, and Puy-de-Dôme regions.

1.69 **stades:** Unit of length equivalent to 600 Greek or Roman feet (or 185 meters).

1.71 **The sea fort:** Perhaps the Tower of Bouc (cf. 1.28) or the Tower of Saint-Jean guarding the port of Marseille, occupied by the Spaniards in 1425 and again in 1536. Cf. 2.14.

1.73 **Sicily's Leon.:** Cf. 1.11.

1.74 **Epire:** Epirus, region on the Ionian Sea, shared by today's Greece and Albania. **Antioch:** Celebrated Syrian city on the river Orontes. **Bronzebeard:** From the Latin *ahenobarbus*, "red-bearded." May refer to the tyrant Nero (who belonged to the *gens* of the Aenobarbi) or to Emperor Frederick Barbarossa, who laid siege to Antioch during the First Crusade. In Nostradamus's day the name would have been associated with Hayreddin Barbarossa (ca. 1478–1546), the Ottoman admiral who dominated the Mediterranean for much of the early sixteenth century.

1.75 **Savona:** Port to the west of Genoa. **Marches of Ancona:** Region on the Adriatric, bordering Tuscany and Umbria.

1.77 **black sail:** May evoke the black sail with which the Greek hero Theseus inadvertently caused his father's death.

1.79 **Car., Bord., Bay.:** Carcassonne, Bordeaux, Bayonne, all in the Protestant stronghold of southwestern France, as are the five towns listed in the first line. For Toulouse and bull sacrifice, cf. 1.44; 9.46.

1.80 **the sixth celestial splendor:** The planet Jupiter.

1.81 **Kappa, Theta, Lambda:** Greek letters gematrically equivalent to 9, 20, 30—which, added together, might point to the 59 Templars who were burned at the stake in Paris in 1310 for heresy. Nine further heretics (see line 1) were summarily executed in Senlis, without the benefit of full trial.

1.82 **Vienna:** The Ottomans besieged Vienna in 1529.

1.84 **Its brother . . . dull as iron rust:** Cf. the ferruginous sun in mourning for the death of Julius Caesar in Virgil's *Georgics* I, 461–68. Also: Acts 2:19–22.

1.86 **the mighty queen:** From Livy's *History of Rome* (II, 13) and Plutarch's "Life of Publicola," which recount how the noble young hostage Cloelia fled the camp of her captor, the Etruscan king Porsena, by traversing the Tiber back to Rome on horseback, thereby violating the terms of agreement between Tarquinius and Porsena.

1.87 **Ennosigaeus:** Neptune, the "earth-shaker." **Arethusa:** Pursued by the river god Alpheus, the nymph Arethusa was changed into a stream to escape him. Ovid, *Metamorphoses* V, 572–641.

1.88 **epilepsy:** Julius Caesar was subject to seizures for the last two years of his life. **shaven head:** Tonsured monk? Cf. 4.66; 5.60; 6.29; 7.13; 7.36.

1.89 **Lerida:** Town in Aragon, Spain.

1.90 **At the toll of the bell:** The tocsin encouraging the peasants of southwestern France to rise up in revolt against Henri II's salt tax in the summer of 1548? **monster is born near Orgon:** Cf. 1.58.

1.93 **The Lion & the Cock:** Venice (?) and France. **Celts:** Portuguese.

1.94 **port Selin:** Cf. 2.1; 4.23.

1.95 **A twin:** Théodore de Bèze (1519–1605), whose twin brother died at age twenty-three, would later become John Calvin's Protestant successor at Geneva. Cf. 7.20.

1.96 **his tongue's golden chains:** This "Gallic Hercules" (cf. 10.79) is described in Erasmus's 1502 translation of Lucian's *The Death of Peregrinus*. An epithet of Henri II—but also known by the name of Ogmion in 2.73; 5.80; 6.42; 8.4; 8.44; 9.89—the demigod is described as "leading on the nations by their ears which are attached by chains to his tongue." Erasmus also used the mythical figure of Ogmion (or "Ognyon") to illustrate the superiority of eloquence over brute force.

1.97 **Smooth tongue:** Possibly Michel de l'Hôpital (1507–1573), adviser to Henri II.

1.100 **Holding in its beak a fresh branch of green:** According to Suetonius (I, 81), one of the omens presaging the death of Julius Caesar was a bird flying with a laurel branch in its beak.

CENTURY II

2.1 **assaults by Britain:** British attacks on La Rochelle were feared during the salt-tax revolt of the summer of 1548 in southwestern France. Cf. 1.90; 2.61.

2.2 **Blue turban:** In his 1566 almanac Nostradamus predicts that within seventy-two years, the "white head" (i.e., the king of the Turks) will enter into great conflict with the "blue head" (the king of the Persians).

2.3 **The fish half-cooked:** From Julius Obsequens's *Book of Prodigies*. **Negrepont:** "Black sea," the medieval name for the island of Euboea and its capital, Chalcis. Cf. 2.21; 5.98.

2.5 **He goes free:** Nostradamus's old acquaintance the Baron de la Garde (ca. 1498–1578), French ambassador to the Ottoman Empire (1541–47), was released from prison in 1552 and rejoined the French fleet that cooperated with the Ottomans in the battles of Corsica and Sardinia. Cf. 2.59; 2.78.

2.7 **born with two teeth in its throat:** Cf. 3.42.

2.14 **the Saint-Jean tower:** Guarding the port of Marseille, where Caterina de' Medici and her uncle Pope Clement VII were received in 1533 as they made their way to her wedding to the future Henri II of France. Cf. 1.71; 9.27.

2.15 **Castor & Pollux:** St. Elmo's fire.

2.20 **Brothers & sisters:** Huguenots. In January 1535, François I had organized a procession of Protestant heretics on their way to the stake.

2.21 **Negrepont:** Cf. 2.3.

2.22 **Asop . . . Eurotas:** Asopia, river in Boeotia; Eurotas, river in Laconia (Sparta). **the navel of the earth:** The *omphalos* of Delphi, site of the oracle of Apollo.

2.23 **Near palace:** Incident from the reign of Tarquin the Elder recorded in Julius Obsequens's *Book of Prodigies*.

2.24 **Ister:** Latin name for the Danube. Due to its old French spelling in the original printing (*Hifter*), the name has been famously read as prophetic of Hitler.   **iron cage:** Cf. 1.10; 3.10.

2.26 **Ticino overthrows Po:** The Ticino River flows into the Po east of Pavia, site of the disastrous French defeat in 1525. Cf. 4.5; 4.75; 8.7; 10.72.

2.27 **The Divine Word:** The consecrated host. Cf. 3.2; 7.36; 8.99.

2.28 **Joveday:** Thursday. Cf. 1.50; 10.71.

2.30 **Hannibal:** Livy's *History of Rome* chronicles the Carthaginian general Hannibal's invasion of Italy in 218–203 B.C.E. Cf. 1.9.

2.31 **Cassiline:** A town in Campania (today's Capua).

2.32 **monster born near & in Ravenna:** Discovered by invading French troops in 1512 and attested by Ambroise Paré in his *Des monstres et prodiges* (1573). Cf. 5.20.

2.35 **Fire shall break out:** In November 1500, a fire broke out at the Hôtel de la Tête d'Argent in Lyon (at the confluence of the rivers Rhône and Saône), killing many of the merchants who were staying there for the annual trade fair.

2.38 **When the monarchs are reconciled:** The brief diplomatic thaw between François I and Charles V in 1538–39?

2.40 **Greek fire:** Incendiary weapons used in naval battles by the Byzantine Empire.

2.41 **The mighty star shall blaze seven days straight:** Drawn from Julius Obsequens's description of the omens following the assassination of Julius Caesar. Could also refer to the comet of 1527.

2.43 **bearded star:** Comet.   **The three great princes:** May refer to the dissensions within the triumvirate of Octavius, Marc Antony, and Lepidus in the wake of Julius Caesar's death.

2.45 **the Androgyne's birth:** A frequent omen in Obsequens's *Book of Prodigies*.

2.46 **The mighty Mover renews the ages:** A paraphrase of Virgil's celebrated Fourth Eclogue. Cf. 3.92.

2.48 **Saturn in Sag.:** The astronomical conjunction coincides with 1545–46, a period that saw the massacre of the Waldensians in the Lubéron mountains (led by the Baron de la Garde) and the hanging of one of their leaders in Avignon.   **Psalmons:** Possible pun on psalms and salmons.

2.49 **Malta now on their mind:** The Knights of St. John were granted refuge in Malta by Charles V in 1530.

2.50 **Ghent, Brussels & Hainaut:** Ghent, chief city of Flanders, Brussels of Brabant; with Hainaut, the three richest provinces of the Netherlands. Cf. 4.19.   **Langres:** Key city on the sixteenth-century frontier between the Netherlands and France.

2.51 **Six times twenty-three consumed by lightning:** Cf. 1.81. During the Affair of the Templars (1307–14), 138 French heretics were burned at the stake (unlike those arrested in England). Cf. the allusions to the Templars in 8.87.

2.53 **The mighty plague:** Marseille and Provence were struck by the plague following the 1545 massacre of the Waldensians of the Lubéron.   **The great dame:** The dame de Cental, patroness of the Waldensians?

2.55 **Adria:** Cf. 1.8.

2.57 **the great wall shall fall:** Just before Rome was sacked by the Imperial forces in 1527, the wall joining the Vatican to the Castel Sant'Angelo collapsed, killing Charles III, Duke of Bourbon in the process.

2.59 **This great Neptune:** I.e., the Baron de la Garde, ambassador to the Ottoman Empire under François I—whose 1543 agreement to allow the Turkish fleet to anchor in the ports of Toulon and Marseille seems to be alluded to in line 3. Cf. 1.18; 2.5; 2.78. **Narbonne of Mars:** The Roman coastal colony of Narbonne was placed under the protection of Mars.

2.60 **The Punic pact now broken:** The breaking of the Ottomans' agreement with France in 1554? **Ganges, Indus:** Paraphrase of the Sibylline oracle: "Ganges, Indus, Tagus erit mutabile visu" ("The Ganges, Indus, Tagus shall change their face").

2.61 **La Rochelle & the Gironde:** Cf. 1.90; 2.1. The Gironde, an estuary of the Garonne, flows about thirty miles south of La Rochelle. **O Trojan blood:** Cf. 1.19. **La Flèche:** Toulon (*Telo-Martius* in Latin)?

2.62 **Mabus:** May allude to the northeast French border town of Maubeuge, also known as Mabuse (as in the nickname of Flemish painter Jan Gossaert). The town was destroyed by François I in 1543 and by Henri II in 1553.

2.63 **Ausonia:** Italy. **Parma:** The War of Parma of 1551?

2.64 **Cévennes:** Huguenot stronghold in southern France.

2.65 **Hesperia:** Western land (sometimes Spain). **Insubria:** Cisalpine Gaul; Lombardy.

2.69 **the three parts:** Cf. Caesar's *Gallic War*: "All of Gaul is divided into three parts"—the Belgian, the Celtic, and the Aquitanian. **the great Hierarchy:** The Church of Rome (symbolized by the "cope," an ecclesiastic garment), as opposed to the secular power of the Monarchy.

2.70 **The spear of the sky:** Comet. Cf. 2.15; 2.41; 2.42; 2.43; 2.62.

2.72 **Rubicon:** Julius Caesar's successful crossing of the Rubicon in 49 B.C.E., here contrasted to French reverses in Italy (as in the disastrous battle of Pavia of 1525). Cf. 2.26; 4.5; 4.75; 8.7; 10.72.

2.73 **Lake Fucino:** East of Rome, in the Kingdom of the Two Sicilies. **Lake Garda:** In northeastern Italy, in the Republic of Venice. **Port'Ercole:** Major French port on the southern Tuscan coast. (For Ogmion = Hercules, see note to 1.96). **Endymion:** The lover of the Moon. Usually identified as Henri II, the lunar (or "Selin") monarch. See notes to 4.77; 6.42; 6.78; 10.53; 10.58.

2.78 **This mighty Neptune:** The Baron de la Garde (believed by Nostradamus to be of mixed French and "Punic" blood), working in concert with the Ottoman fleet, was late in arriving at the 1554 battle in which the Imperial admiral Andrea Doria devastated Corsica and Sardinia. Cf. 2.5; 2.59.

2.79 CHYREN: A standard anagram for Henri II (from "Henryc," the Provençal form of his name). Cf. 4.34; 6.27; 6.70; 8.54; 9.41. Here perhaps conflated with Charles V, who during his expedition to Tunis of 1535 freed thousands of Christian prisoners held by the Ottoman admiral Barbarossa. Cf. 5.69.

2.81 **The Urn:** Aquarius (i.e., midwinter). **Deucalion:** Son of Prometheus; Greek equivalent of the biblical Noah, hence a metonym for the Flood. Cf. 10.6. **Phaëthon:** The Manifest One, epithet applied to the Sun, and to Jupiter and Saturn.

2.84 **Dalmatia:** Held by the Venetians.

2.85 **Ligustic sea:** The waters off the Ligurian coast.

2.86 **Fleet shipwrecked:** News stories of 1538: Barbarossa defeats the fleet of Charles under the command of Andrea Doria at the battle of Preveza (line 1); Vesuvius erupts (line 2); Süleyman the Magnificent dispatches the Ottoman fleet into the Red Sea (line 3); Gaucher de Dinteville is taunted as a sodomite by Jean du Plessis; François I arranges a duel, but when Dinteville fails to appear, the affair of honor is called off (line 4).

2.90 **changing Hungary's regime:** The Ottomans under Süleyman the Magnificent captured the twin cities of Buda and Pest in 1526, killing King Louis II of Hungary; the kingdom was then disputed between John Zápolya and Ferdinand of Hapsburg, presumably the enemy brothers Castor and Pollux of line 4.

2.93 **Libitina:** Roman goddess of death. May allude to the sack of Rome by the Imperial troops in 1527, when the Tiber was in flood and the pope (the "ship captain" of line 3) held prisoner in the Castel Sant'Angelo. Cf. 2.57; 5.81; 10.27.

2.94 **Lion of the seas:** Emblem of Venice?

2.96 **flaming torch:** A meteorite, like the one Nostradamus saw fall near Salon on March 10, 1554.

2.97 **The city where the two rivers pool:** Lyon, at the confluence of the Rhône and the Saône—where Pope Clement V was coronated, under catastrophic circumstances, in 1305.

2.98 **spattered by the blood:** An evil omen, as in Livy's *History of Rome* (XXI, 63).

2.99 **Boreas:** The north wind.

CENTURY III

3.1 **The great Neptune:** Another exploit of the Baron de la Garde: in 1545, he passed through the Strait of Gibraltar with twenty-five galleys on his way to attack the coast of England in July. Cf. 2.5; 2.59; 2.78.   **The enemy red:** The armed forces of the Holy Roman Emperor Charles V wore red crosses as their insignia.

3.2 **the Divine Word:** The consecrated host. A reaffirmation of the Catholic doctrine of transubstantiation, as against the Protestant denial of the Eucharist (most notoriously, in the "Affaire des placards" of 1534). Cf. 2.27; 7.36; 8.99.

3.3 **Mars & Mercury & the Moon conjoined:** This triple conjunction occurred in 1554.   **Corinth, Ephesus:** Cf. 2.52.

3.5 **the failing of these two great lights:** A lunar eclipse was visible in eastern Europe on March 22, 1540, followed by a solar eclipse apparent to the Balkans and Greece on April 7.   **What prices:** François I's new salt tax was introduced in 1541, followed by general inflation.

3.8 **the Cimbrians:** Plutarch's *Parallel Lives* described the invasion of Spain by the Cimbri.

3.12 **Eb. . . . Tib.:** The rivers Ebro, Tagus, Tiber.

3.15 **a child France shall betray:** Should the current king Henri II die, the throne would pass to the twelve-year-old dauphin François, under the regency of Catherine de Médicis.

3.16 **The English prince:** Henry VIII, who had died in 1547?

3.17 **The Aventine Hill seen aflame:** The Great Fire of Rome, 64 C.E.? **Above Flanders skies shall suddenly dim:** The solar eclipse of January 1544?

3.18 **Reims:** A site sacred to French royalty.

3.20 **the great Baetic river:** The river Guadalquivir in Spain.

3.21 **Crustumerium:** Ancient Sabine town on the Conca River. **dragged from the waters by a hook:** Cf. Job 41:1: "Canst thou draw out leviathan with an hook?"

3.23 **France, if you pass beyond the Ligurian sea:** Evokes the disastrous military campaigns of France in Italy under Louis XII, François I, and Henri II. Cf. 3.24.

3.27 **Shall so inflame François for Arab matters:** François I instituted the study of Arabic under the direction of Guillaume Postel at the Collège des Lecteurs Royaux in 1541.

3.28 **A young female reigning on for ages:** The lowborn empress Theodora (ca. 500–548) of the Byzantine Empire?

3.30 **Shall be attacked in bed:** Exemplary assassinations: the Duke of Parma killed in his bed at Piacenza on the orders of Emperor Charles V in 1547; the Byzantine emperor Nicephorus Phocas killed at the behest of his wife in 969.

3.31 **Araxes:** River marking the boundary between Turkey and Persia. May allude to the eastern campaigns of Süleyman the Magnificent (r. 1520–66) in Media and Armenia.

3.32 **He who put all Aquitaine in the grave:** High Constable Anne de Mont-morency, who put down the salt-tax revolt in Aquitaine in 1548? Cf. 9.1.

3.35 **Europe's farthermost western reaches:** The British Isles.

3.36 **When the city condemns the heretic:** According to Prévost, Savonarola, condemned as a schismatic and heretic in Florence in 1498.

3.42 **two teeth in its throat:** Cf. 2.7.

3.44 **pet dog:** Crouzet observes that the dog is traditionally the emblem of Christian fidelity and faith.

3.46 **Plancus town:** Lyon, which had witnessed a meteor falling on the city on April 5, 1528. Cf. 8.6.

3.47 **Mytilene:** The Greek isle of Lesbos.

3.51 **a great murder:** That of Claude de Lorraine, first Duke of Guise in 1550?

3.52 **Cock shall see the Eagle waver on wing:** The cock was the emblem of France, the eagle the emblem of Charles V's Holy Roman Empire.

3.53 **Agrippine:** I.e., the city of Cologne (*Colonia Agrippinensis* in Tacitus).

3.55 **one eye:** Read by some of Nostradamus's contemporaries in 1561 as predicting King Charles IX's loss of an eye. **The lord from Blois shall have killed his friend:** Cf. 3.51.

3.56 **Plague, thunder & hail:** The various omens that appeared at the death of François I in 1547?

3.57 **Seven times you'll see the British people change:** According to Prévost, may allude to the violent deaths of Simon de Montfort, Edward II, Richard II, Henry VI, Edward V, Richard III, and Lady Jane Grey between 1265 and 1555 (i.e., 290 years), the date of the publication of this quatrain. **Bastarnian:** Refers to the region between the sources of the Vistula and the mouth of the Danube.

3.58 **the mountains of Noricum:** Region to the north of the Adriatic. **SAUROM.:** Sarmatians, inhabitants of the region stretching from the Vistula to the mouth of the Danube and eastward to the Volga. **Pannon.:** Pannonians, inhabitants of the region between the former Yugoslavia and Hungary.

3.60 **Mysia, Lysia & Pamphylia:** Regions of today's Turkey.

3.61 **cross-bearers:** Probably alludes to the contemporary Catholic persecution of the Waldensians in the region between the rivers Rhône and Durance (also called "Mesopotamia" in Nostradamus's *Présages*). Cf. 2.48; 2.53; 3.99.

3.62 **From the Duero he shall cross the Pyrenees:** Hannibal's route toward Rome.

3.64 ΟΛΧΑΔΕΣ: Transport ships.

3.65 **When the mighty Roman's tomb is dug up:** According to Bandini's *Dell' obelisco di Cesare Augusto* (1549), the tomb of Augustus Caesar was discovered in 1521, the same year that Pope Leo X died from poisoning, his blood captured in a chalice in which votes were later collected to elect his successor. Cf. 5.7; 6.66.

3.66 **He shall not die a deserved death nor by chance:** Cf. Virgil *Aeneid* IV, 696: "Nam quia nec fato merita nec morte peribat."

3.67 **A new sect of philosophers:** Probably refers to the Anabaptist sects of southern Germany. Cf. 3.76; 4.31; 4.32.

3.68 **Chersonese:** Ancient name of the Gallipoli Peninsula.

3.69 **born back at the Half-Swine:** I.e., etymologically, in Milan.

3.70 **Ausonia:** Italy.

3.71 **Those trapped within towns:** I follow Brind'Amour's reading here. Previous editions read "isles" instead of "towns."

3.73 **When the lame-footed one ascends the throne:** From Plutarch's "Life of Agesilaus." Leotychides was the rival of the lame Agesilaus.

3.77 **October seventeen twenty-seven:** Either October 1727 or October 27, 1700, neither of which corresponds to a specific astronomic conjunction or major historical event.

3.79 **The chain of never-ending destiny:** From Aulus Gellius's *Attic Nights*, quoted in Nostradamus's preface: "Destiny is a certain eternal and immutable series of events that both constantly revolves in a chain and brings with it those unending sequences of consequences to which it is appropriate and attached." **The Phocaeans' port shall be broken:** The breaking of the chains that closed the port of Marseille; could refer to the invasion of the city by Alfonso V of Aragon in 1423.

3.87 **Go not near Corsica:** Allusion to the disastrous defeat of the French fleet by Andrea Doria in Corsica in 1553.

3.88 **That all Marseille shall be trembling with fear:** May refer to the 1524 invasion of Marseille by the renegade Charles de Bourbon on behalf of Charles V.

3.90 **The great Satyr & Hyrcanian Tyger:** Exotic animals sent in 1533 to François I (via the Ottoman privateer Barbarossa) by Süleyman the Magnificent—who was at that point campaigning in Carmania (in Persia)—in order to seal the Franco-Ottoman alliance against Charles V's Holy Roman Empire. Cf. 4.85. **the Tyrrhenian port Phocaean:** Marseille.

3.91 **The tree that was dry as death for years:** Cf. Suetonius, *The Twelve Caesars* (II, 92), announcing the reign of Augustus: "On the isle of Capri the fallen branches of a very ancient oak, already drooping to the ground, sprang to life at his advent." Here rhymed with the death of François I in 1547 and the accession of the young Henri II.

3.92 **Slow Saturn again making a return:** From Virgil's Fourth Eclogue. Cf. 2.46. **Brodde:** From the Latin *Ebrodunum*, a region of the Alps. **the eye:** The monarch (from Horapollo).

3.93 **Tricastin:** Area around Saint-Paul-Trois-Châteaux, north of Orange on the east bank of the Rhône.

3.95 **The Borysthenes:** Inhabitants of the Dnieper region.

3.96 **the Tarpeian Rock:** Steep cliff of the Capitoline Hill in Rome from which those sentenced to death were flung to their doom.

3.97 **Phoebe:** The Moon, whose cycle was to be completed in 1887.

3.99 **Alleins & Vernègues:** Two villages in today's Bouches-du-Rhône. **The conflict between the two camps:** I.e., between Catholics and Protestants in France. **Mesopotamia:** Cf. 3.61.

3.100 **Among the the Gauls:** The victory of Vercingetorix over Julius Caesar at Gergovia in 52 B.C.E.?

CENTURY IV

4.3 **Sagunto:** Halfway down the east coast of Spain, at the foot of the Peñas de Pajarito.

4.4 **Libyans & cocks:** Alludes to the naval alliance between the French ("cocks") and the Ottoman corsairs ("Libyans") against Charles V. Cf. 1.18; 2.5; 2.59.

4.8 **At the vigil of Saint-Quentin:** Falls on October 31, that is, at La Toussaint.

4.10 **Struck in head by a stanchion:** Collapsing structures: cf. 2.92; 3.40; 6.37; 6.51. **lays a healing balm:** The laying on of hands, one of the traditional thaumaturgic gifts of the kings of France.

4.11 **the great cope:** The papacy. **The twelve red ones:** Cardinals.

4.15 **The eye of the sea:** A seaport, via Cicero's *De natura deorum* (III, 91).

4.16 **The frank city:** Protestant stronghold of La Rochelle, pardoned by François I in early 1543 for its opposition to the salt tax. Cf. 2.1; 5.35.

4.18 **those most versed in lore celestial:** Cf. 8.71.

4.19 **Insubria:** Milanese holdings in Lombardy. **Hainaut . . . Liège:** Cf. 2.50.

4.20 **With the lily:** I.e., the fleur-de-lis, traditional emblem of royal France.

4.23 **Chalcis:** Port of the isle of Euboea; cf. 2.3. **Magnesia:** East part of Thessaly, facing Euboea. **Port Selin:** Cf. 1.94; 2.1. **Port'Ercole:** Cf. 2.73.

4.25 **Sublimates:** In alchemy and modern chemistry, fluids in the gaseous state having neither independent shape nor volume and being able to expand indefinitely.

4.26 **The swarming bees:** Quatrain written in Provençal.

4.27 **Mausole:** The ancient Mausoleum of the Julii in Saint-Rémy-de-Provence, situated at the entrance to the ruins of the Greco-Roman city of Glanum. SEX.: From the inscription on the Saint-Rémy mausoleum: SEX.L.M.IULIEI C.F. PARENTIBUS SUEIS (Sextus, Lucius, Marcus, sons of Caius Julius, to their parents). **pyramid:** A spindle of stone in the old quarry at Glanum, locally known as "la Pyramide." **the Danish prince:** Ogier, the son of Godfrey of Denmark, offered as a hostage by the latter to Charlemagne? **Artemis temple:** Queen Artemisia had the original Mausoleum built for her husband.

4.28 **When Venus is blotted out by the Sun:** In alchemical terms, copper and gold.

4.29 **The Sun hidden:** Mercury (a "second heaven," "Hermes") alchemically transformed by fire ("Vulcan") into gold ("Sun").

4.30 **The ☽. ☉ to soar or fall in value:** Fluctuations in the price of precious metals. (Sun and Moon symbols in my version retained from the 1555 edition.) Cf. 1.40; 5.72.

4.31 **midnight on the mountain high:** See the German Anabaptist locale of 3.67.

4.32 πάντα χοῖνα φιλῶν: "All things in common among friends." (Greek letters retained from 1555 edition.) From Erasmus's *Adages*. Cf. 3.67.

4.33 **Jove . . . Venus:** Alchemically, Jupiter (Jove) represents tin, Venus copper, Neptune water, Mars iron.

4.34 **King CHYREN:** Usually Henri II; see note to 2.79.

4.36 **Romagna:** Part of the Papal States.

4.37 **Monech, Gennes:** Monaco, Genoa.

4.39 **The men of Rhodes shall cry out for more aid:** The isle of Rhodes, home of the Knights of St. John of Jerusalem, was seized by the Turks in 1522. **The common cause given new hope by Spain:** Charles V installed the expelled Knights of St. John on Malta in 1530 and captured Tunis in 1535.

4.41 **captured hostage:** A Roman ploy (390 B.C.E.) described by Plutarch ("Life of Romulus," "Life of Camillus").

4.42 **Seyssel:** Town on the Rhône just below the Protestant center of Geneva (and thus not far from Lausanne).

4.44 **For notables:** Quatrain written in Provençal.

4.45 **The conflict:** Probably the French rout at the battle of Pavia (1525), during which François I, momentarily deserted by his brother-in-law, the Duke of Alençon, was captured. Cf. 2.26; 4.75; 8.7; 10.22.

4.48 **The Ausonian plain:** The lands around Milan were invaded by locusts in 1542, the year of a solar eclipse.

4.51 **Ganges:** Village near Montpellier.

4.53 **His son . . . drowned in the well:** Final line of the 1555 edition of the *Prophecies.*

4.54 **The first of the French kings:** François I, who married Eleonor of Austria (and of Castile), the sister of Charles V, in 1530?

4.55 **When the crow shall caw:** Suetonius (XII, 15, 23), describing the omens announcing the death of Emperor Domitian.

4.57 **But shall ban all the writings:** From Suetonius, *The Twelve Caesars* (XII, 1, 10) on Domitian.

4.58 **blood shall lave the Etruscan plain:** Evokes the Ottoman corsair Barbarossa's raids on the Tuscan coast in 1543, during which he married the daughter of the governor of Gaeta, who converted to Islam and followed him back to Turkey. Cf. 5.3.

4.59 **Nira:** Leoni suggests that, given the mention of Geneva, this might be a misprint for "Iura," i.e., the nearby Jura mountains.

4.61 **knocked from his rightful place:** High Constable Anne de Montmorency (1493–1567) fell from power in 1541, replaced by the dukes of Guise, "foreigners" from Lorraine. **Orl.:** Orléans.

4.62 **An ambitious colonel:** The Huguenot sympathizer Gaspard II de Coligny (1519–1572), named Colonel General of the French Infantry in the late 1540s and later admiral of France? Cf. 6.75; 8.57. **discovered beneath the leaves:** Cf. the death of the rebel Absalom in II Samuel 18.

4.67 **Saturn & Mars:** Saturn and Mars were conjoined in Aries and close to the Sun in mid-March 1556. There was a comet that same spring and a major drought during the summer.

4.72 **Arecomicians:** A Volcae tribe of the Narbonne region whose capital was
Nîmes. Cf. 1.79.   **Saint-Félix:** Southeast of Toulouse, in 1167 the seat of
an Albigensian assembly. All the other towns mentioned are located in
Aquitaine.

4.74 **Brunnovices:** Region of Roman Gaul near Mâcon.

4.75 **he shall vanish:** See note to 4.45 on the battle of Pavia.

4.76 **Nictobriges:** People of the region of Agen.

4.77 **SELIN monarch:** The moon-king Henri II (r. 1547–59). "Selene" is the
Greek equivalent of Diana, goddess of the hunt and of the Moon—and
the name of Henri II's confidante and mistress, Diane de Poitiers (1499–
1566), as in her celebrated crest "H-D." To distinguish himself from the
sun emblem of Emperor Charles V, Henri adopted the (crescent) moon as
his device. Cf. 6.42; 6.78; 8.31; 10.53; 10.58.   **Blois:** Ancestral castle of
the royal Valois family.

4.79 **Monhurt . . . Eguillon:** Towns in the region of Agen.

4.80 **great conduit:** Cf. 5.58; 8.27; 8.68; 10.89.

4.82 **The ancient Vandal:** The French term *L'Olestant* is derived from the Greek
olestai, destroyer.   **Romania:** Ancient Roman or contemporary Vatican
lands.

4.85 **The black coal . . . the white coal:** I follow Lemesurier's translation ("The
black plague follows on the white plague's heels"), substituting "coal" for
"plague." While observing that the French *charbon* can mean, in addition
to coal, "also a Carbuncle or Plague-sore," Cotgrave's 1611 *Dictionarie*
further specifies that *charbon blanc* is "a kind of coale made of wood of
the crimson, or pricklie, cedar," hence presumably a higher quality
than black coal.   **The Moorish Camel:** François I had been given a camel
in 1553; it was featured in his ceremonial entry into Rouen in 1550. Cf.
3.90.

4.88 **Antoine:** Antoine Duprat, cardinal of Sens and Chancellor of the Realm,
suspected of having manipulated the metals in coins, dead of gangrene in
1535.   **phthiriasis:** Eyelid infection caused by crab lice.

4.89 **Fries:** Friesland, province in the north of the Netherlands.

4.91 **Mellila:** Moroccan port?

4.92 **dissevered head:** Cf. Plutarch's "Life of Pompey"—whose severed head
was presented to Julius Caesar after he had been assassinated on board
ship by Ptolemy, the last king of Egypt.

4.93 **Near her royal bed . . . A snake:** Cf. Suetonius, "Life of Augustus" (II,
104), for the omens surrounding his birth.

4.97 **Mercury, Mars, Venus retrograding:** The conjunction suggests 1502, date
of birth of the future king of Portugal John III.

4.98 **The troops of Alba:** Fernando, Duke of Alba (1507–1582), chief military
commander of Imperial forces of Charles V. Cf. 7.29; 8.40; 8.60.

4.100 **Rouen, Évreux:** Cf. 5.84.

CENTURY V

5.3 **Sea-Frog:** Probably the Ottoman pirate-admiral Barbarossa, brief ally of
François I against Charles V in Italy in 1533. Cf. 1.74; 4.58; 4.59; 5.95.

5.6 **Laying his hand:** Cf. Livy's account in his *History of Rome* (I, 18) of the
coronation of Numa Pompilius, as described in Guillaume du Choul's
contemporary *Discours de la religion des anciens Romains* (1556). Cf.
5.75.

5.7　**The bones of the Triumvir:** I.e., Octavius, later known as Augustus. Cf. 3.65; 6.66.

5.11　**Solars:** Brind'Amour decodes as follows: Sun = Sunday = Christians; Venus = Friday = Muslims; Saturn = Saturday = Jews.

5.12　**a foreign maid:** Cf. 2.25.

5.13　**Pannonia:** Region between the former Yugoslavia and Hungary.

5.14　**Saturn & Mars in Leo:** 1535–36, or July 1564.

5.16　**Tears of Saba:** Frankincense or myrrh?

5.20　**Just before the ravening monster's born:** The 1512 expulsion of the Medici from Florence by the French, shortly before the discovery of the Ravenna monster that same year? Cf. 2.32.

5.22　**The two red ones:** Cardinals?

5.23　**The two rivals shall then come to unite:** May allude to the brief alliance of François I and Charles V (the Roman "duumvirate") in the summer of 1539—astrologically marked by the conjunction of Mars, Jupiter, Venus, and Mercury in Cancer. A similar conjunction in Leo was foretold for mid-July 1594: cf. the first line of 5.25.　**The African lord:** The sultan of Algiers, object of a projected Spanish invasion in 1541?

5.24　**Venus . . . Sun . . . Saturnine:** Cf. the note to 5.11.

5.27　**Mar Negro:** The Black Sea. The final *o* in the French *Negro* and *alegro* is silent.　**Trebizond:** Black Sea port, capital of the Greek empire from 1204 to 1461.　**Pharos:** Island in the harbor of Alexandria, site of the celebrated lighthouse.　**Mytilene:** The Greek isle of Lesbos.　**Sol allegro:** Joyous Christians?

5.29　**Ister:** The Danube.

5.32　**seventh stone:** The Tarpeian Rock, seventh of the Roman hills?

5.35　**Seline sea:** The lunar (or salty) sea. The Atlantic Ocean?　**Which still bears the name of rock:** Probably alludes to the "free city" of La Rochelle. Cf. 2.1; 4.16.

5.38　**Salic law:** Frankish law excluding women from inheriting property or succeeding to the throne of France.

5.39　**Born of the true branch:** Quatrain composed in honor of Catherine de Médicis after Nostradamus's visit to the court in the summer of 1555. Recycled by César de Nostredame into an inscription celebrating the entry of Marie de Médicis into Salon-de-Provence in 1600.

5.42　**the Allobroges:** Ancient tribe of the Narbonne region.

5.44　**the red one:** Most likely a Church cardinal.

5.45　**Ahenobarbus:** Red-beard, Barbarossa. Nero's family name. Cf. 1.74; 5.59.

5.46　**Cardinals feuding, creating schisms:** May allude to the Great Schism of 1378, although the two popes involved were Neapolitan (Urban VI) and Genevan (Clement VII).　**Alba:** May allude to the Alban War of the seventh century B.C.E., described by Livy—a model civil war, given that the Romans were said to be descended (via Romulus) from the kings of Alba Longa.

5.47　**The Pannonian:** Cf. 5.13; 5.48.

5.49　**the wavering barque:** The "navicula Petri," symbol of the Catholic Church. Cf. 1.4.

5.50　**Romania:** The Papal States around Rome.

5.51　**Dacia:** Present-day Romania.　**Pillars of Hercules:** Strait of Gibraltar.　**Barcino:** Barcelona.

5.53 **The creeds of Sol & Venus:** Christianity and Islam. See note to 5.11.

5.54 **Alany:** Sarmatian Scythia.

5.56 **When the Pope dies:** Pope Paul III died in 1549 at the age of eighty-one, succeeded by the controversial Julius III, age sixty-two.

5.57 **Aventine:** One of the seven hills of Rome.   **Mount Gaussier:** Just south of Saint-Rémy (Nostradamus's birthplace in Provence), this mount features two holes through which the troops of Charles V were espied during the Imperial invasion of Provence in 1536.   **Saint-Paul-de-Mausole:** For the Latin inscription on this local Saint-Rémy mausoleum, see note to 4.27.

5.58 **the aqueduct:** The Pont du Gard, Roman aqueduct over the river Gardon between Uzès and Nîmes. Cf. 4.80; 8.27; 8.68; 10.89.

5.59 **Ahenobarbus:** See note to 5.45.

5.60 **His tongue shall run:** The current pope, Paul IV (1476–1559), a former monk and extreme proponent of the Inquisition?

5.61 **Mount Cenis:** Mountain in French Savoy.

5.62 **Orgon:** Command post on the river Durance in the Alpilles, north of Nostradamus's Salon.   **Tridental:** Ship with trident; alluding to Neptune. Or perhaps Tridentine: i.e., pertaining to the Council of Trent (1545–63).

5.66 **Sun & Moon:** Gold and silver.   **the golden goat:** Local legend had it that the ancient Roman ruins of Saint-Rémy (which included an aqueduct) contained a buried treasure guarded by a golden goat (*tragos* in Provençal). Cf. 8.28; 9.9; 9.12; 9.32; 10.6.

5.68 **The mighty Camel:** An Arab leader?   **the Cock:** Emblem of the Kingdom of France.

5.69 **Conquer Africa:** Charles V's triumph over the forces of Barbarossa at Tunis in 1535?

5.72 **Venus:** Muslims? Cf. note to 5.11.

5.73 **Polonians:** Poles? Inhabitants of Saint-Paul-de-Mausole?

5.74 **a German great:** The Hapsburg Charles V, born in Flemish Ghent, grandson of the "Trojan" (i.e., French) Mary of Burgundy?

5.75 **seated on the squarish rock:** Charles V's triumphal entry into Rome in 1536, recalling Numa Pompilius's inauguration as second king of Rome? Cf. 5.6; 6.78.

5.76 **he shall pitch his camp:** Charles V's raids throughout Provence? Cf. 5.57.

5.77 **Quirinal:** From Quirinus, an early Sabine god of war and, in Augustine Rome, an epithet of Janus. A play on the Roman priests who went by such names as *flamen quirinalis, flamen martialis, flamen vulcanalis.* Prévost sees an allusion to Constable Anne de Montmorency's fall from grace during the reign of François I in 1540–41. Cf. 4.61.

5.78 **allies thirteen years:** The thirteen-year alliance (1534–47) between Emperor Charles V and Pope Paul III against the Ottoman corsair Barbarossa?   **the barque & its cope:** The Vatican and the pope's ecclesiastical cloak.

5.79 **the great legislator:** Cf. 1.50; 10.71; 10.73.

5.80 **Ogmion:** The Gallic Hercules. See the note to 1.96.

5.81 **solar city:** Cf. 1.8. The sack of Rome by Imperial forces in early May 1527, linked to the omens (reported by Suetonius) surrounding the assassination of Julius Caesar? Cf. 2.57; 2.93; 10.27.

5.82 **Arbois . . . Dole:** Towns on France's eastern border with Savoy.

5.84 **Rouen & Évreux:** Cf. 4.100.

5.85 **the latest rage:** Protestantism, associated with a plague of locusts around Lake Geneva in lines 3–4.

5.87 **Trojan blood:** See note to 1.19.

5.88 **A sea monster:** Cf. 1.29.

5.90 **Perinthus, Larissa, Cyclades:** Town in Thrace, town in Thessaly, Greek island group, respectively.   **Chersonese:** Today's Gallipoli Peninsula.

5.91 **marketplace of lies:** Hippocrates and Galen describing the forum of Athens.

5.95 **The Sea-Frog:** Cf. 5.3. Barbarossa?

5.96 **The rose:** Cf. 5.31. Crouzet compares this to the "candida rosa" that Beatrice offers Dante when he reaches the final circle of Paradise (*Paradiso* XXXI, 1–3).

5.97 **Condom:** Town in southwestern France on the pilgrimage route to Compostela.

5.98 **Scrawny fish:** Cf. 2.3.   **Béarn & Bigorre:** Towns in Gascony, southwestern France.

5.99 **an old Britannic chief:** Adrian IV was the sole pope of British origin. During his reign (1154–59), Milan rebelled, Emperor Frederick Barbarossa invaded northern Italy, Capua burned, and the Norman king William I of Sicily took Brindisi.

5.100 **Carcas.:** Carcassonne. Comminges was ancient county seat of Bigorre in Gascony.   **Foix, Auch, Mazères:** Towns in the Pyrenees.   **Hessians, Saxons, Thuringians:** Inhabitants of three regions of Germany.

CENTURY VI

6.2 **In the year fifteen eighty:** Contemporary astrologers predicted great changes around the year 1580. In January of that year, as well as in January of 1703 (line 3), there was to be a conjunction of Saturn and Jupiter in Aries.

6.3 **The stream:** The Rhine? According to Garencières, "The ancient Frenchmen when they had a King newly born, they used to put him upon a Target [i.e., a shield] to make him swim up on that River [Rhine], to try whether by his swimming he was lawfully begotten or no."

6.4 **Agrippine's city:** Cologne. Cf. 3.53.   **Saturn, Leo, Mars, Cancer:** In 1594, Saturn would be in Leo and Mars in Cancer.

6.5 **Samarobryn:** Amiens (from the Latin *Samarobriva*).

6.6 **the star with the beard:** Halley's comet was visible from August to September 1531, traversing Cancer, Leo, Virgo, and Libra. More likely, however, the comet referred to here is the one that was visible between June and August 1533, moving from Gemini toward Aries, contiguous to Cancer. During this same year the Ottoman corsair Barbarossa, having plundered the Ligurian and Tuscan coast, withdrew to Thrace.   **Susa:** Cf. 2.16.   **Boeotia:** Region of Greece north of Attica and the Gulf of Corinth.   **Eretrion:** Erythrea, in Ionia.   **Rome's lord shall die the night it disappears:** Following the ominous comet and ensuing eclipse of 1533, Pope Clement VII died in 1534.

6.7 **Norneigre:** Norway?   **Dacia:** Roughly corresponds to modern Romania.

6.8 **Scholars & letters to be held quite cheap:** Cf. 1.62.

6.12 **Aspire:** The town of Spire in the German Palatinate?

6.15 **when Capricorn is thin:** The period from December 10 to January 10.

6.16 **Milve:** French term for a female kite. Also a pun on the city of Milan (French *milan* = kite)? **Negresilve:** Black Forest (from the Latin *nigra sylva*).

6.17 **the Saturnines:** The Jews? Cf. 5.11; 5.24.

6.20 **The sham alliance:** The Holy League of 1538, which allied Pope Paul III, Emperor Charles V, and the Republic of Venice against the Ottoman emperor Süleyman the Magnificent? Cf. 5.78.

6.22 **The barque:** Here, as elsewhere, the "navicula Petri," the barque of St. Peter, i.e., the Vatican. Cf. 1.4; 5.49.

6.23 **Rapis:** Anagram for Paris?

6.24 **When Mars & Jupiter come to conjoin:** Mars and Jupiter were conjoined in Cancer in 1539, 1551, 1575, 1586, and 1611, here announcing the anointment of the Messianic King.

6.25 **the fisherman:** St. Peter.   **the hierarchy:** Cf. 2.69.

6.27 **Chyren Selin:** Henri II. See notes to 2.73; 2.79; 4.77.

6.28 **the Cock:** Symbol of France.

6.32 **Berich:** The Berry region of France?

6.33 **Alus:** Roman divinity, according to Petey-Girard; or perhaps Halus, the Parthian town mentioned by Tacitus in his *Annals of Imperial Rome*.

6.35 **Trion:** The Bear constellations (from the Latin *Triones*).

6.39 **Trasimen:** Lake Trasimeno in Umbria.

6.42 **Ogmion:** The Gallic Hercules (see note to 1.96). To Henri II (the "great Selin" of line 2) was born a son by the name of Hercule on March 18, 1555; his name was later changed to François, given his sickly, that is, less than Herculean, constitution.

6.46 **Nonseggle:** From *Nom-de-sceau* (*sigilla* in Latin, as in the *Sigillaria* [Market of Seals] in Rome)? **Frog:** Cf. 5.3.

6.49 **Mammer:** Messina (*Mammertina* in Latin).

6.51 **Pillars, walls fall:** Cf. 3.40; 6.37.

6.54 **Bougie:** Coastal city four hundred miles west of Tunis, the stronghold of the Barbary pirates (taken by the Spanish in 1535). **the Moroccan King:** Probably alludes to the assassination of King Mohammed al-Mahdi by the pasha of Algiers in 1557, following Turkish military operations in the Maghreb—projected fifty years into the future in the last line.

6.55 **Tripolis:** Modern Tirebolu, port on the Black Sea. **Chios:** Aegean island off the coast of Asia Minor. **Trebizond:** City on the northeastern coast of the Black Sea; traditional rival of Constantinople until it fell to the Turks in 1462.

6.57 **the hierarchy:** Cf. 6.25.

6.58 **When the sunlight is eclipsed:** The solar eclipse of the summer of 1551? This marked a period of growing conflict between King Henri II (the moon) and Emperor Charles V (the sun), leading to the French-sponsored rebellion of Siena in 1552 and a pact between Henri and the Turkish pirate Turgut that allowed French forces to land in Corsica in 1553.

6.59 **The lady enraged:** Perhaps Diane de Poitiers, furious upon discovering King Henri II's liaison with Lady Fleming in 1550, which resulted in the birth of a child the following spring. **Seventeen shall be denied survival:** The Edict of Châteaubriant, proclaimed in 1551, accelerated the burning at the stake of heretics.

6.60 **Rochelle . . . Blaye:** The Aquitaine salt-tax revolt of 1548?

6.61 **so fierce shall he grow:** The Duke of Guise, who broke Emperor Charles V's siege of Metz in 1552?

6.63 **The lady left alone upon the throne:** Usually taken to refer to Catherine de Médicis, who lost her husband Henri II in July 1559 (two years after the publication of this quatrain) and then remained in mourning for seven years.

6.66 **They shall dig up the great Roman's remains:** Cf. 3.65; 5.7 for the unearthing of Augustus's tomb in 1521. Luther had been threatened with ex-communication the previous year.

6.70 **great Chyren:** Henri II as successor to the empire of Charles V. See notes to 2.73; 2.79; 4.77.   **Plus ultra:** The device of Emperor Charles V was "PLVS VLTRA CAROL' QUINT" accompanied by the two columns of Hercules (signifying Gibraltar). This motto, "Plus Outre," ambitiously contradicts Dante's description of the columns as a limit for Ulyssean ambitions: "a ciò che l'uom più oltre non si metta" (*Inferno*, XXVI).

6.71 **Before he has even drawn his last breath:** The abdication of the fifty-five-year-old Charles V in 1555, opening the way for the supremacy of Henri II?

6.75 **the mighty pilot:** Probably refers to the career of Gaspard II de Coligny (1519–1572), raised to the rank of admiral of France by Henri II in 1552. Cf. 4.62; 8.57.

6.76 **The ancient town founded by Antenor:** Padua.

6.78 **great Crescent Selene:** Usually refers to the moon-king (see note to 4.77). Here, more likely the Turkish (i.e., crescent) ruler Süleyman the Magnificent.   **Eagle:** Charles V, making his triumphant entry into Rome in 1536, after his victory over Barbarossa at Tunis the previous year. Cf. 5.6; 5.78.   **Basil:** King (from the Greek *basileos*). I.e., a French king?

6.80 **Blue turbans:** Persians? Cf. 2.2.

6.83 **a great celebrity:** Philip II, who succeeded Charles V as king of Spain in 1556 and who lived in the Netherlands during the early years of his reign? **the flower:** France's fleur-de-lis?

6.84 **He who's too lame:** Cf. 3.73.

6.85 **Tarsus:** City in south-central Turkey.   **St. Urban's Day:** May 25.

6.87 **Frankfurt:** Charles V's brother, Ferdinand of Hapsburg, would be coronated Holy Roman Emperor in Frankfurt in 1558.   **Milan:** Philip had been invested with Milan by Charles V in 1542, but never drove Ferdinand out of Germany as lines 3–4 would suggest.

6.89 **The faithless lover:** I follow Brind'Amour's emendation ("furtive amour").

6.90 **Neptune:** May refer to the Baron de la Garde, as in 2.5; 2.59; 2.78; 3.1.

6.91 **in a bale:** Cf. 6.27.   **an Agrippan son:** Term for a male child whose birth was difficult.

6.94 **wreckers of the see:** I.e., Protestant heretics.

6.98 **Volcae:** A Gallic people from the Narbonne region who conquered most of southern Europe and part of Asia in the late fourth and early third centuries B.C.E.   **Their great city:** Toulouse, plundered by the Roman army under Consul Caepio in 106 B.C.E., as recounted by Strabo. Cf. 1.27; 8.29.

6.99 **Pennines:** The section of the Alps between the St. Bernard and St. Gotthard passes, associated with Hannibal.

6.100 **Incantation of the Law:** Latin quatrain lifted from Petrus Crinitus, *De honesta disciplina* (1543), here rendered into alexandrines.

CENTURY VII

7.1 **The treasure arch:** Cf. 4.27 and 5.66, for the reference to the ancient Mausoleum of the Julii at Glanum, whose western facade contains a representation of the death of Achilles, a panel presumably hiding the treasure guarded by the golden goat.

7.3 **Barchinons:** Inhabitants of Spanish Barcelona or French Barcelone (in today's Drôme). **Salians:** Inhabitants of Provence. **Phocaeans:** Inhabitants of Marseille. **Ptolon:** Toulon?

7.4 **Langres:** In eastern Champagne, Guise territory. **Dole:** In Spanish-held Franche-Comté. **Ostun:** Autun? **Augsburg:** In southwest Germany, scene of the diet that produced the Augsburg Confession (1530). **Mirandole:** Town in the duchy of Modena. **Ancona:** Town in the Papal States.

7.8 **Flora:** Florence. Fiesole lies on its outskirts.

7.9 **the great prince from Bar:** The Duke of Guise, born at the castle of Bar, who had an illicit affair with Diane de Poitiers, mistress of Henri II?

7.10 **Barcelona's isle:** One of the Balearics.

7.12 **Moissac . . . Agen:** Towns in Aquitaine, southwest France.

7.13 **The shaved head:** Most likely the cleric Thomas de Grailly de Foix-Lautrec, who took over the government of Genoa in the name of France between 1508 and 1522.

7.15 **the city of the Insubrian plain:** Milan. For seven years (1515–22) François I dominated Lombardy until his defeat at La Bicoque.

7.16 **The army of three lions:** The British army (defeated at Calais by the Duke of Guise four months after the publication of this quatrain).

7.17 **this king:** The late François I (died 1547), defeated and captured at the battle of Pavia in 1525?

7.19 **the fort of Nice:** The fall of Savoyard Nice to a combined force of French and Turks in 1543?

7.20 **He of Vaud:** Théodore de Bèze, disciple of John Calvin and professor of Greek in Lausanne, exposing Imperial plans to attack France from the southeast? Cf. 1.95.

7.21 **Volcae:** Celtic people from the Narbonne region. **Sorgues:** Town in the Vaucluse.

7.22 **Mesopotamia:** Cf. 3.61; 3.99; 8.70. Usually, the region between the rivers Rhône and Durance. **Tarragona:** City in Catalonia. **Ausonia:** Italy.

7.24 **Marquis du Pont:** The marquis de Pont-à-Mousson, heir to the duchy of Bar? Cf. 7.9.

7.25 **sign of the crescent Moon:** See note to 4.77.

7.27 **Vasto:** Adriatic port. **Ferrajo:** Capital of the isle of Elba.

7.29 **Duke of Alba:** Fernando, Duke of Alba, chief military commander of the forces of Charles V, just as François, Duke of Guise, was the principal general of Henri II. Cf. 4.98; 8.40; 8.60.

7.30 **Fossano . . . Savigliano:** Towns in the Italian Piedmont.

7.31 **Allobrogian men:** Inhabitants of the Narbonne region.

7.32 **One who shall tyrannize vault & account:** Taken to refer to one of the Medici banking family.

7.36 **the Divine Word:** The holy monstrance. Cf. 2.27; 3.2; 8.99. **Trebizond:** Port on the Black Sea, capital of the Greek empire from 1204 to 1461.

7.37 **Lérins, Hyères:** Islands off the southern French coast.

EPISTLE TO HENRI II
First published in the posthumous 1568 Rigaud edition of the *Prophecies* as the introduction to the final three Centuries. As in the case of the 1555 preface Nostradamus wrote to his son César, I have paragraphed the text in order to facilitate reading (while scrupulously following his ampersands and punctuation). The phrases in italics are in Latin in the original.

that day when I first presented myself before a Majesty so unique: Nostradamus had been received at the French court in mid-1555, shortly after the publication of the first edition of his *Prophecies*.

Minerva was free & well-disposed: Cf. Horace, *Ars poetica* 385. *As for the future, the truth cannot entirely be determined:* Quoted by Savonarola in the *Mirabilis liber*. See Nostradamus's borrowings from Savonarola in his 1555 prefatory letter to his son César.

by means of the bronze tripod: See 1.1 and note on Iamblichus.

Kings of France cured people of scrofula: See the thaumaturgic prince of 4.10.

Varro: Marcus Terentius Varro (116–27 B.C.E.), known for his year-by-year chronology of Roman history up to his time.

Eusebius: Eusebius of Caesarea (ca. 260–ca. 339), ecclesiastical historian.

I will pour out my spirit upon all flesh: Joel 2:28.

the long-barren Great Lady: Leoni suggests that this prophecy (which occupies the remainder of the epistle) may refer to the reigning queen, Catherine de Médicis, who had been married to the future Henri II for nine years before conceiving—although she would go on to have nine children. Her eldest child, François (the current dauphin), had just married Mary Stuart in April 1558, which conceivably could also make the latter a candidate for this mysterious "barren lady." Cf. 10.55 and 10.56. Lemesurier, by contrast, reads this entire section as a compilation of prophecies from the *Mirabilis liber*, a patchwork of allusions to texts by Pseudo-Methodus, the Tiburtine sibyl, Joachim of Fiore, St. Bridget of Sweden, etc. Crouzet in turn suggests that this "barren lady" may be allegorical of the contemporary Church of Rome.

Mount of Jove: The Latin *Mons Jovis*, the Great St. Bernard Pass, or possibly the *Mons Capitolinus* in Rome, sacred to Jupiter.

Romania: Roman Italy.

Pannonia: Turkish-dominated southern Hungary.

Attila, & Xerxes: Attila the Hun (whence Hungary); the Persian emperor Xerxes (ca. 519–465 B.C.E.).

one who shall renew the whole Christian Church: Sometimes identified as the "Angelic Pastor" of Joachim of Fiore's prophecies.

Mesopotamia: In the quatrains of the *Prophecies*, Mesopotamia most usually refers to the papal Venaissin enclave, situated between the Durance and Rhône rivers.

the second Thrasybulus: Athenian general who restored democracy to the city in 404 B.C.E.

the three sects: Usually identified in order as Protestantism, Catholicism, and Islam.

Dog & Dogam: An allusion to the Gog and Magog of Ezekiel 38:2–3?

the reds nor the whites: Cf. 1.3.

the port which takes its name from the sea-calf: Phocaea (from the Latin *phocus*, seal), i.e., Marseille. Cf. 3.79.

the Sierra Morena: East-west mountain range stretching across southern Spain.

the Jovialists: Cf. 10.73 and note.

Ashem: A garbled version of "Shechem," visited by Abraham, site of an altar built by Jacob?

That he hear the groaning of the prisoners: a reminiscence of Psalm 102:20.

the year seventeen ninety-two: Roussat in his *Livre de l'estat et mutation des temps* (1550) had mentioned 1789 and 1791 as dates of the "future renovation of the world."

Pampotania: From the Greek *pan* (all) and Latin *potens* (powerful) or the Greek *pan* (all) and *potomos* (river, sea).

the city of Plancus: Lyon, founded by Lucius Munatius Plancus in 43 B.C.E. Cf. 3.46.

Modona Fulcy: Possibly Modena and the house of Este.

the Ligurians of the Adriatic: The Venetians.

the Gallic Ogmion: The French Hercules; see note to 1.96.

the great vicar of the cope: The pope.

Huy huy: In French, "Today, today" (or in Hebrew, "Woe, woe").

CENTURY VIII

8.1 OLORON, PAU, NAY ... **Aude:** Towns in the southwestern French region of Béarn, through which the river Aude runs. Béarn was the heartland of the Kingdom of Navarre, birthplace of Henri IV. "PAU, NAY, OLORON" was read as an anagram for Napoléon in the nineteenth century. **magpies:** A play on the papal name Pius? **Pompon, Durance:** The "plenipotentiary" of the river Durance (which runs through Avignon, city of the popes)?

8.2 **Condom & Auch ... Mirande ... Marmande:** Towns in the department of Gers, southwestern France. Cf. 1.46. **Sun, Mars in Leo:** Reoccurs astrologically roughly every two years. **wall falling into Garonne:** Cf. the flooding in 9.37.

8.3 **Viglanne & Resviers:** San Vigilio and Riviera in the Lake Garda region? **Nancy:** Capital of Lorraine. **Turin:** Capital of the duchy of Savoy, under French occupation in Nostradamus's day.

8.4 **Monaco:** Bound by a 1524 treaty to assist the Spanish in all wars against France. **The Cardinal of France:** Charles, second cardinal of Lorraine (1524–1574), responsible for an alliance between France and the Papacy in 1556? **Ogmion:** The French Hercules. Cf. 1.96; 2.73; 5.80; 6.42; 10.79. **The eagle ... the cock:** Spain and France.

8.5 **At Bornel, Breteuil, lamps & candles bright:** May allude to the 1547 funeral cortege of King François I (the "cock" of the last line), which visited a number of illuminated Catholic churches across the land before his final burial in the Saint-Denis Basilica.

8.6 **A blazing light at Lyon:** Cf. 3.46. **Malta seized:** Cf. 2.49.

8.7 **Ticino:** From the Latin name (*Ticinus*) for Pavia, site of the disastrous February 1525 battle during which François I was captured and subsequently imprisoned in Madrid in May. Cf. 2.26; 4.45; 4.75; 10.72. **Maying:** Taking part in the festivities of May Day; gathering flowers or pleasures during the month of May (*Oxford English Dictionary*).

8.8 **Cisterna:** Town in Lazio in central Italy. **Chivas:** Chivasso, Piedmont commune north of Turin.

8.9 **Savona:** Seaport west of Genoa, here fought over by France and Spain. **Barbar:** "Barbarian," or possibly an aphaeresis of the mysterious "Aeno-barbe." Cf. 5.45.

8.10 **Lausanne:** Metonym for Calvinist Switzerland.

8.11 **Vicenza ... lord Valenza:** May allude to the partial destruction of the Palazzo della Ragione at Vicenza in 1496 and the defeat of Cesare Borgia, Duke of Valentinois, in Urbino in 1502. **Lunigiana:** Strategic valley in eastern Liguria.

8.12 **Buffalora:** Town near Milan. **St. Maur:** Legendary founder of the Benedictine order in Gaul.

8.13 **Shall like Proetus make Bellerophon die:** Accused of trying to seduce the wife of King Proetus, Bellerophon was sent to his death in the land of King Iobates of Lycia. Iobates, hesitating to murder him, instead dispatched him on a mission to kill the Chimera, astride his flying horse, Pegasus.

8.15 **A mannish northern female:** May allude to Isabella, daughter of the king of Poland, who married the satrap of Pannonia (modern Hungary) in 1539 and subsequently became an active ally of Süleyman the Magnificent.

8.16 HIERON: Jason. **Olympian Fiesole:** Mount outside of Florence, with a pun on Thessaly, home of Mount Olympus.

8.18 **Flora:** Florence. **lilies:** Traditional symbol of France.

8.19 **the great cope:** The pope? **The reddest reds:** Cardinals? Spaniards?

8.20 **The election:** Of the pope? Of the Holy Roman Emperor?

8.21 **Agde:** Seaport between Narbonne and Marseille in southern France. **foists:** Light galleys.

8.22 **Coursan ... Tuchan ... Perpignan:** Towns in the vicinity of Narbonne involved in the southwestern salt-tax revolt of 1548. Cf. 1.90; 3.21; 9.1.

8.24 **Montpertuis:** The Perthus Pass in the Pyrenees, south of Perpignan? **Lusignan:** Seat of the illustrious medieval clan that provided the kings of Jerusalem and ruled Cyprus until 1489.

8.26 **Cato:** A grandson of the famous censor Cato died in Tarragona, Spain, in the second century B.C.E. **Montserrat:** Benedictine abbey west of Barcelona.

8.27 **aqueduct:** An ancient Roman aqueduct near Le Muy fed the coastal town of Fréjus in southern France. Cf. 4.80; 5.58; 8.68; 10.89.

8.28 **The idols:** Severe flooding in September 1557 led to the discovery of various pagan artifacts from the ruined temple of Diana that had originally been thrown into the Sacred Lake at Nîmes with the coming of Christianity. Cf. 9.9; 9.12; 10.6.

8.29 **Caepio:** The Roman consul Caepio, dispatched to fight the local Cimbri tribes, plundered Toulouse in 106 B.C.E. Cf. 1.27; 6.98.

8.30 **Bazacle:** Name of the milling section of Toulouse. Cf. 1.27; 8.29, 9.7.

8.31 **Pescara's prince:** The marquis di Pescara commanded the Imperial Hapsburg troops who defeated François I at the battle of Pavia in 1525. **Selin:** The moon-king; usually refers to Henri II. See note to 4.77.

8.32 **your own cousin:** Presumably Louis XII (1462–1515), nephew of Charles VIII and sole monarch from the Valois-Orléans branch of the house of Valois. After his uncle's death in 1498, he quickly married the latter's widow, Anne de Bretagne.

8.33 **Verona or Vicenza:** Towns within the Venetian republic.

8.34 **mausoleum:** Saint-Paul-de-Mausole, near Nostradamus's birthplace at Saint-Rémy? Cf. 4.27.

8.35 **Damazan:** In the Aquitaine region of southwestern France.

8.36 **Saulne [i.e., Lons-le-Saulnier] ... Saint-Aubin ... Bletterans:** Locations in the Franche-Comté, where in the fifteenth century a project was launched to connect the roads of this region with the duchy of Burgundy by using materials recycled from watchtowers built by the Romans.

8.37 **Tamise:** French name of the river Thames. Could refer to the imprisonment in the Tower of London of Henry VI of England, although it's been read from Garencières onward as predicting the imprisonment and eventual beheading of Charles I in 1649. Cf. 9.49.

8.40 **Dorade & Taur:** Two major churches in Toulouse, Saint-Saturnin-du-Taur and Sainte-Marie-de-la-Dorade. **Saturnines:** Cf. 6.17. **Albanines:** The Spanish troops of the Duke of Alba? Cf. 4.98; 7.29.

8.41 **The Fox:** The reign of Pope Julius III (1550–55)?

8.42 **Saint-Memire:** Saint-Mamert-du-Gard in the Languedoc-Roussillon region of southern France?

8.43 **Lectoure:** Town in the Midi-Pyrenees, north of Auch, on the pilgrimage route to Compostela.

8.44 **Ogmion:** The French Hercules. See note to 1.96.   PAU: Birthplace in 1553 of the future Henri IV, who would later marry Marguerite de Valois, daughter of Henri II and Catherine de Médicis.

8.46 **Pol-Mausole:** I.e., Nostradamus's Saint-Rémy-de-Provence? Cf. 4.27. **Cock vs. eagle:** France vs. the Holy Roman Empire.

8.47 **The Transmenian lake:** Lake Trasimeno, west of Perugia (*Perouse* in French).

8.48 **Salvatierra . . . Briviesca:** Towns in the Basque Country and in the province of Burgos, Spain. May refract Nostradamus's readings of Froissart's account of the military campaigns of Edward the Black Prince in the fourteenth century.

8.49 **Saturn in Bull:** The astrological configuration could describe 1499 or, according to Brind'Amour, 1736.   **Ponterosso:** The "Red Bridge" of Florence built in the early sixteenth century (here rhymed with the celebrated bridges of Bruges).   **Barb.:** Barbarian.

8.50 **Capellades:** Town in Catalonia.   **Sagunto:** Seaport in Valencia.

8.51 **The Byzantine:** Here, perhaps, the Turks of Constantinople, attacking Spain.   **pampination:** The pruning or trimming of vines (*Oxford English Dictionary*).   **the Pillars:** The Pillars of Hercules; Gibraltar.

8.52 **In Avignon:** Cf. 8.38.   **Blois . . . Amboise . . . Bonny:** Towns on the river Loire, which meets with the Indre farther south. An incomplete quatrain.

8.54 **Great Selin Chyren:** See notes to 2.73; 2.79; 4.77.   **Quentin, Arras:** Sites of major military defeats of the French by the Spaniards in 1557. At that time a marriage between Henri II's daughter Elisabeth de Valois and Philip II's son Don Carlos was in the offing. Philip II would marry her himself in 1559 after the Treaty of Cateau-Cambrésis.

8.56 **Ebro:** River in Spain.

8.57 **From simple soldier:** Most likely evokes the meteoric rise to power of Gaspard II de Coligny, admiral of France and hero of France's defeat at the 1557 battle of Saint-Quentin. Soon thereafter, having converted to Protestantism, he became an important leader of the French Huguenots. Cf. 4.62; 6.75.

8.58 **twixt brothers divided:** Probably alludes to the rivalry between Edward Seymour, Duke of Somerset (ca. 1506–1552), and John Dudley, Duke of Northumberland (ca. 1504–1553). The latter, after engineering Seymour's decapitation in 1552, became the chief backer of evangelical Protestants (the "Anglican" of line 3) among the clergy.   **Seized by night:** During Dudley's regency, Boulogne was surrendered to the French and the dauphin François allowed to marry Mary, Queen of Scots, thus allowing Henri II to claim sovereignty over both Scotland and England.

8.60 **Romania:** Probably the Holy Roman Empire, given that the quatrain would appear to evoke the counterattack by François, Duke of Guise (1519–1563), against the forces of Charles V in 1558, during which Calais was recaptured from the English and Paris spared. Cf. 7.29.   **NOLARIS:** Usually read as an anagram for Lorraine.

8.61 **host:** Translates Nostradamus's "TAG[ma]" ("legion" in Greek).

8.64 **Nompelle:** Montpellier?

8.65 **The old one:** Pope Adrian VI (1459–1523), who reigned eighteen months between 1522 and 1523?

8.66 **D.M.:** From the Latin *Diis Manibus* ("In the hands of Pluto"), a common inscription on Roman tombs. **Ulpian:** Having to do with Roman jurisprudence, after the celebrated jurist Domitius Ulpianus (ca. 170–228).

8.67 **PAR., CAR., NERSAF:** Paris, Carcassonne, France (anagram). **Colonna:** Powerful Italian noble family in medieval and Renaissance Rome. Cf. 9.2; 10.64.

8.68 **Liqueduct:** Nostradamian compound, variously interpreted as "the water-borne one" (from the Latin *ille acqua ductus*) or "the rotted one" (from the Latin *liqueducere*). Lemesurier reads it as "aqueduct," given Nostradamus's financial investment in his friend Adam de Craponne's project to dig an irrigation canal from the river Durance to Salon and as far as Arles. Cf. 4.80; 5.58; 8.27; 10.89.

8.70 **Mesopotamia:** Usually refers to the area between the Rhône and Durance rivers. Cf. 3.61; 3.99; 7.22. Lemesurier, however, reads the quatrain as alluding to the Great Whore of Babylon and the coming of the Antichrist.

8.71 **astronomers:** Cf. 4.18. No such decision was made by the Church in 1607.

8.72 **Ravenna:** The French victory in the battle of Ravenna of April 11, 1512?

8.74 **the King enters the new land:** Cf. 6.83. Philip II of Spain's takeover of the Netherlands in 1556?

8.77 **The Antichrist:** Sometimes read as referring to the Protestant leader John Calvin.

8.78 **A soldier of fortune:** Michel de l'Hôpital? Cf. 1.97.

8.79 **whoreson father:** The French, *nay de Nonnaire* (born of a Nonnaire), derives from the Latin *nonaria*, or strumpet (because harlots appeared at the ninth hour, our three o'clock in the afternoon). **Gorgon:** In Greek mythology, a terrifying female creature (from *gorgos*, "inspiring dread").

8.80 **Great Red:** The French, *grand roge*, may also be read as an anagram of "ogre."

8.81 **The new empire:** An apparent prediction of a major Hapsburg civil war between Philip II and his uncle, the Holy Roman Emperor Ferdinand (both of whom had come to power in 1556 after the abdication of Charles V).

8.83 **Zara:** As reported in Villehardouin's eyewitness account of the Fourth Crusade, the Crusaders captured Zara, a seaport on the Dalmatian coast, for the Venetians in 1202 before going on to capture Constantinople two years later.

8.84 **Paternò:** Town north of Catania in Sicily. **Trinacria:** The name of the island kingdom of Sicily after 1302 ("Triangle" in English).

8.85 **Bayonne & port Saint-Jean-de-Luz:** Towns in the far southwestern corner of France.

8.86 **Ernani . . . Adrian mounts:** The three towns of the first line and the Sierra San Adrián of line 2 all lie near the western tip of the Pyrenees in Spain. **Bichoro:** The war cry of Navarre (or, more specifically, of Bigorre), launching its attack on Bayonne.

8.88 **Into Sardinia:** The King of Aragon invaded Sardinia between 1323 and 1326.

8.89 **Peloncle:** Unclear. From Pellonia, the goddess of victory? Or Mount Pelion in Thessaly? **dragged along:** Cf. 7.38.

8.90 **a horned ox in the holy church:** The identical apocalyptic image occurs in the Prophecy of the Blessed Vincent included in one of Nostradamus's sourcebooks, the *Mirabilis liber* (1522).

8.91 **The two braziers:** Mars and Venus, following the legend that Venus had been bound to husband Mars by a thread produced by Vulcan.

8.94 **Alba's troops:** Cf. 4.98; 7.29; 8.40.

8.96 **The barren, fruitless synagogue of yore:** As Leoni notes, during Nostradamus's own lifetime thousands of Jews, fleeing persecution in Catholic lands, accepted the hospitality of Süleyman the Magnificent and settled in Constantinople, Salonika, and Adrianople. See also Isaiah 54:1.

8.97 **Var:** River in southeastern France.

8.99 **change the site of the Holy See:** The Holy Council was transferred to Trent, where, in 1551, reacting to Protestant assertions to the contrary, it officially reaffirmed the doctrine of the literal transubstantiation of Christ's blood and body in the Eucharist (the "corporal substance of the spirit" of line 3). Cf. 2.27; 3.2; 7.36.

CENTURY IX

9.1 **the translator:** In his youth, Étienne de La Boétie (1530–1563), translator and humanist (and Montaigne's best friend), wrote a pamphlet, *Discourse on Voluntary Servitude, or the Anti-Dictator,* directed against Anne de Montmorency, constable of France, criticizing the latter's savage suppression of the salt-tax revolt in southwestern France in 1548. Cf. 3.32.

9.2 **Aventine Hill:** One of the seven hills of Rome, which would indicate that the "red ones" of line 3 might be cardinals.   **the Colonna:** One of the most influential families in Rome; during Nostradamus's day, they favored Spain's hegemony over Italy. Cf. 8.67; 10.64.

9.3 **magna vaqua:** From the Latin, "big cow." Magnavacca was also the name of a canal between Ravenna and Ferrara.   **Fornase:** Probably *Farnese,* initially a castle (or *rocca*) acquired and improved in 1504 by Cardinal Alessandro Farnese, the future pope Paul III. Or Fornase, a village west of Venice?

9.6 **Anglaquitania:** Aquitaine had become an English possession as early as 1152, when Eleanor of Aquitaine married Henry II of England. It was not annexed to France until 1453, at the end of the Hundred Years' War.   **Barboccitania:** The feared occupation of southwestern France (from Bordeaux to the Languedoc region of Occitania) by "Barbarians" (Muslim Turks? Barbary pirates? Spaniards?).

9.7 **newly found trove:** Cf. 1.27.

9.9 **the Temple of Diana's walls:** Cf. note to 8.28. The Temple of Diana was associated with the cult of the Vestal Virgins. Cf. 10.6.

9.10 **Pamiers:** A town lying north of Foix, in the same general southwestern area of France as Toulouse and Carcassonne.

9.12 **unearth silver likenesses:** Cf. 8.28; 9.9.

9.13 **Sologne:** Town in the upper Loire region.   **Auxois:** Region of Burgundy to the west of Dijon.   **Burançoys:** Buzançais, just south of Sologne? Byzantines?

9.15 **Perpignan:** Chief city of Roussillon, held by the Spanish ("the red ones") until 1659.

9.16 **Castelfranco:** An attack from Castelfranco (west of Modena) on the Italian Riviera? Read by some twentieth-century commentors as alluding to France's Riviera in the Spanish Civil War.

9.17 **Nero:** Roman emperor from 54 to 68 C.E., known for his cruelty and orgiastic excess. Cf. 9.53; 9.76.

9.18 **the great Montmorency:** Constable Anne de Montmorency (1493–1567) had been captured and imprisoned by the Spaniards at the battle of Saint-Quentin in 1557. Cf. 9.1; 9.29; 9.40.

9.19 **Mayenne:** Town in the province of Maine in northwest France belonging to the house of Guise; Fougères (line 4), slightly to the west of it, belonged to Diane de Poitiers, Henri II's mistress.

9.20 **the woods of Reines:** The city of Rennes? Nineteenth-century Nostradamus scholar Anatole Le Pelletier derives the old French spelling of *forest* from the Latin *foris* (gate), thus arriving at "through the gates of Queens," i.e., the secret doors of Queen Marie Antoinette's apartments through which the royal couple escaped from the Tuileries on June 21, 1791, during their celebrated flight to Varennes (line 3). But like all the other place-names in this quatrain (Pierre Blanche, Herne, Vaultorte, Varennes), the forest of Rennes-en-Grenouilles (spelled "Raines" in the sixteenth century) was lifted from the pages of Charles Estienne's *Guide des chemins de France* (1552). This particular area (cf. the previous quatrain) was a site of numerous skirmishes between Protestants and Catholics during Nostradamus's lifetime. **The black monk all in gray:** Identified by Le Pelletier as Louis XVI, disguised in drab (monkish?) gray during his flight to Varennes. Provides the title for the historian Georges Dumézil's razzle-dazzle reading of this quatrain, *Le moyne noir en gris dedans Varennes* (1984), translated into English as *The Riddle of Nostradamus* (1999). Prévost specifically identifies this figure as the pro-Catholic captain Antoine du Plessis de Richelieu. **cap.:** Abbreviation for captain? For those looking for Louis XVI here, it would read "Capet"—with the final "sang tranche" ("blood slice") clearly alluding to the guillotine.

9.21 **church of Saint-Solenne:** The cathedral of Blois. Cf. 9.23. **Olonne:** Les Sables d'Olonne and Olonne-sur-Mer, on the seacoast north of La Rochelle.

9.23 **The roof collapsing:** According to Prévost, alludes to the accidental death of the young comte d'Enghien in February 1546, followed by François I's expiatory Easter pilgrimage to the abbey of Ferrières in Sologne, south of Blois. Cf. 3.40; 9.83.

9.25 **Rosiers:** Town in the Limousin. **Béziers:** Languedoc town near the Spanish border.

9.26 **Nice:** Territory of the duchy of Savoy. **Voltri:** On the Ligurian coast between Genoa and Savona. **Piombino:** Further down the coast, opposite Elba.

9.27 **the young Dauphin:** Refracts events during Pope Clement VII's trip to Marseille in the autumn of 1533 to celebrate the nuptials of the dauphin Henri (subsequently Henri II) to Caterina de' Medici. Cf. 2.14. **the duke's demesne:** The pope returned to Rome via Nice, in the duchy of Savoy.

9.28 **Pannonia:** Roughly coincides with present-day Hungary, held by the Turks. **the gulf & Illyrian bay:** I.e., the Adriatic Sea.

9.29 **Saint-Quentin, Calais:** Saint-Quentin had been taken by the Spanish on August 10, 1557. Calais, held by the British since 1347, was recaptured by the Duke of Guise, along with Saint-Quentin, in early 1558, just as Nostradamus was completing his *Prophecies*. Cf. 9.18; 9.40.

9.30 **Pula & Saint Nicholas:** Pula, port on the Istrian Peninsula at the head of the Adriatic; Saint Nicholas, across the bay from Porec on the north of the peninsula.   **Phanatic Bay:** Pun aside, probably the Gulf of Quarnero (*Sinus Flanaticus* in Latin) on which Fiume (now Rijeka) is located.   **the Philippine great:** Philip II?

9.31 **Mortara:** Town just southwest of Milan.   **St. George Caltagirone:** A church near Catania in Sicily destroyed by the great earthquakes of 1542.

9.32 **A porphyry column:** The discovery of the obelisk of Augustus Caesar in 1502 toward the end of the reign of Pope Alexander VI. The latter pursued an aggressive foreign policy against the Turks (the "scraggly" or "twisty" beards of line 3). Cf. 8.66.   **Mytilene:** The Greek isle of Lesbos.

9.33 **Hercules:** The figure of the universal monarch; see note to 1.96 concerning Ogmion, the Gallic Hercules.   **St. Mark's seas:** The territories and sea routes of the Republic of Venice.

9.34 **The mitered one:** According to Prévost, French foreign minister Cardinal Georges d'Ambroise, furious with the Spaniards for having reneged on their secret agreement to divvy up Italy with France, launched a campaign of retribution in 1503 against Spain (country of tile roofs, line 2).   **Salces:** A town on the border near Narbonne, besieged over the course of the campaign, but the provisions of oil and candles intended for the French were allowed to fall into Spanish hands—leading to the dismissal of Marshal Rieux, commander of the French company of five hundred men (line 3).

9.35 **Ferdinand:** As in 8.81, tensions are predicted between the new Holy Roman Emperor Ferdinand I and his nephew Philip II of Spain (here as elsewhere referred to by the memory of his namesake, Philip II of Macedon, father of Alexander the Great). Cf. 9.38; 9.64; 9.93; 10.7.   **the flower:** Usually refers to Florence.   **Myrmidon:** The tribe of Achilles, known for their obedience, here equated to Philip II, the "Macedon."

9.36 **three brothers:** Cf. 8.17; 8.46.

9.37 **flooding Garonne:** The *Annales de Toulouse* of 1536 recorded major flooding during December of that year.   **Matronne:** The river Marne (*Matrona* in Latin).

9.38 **the Macedonian:** The French *Aemathien* derives from the Latin *Emathia*, synonym for Macedonia, hence Philip II of Spain again (cf. 9.35). Further (this time, Anglo-Spanish) military maneuvers against the French.

9.39 **Albisola, Veront [?], Carcari [i.e., Caracara] . . . Savona:** Towns along the northern Ligurian coast.   **Turbie, & La Scerry:** La Turbie and L'Escarène, north of Monaco.

9.40 **Near Saint-Quentin:** Revisiting France's major military disaster at Saint-Quentin on August 10, 1557. Cf. 9.18; 9.29.

9.41 **The great Chyren:** Usually Henri II (see note to 2.79). Here conflated with his father, François I, who had temporarily seized Avignon from the papacy in 1536, provoking diplomatic protests from Pope Paul III (line 2). **Chanignon:** Canino, a town adjacent to the pope's fortress at Farnese (see note to 9.3)?   **Carpentras:** Northwest of Avignon, part of the papal possessions in France.

9.42 **Barbar fleet:** Recollections of the fleet of the Ottoman corsair and admiral Hayreddin Barbarossa, driven out of Tunis by Charles V's expedition of 1535.

9.43 **Ishmaelites:** Biblical name for the Arvim, or Arabs, direct descendants of Ishmael, son of Abraham and Hagar (Book of Jubilees 20:13). Cf. 9.60.

9.44 RAYPOZ: According to Leoni, an anagram for Zopyra. Herodotus (III, 153–60) recounts how during Darius's siege of Babylon, his friend Zopyra decided to cut off his nose and ears and to introduce himself into the city as a deserter, claiming he had been cruelly mutilated by his king. Gaining the confidence of Babylon's defenders, Zopyra thus managed to deliver the city over to the Persians. Philip II of Spain adopted the name of Zopyra in one of his devices—two scepters passed in saltire through a crown over an open pomegranate, bearing the motto "Tot Zopiro."

9.45 **Mendosus:** Latin *mendosus*, "full of faults, erroneous." Anagram for Vendôme? Cf. 9.50. **Tyrron:** Likely from the Latin *Tyrrhenia*, i.e., Etruscan, Tuscan.

9.49 **The senate of London its king shall slay:** Read by Le Pelletier as predicting the fate of King Charles I of England, beheaded in 1649. Others prefer to see this quatrain as alluding to the unhappy fate of Edward II of England (1284–1327).

9.50 **Mandosus:** Cf. 9.45. **Norlaris:** Anagram for Lorraine? **Barbaries:** Barbary pirates.

9.53 **Nero:** Cf. 9.17; 9.76.

9.56 **Goussonville, Houdan:** Towns to the west of Paris. **Maiotes:** Mantes?

9.57 DRUX: Dreux, westward of Paris in Normandy?

9.58 **Vitry:** Vitry-le-François in Champagne, southeast of Paris?

9.59 **Nicholas:** The context would suggest Nicholas de Lorraine (1524–1577), whose daughter Louise, born in 1553, would later marry Henri III, the last Valois king.

9.60 **Mighty Ishmael:** Cf. 9.43. **frogs:** Often used by Nostradamus for sea admirals or pirates. Cf. 5.3; 5.95.

9.61 **Cittanova . . . Messina:** Part of the Hapsburg Kingdom of the Two Sicilies. Malta, also a Hapsburg protectorate, had been the seat of the Knights of St. John since 1530.

9.62 **Cheramon:** Ceramon-agora, a Greek town in Asia Minor, today's Usak.

9.63 **Mars:** Each revolution of Mars takes 687 days.

9.64 **The Macedonian:** Philip II of Spain. Cf. 9.35; 9.38. **Cap.:** Captain?

9.65 **Luna:** A place-name or simply a patch of moonlight?

9.67 **Isère:** The river Isère flows into the Rhône at Valence. Romans, Crest, Pierrelatte, Donzère, Châteauneuf all lie nearby in this area of the Dauphiné, a part of the papal enclave of Venaissin.

9.68 **Montélimar:** In the Drôme (cf. the geography of the previous quatrain). **where Saône meets Rhône:** The city of Lyon. **Lucy's day:** December 13.

9.69 **Sain-Bel & L'Arbresle . . . Grenoble:** Towns in the Dauphiné. **Vienne:** South of Lyon on the Rhône.

9.70 **Latin cantons:** The Swiss Grisons?

9.72 **churches shall be defiled:** A takeover of Toulouse by the Protestants (the "folk of a new leaven" of line 4)? **two three cycles:** If this is read as six revolutions, it would come to 177 years. **leaven:** Matthew 16:6: "the leaven of the Pharisees and of the Sadducees."

9.73 **one of Saturn's turns:** Twenty-nine years and 167 days. **the Urn:** Aquarius. The astrology points to the year 1586.

9.74 **Fertsod:** Read by some as a distant anagram for Sodom—or as Toulouse, traditional site of the pagan sacrifice of bulls and a Protestant stronghold. Cf. 1.79; 9.46.

9.75 **Ambracia:** Arta in western Greece; Thrace lies in northeastern Greece.

9.76 **Nero:** Cf. 9.17; 9.53. **the young bald one:** Lemesurier reads the French ("Joyne chaulberon") as homophonic with Jean Chauvin (i.e., John Calvin), a Protestant leader who had the heretic Michael Servetus burned alive in Geneva (between the rivers Arve and Rhône) in 1553.

9.77 **the King:** Henry VIII of England?

9.78 **The damsel Greek:** According to Prévost, Helen of Epirus, daughter of the Emperor of Constantinople, courted by numerous suitors, eventually marrying the son of Emperor Frederick II of Hohenstaufen, then widowed and captured on her way back to Greece and imprisoned in Spanish-controlled Naples, where she died in 1271.

9.79 **chrism:** Oil mingled with balm, consecrated for use as an unguent in the administration of certain sacraments of the Christian churches (*Oxford English Dictionary*).

9.81 **coqueluches:** "A hood; also the Coqueluchoe [*sic*], or new disease [i.e., whooping cough], which troubled the French about the yeares 1510 and 1557; and us but a while agoe" (Cotgrave's *Dictionarie* of 1611). By extension, hooded monks? **Translator:** Alternate reading: "traducer."

9.83 **crowded theater:** Cf. 3.40.

9.84 **The flood unearths:** Cf. 5.7; 5.66; 8.66; 9.9.

9.85 **Guyenne:** Large province of southwestern France, adjacent to Languedoc. **Agen ... Marmande ... La Réole:** Towns on the river Garonne in Guyenne. **Phocaean:** Latin adjective for Marseille. **Saint-Paul-de-Mausole:** Nostradamus's Saint-Rémy. See note to 4.27.

9.86 **Bourg-la-Reine:** A few miles south of Paris. All five place-names (except Paris) in this and the following quatrain occur on a single page (p. 92) of Charles Estienne's 1552 *Guide des chemins de France.*

9.88 **Calais ... Thérouanne:** The port of Calais had belonged to the English since 1347, but was seized by the French in early 1558 under the Duke of Guise. Cf. 9.29. Nearby Thérouanne was destroyed by Charles V in 1553. **Roanne:** Northwest of Lyon on the Loire, thus not far from the duchy of Savoy.

9.89 **Fortune shall favor Philip seven years:** If Philip II of Spain's fortunate years dated from 1554 (when he married Queen Mary of England), then his defeat by Henri II, the young French Hercules ("Ogmion," line 4), would have fallen in 1561. (Henri II died in 1559.) **Ogmion:** Cf. note to 1.96.

9.90 **Pannonia:** Present-day southern Hungary.

9.91 **Perinthus:** Town in Thrace. All the other place-names in this quatrain are located in Greece. **Anthony:** St. Anthony? Antoine de Bourbon, Duke of Vendôme, king of Navarre, father of Henri IV?

9.92 **the new city:** Naples (from the Greek *Neapolis*)?

9.93 **Hercules ... Macedon:** Henri II vs. Philip II.

9.94 **Bratislava:** One of the capitals of Hapsburg Hungary. **Lübeck:** Imperial free city on the Baltic. **Meissen:** On the Elbe in Saxony.

9.98 **Molite:** From the Greek *molos* (war) or the Latin *Melita* (Malta)?

CENTURY X

10.5 **Albi:** A center of the Albigensians in thirteenth-century France; Castres lies nearby. **Arrianus:** Military commander and historian of Alexander the Great's campaigns (ca. 86–160). **Lauraguès:** Albigensian village in the Aude.

10.6 **Deucalion:** Greek mythological figure associated with the Deluge. Heavy flooding occurred throughout southern France in September 1557. Cf. 2.81. **coliseum:** The Arena of Nîmes. **Vesta's tomb:** Cf. 8.28.

10.7 **Macedon:** Philip II. Cf. 9.35; 9.38; 9.64; 9.93. **two Phi.:** Apocope for Philip II? **Metz:** Town in French-occupied Lorraine.

10.8 **Senigallia:** Above Ancona in the Papal States.

10.11 **Junquera:** On the Spanish side of the Perthus Pass; Perpignan lies to the east, with the route leading to Tende, above Nice.

10.13 **Antipolis:** Antibes, port between Cannes and Nice.

10.14 **Urnel Vaucile:** Prévost reads as "Humil. Vacil." (i.e., humilated, vacillating). **Chartreux:** Carthusian convent.

10.15 **To the agèd duke:** An anecdote drawn from Book IV of Philippe de Commynes' *Mémoires*, involving the Duke of Guelders's torturing of his own father in the 1470s?

10.17 **The scheming queen:** Perhaps Anne de Bretagne (1447–1514), queen of France, machinating to get her daughter Claude married off, first to the future emperor Charles V and then to the future François I, all the while attempting to get herself pregnant to preclude the latter from acceding to the throne. Cf. 8.32.

10.18 **Vendôme:** Usually read as predicting the rise to power of the future Henri IV, the Duke of Vendôme, a Protestant. **Hamon:** Jupiter.

10.20 **The Roman people:** The sacking of Rome in 1527 by Imperial troops. Cf. 2.57; 5.81; 10.27.

10.23 **Antibes . . . Monaco . . . Fréjus:** Towns along France's southern coast.

10.25 **Ebro:** River in northeastern Spain. **Pézenas:** North of Narbonne, on the border with Spain. Leoni's reading of *Brisanne*. **el Tago fara muestra:** Spanish: "The Tagus [river in central Spain and Portugal] shall make a show." **Pelligouxe:** Périgueux, in the Dordogne? **orchestra:** In Roman theaters, the area in front of the stage containing the seats of senators and other notables.

10.27 **the fifth & mighty Hercules:** The Holy Roman Emperor Charles V (symbolized by the eagle), whose forces sacked Rome in 1527, humiliating the papacy (symbolized by keys). **Clement:** Pope Clement VII (1478–1534). His first name, Julius, was modeled after Julius Ascanius, the son of Virgil's Aeneas. Held prisoner in the Castel Sant'Angelo for six months in 1527. Cf. 2.57; 5.81; 10.20.

10.29 **Saint-Paul-de-Mausole:** Adjacent to Nostradamus's Saint-Rémy-de-Provence. See note to 4.27. **Tarbes:** Town in Gascony, southwestern France. **Bigorre:** The specific region of Gascony within which Tarbes is situated.

10.31 **Ishmaelites:** Cf. 9.43; 9.60. **Carmania:** Used by Ptolemy and others to refer to the northern Persian deserts of Parthia and Aria; also a satrapy on the Persian Gulf, west of Hormoz.

10.33 **the diphthong town:** Fiesole, nearby to Florence?

10.36 **Harmotic:** From the Greek *harmotikos* (fit for joining)? Hermetic?

10.37 **Bourget:** All the place-names in this quatrain were located in the duchy of Savoy.

10.38 **Santa Barbara:** Her feast day on December 4? Place-name? "Barbarian saint"? **Orsini:** Major Roman family, rivals of the Colonna. **Adria:** Venice.

10.39 **Before he turns eighteen:** Read by at least one contemporary of Nostradamus (the Venetian ambassador to France in a secret diplomatic dispatch of November 1560) as predicting the future demise of the sickly dauphin of France, François, who was fourteen years old at the time of the composition of this quatrain (1558) and had just married Mary, Queen of Scots. After the accidental death of his father, King Henri II, in July 1559, the fifteen-year-old François II succeeded him on the throne, only to die eighteen months later (without issue) of an ear infection. He in turn was succeeded by his ten-year-old brother, Charles IX, in December 1560.

10.40 **The young prince:** From Froissart's account of the troubled reign of Edward II of England, son of Edward I? Cf. 9.49. LONOLE: London?

10.41 **Caussade & Caylus:** All the place-names in this quatrain are located in the Agen region, where Nostradamus briefly resided.

10.44 **Blois:** Cf. 8.38 and 8.52. Blois was the ancestral seat of the Orléans branch of the house of Valois. **Memel:** Important port of the Hanseatic League (in today's Lithuania).

10.45 **The Kingdom of Navarre:** May allude to the mercurial Antoine de Bourbon, Duke of Vendôme and king of Navarre from 1555 to 1562. **The vow made in Cambrai:** With the Treaty of Cambrai of 1529, King François I renounced his claims to Naples, Artois, and Flanders; but the French broke this agreement in 1556 under Henri II, after the abdication of Charles V.

10.46 **Elector of Saxony:** Probably Maurice, elector of Saxony (1547–53), known as "Judas" for his shrewd manipulation of alliances in Germany. Initially aligned with the anti-Protestant Charles V, he shifted to Henri II's side in 1552, then reverted to the Imperial cause.

10.47 **Burgos:** In the province of León in Spain. **Formande:** Formentera, in the Balearic Islands?

10.48 **Laigne:** The river Aisne, near the area of the Netherlands invaded by the Spanish in 1557?

10.49 **new city:** Naples (*Neapolis* in Greek)?

10.50 **urn:** Aquarius. **Lorraine:** The Meuse flows through the Lorraine, site of major flooding in 1523.

10.51 **the low Germans:** I.e., the Palatinate and the bishopric of Strassburg? **Picardy, Normandy, Maine:** All in northern France.

10.52 **Leie & Schelde:** The rivers Leie (*Lys* in French) and Schelde (*Escaut* in French) meet in Ghent, heart of the Spanish Netherlands. The port of Antwerp lies to the northeast.

10.53 **The great Selin:** If "Selin" is Henri II here, then the "first" mistress could be Diane de Poitiers, dealing with her rivals.

10.54 **Malines:** A lordship just north of Brussels.

10.55 **the ill-starred wedding vows:** Probably refers to the marriage of the fourteen-year-old future François II to sixteen-year-old Mary, Queen of Scots (with a possible pun on her name in line 3), in April 1558, just around the time of the composition of this quatrain. Cf. 10.39. **Phoebus:** Has been read as a cryptic reference to F[rançois] II (from the Greek *phi* [i.e., *F*] + *beta*, the second letter of the Greek alphabet = II), upon whose untimely death in 1560 the Catholic Mary returned to Scotland.

10.56 **saved by a queen:** Mary Stuart, Catholic queen regnant of Scotland in 1542–67? **Tunis:** Ruled from 1535 to 1570 by a Muslim puppet of the Hapsburgs.

10.58 **the Selene monarch:** Henri II. See notes to 2.73; 4.77. **the new Macedon:** Philip II of Spain. Cf. 9.35; 9.38; 9.64; 9.93. **Peter's barque:** The Vatican. After the French defeat at Saint-Quentin in 1557, Spanish troops were menacing Rome and Marseille.

10.59 **Bressans:** From the province of Savoy north of Lyon.

10.60 **Nice . . . Malta:** Nice was in Savoy, Monaco and Malta independent Hapsburg protectorates, Modena an independent duchy, Savona and Genoa in the Genoese republic, Pisa and Siena in the duchy of Tuscany, and Capua in the Hapsburg Kingdom of the Two Sicilies. **Nolita:** A personified imaginary place-name, from the Latin ("she who is unwilling")?

10.61 **Betta:** From the Latin *Baetis*, the Guadalquivir River in Spain; or *Baetica*, one of the Roman provinces in Spain? **Emorra:** From *Agusta Emirita*, Mérida, the capital of the Spanish province of Extremadura. **Scarabantia:** Modern Sopron, city on the western borders of Hungary, at the foot of the Alps. **Pannonia:** Southern region of modern Hungary.

10.62 **Sorbia:** Also known as Lusatia, region between the Elbe and Oder rivers, encompassing Saxony and Prussia. **Buda:** Capital of Turkish Hungary. **Salona:** Now Solin, in Dalmatia. A play on Nostradamus's Salon-de-Provence?

10.63 **Cydonia:** Chania, second-largest city of Crete? **Ragusa:** Today's Dubrovnik, on the Adriatic coast; a Venetian colony. **city of St. Jerome:** He was born in Stridon, in the Roman province of Dalmatia.

10.64 **the Colonnas:** Powerful family of Renaissance Rome (and supporters of Charles V), rivals of the Orsini. Cf. 8.67.

10.65 **The rough-lettered one:** According to Lemesurier, the southern German knight Georg von Frundsberg (1473–1528), who, in the service of the Hapsburg dynasty of Charles V, led some twelve thousand Landsknechts in an advance on Rome in 1527, suffering a stroke in Modena just before the sacking of the city. Cf. 2.57; 2.93; 3.89; 10.20; 10.27.

10.66 **American:** Dubious. More likely derived from *Amorica* (place by the sea), traditional name given that part of Gaul that includes the Brittany peninsula and the territory between the rivers Seine and Loire. **Reb:** Apocope for "rebel"? Variously identified as Edward I ("Hammer of the Scots") and Oliver Cromwell.

10.67 **earthquake in the month of May:** The astrological conjunction of lines 2 and 3, according to Brind'Amour, perfectly describes the time of the earthquake that took place at Montélimar (in the Drôme) on May 4, 1549, between ten and eleven in the evening. **Annonay:** North of Montélimar, beyond Valence.

10.68 **the pirate ships:** The Barbary pirates raided the coast just south of Nostradamus's Salon throughout the late 1520s and into the mid-1530s.

10.69 **Ambellon:** Amiens (*Ambianum* in Latin)? Ambel, a commune in the Isère?

10.70 **Reggio:** Reggio di Calabria in the south of Italy, or Reggio Emilia in the north?

10.71 **Thursday:** Cf. the celebrations of Thursday at 1.50; 10.73.

10.72 **nineteen ninety-nine:** One of only nine actual dates provided in the *Prophecies*. Brind'Amour notes that this coincides with the total solar eclipse of August 11 of that year. **The sky shall send a great King to defray:** Leoni translates this as "From the sky will come a great King of Terror," reading the French as *un grand Roi d'effrayeur* (where *effrayeur* indeed would mean: causing amazement, dismay, fright). Brind'Amour reads it the same way. The original, however, reads *un grand Roi deffraieur* (with no apostrophe). The noun *defrayeur*, as defined by Cotgrave's 1611 *Dictionarie of the French and English Tongues*, is cognate to our "defray" and in sixteenth-century French means: "A Cater, or Steward; one that in a journey furnishes, and defrayes the provision, and expence of the whole companie." Lemesurier therefore translates this as "a great King and host" and reads the second and third lines as referring to the miraculous restoration to health, in his Madrid prison, of the dying king François, Duke of Angoulême, captured six months earlier by the Imperial forces at the battle of Pavia (cf. 2.26; 4.45; 4.75; 8.7). His recovery (as recounted in Guicciardini's *History of Italy*) resulted from a magnanimous personal visit from his "steward" and jailer, Charles V, in August 1525—who (here at least) takes on the allegorical features of a Savior King. **Before, after March:** After signing the Treaty of Madrid in January 1526 (in which he renounced all claims over Italy, Flanders, and Artois and surrendered Burgundy), François I was officially set free on March 6, handing over his two young sons (the future Henri II and François III) as hostages to Charles V to guarantee the terms of the treaty—which, in the event, he did not honor.

10.73 **Jovialist:** Often used by Nostradamus to refer to legislators (born under the influence of Jupiter). According to Lemesurier, this figure represents the "Angelic Pastor" predicted by the *Mirabilis liber*. Cf. 1.50; 5.79; 10.71.

10.74 **The mighty number seven:** The end of the seventh millennium (since the world's creation)—which, according to Roussat and others, would fall in 1800 or 1887 . . . or 4722. **at the Games of the Hecatomb:** The Olympic Games of ancient Greece were celebrated during the month of Hecatombaion, that is, in midsummer.

10.77 **Quirites:** Citizens of ancient Rome.

10.78 **Rome:** The sack of Rome of 1527? Cf. 2.57; 2.93; 5.81; 10.20; 10.27; 10.65.

10.79 **Gallic Hercules:** The Ogmion figure. See note to 1.96.

10.81 **Hesperians:** People of the West, Spaniards.

10.83 **Ghent:** Major commercial center of the Spanish Netherlands. Cf. 10.52.

10.84 **The lord's bastard girl:** Possibly Elizabeth Tudor, daughter of Henry VIII, but declared illegitimate at the age of two and a half after the execution of her mother, Anne Boleyn. When this quatrain was composed in the spring/early summer 1558, her accession to the English throne was virtually assured.

10.85 **The aged tribune:** The fifty-five-year-old Cicero, intimidated by Pompey's mob as he attempted to deliver a speech in defense of his friend Titus Annius Milo, who was accused of having murdered Publius Clodius Pulcher—subsequently rewritten into one of his most celebrated orations, *Pro Milone*.

10.86 **King of Europe:** Lemesurier hears echoes of the Third Crusade's attempts to reconquer the Holy Land from Saladin, known as "the King of Babylon."

10.89 **In marble shall the walls of brick now rise:** On his deathbed the Roman emperor Augustus boasted that "I found a Rome of bricks and left it to you of marble"—a metaphor for the empire's strength, according to Cassius Dio. **Seven & fifty years:** Augustus (then known as Octavius) came to power in the Second Triumvirate in 43 B.C.E. and ruled fifty-seven years until his death in 14 C.E.—a period known as the Pax Augusta. **Aqueducts:** Cf. 4.80; 5.58; 8.27; 8.68.

10.90 **a learnèd man of good counsel:** Emperor Claudius (r. 41–56 C.E.), successor to the assassinated Caligula?

10.91 **sixteen nine:** No pope was elected in 1609.

10.92 **Their leader:** Presumably John Calvin (1509–1564).

10.93 **The new barque:** The mobility of the Vatican (the barque of St. Peter), as illustrated by the transfer of part of its empire to Avignon during the Great Schism of 1378–1417? Cf. 1.32; 5.45.

10.94 **Hesperia:** Cf. 10.81.

10.95 **those who worship Fridays:** I.e., Muslims (further symbolized by the crescent in line 3).

10.96 **the faith with the sea's name:** Lemesurier suggests that the "religion du nom des mers" may punningly refer to the *Mar*ranos (or "secret Jews") from whom Nostradamus's family descended. **Adaluncatif:** Printer's garbling of something on the order of "Andalus-caliph"? "Abdallah-caliph"? **Aleph & Alif:** Aleph is the first letter of the Hebrew alphabet, while alif (see probable rhyme on "caliph") is the first letter of the Arabic alphabet.

10.97 **which way the wind makes feather fall:** From the old French expression "jeter la plume au vent" or "mettre sa plume au vent." Cotgrave's 1611 *Dictionarie* glosses this: "To grow carelesse, let the world runne; weigh not how matters passe, which way he goes, what course he takes, what thing he does."

10.99 **dogs:** The dogs here are *mâtins*, that is, mastiffs, large watchdogs, suggestive of Cerberus, the Hound of Hell.

Printed in the United States
by Baker & Taylor Publisher Services